Macro Express

Explained

Joseph Weinpert

Printed in Victoria, Canada

National Library of Canada Cataloguing in Publication Data

A cataloguing record for this book that includes the U.S. Library of Congress Classification number, the Library of Congress Call number and the Dewey Decimal cataloguing code is available from the National Library of Canada. The complete cataloguing record can be obtained from the National Library's online database at: www.nlc-bnc.ca/amicus/index-e.html

ISBN: 1-4120-3199-0

TRAFFORD

This book was published *on-demand* in cooperation with Trafford Publishing.
On-demand publishing is a unique process and service of making a book available for retail sale to the public taking advantage of on-demand manufacturing and Internet marketing. **On-demand publishing** includes promotions, retail sales, manufacturing, order fulfilment, accounting and collecting royalties on behalf of the author.

Suite 6E, 2333 Government St., Victoria, B.C. V8T 4P4, CANADA

Phone	250-383-6864	Toll-free	1-888-232-4444 (Canada & US)
Fax	250-383-6804	E-mail	sales@trafford.com
Web site	www.trafford.com	TRAFFORD PUBLISHING IS A DIVISION OF TRAFFORD HOLDINGS LTD.	
Trafford Catalogue #04-1026		www.trafford.com/robots/04-1026.html	

10   9   8   7   6   5   4   3   2   1

Table of Contents

Table of Contents iii

End-User License Agreement... xv

Acknowledgments xvi

About this Book.. xvii

Introduction to Macro Express 1

Starting Macro Express 2

Startup Preferences... 3

Create a Macro 4

Playing Macros 7

Scoping Macros 8

Macro Commands.. 8

Installation...9

Basic Installation 9

Welcome..9

License Agreement 10

Installation Type 10

Select Components.. 10

Editor..10

Help..10

Quick Start Guide 11

Icons...11

Install Older Files..11

Search for Existing Versions.. 11

Search Results 11

Choose Destination Location 12

Select Start Menu Folder 12

Run on Windows Startup.. 13

Start Installation 13

Installing 13

Installation Complete 14

File Association Notification.. 14

What was installed?... 14

Advanced Installation... 16

NoEditor.. 16

NoHelp 16

NoQuickStart 16

NoIcons 17

InstallOlder.. 17

InstallPath... 17

StartMenuFoldr.. 17

Startup... 17

LaunchNow... 17

QuickStartNow... 18

Reboot...18
LicenseName..18
LicenseCode...19
ConfigFilePath..19
MacroFileDest..20
Special Installation Files...21
PrgLoad.chk...21
NoQuickStart..21
NoIcons..21
NoStartup...21
NoQuickStartNow...21
Summary..22
Macro Express Editor **23**
Main Menu 25
Navigating the Main Menu...26
Menu Toolbar...28
Actions Toolbar..29
Categories Pane...30
Add a Category..31
Rename a Category..31
Delete a Category..31
Move a Category...32
Navigating the Categories Pane...32
Placing Macros in Categories..33
Macros Pane...34
Columns...34
Views..35
Sorting..35
Navigating..38
Add Macros..40
Copy Macros..40
Rename Macros..41
Delete Macros..42
Editing a Macro..42
Running a Macro..43
Enable and Disable Macros...43
Macro Properties...44
General Tab..44
Activation Tab..45
Scope Tab...46
Script Tab...46
Security Tab..46
Notes Tab...47
Log Tab..47
System Macros...49
Menu of Macros for Topmost Window...49
Resume Pause..50
Run Macro Express Editor..50
Start / Stop Capture...51

Suspend / Resume Macro Express 51
Terminate Macro Express 51
Macro Recycle Bin 52
Main Menu 54
Menu Toolbar 55
Actions Toolbar 55
Options Pane 55
Deleted Macros Pane 55
Restore Macro(s) 56
Delete Macro(s) 56
Empty Recycle Bin 56
Summary 57

Creating and Editing Macros **59**
Scripting Editor 61
Commands Pane 63
Search Box 66
Macro Script Pane 67
Selecting Lines 68
Moving Lines 68
Duplicating Lines 68
Inserting Lines 68
Deleting Lines 69
Changing Lines 69
Disabling Lines 69
Breakpoints 69
Stepping Through a Macro 70
Running a Macro 70
Change Focus Automatically 70
Test Window 71
Viewing Variables 71
Syntax Checking 72
Go To Line 72
Finding Text 73
Saving a Macro 73
Printing a Macro 73
Copy Command Text 74
Direct Editor 75
Commands Pane 76
Search Box 76
Macro Text Pane 77
Separator Character 77
Text Type 78
Running a Macro 79
Test Window 79
Finding Text 79
Search and Replace Text 80
Saving a Macro 80
Printing a Macro 80
Properties Tab 80
Nickname 80
Icon 81
Active 82
Use Log File 82
Scope Tab 83
Security Tab 83
Main File Passwords 84

Notes Tab 86
External Editor.. 87
Capturing Macros 88
   Capture Settings.. 88
   Capture Options... 91
      System HotKey...91
      Capture Icon 93
      Recapture Macro..94
      Capture Wizard 95
      Notes on Capturing Macros... 100
Quick Wizards.. 101
Summary.. 103
Running and Activating Macros.. **105**
Running Macros 105
   Components.. 105
   Command Line Parameters 106
      /A<nickname> 106
      /MXE<\path\filename>.. 106
      /V<variable:value> 106
      /F<\path\filename> 107
      /IC<filename> 107
      /delay:<seconds>... 108
      /N... 108
      /S... 108
      /SM<minutes> 109
      /T... 109
      /H... 109
      /B... 110
      /EY... 110
      /EN... 110
      /NQS 110
   Windows Explorer.. 110
   Desktop 111
   Macro Express Explorer and Editors 111
Activating Macros 112
   HotKey.. 113
   Schedule 115
      Preferences... 116
      Common Fields... 117
      At Startup... 117
      Once 118
      Hourly 118
      Daily... 119
      Weekly.. 120
      Monthly.. 121
      Time Out... 122
      Other 122
      Load File 122
   ShortKey 123
   Window Title 126
   Mouse Click.. 128
      Area on Screen... 128
      Window Part 128
   Window Control... 129
   Scope 129
      Global... 130

Global Except 130
Windows Specific 131
Program Specific 132
Popup and Floating Menus 133
Building a Menu 134
Setting Menu Features 135
Scoping a Menu 139
Switching Menu Types 139

Stopping Macros 140
Dynamic Macros 141
Load Macro Text File 141
Run Macro in Variable 145
Advanced Options 148
Online Delay 148
Activation Prefix 148
Scope Prefix 149
ShortKey Punctuation Chars 149
ShortKey Invalid Chars 149
Macro Stop Abort Message 149
Hotkey Abort Message 149
Right Click Abort Message 149
Display Gradients 149
Macro Priority 150
Show Pixel Color in Hex in Mouse Locator 150
Banker's Rounding 150
Summary 151

Program Logic and Flow **153**
If 153
Else 153
End If 153
AND 154
OR 154
XOR 154
If Variable 156
If OS Version 158
If Macro Enabled 159
If Macro Disabled 159
If Message 160
If Clipboard 161
If Control 161
If Mouse Cursor 161
If Not Mouse Cursor 161
If File Exists 162
If Not File Exists 162
If File Ready 162
If Not File Ready 162
If Folder Exists 162
If Not Folder Exists 162

If Registry 162
If Program 162
If Not Program 162
If Window 162
If Not Window 162
Switch 162
End Switch 162
Case 162
Default Case 162
End Case 162
Repeat 164
Repeat End 164
Repeat Exit 164
Break 164
Repeat Start 166
Repeat with Variable 168
Repeat Prompt Start 169
Repeat Until 170
Repeat with Processes 172
Repeat Counter 172
Repeat with Folder 173
Repeat with Windows 173
Multiple Choice Menu 174
Text Box Display 177
Text Box Close 177
Pause 180
Summary 181

Variables..**183**
Types of Variables 185
   String Variables..185
   Integer Variables 185
   Decimal Variables 185
   Environment Variables 185
Scope of Variables 186
Literal Values vs. Variables 187
Common Variable Dialogs 189
   Drop-Down List 189
   Dialog Positioner...189
   File-Picker 191
   Bypass File Existence Check...191
String Variable Commands 192
   Set Text String Variables 192
      Set Value Now 192
      Prompt for Value..192
      Set Value from Clipboard 193
      Set Value from File 194
      Set Value to Topmost Program Name 194
      Set Value to Topmost Window Title 194

Set Value to Current Folder Name 195
Set Value from INI File 195
Set Value from Environment Variable 196
Set Value to File Name (Prompt) 196
Set Value to Folder Name (Prompt) 196
Set with a Random Letter 197

Modify String Variables 197
Trim 197
Left Trim 197
Right Trim 198
Strip CR/LF 198
Convert to Integer 198
Convert to Decimal 199
Append Text 199
Append Text String Variable 199
Copy Whole Text 200
Copy Part of Text 200
Delete Part of Text 200
Uppercase 201
Lowercase 201
Pad Left 201
Pad Right 201
Replace Substring 202
Save to Clipboard 203
Save to Text File 203
Append to Text File 204
Save to INI File 204
Save to Environment Variable 204

Integer Variable Commands 205
Set Integer Variables 206
Set Value Now 206
Prompt for Value 206
Set Value from Mouse X Position 207
Set Value from Mouse Y Position 207
Set Value from the Size of a File 208
Set a Random Value 208
Set Value from Screen Width 208
Set Value from Screen Height 208
Set Value from Current Window Left 208
Set Value from Current Window Top 208
Set Value from Current Window Width 209
Set Value from Current Window Height 209
Set Value from Clipboard 209
Get Length of a Text Variable 209
Get Position of Text in a Text Variable 209
Set Value from Current Day 210
Set Value from Current Month 210
Set Value from Current Year 210
Set Value from Current Day of Week 210
Set Value from Current Hour 210
Set Value from Current Minute 210
Set Value from Current Second 210
Set Value from Control Left 210
Set Value from Control Top 210
Set Value from Control Width 210
Set Value from Control Height 210
Set Value from Monitor Width 210
Set Value from Monitor Height 210

Modify Integer Variables 211
Add 211
Subtract 211

Multiply 211
Divide 211
Convert to Text String 211
Convert to Decimal 212
Copy Value 212
Increment 212
Decrement 212

Decimal Variable Commands 213
Set Decimal Variables 213
Set Value Now 213
Prompt for Value 214
Set Value from Clipboard 215
Modify Decimal Variables 215
Add 215
Subtract 215
Multiply 215
Divide 215
Round 216
Convert to Text String 217
Truncate to Integer 217
Remove Integer 218
Copy Value 218

Clearing, Saving, and Restoring Variables 219
Clear Variables 219
Save Variables 220
Restore Variables 220

Other Variable Dialogs 223
Variable Set from Misc 223
ASCII Values and Variables 223
Set Variable to ASCII Character 224
Set Variable to ASCII Value 224

Running Macros from Variables 225
Special Characters 225

Using Environment Variables 228

Summary 229

Keyboard 231
Text Type 231
Wait Text Playback 236
Keystroke Speed 237
Encrypted Text 237
Set Keyboard Repeat Delay 238
Set Keyboard Repeat Speed 238
Wait for Key Press 238
Wait for Text 238
Alt Key 240
Control Key 240
Shift Key 240
Win Key 240
Caps Lock 240
Num Lock 240
Scroll Lock 240

Restore Keyboard Hooks 241
Auto Restore Keyboard Hooks 241
Remap Keyboard 242
Summary 244

Mouse **245**
Mouse Left 245
Mouse Right 245
Mouse Middle 245
    Button Click 245
    Button Double Click 245
    Button Down 245
    Button Up 245
Mouse Wheel Forward 246
Mouse Wheel Backward 246
Get Mouse Position 247
Mouse Move 247
    Mouse Locator 248
Move Mouse to Tray Icon 249
Mouse Speed 251
If Mouse Cursor 252
If Not Mouse Cursor 252
Wait for Mouse Cursor 253
Wait for Not Mouse Cursor 253
Wait Left Mouse Click 254
Wait Right Mouse Click 254
Wait Middle Mouse Click 254
Restore Mouse Hooks 255
Summary 255

Clipboard **257**
Global Clipboard Delay 257
Nonfile Clipboard Commands 258
    Start Clipboard Copy 258
    End Clipboard Copy 258
    Type Out Text from the Clipboard 258
    Empty the Clipboard 259
    Issue Clipboard Cut Command (Ctrl+X) 259
    Issue Clipboard Copy Command (Ctrl+C) 259
    Issue Clipboard Paste Command (Ctrl+V) 259
File Clipboard Commands 260
    File Opening Error Options (Graphic Files Only) 260
        Halt the Macro 260
        Continue the Macro 260
        Be Asked What to Do 261
    Common Options 261
    Copy Text File to Clipboard 261
    Save Clipboard to a Text File 261
    Append Clipboard Text to the End of a Text File 262

Copy Graphic File to Clipboard...262
Save Clipboard Graphic to a Graphic File 263
If Clipboard Text Equals 263
If Clipboard Contains...263
Summary..264

Using the Registry..265
Registry Overview..265
What is the Registry?...265
HKEY_CLASSES_ROOT...265
HKEY_CURRENT_USER..266
HKEY_LOCAL_MACHINE..266
HKEY_USERS..266
HKEY_CURRENT_CONFIG...266
What is a Hive?...266
What are Values?..267
REG_SZ...268
REG_EXPAND_SZ (Read-Only)..268
REG_DWORD..268
REG_BINARY...268
Commands..269
Registry Picker...269
Create Registry Key...270
Delete Registry Key...270
Write Registry String...270
Write Registry Integer...270
Write Registry Decimal..270
Read Registry String..271
Read Registry Integer..271
Read Registry Decimal...271
Delete Registry Value...272
If Registry..272
Saving and Restoring Variables..274
Common Data..274
Temporary Variables...275
Passing Parameters...275
Reusable Macros 276
Summary..281

Windows and Programs...283
Common Dialogs..283
Window Activate..285
Program Launch...285
Launch and Activate...285
Activate or Launch 285
Maximize Window..290
Minimize Window...290
Restore Window..290
Hide Window..290
Show Window (unhide)...290
Close Window...291

Shut Down Program 291
Terminate Process... 292
Window Resize 293
Window Reposition 294
Set Window Order 296
Window Sizing Border.. 297
Repeat with Windows 298
If Window On Top 299
If Window Not On Top.. 299
If Window Running 299
If Window Not Running 299
If Program On Top.. 300
If Program Not On Top.. 300
If Program Running 300
If Program Not Running 300
Summary 302

Files and Folders.. **303**
Common Dialogs 303
Disk Operations... 305
Change Default Folder 305
Create Folder..306
Rename Folder..306
Delete Folder..307
Copy File or Files 307
Rename File or Files 309
Move File or Files 311
Delete File or Files 312
File Information.. 313
Convert Filename..313
File Attributes...313
Archive Attribute 314
System Attribute 314
Hidden Attribute 315
Read-Only Attribute...315
Variable Set from File 315
Get File Date/Time...316
Get File Path Info..316
Get File Version...317
Set Value from the Size of a File 318
Program Logic 319
If File Exists...319
If Not File Exists...319
If Folder Exists...319
If Not Folder Exists 319
If File Ready 320
If Not File Ready...320
Wait for File Exist 320
Wait for Folder to Exist 320
Wait for File Ready...321

Data Processing 322
    Repeat with Folder 322
    Text File Begin Process 323
    Text File End Process..323
    ASCII File Begin Process 326
    ASCII Text File End Process...326
        Comma Delimited Text (.csv) 327
        Tab Delimited Text (.txt) 327
        ASCII Delimited Text (.txt) 328
  Summary 328
Window Controls **329**
  Window Control Variables 330
  The First Big Step 331
    Get Control 331
    Capture Control 339
  Manipulating Window Controls...341
    Variable Get Control Text 341
    Variable Set Control Text 341
    Variable Get Control Class 342
    Variable Modify Control 343
  Engage! 345
    Mouse Click on Control 345
    Set Focus..346
  What if? Wait a minute! 349
    If Control 349
    Wait for Control 349
  And the rest of the commands...351
    Set Integer to Control Left..351
    Set Integer to Control Top..351
    Set Integer to Control Width 351
    Set Integer to Control Height 351
    Send Text to Control 351
    Window Control Activation 352
    Clear Control Variables 353
    Save Control Variables..354
    Restore Control Variables 354
  Summary..355
List of Commands **357**
Companion CD **367**
Conclusion **371**
Index **373**

End-User License Agreement

All other product names and services identified throughout this book are trademarks or registered trademarks of their respective companies. They are used throughout this book in editorial fashion only and for the benefit of such companies. No such uses, or the use of any trade name, is intended to convey endorsement or other affiliation with the book.

EXCEPT FOR THE LIMITED WARRANTY COVERING THE PHYSICAL COMPANION CD PACKAGED WITH THIS BOOK AS PROVIDED IN THE END-USER LICENSE AGREEMENT, THE INFORMATION AND MATERIAL CONTAINED IN THIS BOOK ARE PROVIDED "AS IS," WITHOUT WARRANTY OF ANY KIND, EXPRESS OR IMPLIED, INCLUDING WITHOUT LIMITATION ANY WARRANTY CONCERNING THE ACCURACY, ADEQUACY, OR COMPLETENESS OF SUCH INFORMATION OR MATERIAL OR THE RESULTS TO BE OBTAINED FROM USING SUCH INFORMATION OR MATERIAL. NEITHER PROFESSIONAL GRADE MACROS NOR THE AUTHOR, JOSEPH L WEINPERT, SHALL BE RESPONSIBLE FOR ANY CLAIMS ATTRIBUTABLE TO ERRORS, OMISSIONS, OR OTHER INACCURACIES IN THE INFORMATION OR MATERIAL CONTAINED IN THIS BOOK, AND IN NO EVENT SHALL PROFESSIONAL GRADE MACROS OR THE AUTHOR, JOSEPH L WEINPERT, BE LIABLE FOR DIRECT, INDIRECT, SPECIAL, INCIDENTAL, OR CONSEQUENTIAL DAMAGES ARISING OUT OF THE USE OF SUCH INFORMATION OR MATERIAL.

END-USER LICENSE AGREEMENT

READ THIS AGREEMENT CAREFULLY. BY BUYING THE BOOK AND USING THE PROGRAM LISTINGS, COMPANION CD, AND PROGRAMS REFERRED TO BELOW, YOU ACCEPT THE TERMS OF THIS AGREEMENT.

The program listings included in this book and the programs included on the companion CD contained in the package in this book ("CD") are proprietary products of Professional Grade Macros and/or third party suppliers ("Suppliers"). The program listings and programs are hereinafter collectively referred to as the "Programs." Professional Grade Macros and the Suppliers retain ownership of the CD and copyright to the Programs, as their respective interests may appear. The Programs and the copy of the CD provided are licensed (not sold) to you under the conditions set forth herein.

License. You may use the CD on any computer, provided that the CD is used on only one computer and by one user at a time.

Restrictions. You may not commercially distribute the CD or the Programs or otherwise reproduce, publish, or distribute or otherwise use the CD or the Programs in any manner that may infringe any copyright or other proprietary right of Professional Grade Macros, the Suppliers, or any other party or assign, sublicense, or otherwise transfer the CD or this agreement to any other party unless such party agrees to accept the terms and conditions of this agreement. This license and your right to use the CD and the Programs automatically terminates if you fail to comply with any provision of this agreement.

U.S. GOVERNMENT RESTRICTED RIGHTS. The CD and the Programs are provided with **RESTRICTED RIGHTS.** Use, duplication, or disclosure by the Government is subject to restrictions as set forth in subparagraph (c)(1)(ii) of the Rights in Technical Data and Computer Software Clause at DFARS (48 CFR 252.277-7013). The Proprietor of the compilation of the Programs and the CD is Professional Grade Macros, PO Box 5035, Timberlake, OH 44095.

Limited Warranty. Professional Grade Macros warrants the physical CD to be free of defects in materials and workmanship under normal use for a period of 30 days from the purchase date. If Professional Grade Macros receives written notification within the warranty period of defects in materials or workmanship in the physical CD, and such notification is determined by Professional Grade Macros to be correct, Professional Grade Macros will, at its option, replace the defective CD or refund a prorated portion of the purchase price of the book. **THESE ARE YOUR SOLE REMEDIES FOR ANY BREACH OF WARRANTY.**

EXCEPT AS SPECIFICALLY PROVIDED ABOVE, THE DISKS AND THE PROGRAMS ARE PROVIDED "AS IS" WITHOUT ANY WARRANTY OF ANY KIND. NEITHER PROFESSIONAL GRADE MACROS NOR THE SUPPLIERS MAKE ANY WARRANTY OF ANY KIND AS TO THE ACCURACY OR COMPLETENESS OF THE CD OR THE PROGRAMS OR THE RESULTS TO BE OBTAINED FROM USING THE CD OR THE PROGRAMS AND NEITHER PROFESSIONAL GRADE MACROS NOR THE SUPPLIERS SHALL BE RESPONSIBLE FOR ANY CLAIMS ATTRIBUTABLE TO ERRORS, OMISSIONS, OR OTHER INACCURACIES IN THE CD OR THE PROGRAMS. THE ENTIRE RISK AS TO THE RESULTS AND PERFORMANCE OF THE CD AND THE PROGRAMS IS ASSUMED BY THE USER. FURTHER, NEITHER PROFESSIONAL GRADE MACROS NOR THE SUPPLIERS MAKE ANY REPRESENTATIONS OR WARRANTIES, EITHER EXPRESS OR IMPLIED, WITH RESPECT TO THE CD OR THE PROGRAMS, INCLUDING BUT NOT LIMITED TO, THE QUALITY, PERFORMANCE, MERCHANTABILITY, OR FITNESS FOR A PARTICULAR PURPOSE OF THE CD OR THE PROGRAMS. IN NO EVENT SHALL PROFESSIONAL GRADE MACROS OR THE SUPPLIERS BE LIABLE FOR DIRECT, INDIRECT, SPECIAL, INCIDENTAL, OR CONSEQUENTIAL DAMAGES ARISING OUT THE USE OF OR INABILITY TO USE THE CD OR THE PROGRAMS OR FOR ANY LOSS OR DAMAGE OF ANY NATURE CAUSED TO ANY PERSON OR PROPERTY AS A RESULT OF THE USE OF THE CD OR THE PROGRAMS, EVEN IF PROFESSIONAL GRADE MACROS OR THE SUPPLIERS HAVE BEEN SPECIFICALLY ADVISED OF THE POSSIBILITY OF SUCH DAMAGES. NEITHER PROFESSIONAL GRADE MACROS NOR THE SUPPLIERS ARE RESPONSIBLE FOR ANY COSTS INCLUDING, BUT NOT LIMITED TO, THOSE INCURRED AS A RESULT OF LOST PROFITS OR REVENUE, LOSS OF USE OF THE CD OR THE PROGRAMS, LOSS OF DATA, THE COSTS OF RECOVERING SOFTWARE OR DATA, OR THIRD-PARTY CLAIMS. IN NO EVENT WILL PROFESSIONAL GRADE MACROS' OR THE SUPPLIERS' LIABILITY FOR ANY DAMAGES TO YOU OR ANY OTHER PARTY EVER EXCEED THE PRICE OF THIS BOOK. NO SALES PERSON OR OTHER REPRESENTATIVE OF ANY PARTY INVOLVED IN THE DISTRIBUTION OF THE CD IS AUTHORIZED TO MAKE ANY MODIFICATIONS OR ADDITIONS TO THIS LIMITED WARRANTY.

Some states do not allow the exclusion or limitation of implied warranties or limitation of liability for incidental or consequential damages, so the above limitation or exclusion may not apply to you.

General. Professional Grade Macros and the Suppliers retain all rights not expressly granted. Nothing in this license constitutes a waiver of the rights of Professional Grade Macros or the Suppliers under the U.S. Copyright Act or any other Federal or State Law, international treaty, or foreign law.

Acknowledgments

There are several people who have been involved with making this book, and each deserves to be acknowledged for their contribution.

Chief among them is my wonderful wife JoAnn. In a very real way, she spent as much time on this book as I did … she is a very patient person.

You, the reader. Thank you for buying this book. I am positive that you will find it useful.

Insight Software Solutions has provided a wonderful product. But a product is only as good as the people behind it, and I must thank Kevin Heaton. There is no other person that contributed as much to this important book. I do not recall ever asking a single person so many times "Is this what it is supposed to do?" And each time, I received a prompt, professional answer. No exceptions. Period.

M. Stanton Jones, President of Insight Software Solutions. He also contributed much to the success of this book, and it would have nearly been impossible to write it without his support.

Matthew Frandsen of Formaquest Technologies in Utah. You may have already viewed his videos made only for this book. He gave me plenty of ideas, and more importantly, his time. I am sure you agree his videos are a good addition to this book and that they enhance our ability to learn about Macro Express.

Danielle Wilber of ImageFirst Graphics in Pennsylvania who helped this poor, nearly color-blind soul out. She went way above the call-of-duty to help. When you are looking at the cover of this book and the companion CD, you are looking at her work.

Patricia Graham of Trafford Publishing who went out of her way to get this novice writer answers to publishing questions. And Sydney Richardson who kept everything moving forward.

And then there is Floyd, who helped keep other projects moving forward for Professional Grade Macros while I was writing. Sometimes I think Floyd and I are spun from the same mold.

My thanks to the Macro Express newsgroup regulars, who, during my extended absences, stepped up to the plate to answer questions. You know who you are!

Finally, this has been a great experience, and I am looking forward to working with the good folks at Insight Software Solutions again on whatever project happens by next.

Joseph Weinpert
Timberlake, Ohio
April, 2004

About this Book

The purpose of this book is to explain Macro Express. It is not meant to teach you about macros. You already know what a macro is, or if you have never created one, at least what the concept is. *"If it can be done with a keyboard and mouse, do it with Macro Express"*. You will see our (Professional Grade Macros) theme elsewhere in this book. It is our concept of what a macro is.

Macro Express software

Writing a book about Macro Express as it is being built is like nailing gelatin to a tree and takes a huge time commitment. This book was started before the release of Macro Express 3.4, which, at the time of this writing, was about a year ago. Well, one year, two releases (3.4a and 3.4b), and two-dozen 3.5 beta-test builds later, Macro Express 3.5 has been released … and so has this book.

To keep information up-to-date during the writing process, and as accurate as possible during the time frame, beta releases of Macro Express 3.5 were used (24 of them) for descriptions, testing, and examples. This process continued right up to the last minute. Insight Software Solutions officially released Macro Express 3.5.0.1 to the public on April 7th, 2004. Or yesterday, as I write this.

Still, there may be changes in Macro Express that I have overlooked which could affect this book. Indeed, I have no doubts that as Macro Express moves forward, existing information will change and new commands will be added. This is why, as a buyer of this book, you are invited to log on, and download changes as they are placed on our web site. For more information, please read the *Conclusion* chapter towards the end of this book.

What you need to know

This book assumes that your computer skills have reached a certain level. You should have more than just a basic understanding of how to operate your computer, keyboard, and mouse. You need to be aware of how your monitor works. Understand the term "display resolution" as well as "X and Y coordinates". You will need to know how to use the Windows Explorer program (Start | All Programs | Accessories | Windows Explorer) as well as the *Run* dialog window (Start | Run). Please be familiar with file and directory (folder) structures. Know what "folder hierarchy" means. Know how to create, move, and delete files as well as folders. Know how to use file-picker style dialogs, and be familiar with making choices from menus, toolbars, and drop-down lists. These basic tools are used by almost every software package written for Windows. Finally, it is helpful to be familiar with any programming or script language, even if it is just in passing.

What is inside?

This book was originally intended to be just a reference guide that detailed each Macro Express command; however, it quickly expanded into other subjects. Early in the process, it became clear that, to understand the commands, a greater understanding of Macro Express *basics*, such as how macros are created, run, activated, and so forth, would be necessary. So, I added what are now the beginning chapters of the book. They are organized around the Macro Express Editor, which is the main link between you and Macro Express.

Do not skip over the beginning chapters, even if you have been using Macro Express for a while. You may find options and features that you did not already know about. I sure did!

For the latter chapters, the book organizes Macro Express commands by subject matter such as logic, variables, hardware, the Registry, Window programs and applications, and so forth. What follows is a short description of each chapter.

Introduction to Macro Express

This chapter introduces you to Macro Express and discusses the basics of launching and setting its startup preferences. It steps you through creating a macro and covers different methods used to edit macros, set activations and scopes, and play macros (what you can and cannot do). It also points to other areas in the book containing more information about subjects that have just been touched on.

Installation

For basic installations, this chapter shows step-by-step how to install Macro Express. However, most of the chapter is devoted to explaining the advanced installation tools available for network, multiple user, and client setups.

Macro Express Editor

This chapter is a thorough examination of the *Macro Explorer* window which is the primary interface of the Macro Express Editor. It shows how to use macro categories and how to manage the macro list. It explains available preference option settings and how to change them. There are charts containing navigation and shortcut keys for each window section, including the Categories Pane and the Macros Pane.

Creating and Editing Macros

This chapter is an exhaustive study of five different methods used to create and edit macros, which include the Scripting Editor, Direct Editor, an external editor, capturing macros, and using the Quick Wizards tool. The *Scripting Editor* window and *Direct Editor* window are two more tools of the Macro Express Editor. This chapter shows how to use the commands and command categories to create macros. It explains what preference option settings are available, and how to change them. There are charts containing navigation and shortcut keys for each window section, including the Commands Pane, Macro Script Pane, and the Macro Text Pane.

Running and Activating Macros

This chapter examines what is needed to run macros from inside and outside the Macro Express Editor. Macros can be launched from your Desktop, the Windows *Run* dialog, batch files, and so forth. There is an in-depth discussion of command line parameters, which shines a light on Macro Express features you might not know existed. Also, every possible activation type and scope is explained in detail, including Popup and Floating Menus. This chapter also explains how to create, and use, one of the best features of Macro Express, *dynamic macros*. Plus there is a great section about advanced Macro Express preference settings, that are not accessible from the *Preferences* dialog.

Program Logic and Flow

This chapter explains the finer points of commands that add structure to your Macro Express scripts. The *If / Else / End If* construct, Boolean operators, *Switch / End Switch* construct, *Repeat / Repeat End* loops, and so forth, are all detailed, as well as the *Multiple Choice Menu* and *Text Box Display* dialogs.

Variables

This chapter discusses variables and variable types within Macro Express. It explains each of the variable commands that deal with string, integer, decimal, and environment variables. It shows dialogs that are common to each type, how to create and change variables, how to save and restore them, and how they can be passed to other macros between sessions. It also examines commands to manipulate ASCII values and special characters that are built in to Macro Express, and shows you how to create macro command strings that can be run from variables.

Keyboard

This chapter covers macro commands that are specific to your keyboard such as *Text Type*, *Wait for Text*, *Keystroke Speed*, and so forth. It also shows how to remap your keyboard and discusses keyboard hooks.

Mouse

This chapter examines macro commands that are specific to your mouse. You are shown how to use commands to click, spin the wheel, and move the mouse. It also details commands used to control the flow of your macro by waiting for the mouse cursor to change. The newer *Move Mouse to Tray Icon* command is explained, too.

Clipboard

This chapter explains the file and nonfile clipboard commands. Plus it shows how to use its logic commands to control the flow of your macro.

Using the Registry

Every macro project we create here at Professional Grade Macros makes use of the Registry commands. This chapter explains them, but also shows how they can be used to create reusable macros (those having black-box functionality), which can be called like any built-in command. There is an overview of the Registry and the types of Registry variables that Macro Express supports. This chapter explains how to create Registry Keys and Values, how to read them from the Registry and store them as variables. You will also learn how to write variables to the Registry, and how to delete Keys and Values.

Windows and Programs

Macro Express has commands that control other programs such as those that launch applications, stop them from running, and manipulate them. This chapter discusses those commands, and how to set focus to application windows, hide them, and make them reappear, change window sizes, move them around, and restack them. This chapter also teaches about the *If Window* and *If Program* logic commands so you can use them to control the flow of your macro.

Files and Folders

This chapter explains Macro Express commands that are designed to manipulate files and folders on your computer system. It covers commands dealing with disk operations, file information, program logic, data processing, and dialogs that are common to all four areas. Disk operations include commands that copy, move, rename, and delete files and folders. File information commands are those that retrieve paths, versions, and date and time stamps, and those that change file attributes and convert long and short file names. Program logic commands control the flow of your macro based on different file and folder statuses. Data processing commands extract data from text files and then converts it to variables. In turn, these variables can be used in any imaginable manner.

Window Controls

This chapter examines the Window Control commands. Window Controls are objects inside any window on your computer such as command buttons, text boxes, radio buttons, menus, drop-down lists, and so forth. These commands allow you to capture and control them directly. Each command is detailed and the whole process of capturing controls is exhaustively studied. Included is a good example that uses the Window's calculator.

List of Commands

This chapter contains an alphabetical list of all Macro Express commands and a short description of what each one does.

Companion CD

This chapter explains what is contained on the companion CD that included with this book.

Conclusion

This chapter contains a few parting thoughts about the book and about Macro Express. It also has instructions on how to log on to our web site to get updates.

Credits

This book was written by **Joseph Weinpert** at Professional Grade Macros www.pgmacros.com

Technical editing was completed by **Kevin Heaton** at Insight Software Solutions www.wintools.com

The videos were written, produced, and edited by **Matthew Frandsen** at Formaquest Technologies www.formaquest.com

Book cover and companion CD artwork designed by **Danielle Wilber** at ImageFirst Graphics

Publishing consultant for this book was **Patricia Graham** at Trafford Publishing www.trafford.com

Macro Express Explained printed by **Trafford Publishing** www.trafford.com

Technical tools

This book was written using **Microsoft Word** *2002* from Microsoft Corporation www.microsoft.com

Drafts were prepared using **UltraEdit-32** *Professional Hex/Text Editor* from IDM Computer Solution www.ultraedit.com

Primary editing performed using **StyleWriter** *the Plain English Editor* from Editor Software (UK) Ltd www.editorsoftware.com

Draft pictures were produced using **Capture Express** *Quick & Easy Image Capture* from Insight Software Solutions www.captureexpress.com

Pictures were produced using **SnagIt** *the Windows Screen Capture Utility* from TechSmith Corporation www.techsmith.com

Macros for writing and editing this book were created using **Macro Express** *The Windows Automation Tool* from Insight Software Solutions www.macroexpress.com

Macro Express Explained PDF document generated using **Adobe Acrobat Professional** from Adobe Systems Incorporated www.adobe.com

Fonts used in book

Body Text, Body Text Indent - Myriad Roman 10 pt

Emphasis (Window, dialog, and chapter titles) - Myriad Roman Italic 10 pt

Strong - Myriad Roman Bold 10 pt

Caption - Myriad Roman Bold 8 pt

Command, Function Name - MyriadPro Condensed Italic 10 pt

Macro Text, Block Text - MyriadPro Condensed 9 pt

Macro Comment - MyriadPro Condensed 9 pt (50% grey)

Field Name, Variable, Keyboard - MyriadPro Condensed 10 pt

Registry Value - Myriad Roman Bold Italic 9 pt

Header - MyriadPro Condensed 12 pt

Page Number - MyriadPro Condensed 14 pt

Heading 2 - Myriad Roman Bold 18 pt (shadow)

Heading 3 - Myriad Roman Bold 14 pt

Heading 4 - Myriad Roman Bold 12 pt

Heading 5, Syntax - MyriadPro Condensed 11 pt

Introduction to Macro Express

Welcome to Macro Express! The purpose in using Macro Express is to create automation macros, which at the very least, are script files that send keystrokes to your keyboard and move and click your mouse for you … or rather, instead of you.

If it can be done with a keyboard and mouse, do it with Macro Express … is a theme we here at Professional Grade Macros truly believe, and have built many macro application based on. Some small, some large, and a whole bunch between.

Look at it like this; You may run a few different types of software applications on your computer, each performing a separate task or service, and each having a different purpose. Word processing, spreadsheets, databases, internet browsers, graphic programs, specialized applications like accounting and legal packages, buying and selling stuff on the internet, playing games, and so forth. Or you may run just one or two applications. It does not matter, because as different as these applications are, they all have one thing in common. They require *your* input from *your* keyboard and *your* mouse. It is like your automobile. You may only have one, but you drive it to many different places using the *same* steering wheel and the *same* gas pedal. Likewise, you use the *same* keyboard and the *same* mouse to drive your computer, no matter what it is running. So, since it *must* be done with a keyboard and mouse, do it with Macro Express.

We think that Macro Express *is* the premier macro utility on the market today. Its powerful tools and robust features will noticeably boost your productivity … if productivity is what your goal is. It may not be. Maybe you just want to turn over to Macro Express some of the mundane tasks you must perform everyday. Get the e-mail, get to the internet, look at your bank account, read the news, go to your favorite auction site, and anything else you can think of. This is what makes Macro Express such a premier utility. It can be used to create single-line macros to do the drudgery work. But it can also be used to produce macros containing thousands of lines of code, spanning hundreds of macros, and linking with many applications at once, all to complete a particular task. And it is free for the first 30 days. And it is cheap. Nirvana!

Macro Express comes with a tutorial and an extensive help system to get you started. As you familiarize yourself with these tools you will learn that it contains over 260 commands in 24 categories, recognizes over 700 HotKeys, 6 different kinds of automatic activations, 9 different types of scheduling tasks, and 4 different scope classes.

Stating the obvious, you must install Macro Express before you can use it. Read the *Installation* chapter, which has two sections called *Basic Installation* and *Advanced Installation*. If you have not yet installed Macro Express then at least read the *Basic Installation* section. However, there is a lot to be learned about Macro Express from reading the *Advanced Installation* section, too, even if you have already installed it.

Starting Macro Express

You can start Macro Express by choosing it from the Start Menu or by clicking on its Desktop icon, which was placed there during installation.

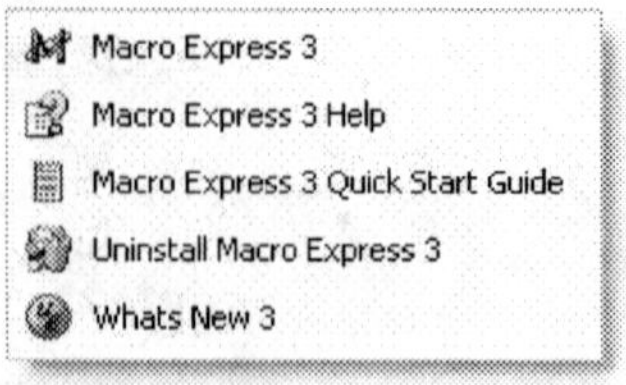

If the Macro Express icon is in your System Tray then Macro Express has been launched. Depending on the installation choices you made, you may or may not see the window titled *Macro Explorer*. Chances are you will, but if you do not, click on the Macro Express icon in your System Tray or just press the **Ctrl+Alt+Shft+W** system HotKey to launch it.

The Macro Express Editor's main window pops up, which is titled *Macro Explorer*. This is the main link between you and  Macro Express and is detailed in the *Macro Express Editor* chapter. The top portion is shown here with the *samples.mex* macro library file loaded. This file was placed in the Macro Express home folder during installation and contains plenty of samples to go with the tutorial.

The term "library file" is what we at Professional Grade Macros call a Macro Express *.mex* file because it is a repository for macros that you create. You can have many different library files containing many different macros for many different purposes. Or just one library file that contains all of your macros. Macro library files are discussed in the *Running and Activating Macros* chapter.

Startup Preferences

You may want to change some of the Macro Express startup features, which can be done by choosing (Options | Preferences | Startup) from the main menu. The *Startup* dialog panel is shown on the right.

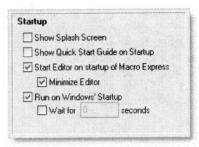

The splash screen can be turned off (the default is on) by unchecking the **Show Splash Screen** checkbox. To turn it back on for launching, put a checkmark in the box.

The Quick Start Guide can be turned off by unchecking the **Show Quick Start Guide on Startup** checkbox. Depending on the choices made during installation, it may already be turned off. To turn it back on for launching, check the box here or in the Quick Start Guide itself.

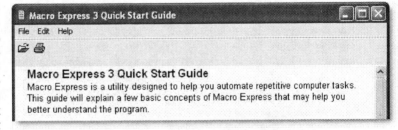

The **Start Editor on Startup of Macro Express** checkbox controls whether the Macro Express Editor (*MacEdit.exe*) will be launched with the Macro Express player program (*MacExp.exe*). If the **Minimize Editor** checkbox is checked, it will be minimized to your Taskbar when launched;

otherwise, it will be displayed normally. When you installed Macro Express, you were asked whether it is to be launched whenever Windows starts. For example, on boot-up. You can change the decision you made here. To prevent Macro Express from launching automatically, uncheck the **Run on Windows Startup** checkbox.

The **Wait for XX Seconds** checkbox, if checked, forces Macro Express to delay the number of specified seconds before executing its internal startup procedures such as establishing hooks and shared memory. You probably do not need to use this option. However, on some computers, Windows may not be fully loaded when Macro Express begins to launch. If that is the case on your computer, check the **Wait for XX Seconds** box and try different values.

Create a Macro

Let's create a macro to open your *Control Panel* dialog. The first thing we are going to do is to create a new library file so that you are not adding macros to the default macro library file *macex.mex*, or the sample macro library file *samples.mex*. Click on the New Macro File icon in the toolbar or choose (File | New Macro File) from the main menu (**Alt+F,N**). The *Create*

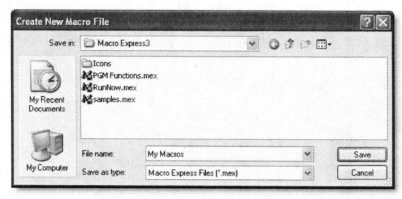

New Macro File dialog appears. Let's name the file "My Macros.mex". When you click on the **Save** button, Macro Express will generate the file and load it into the Macro Express Editor. You can create any number of macro library (*.mex*) files in this manner. And there is no limit to the number of macros that each can hold (but there is sure to be a practical limit).

To reload the previous macro library file, click on the Open Macro File icon in the  toolbar or choose (File | Open Macro File) from the main menu (**Alt+F,0**). When the *Open Macro* dialog appears, simply navigate to the file and pick it. This is the same method used to load any macro library file. Only a single file can be loaded into the Macro Express Editor at any given time.

So now the *Macro Explorer* window looks like this with the *My Macros.mex* file loaded:

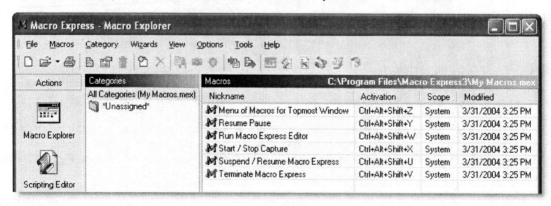

Notice the library already contains six macros. These are system macros that are generated automatically with each new macro library file. See the *Macro Express Editor* chapter for more information on system macros.

To create a new macro, click on the New Macro icon in the toolbar or choose (Macros | Add Macros) from the main menu (**Alt+M,A**). The *Add Macro* dialog pops up with the left-hand section containing macro activation types. Click on the **No Activation** radio button. You can change the activation type later. As a matter of fact, multiple activations can be added to any macro after it is created. Activation types are explained in the *Running and Activating Macros* chapter.

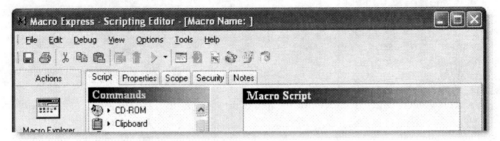

The right-side of the dialog provides three ways to create a macro. The buttons are named **Scripting Editor**, **Direct Editor**, and **Capture Macro**. These choices, and more, are detailed in the *Creating and Editing Macros* chapter. Click on the **Scripting Editor** button and the *Scripting Editor* window appears.

The Commands pane on the left holds all the Macro Express commands (over 260 of them), separated into in 24 categories. The Macro Script pane on the right is where the macro, any macro, is created. The concept is simple. Find a command in the Commands category then, if the command has options or features (and most do), set them. Click the **OK** button and the command will be placed into the Macro Script pane. The Scripting Editor is fully explained in the *Creating and Editing Macros* chapter.

Scroll down through the categories until you find a category named **System**, and then click on it. Now look for the **Control Panel Open** command. Double-click on it and an options dialog pops up named *Control Panel*. Make sure the **Open Main Control Panel** radio button is chosen and then click the **OK** button. The command is added to the Macro Script pane.

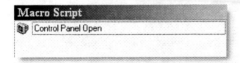

Name the macro before saving it. There is a set of tabs above the Commands pane. Click on the **Properties** Tab. The **Nickname** field is used for the macro name. Let's call it "Open My Control Panel". Enter the name and then click on the Save icon in the toolbar or press **Ctrl+S**.

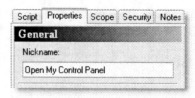

Now we can go back to the *Macro Explorer* window. Click on the large Macro Explorer icon in the Actions toolbar and you will see that the macro has been added to the list of macros.

The macros are sorted alphabetically with the macro we added highlighted. The **Activation** column displays which activation type the macro is set for. Multiple activations are strung together on the same line. We had chosen **No Activation** before creating the macro in the Scripting Editor. The **Scope** column shows how the macro is scoped. In this case it is **Global**, meaning that it can be run anytime and anywhere. This is the Macro Express default

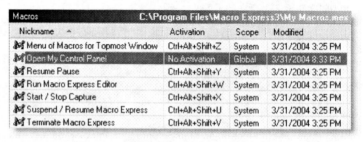

setting. Everything you want to know about scope and activation are covered in the *Running and Activating Macros* chapter.

That is it! You have created a macro. Now let's run it. Right-click on the macro and then choose "Run Macro Now" from the menu list (or press "**R**") and your *Control Panel* dialog pops up.

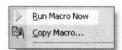

With a single-line macro, we have created a tool that replaces the steps you would normally have taken to open your *Control Panel* dialog. Everybody does it different, but one way is to double-click on the My Computer icon on your Desktop, which will pop up the *My Computer* dialog containing the Control Panel icon. Double-click on it and the *Control Panel* is displayed. You can create a macro to do it this way, too.

So you do not need the Macro Express Editor

program to be running to launch the ***Open My Control Panel*** macro, change the activation from **No Activation** to **HotKey** activation. Read the *Running and Activating Macros* chapter to learn how to change, or add activations to a macro. Let's just say for now it is changed to **Win+Alt+C**. With the HotKey set, you can invoke the macro to launch the *Control Panel* dialog anytime, and from almost anywhere.

The Scripting Editor is only one way to create a macro. It is menu-driven, structured, and easy to read. The Direct Editor is a text editor and the macro within in it is a single unbroken line of mnemonic commands, which is its natural state. An external text editor can also be used. Macros can be captured "on-the-fly" using the Capture tool to record keyboard and mouse activity. And finally, they can be created using the 28 built-in Quick Wizards, which are internal macro builders. These methods are explained in the *Creating and Editing Macros* chapter.

Playing Macros

Macro Express works by reading and processing command lines in a macro, one at a time, and from top to bottom. Of course there are programming construct commands like ***If / End If***, ***Switch / End Switch***, ***Repeat / Repeat End***, and so forth that affect the processing sequence and add power to your macros.

No matter how many times you click on the Macro Express icon in the System Tray, only a single instance of the Macro Express player program (*MacExp.exe*) will run on your computer. However, and this is -NOT- recommended, you may have success on Windows XP running another instance as a different logged-in user. But be warned … your computer is at risk -AND- you are on your own. Do not call Insight Software Solutions to ask for support when doing this. By logging in under multiple names, you may get Macro Express to run concurrently for each user on your computer -BUT- you only have -ONE- keyboard and -ONE- mouse for Macro Express to access.

Only a single macro can run at any given time. One macro may call another macro using the ***Macro Run*** command, but it is still only one macro that is running. When a ***Macro Run*** command is finished, the calling macro will begin where it left off, which is at the line following the ***Macro Run*** command. It may be that a scheduled macro will attempt to run when you are running a different macro manually, say while editing and testing. If this happens, the scheduled macro will be placed in a queue and run when the current macro finishes.

With proper licensing, macros can be run over a network. Users can create, edit, and run macros stored on a server. Networking is set up in the (Options | Preferences | Network) dialog and is explained in the *Running and Activating Macros* chapter.

There are two types of macros, those contained within a macro library (*.mex*) file and those that are external to it. The latter are called playable macros and are individual text files that end with a *.mxe* file extension. These are played back by double-clicking on them or by using the command line arguments explained in the *Running and Activating Macros* chapter. The internal macros are played back by running them manually (No Activation), or by picking them from Popup and Floating menus. They can also be invoked using HotKeys, ShortKeys, or clicking on an area of your screen or a window. Playing them back automatically is done using scheduling or when particular windows or window objects gain focus. All activation types are explained in the *Running and Activating Macros* chapter.

Scoping Macros

Scoping is the method used to prevent macros from being launched in an untimely fashion. Setting the scope allows you to specify what applications must be running, or not running, for a macro to launch. Say, for example, you have created a macro to handle some task in a Microsoft Word document. It does not make sense to let the macro launch unless Microsoft Word is running.

The default scope for any macro is Global, which means it can be run from anywhere. There are three other scope choices named Global Except, Window Specific, and Program Specific.

For example, a macro can be prevented from being launched unless a certain window title is running, or unless this window title *and* that window title is running. You also choose if one or all the window titles must match exactly, character for character, or use a partial match. Furthermore, you decide if at least one of the window titles has to have focus before the macro will launch. This, and the rest of the scope options, are explained in the *Running and Activating Macros* chapter.

Macro Commands

As mentioned before, Macro Express contains over 260 commands spread throughout 24 default categories. The diversity of these commands is one of the main strengths of Macro Express. After all, the commands *are* the macros.

Naturally there are commands that control and gather data from your keyboard, mouse, and monitor. But also:

- There are commands for your clipboard, Windows Explorer, Internet Explorer, internet web pages and FTP sites.
- There are commands to read from, and write to, your Registry, and to create, delete, and process data in text files … delimited, CSV, or otherwise.
- There are categories of commands to control other software applications such as launching and terminating them, or running them much the same as you do.
- Commands are available to capture and control objects like command buttons and text fields. Also to get pixel colors from your screen.
- There are variable commands, program logic commands, Boolean operator commands, and repeat loop commands.
- Commands exist to control your Desktop, network, screen savers, wallpaper, to run links in your Control Panel or use the system Run dialog.
- You can shut down, logoff, reboot, hibernate, lock, suspend, and undock your computer.
- You will also find multimedia commands for your CD-ROM player, audio controls, MIDI controls, and WAV and AVI players.
- There are categories of commands that control Macro Express, or the macros themselves, including debugging commands.

See the *List of Commands* chapter for Macro Express commands and a short description of each.

Installation

Installation? Well, even if this is something most of you have already done, it is a good place to begin because of the advanced features. You will like these, especially if you have many customers, or are charged with the demanding task of keeping a network up-to-date. So let's quickly get through the Macro Express standard installation stuff.

If you are installing Macro Express on Windows NT, 2000 or XP then you will need administrative rights to write to the **HKEY_LOCAL_MACHINE** section of your Windows Registry. Windows 95, 98, and ME give each user administrative rights by default.

Basic Installation

To install Macro Express you first need to get it … and you can get it from the Macro Express web site at www.macros.com/download. Once there, download either macex.zip or macex.exe. There is no right or wrong choice, only your choice.

If you decide on macex.zip, then you will need to unzip it with either WinZip or PKZip to get to the real setup file called macex.exe. On the other hand, macex.exe is already good to go, so why bother with the zip file? The rest of this chapter refers to the macex.exe setup file.

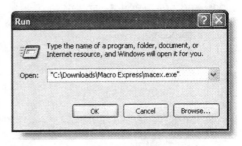

Use the *Run Command* dialog to start the setup. Click on your **Start** button and then **Run**. Use the **Browse** button to find the setup file then click **Open**. Now click **OK** to run it.

Welcome

Reading this, you will see a suggestion to shut down any running programs before continuing forward. It is an excellent idea so do it, especially any screen savers. Also, shut down Macro Express if you are upgrading. You can leave the installation file running while closing the other programs. Click **Next** when you are ready to move on.

License Agreement

Standard stuff. Use the **elevator bar** to read through it and then do yourself a favor and agree to it. Disagreeing causes the installation to stop. So there you go, not much left to say.

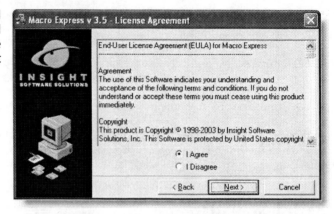

Installation Type

You are given a choice of a default or custom installation. The default is to install the *Editor*, *Help files*, a *Quick Start Guide*, all *Icons*, and *not* overwrite any newer files. If you want to override these defaults, choose **Custom Installation**.

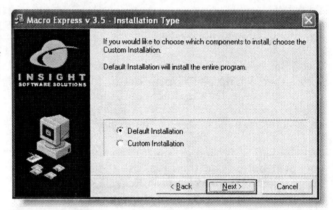

Select Components

If you want to perform a custom installation, here is a short explanation of each choice:

Editor

You are going to need this program (*MacEdit.exe*) to create and edit macros. If your installation is only for running previously created macros then you do not need it.

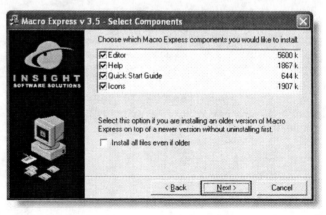

Help

The help file (*MacExp3.chm*) is extensive and contains nearly 400 pages of help topics.

Quick Start Guide

This is a two-page document (*MEQuickStart.doc*) explaining basic Macro Express concepts. It can be viewed with the *QkStart.exe* program that was installed with Macro Express or with Microsoft Word. Although short, it is a well-designed document for brand-spanking new users.

Icons

Over 200 icons for you to stamp your macros with.

Install Older Files

Check this option if you are reinstalling an older version on top of a newer version. Normally this is not done, is it? Although sometimes it may be necessary if a newer release does not, for whatever reason, run a macro that clearly ran in an older version. I think it would be better to uninstall the newer version before reinstalling the older one.

If you clear all of these choices, you will, in effect, be installing a read-only system. This is a nice feature for those of you that have network users needing only to run macros.

Search for Existing Versions

This tries to set the install path for you by finding an existing Macro Express installation. Unless you have a real compelling reason to do so, answer **No** because this search can take a longtime to complete. It is one of those get-a-cup-of-coffee-and-a-sandwich searches. The only reason to answer **Yes** is if you forgot where your current version of Macro Express is installed and you cannot find it using *Windows Explorer*, which would be unlikely.

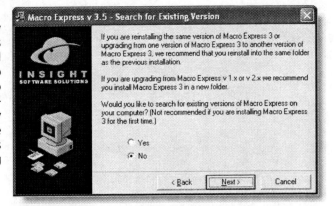

Search Results

If you decide to do a search, then at some point you will see this dialog. Did I mention the search takes a real longtime?

Choose **Yes** to the highlighted install path that was found. Answering **No** means that you did not want to do the search anyway. How was the sandwich?

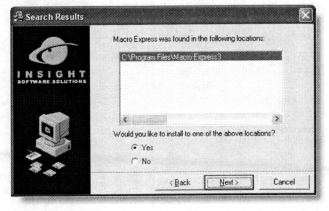

Choose Destination Location

If you searched for an existing installation in the previous step then the path will be displayed here for your confirmation. On the other hand, the default path for your workstation is displayed. Either way, this dialog is telling you where it wants to install Macro Express. If you are not happy with the choice then change it by clicking on the **Browse** button. Macro Express does not care where it is installed and will work wonderfully wherever you decide its home should be.

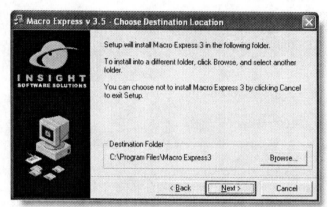

If you clicked **Browse** in the last step then you want to find a place to install Macro Express. Here you see a standard folder search dialog named *Select Destination Directory*. Use it to choose where you want to install Macro Express then click **OK**.

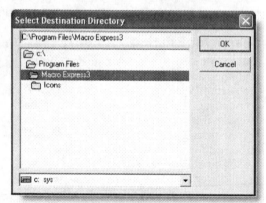

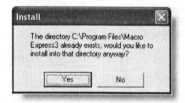

This *Install* dialog may appear once you have chosen a location. It is a warning that Macro Express exists and that you are about to overwrite it. Time to make a decision … choosing **Yes** will take you back to the *Destination Location* dialog. **No** will allow you to select a different installation folder.

Select Start Menu Folder

Now you are being prompted for a Macro Express installation name to place in the list of available programs menu (Start | Programs). Choose the default, pick one from the list, or type in anything that you like. "*Macro Express*" would be my choice.

Run on Windows Startup

This dialog let's you decide whether to start the Macro Express player each time you reboot your workstation. Your answer can always be changed from within Macro Express with the (Options | Preferences | Startup) dialog.

Start Installation

This is it! This is the dialog you have been looking for. The last one ... well, almost. If you want to install Macro Express then click **Next** otherwise you can **Cancel** now and start the whole process again.

Installing

You can watch your choices displayed as they are installed. When completed, this "reboot" dialog may, or may not, appear. It means that a file currently in use needs to be updated by the installer, which can only be done when your computer reboots. Choose **OK** to restart your computer and allow the installer to finish.

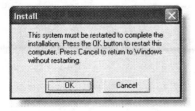

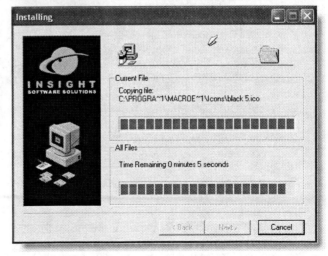

Installation Complete

If, on the other hand, you are able to forge right into Macro Express (and if the installer does not need to reboot), then you are given a couple of choices. If you want to start Macro Express right away, then check the **Launch Macro Express** checkbox. If you want to read the Quick Start Guide, then check the **View Quick Start Guide** checkbox. Click **Finish** to complete the installation.

File Association Notification

One more thing. This dialog may, or may not, appear when you start Macro Express for the first time. It depends on if this is your first Macro Express installation. It wants to know whether to associate *.mex* and *.mxe* files with Macro Express. Do it. Period. And put a checkmark in the **Don't Ask Again** box. From this point forward, your operating system will know that any *.mex* or *.mxe* files are to be handled by Macro Express.

What was installed?

In my example these files are installed into the C:\Program Files\Macro Express folder.

CapUtil.exe - Window Controls capture utility program.
HHActive.ini - Configuration for the HTML help file.
HHActiveX.dll - Dynamic link library for the HTML help file.
iCapture.dll - Dynamic link library used for the **Wait for Web Page** command in *previous* versions. It may be in the folder, but it is not installed with version 3.5.
Icons - Folder containing billions of icons … well, at least a couple of hundred.
Install.log - File containing what was installed. Used by the uninstaller program *UnWise.exe*. Leave it alone.
MacDef.exe - Utility program to reset Macro Express preferences back to their default state after you have messed them up.
MacEdit.exe - Macro Express editor program.
MacEx.mex - Your macro library (see the advanced **MacroFileDest** option).
MacExp.exe - Macro Express player program.
MacExp3.chm - Macro Express compiled HTML help file.
MeProc.exe - Macro Express process program to launch *.mxe* macro files. Quick little bugger!
MeQuickStart.doc - Macro Express Quick Start Guide document for the uninitiated.
MexHook.dll - Macro Express dynamic link hook library.
MSLocate.exe - Mouse cursor locator program.
MSLocHK.dll - Mouse locator dynamic link hook library.

PostCommCtrl.ini - Constant reference file for the Window Controls PostMessage command.
PostMessage.ini - Constant reference file for the Window Controls PostMessage command.
PostRichEdit.ini - Constant reference file for the Window Controls PostMessage command.
Restart_MacExp.exe - Executable called by the **Restart Macro Express** command.
RunNow.mex - Not installed, but may be placed in your folder when running macros from the debug window. It is an internal work file for Macro Express.
Samples.mex - Great macro library containing how-to macro samples.
SweepWiz.exe - Wizard for creating macros to use when entering sweepstakes.
SwpKey.mes - Contains remapped keyboard definitions as defined in (Tools | Remap Keyboard).
UnWise.exe - Macro Express uninstaller program.
WhatsNew.txt - Log file containing the Macro Express changes from revision to revision.

And these files are installed into the C:\Program Files\Common Files\Insight Software Solutions folder. They are common files used by other Insight Software Solutions products such as Keyboard Express, Zip Express, ShortKeys, and so forth:

ISSBugRp.exe - A bug reporter program called automatically when Macro Express detects an error, which allows you to send a report about the nasty thing that just happened.
QkStart.exe - Program to launch the Quick Start Guide for various Insight Software Solutions products.

Finally, these link files are installed into your Start button program list (on my system this is contained in the C:\Documents and Settings\All Users\Start Menu\Programs\Macro Express folder). These files are what you see when you choose (Start | Programs | Macro Express):

Macro Express 3.lnk - The Macro Express player *MacExp.exe*
Macro Express 3 Help.lnk - The Macro Express compiled HTML help file *MacExp3.chm*
Macro Express 3 Quick Start Guide.lnk - The Quick Start Guide program *QkStart.exe*
Uninstall Macro Express 3.lnk - The Macro Express uninstaller program *UnWise.exe*
What is New.lnk - The Macro Express change log text file *WhatsNew.txt*

Advanced Installation

Advanced installation is a way to answer all the basic installation questions without needing to prompt you, or your users, for answers. This is great for installing Macro Express across a network or even ... and get this ... *from another setup.exe program*. If you have macro libraries, graphics, programs, and so forth that need to be installed on individual workstations, pack them into a *setup.exe* program, and have the installation done from a single file. There are hundreds of *installer* packages available in the market.

Taking advantage of the advanced installation feature is easy. Just add a **/S** and/or **/M** flag to the *macex.exe* command line. For example "macex.exe /S /M=<Your Install File>". Case does not matter but the "/" slash character does. Do not use a "-" dash, it will not work. Also, **/S** must precede **/M** when used together.

The **/S** flag tells Macro Express to install silently without screen prompts and questions, using default choices. If you do not want to use the defaults, then install Macro Express with the **/M**=<Your Install File> flag. For those of you who do not care about a silent install, and still do not want to use the defaults, then use **/M** without **/S**. Your choices will be conveniently displayed during installation.

Although any path and filename will do for your installation text file, we will use "C:\YourChoices.txt" for our example. An installation text file can be created with any text editor. The Macro Express help system says not to place any invalid options or comments in it. A comment is simply a line in the text file that does not begin with one of the legal option names. This is good advice. On the other hand, I must confess to putting comments into the file without anything bad happening.

There are 15 different options. The following five options are related to the *Select Components* dialog. Note the default answer for each option is shown first. If any options are left out of your file, or do not contain a specific "**Y**" or "**N**", then the default for that option will be used automatically by the installer. The option name may be upper, lower, or mixed case. There can be no spaces between it, the equal sign, and the answer. Last, but not least, some, but not all Macro Express installation options are double-negative type questions, so be careful.

NoEditor

N or **Y**. If (**N**)o then the macro editor (*MacEdit.exe*) will be installed. You are going to need this program to create and edit macros. If your installation is for only running previously created macros, then you do not need it, and you would answer (**Y**)es, do not install it.

NoHelp

N or **Y**. If (**N**)o then the Macro Express help (*MacExp3.chm*) will be installed. The help system is extensive and contains nearly 400 pages of help topics. If you do not need or want it, then you would answer (**Y**)es, do not install it.

NoQuickStart

N or **Y**. If (**N**)o then the Quick Start Guide will be installed with the program to display it (*MEQuickStart.doc* and *QkStart.exe*). This is a two-page document explaining basic Macro Express concepts. Although short, it is a well-designed document for brand-spanking new users. If you do not need or want it, then you would answer (**Y**)es, do not install it, and ignore the *QuickStartNow* option below.

NoIcons

N or **Y**. If (**N**)o then over 200 icons, which can be used to stamp your macros, will be installed into the Macro Express Icons subfolder. If you do not need or want them, then you would answer (**Y**)es, do not install them. You can create your own icons and place them in this same Icons subfolder regardless of what you decide here.

InstallOlder

N or **Y**. If (**N**)o then newer files within the target installation folder will not be overwritten with older files from the installation program during a reinstall procedure. Answering (**Y**)es will assure that all files are overwritten. Period. Which is what you would want if your installing an older version of Macro Express over a newer version without doing an uninstall first. On the other hand, it is nice to know that you can do a reinstall and preserve changes that you have made at the same time.

Now here is something interesting. If all options are set to (**Y**)es, you will, in effect, be installing a read-only system, which is a great feature for those of you that have network users that only need to run macros.

The next three options are related to the *Choose Destination Location*, *Select Start Menu Folder*, and *Run on Windows Startup?* dialogs.

InstallPath

<drive:\Macro Express Folder>. Macro Express will be installed into whatever path is entered here. If you leave this option out, or it remains blank, then the default C:\Program Files\Macro Express3 installation folder will be used. Any trailing "\" backslash characters are ignored.

StartMenuFoldr

<Folder Name>. The name that you enter here is the name that will be listed in the Program menu (from your Start button on your Desktop) containing the Macro Express programs. If you leave this option out, or it remains blank, then the default "Macro Express" name will be used.

Startup

Y or **N**. If (**Y**)es then Macro Express will start automatically when Windows starts. If you do not want this to happen, then you would answer (**N**)o, do not start Macro Express automatically. This feature is independent of the *LaunchNow* option, which controls only what happens immediately after installation.

The following two options are related to the *Installation Complete* dialog.

LaunchNow

Y or **N**. If (**Y**)es then Macro Express will launch immediately after the installation completes. If you do not want this to happen, then you would answer (**N**)o, do not launch Macro Express. This option, by the way, has no effect on the *QuickStartNow* option. The Quick Start Guide is independent of this, meaning that you can display the Quick Start Guide without Macro Express being launched.

QuickStartNow

Y or **N** or **P**. These choices control when the Quick Start Guide is, or is not, displayed. The **Y** and **N** choices affect only the installer, while the **P** choice affects Macro Express at startup.

If (**Y**)es, and if you have installed the Quick Start Guide (*NoQuickStart*=N), then it will be displayed after the installation is complete regardless of the *LaunchNow* setting. That is right; it will be displayed even if Macro Express is not launched.

(**N**)o will not display it after the installation however, when Macro Express is launched, it may still be displayed. The **Y** and **N** choices affect only the installer, not Macro Express. By default, when Macro Express first launches, it displays the Quick Start Guide.

(**P**)revent tells Macro Express to not display the Quick Start Guide when it first launches. Windows XP, 2000 and NT users: This option only applies to the person who is logged on when Macro Express is installed. If an administrator installs Macro Express using *QuickStartNow*=P, then Quick Start Guide will still be displayed when another user logs on.

The **P** option can be combined with either the **Y** or **N** option. **NP** tells the installer to not display the Quick Start Guide and tells Macro Express to not display the Quick Start Guide. **YP** tells the installer to display the Quick Start Guide and tells Macro Express to not display the Quick Start Guide.

One more point covering this option. The **/S** flag tells Macro Express to install silently without screen prompts and questions, using default choices. However, depending on the *QuickStartNow* options you have selected, the Quick Start Guide may be displayed even when the **/S** option is used.

Once the Quick Start Guide is displayed, the **Do not show this the next time Macro Express runs** checkbox controls whether the Quick Start Guide will be displayed the next time Macro Express is launched. This setting can also be changed from the Startup section of the Preferences dialog, which is accessed from the main Macro Express menu (Options | Preferences).

> ☑ Do not show this the next time Macro Express runs
>
> c:\program files\macro express3\MEQuickStart.doc

Reboot

N or **Y**. Sometimes it is necessary to reboot your system after installing Macro Express. If this is true during the basic install, a dialog window appears. Setting this option to (**N**)o, which is the default choice, will prevent the dialog from appearing even if the installer says that it should. Setting it to (**Y**)es will allow it to appear if it is needed.

> **Install**
>
> This system must be restarted to complete the installation. Press the OK button to restart this computer. Press Cancel to return to Windows without restarting.
>
> [OK]   [Cancel]

LicenseName

<Name>. This is the name that your Macro Express license was registered to. Make sure you enter it exactly as it appears; case, spaces … everything.

LicenseCode

<Code>. This is the code that you were given with the above name and just like the name, enter it exactly as it appears … dashes and all.

You must use both the *LicenseName* and *LicenseCode* options together. Placing one in the installation text file without the other will quash both of them, as if neither one exists.

ConfigFilePath

<Name>. For example, "*C:\YourConfig.mcf*". All the previous options concentrated what and where to install, and what to do afterwards. This next one is meant for those of you that have network users, or clients for whom you want to create a consistent Macro Express installation containing identical preferences. It uses an existing Macro Express configuration (*.mcf*) file to feed Macro Express Windows Registry settings during the installation process.

If you have any experience importing and exporting data from your Windows Registry, you know that a file extension of *.reg* is used for storage. The Macro Express configuration file is similar except that it uses a *.mcf* extension, although you can name the file anything you wish.

To use this option, you first need to install Macro Express, and then set the *Preferences* dialog features to your liking. Once set, you can export them from the *Tools* menu inside Macro Express, or from the *System Tray* icon, then type in the name of the configuration file.

The output is a text file that contains almost 2,000 configuration lines. Do not try to change the file in any way. If you want to change, or fix something, then adjust the *Preferences* dialog and export the file again.

```
<[Macro Express]>
<<Windows 5.1.2600>>
<HKEY_CURRENT_USER>
[Software\Insight Software Solutions\Macro Express]
integer    Report Number  10
[Software\Insight Software Solutions\Macro Express\AdvOptions]
string     Menu Style XP
integer    Macro Priority   0
[Software\Insight Software Solutions\Macro Express\Backup]
integer    Schedule   0
integer    Prompt     1
integer    Days 3
integer    Def Path   1
string     Path
integer    Count      99
binary     Last Time  00 00 00 00 00 00 00 00
integer    Timeout    0
integer    Timeout Value   10
integer    Answer Yes 1
```

```
[Software\Insight Software Solutions\Macro Express\Bypass]
string     SetInt     0
string     SetStr     0
string     ActivateLaunch  0
string     GetControl 1
string     OpenFolder     1
string     VidClip    0
[Software\Insight Software Solutions\Macro Express\Capture]
integer    Clicks Only 0
integer    Double Alt 1
integer    Global     1
integer    Keys 1
integer    Window Size     1
```

But wait, there's more!

Get this ... you can create another configuration file specifically named "*defprefs.mcf*" and place it in the folder where you installed Macro Express to accommodate *first-time* users.

Why would you want to do this? By default when a first-time Macro Express user runs Macro Express their HKEY_CURRENT_USER preferences are set to the default values built into Macro Express. As a systems administrator, these may not be the ones that you want the user to have. This option allows you to set the default preferences for these first-time users. When they run Macro Express for the first time, it will set their preference from this file. Once set, this file is not used again for that user.

MacroFileDest

<drive:\path\name of Macro Express library.mex>. Macro Express will install a macro library (.mex file) for you, and you do not even need this option for it to happen. Simply place your macro library in the same folder as the "*macex.exe*" installer and rename it "*macexinstall.mex*".

Without this option line, Macro Express will copy the "*macexinstall.mex*" file to the destination folder and rename it "*macex.mex*".

With this option line, Macro Express will copy the "*macexinstall.mex*" file to the named path and will rename it to the specified name. *Be careful with this option*. If you specify an illegal path or file name, say one with illegal characters, then the installer will not be able to rename it. Worse than that, the installer may not finish so the uninstall data is never written. In other words, you may not be able to easily uninstall Macro Express.

Special Installation Files

Before I explain these undocumented files and what they do, you need to know that Insight Software Solutions will not accept support calls about them. They are undocumented for a reason, which is they are subject to change without notice. However, I found that my installations are easier because I do not have to change options in an installation text file.

These are physical files, which take precedence over their counterparts in the installation text file. They can be placed in either the same folder as the installer file "*macex.exe*" or the destination folder. Their contents do not matter. The installer only checks to see if the filename exists in one of the two folders.

PrgLoad.chk

If Macro Express is running, an attempt is made to stop it before the installation continues. It does not always work. If the Scripting Editor or Direct Editor window is open, and a macro has not been saved at the time you try to install, funny things happen. Maybe not so funny, depending on your point-of-view. Do not leave either editor open when installing a Macro Express upgrade. Period.

NoQuickStart

The Quick Start Guide (*MEQuickStart.doc*) will not be installed. This is the same as setting the installation text file *NoQuickStart* option to (**Y**)es.

NoIcons

None of the over 200 icon files will be installed. This is the same as setting the installation text file *NoIcons* option to (**Y**)es.

NoStartup

Macro Express will *not* automatically start when your computer starts. This is the same as setting the installation text file *Startup* option to (**N**)o.

NoQuickStartNow

Do not display the Quick Start Guide. This is the same as setting the installation text file *QuickStartNow* option to (**N**)o.

Summary

- You must have administrative rights to install Macro Express.
- Close all applications before installing, including screen savers.
- There is both a standard and custom installation choice.
- Turning off all installation options results in a read-only Macro Express system.
- Do not let the installation program search for an existing Macro Express version unless you have too much time on your hands.
- The Macro Express setup program may be combined with other setup programs.
- The advanced installation technique answers questions posed in the basic installation dialogs for silent and network-wide installations.
- Some of the configuration option choices have double negative meanings, so be careful.
- You can include your User ID and Key Code in the installation.
- A system-wide preferences file can be created and spread throughout your network using the advanced installation techniques.
- A default preferences file may be used to accommodate any user of Macro Express even if they have never logged on to a particular workstation before.

Macro Express Editor

Did you know the only thing needed to create and run macros is any plain old text editor and the Macro Express player program (*MacExp.exe*)? Of course other files (like a few .dlls) are required but, technically, that is all that is needed! It can be done. And it has been done. But why? Why would you want to do it this way when there is a great big editor and interface specifically designed, built-in, and waiting for you to use, as part of Macro Express?

And this is it. This is the Macro Express primary interface window. It is from here that you access other windows and dialogs for creating, editing, running, importing, printing, and anything and everything else to do with macros.

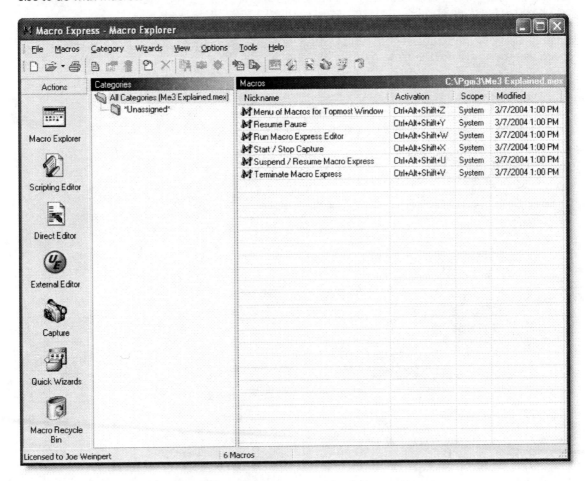

It generates and controls your macro library files (*.mex*). Although titled *Macro Explorer*, it is the Macro Express Editor program *MacEdit.exe*. Throughout this book when referring to the *Macro Explorer*

window, we are referring to the title of the main window of the Macro Express Editor. In fact, the Macro Express Editor consists of four different windows, which are Macro Explorer, Scripting Editor, Direct Editor, and Macro Recycle Bin. The Scripting Editor and Direct Editor windows are detailed in their own sections within the *Creating and Editing Macros* chapter. The Macro Recycle Bin window is discussed later in this chapter.

You control whether or not the Macro Express Editor appears when launching Macro Express by using the **Start Editor on Startup of Macro Express** checkbox, which is found in the (Options | Preferences | Startup) dialog. If checked, it will be launched with the Macro Express Player program named *MacExp.exe*. If the **Minimize Editor** checkbox is checked, it will be minimized to your Taskbar when  launched; otherwise, it will be displayed normally. More information about the relationship between *MacEdit.exe*, *MacExp.exe*, and another program called *MeProc.exe* can be found in the *Components* section within the *Running and Activating Macros* chapter.

Regardless of how you set the startup feature, the Macro Express Editor can be launched any time using the *Run Macro Express Editor* system macro by pressing **Ctrl+Alt+Shft+W**.

The *Macro Explorer* window is separated into five sections:

1. Main Menu

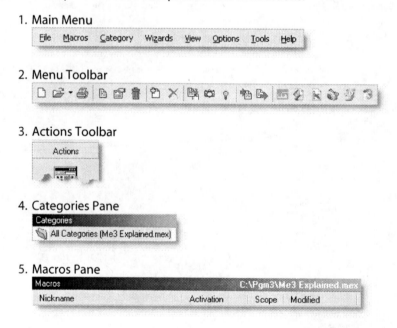

2. Menu Toolbar

3. Actions Toolbar

4. Categories Pane

5. Macros Pane

Main Menu

We will not go into any great detail here; after all, a menu is a menu. But there are some features to be aware of.

You can control how the drop-down menus look by using the **Menu Style** drop-down list, which is found in the (Options | Preferences | Appearance) dialog. There are three choices, **Flat** (the default), **Standard**, and **Enhanced**.

Examples of the three styles are, from left to right, **Flat**, **Standard**, and **Enhanced**. There is not much difference between the **Standard** and **Enhanced** styles, just the length of the menu separator lines. And there is little difference in functionality between the styles with one exception, the Menu Toolbar extension icon (shown here to the left) is disabled when using the **Standard** style. On the other hand, some text-to-speech software packages work better when using the **Standard** menu style.

The Main Menu can be moved. It does not have to remain at the top of the window. It can also be placed on the bottom, left, or right side of the window. Do this by moving the mouse cursor over the menu's resize bar highlighted here on the right. Your mouse cursor will change to a "Size All" arrow. Click and hold the left mouse button down and drag the menu over top of one of the other locations. It will automatically settle and position itself in place. Let go of the mouse button. The picture on the next page shows the menu positioned on the left side of the window. Because the Actions Toolbar takes precedence, it is positioned next to it.

You are not limited to moving the Main Menu around just inside the *Macro Explorer* window. It can also be moved to your Desktop. Take the same steps to grab the menu's resize bar, drag the menu to your Desktop, and then let it go. When the Main Menu is placed on your Desktop, it will be visible only when the *Macro Explorer* window has focus. Grab the menu by the "Main Menu" titlebar to move it back into the *Macro Explorer* window.

Be careful when moving the Main Menu. You can move it where it is no longer accessible. If that happens, you will need to reset the preferences. To do this, close the *Macro Explorer* window, right-click on the Macro Express icon in the System Tray, click "Tools" and then "Restore Program Defaults". When you launch the Macro Express Editor, the Main Menu will be restored to its default location.

Navigating the Main Menu

The following charts detail navigation keys for each menu within the main menu.

File Menu		
Shortcut	**Action**	**Icon**
Alt+F	File menu	
Alt+F N	New Macro File	
Alt+F O	Open Macro File	
Alt+F A	Save Macro File As	
Alt+F R	Reopen	
Alt+F R 1 - 7	Most recent files 1 - 7	
Alt+F B	Backup	
Alt+F I	Import	
Alt+F I I	Import Macros	
Alt+F I T	Import Text File	
Alt+F I P	Import a Playable Macro	
Alt+F E	Export	
Alt+F E E	Export Macros	
Alt+F E O	Output Macro Information	
Alt+F E P	Export as Playable Macro	
Alt+F P Ctrl+P	Print Macro List	
Alt+F F	Printer Font	
Alt+F U	Printer Setup	
Alt+F T	Terminate Macro Express Editor	
Alt+F X **Ctrl+Alt+Shft+V**	Terminate Macro Express Editor & Player	

Macros Menu		
Shortcut	**Action**	**Icon**
Alt+M	Macros menu	
Alt+M A	Add Macro	
Alt+M C	Copy Macro	
Alt+M N	Run Macro Now (icon not in toolbar)	
Alt+M S	Scripting Editor	
Alt+M D	Direct Editor	
Alt+M B	Menu Builder	
Alt+M E	Recapture Macro	
Alt+M B B	Disable Macro or Enable Macro	
Alt+M H Ctrl+F	Search or Find	
Alt+M G F3	Search Again	
Alt+M R Delete	Delete Macro(s)	
Alt+M L	Place on Desktop	
Alt+M M	Move to Category	
Alt+M P	Properties	

Category Menu		
Shortcut	**Action**	**Icon**
Alt+C	Category menu	
Alt+C A	Add Category	
Alt+C R	Rename Category	
Alt+C B	Enable/Disable Macros	
Alt+C D	Delete Category	

Wizards Menu	
Shortcut	**Action**
Alt+Z	Wizards menu
Alt+Z T	Text
Alt+Z I	Internet & Networking
Alt+Z M	Macro
Alt+Z U	Multimedia
Alt+Z S	System & Files

View Menu		
Shortcut	**Action**	**Icon**
Alt+V	View menu	
Alt+V E	Macro Explorer	
Alt+V S	Scripting Editor	
Alt+V D	Direct Editor	
Alt+V Q	Quick Wizards	
Alt+V R	Recycle Bin	

Options Menu	
Shortcut	**Action**
Alt+O	Options menu
Alt+O O	Sort Macros
Alt+O O N	By Nickname
Alt+O O A	By Activation
Alt+O O S	By Scope
Alt+O O D	By Date
Alt+O O C	Custom
Alt+O V	View
Alt+O V G	Large Icons
Alt+O V M	Small Icons
Alt+O V I	List
Alt+O V D	Details
Alt+O B	Configure Bug Reporter
Alt+O P	Preferences

Tools Menu	
Shortcut	**Action**
Alt+T	Tools menu
Alt+T L	Mouse Locator
Alt+T R	Remap Keyboard
Alt+T E	Error Log Viewer
Alt+T D	Restore Program Defaults
Alt+T I	Import Program Configuration
Alt+T X	Export Program Configuration
Alt+T F	Restore File Associations
Alt+T K	Restore Keyboard Hooks
Alt+T M	Restore Mouse Hooks

Help Menu	
Shortcut	**Action**
Alt+H	Help menu
Alt+H H	Macro Express Help
Alt+H T	Tutorial
Alt+H W	On the Web
Alt+H W H	Home Page
Alt+H W C	Check for Update
Alt+H W K	Knowledge Base
Alt+H W S	Support
Alt+H Q	Quick Start Guide
Alt+H B	Buy Macro Express
Alt+H L	License Information
Alt+H A	About Macro Express

Menu Toolbar

The Menu Toolbar contains 19 icons each matched with a choice within the Main Menu. Well, all but one … the Capture icon. Refer to the chart below.

Just like the Main Menu, the Menu Toolbar can be moved to the bottom, left, or right side of the *Macro Explorer* window. And it can be placed on your Desktop. It is done in the same manner as with the Main Menu. Grab the toolbar's resize bar with your mouse and drag it into position.

When placed on your Desktop, the Menu Toolbar is resizable, but will be visible only when the *Macro Explorer* window has focus. Grab the toolbar by the "Explorer" titlebar to move it back into the *Macro Explorer* window.

Be careful when moving the Menu Toolbar. You can move it where it is no longer accessible. If that happens, you will need to reset the preferences. Do it in the same manner as you would for the Main Menu.

Icon	Action	Shortcut	Icon	Action	Shortcut
	New Macro File	Alt+F N		Disable Macro or Enable Macro	Alt+M B B
	Open Macro File	Alt+F O		Import Macros	Alt+F I I
	Print Macro List	Alt+F P		Export Macros	Alt+F E E
	Add Macro	Alt+M A		Macro Explorer	Alt+V E
	Properties	Alt+M P		Scripting Editor	Alt+V S
	Delete Macro(s)	Alt+M R		Direct Editor	Alt+V D
	Add Category	Alt+C A		Capture	(none)
	Delete Category	Alt+C D		Quick Wizards	Alt+V Q
	Copy Macro	Alt+M C		Recycle Bin	Alt+V R
	Recapture Macro	Alt+M E			

Actions Toolbar

The Actions Toolbar contains 6 or 7 icons depending on if you use an external editor (see the *Creating and Editing Macros* chapter). You control whether or not to display this toolbar by using the **Show Actions Bar** checkbox, which is found in the (Options | Preferences | Startup) dialog. If checked, it will be displayed along the left-hand side of the *Macro Explorer* window.

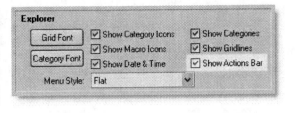

Action	Shortcut
Macro Explorer	Alt+V E
Scripting Editor	Alt+V S
Direct Editor	Alt+V D
External Editor	(none)
Capture	(none)
Quick Wizards	Alt+V Q
Recycle Bin	Alt+V R

Categories Pane

If you have several macros in your library, you may want to separate them into categories to be more manageable. This is the purpose of the Categories Pane. Only the macros that belong to the current category are displayed in the Macros Pane. This is similar to the way Windows Explorer works where only the files belonging to the current folder are listed.

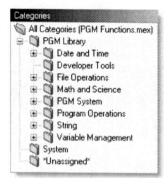

You control whether to use the Categories Pane by setting the **Show Categories** checkbox, which is found in the (Options | Preferences | Appearance) dialog. If checked, the Categories Pane will be positioned to the left of the Macros Pane.

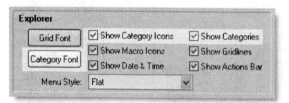

Another feature found in the *Preferences* dialog controls whether icons are used in the Categories Pane. If the **Show Category Icons** checkbox is checked (the default), they will be used, otherwise they will not. You can compare the difference in the two pictures on the right. Macro Express uses a single "blue folder" icon for every category. There is no mechanism to choose different icons for each category.

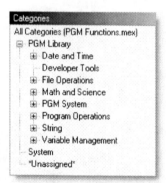

The **Category Font** button, which is also found in the *Preferences* dialog, allows you change the default font in the Categories Pane. Macro Express uses MS Sans Serif, Regular, 8 points, and Black as the default font. Here is what the Categories Pane looks like using Times New Roman, Bold, 10 points, and Black.

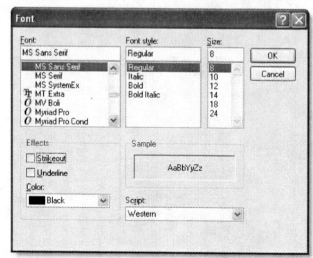

When a new macro library (*.mex*) file is created, Macro Express automatically generates two default categories. The main category is named "All Categories (<your macro library name here>)" and a single subcategory within it named *Unassigned*. These two default categories cannot be renamed or deleted like other categories you create. And the *Unassigned* category cannot have subcategories placed within it. If you already have macros in the library before enabling categories, they will be placed within the *Unassigned* category when categories are enabled.

Categories serve as folders for your macros. There is limit of 255 total categories and subcategories that you can create. Let's discover how to manipulate the categories before we discuss placing macros into them.

Add a Category

The key to adding a new category is to first highlight where you want to add it. If you want to add a main category, highlight the "All Categories (<...>)" name at the top. To add a subcategory, highlight the category that it will be placed in. Click on the Add Category icon. A line named "New Category" is added and is made ready for renaming. Change the name (25 characters maximum) and hit **Enter**. The category is immediately re-sorted alphabetically into the tree branch. If you just press **Enter** without changing the name, it will remain at the bottom of the list until you change it or the *Macro Explorer* window is refreshed internally. On the other hand, if you type "New Category" as the name it will be sorted normally. You can enter as many duplicate names as you want because multiple categories with the same name are acceptable.

The Add Category icon is not the only way to add a category. You can also press the **Alt+C,A** shortcut. And you can right-click your mouse on the highlighted category, or press the **App** key on your keyboard (the one that looks like a menu list), which pops up a menu. Now choose **New Category** or just press "**C**" then enter the new name.

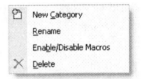

Rename a Category

Renaming a category is similar to adding a category. Highlight the category you want to rename. Press the **Alt+C,R** shortcut. Change the name and hit **Enter**. The category is immediately re-sorted alphabetically into the tree branch. You can also right-click your mouse (or press the **App** key), which pops up a menu. Then choose **Rename** or just press "**R**".

Delete a Category

Deleting a category will delete any subcategories beneath it, but will *not* delete any macros. They will be moved to the *Unassigned* category before the target category is deleted. Highlight the category you want to delete. Click on the Delete Category icon. The *Confirm Delete* dialog

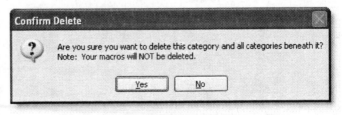

pops up. If you choose **No**, the operation is canceled. If you choose **Yes**, the category will be deleted and the rest will be re-sorted alphabetically into the tree branch. You can also just press **Delete** or the **Alt+C,D** shortcut. Optionally, you can right-click your mouse (or press the **App** key), then choose **Delete** or just press "**D**".

Move a Category

Moving a category is done by dragging it to another category. Click and hold the left mouse button down on the category to be moved. Drag it over top of the category you are moving it to and then let go of the mouse button. It will automatically settle in and position itself alphabetically. Let go of the mouse button. While you are dragging, the mouse cursor changes to a Drag icon. When you let it go, it changes back. The macros within the category will be seamlessly moved with the category.

Navigating the Categories Pane

Using the keyboard to navigate through the Categories Pane is similar to using the keyboard in the Windows Explorer Folders pane. Here is a chart showing what the keys do.

Categories Pane	
Key	**Action**
Home	Move to the top of the category list
End	Move to the bottom of the category list
Page Up	Move up a full pane
Page Down	Move down a full pane
Up Arrow	Move to previous line in category list
Down Arrow	Move to next line in category list
Character	Move to next category starting with character (will wrap at the end)
Right Arrow	If not expanded, expands category, or goes to next line in category list
Left Arrow	If not collapsed, collapses category, or goes to previous line in category list
Keypad Plus Sign (+)	Expands current category to show underlying categories
Keypad Minus Sign (-)	Collapses current category to hide underlying categories
Keypad Asterisk (*)	Expands current category including all of its subcategories
Tab	Move cursor from the Categories Pane to the Macros Pane

Please note that moving up and down through the list is done line-by-line. In other words, moving up and down does not automatically expand or collapse subcategories, but simply highlights whatever is on the next, or previous line.

Placing Macros in Categories

Placing a macro in a category is the process of moving a macro from one category to the next.

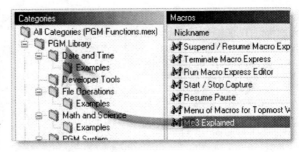

All macros belong to a category whether or not the Categories Pane is enabled. If this were not true, every time you disabled and then at some point, enabled the Categories Pane, you would need to place the macros back into their respective categories. Thankfully this is not so! If nothing else, a category will always belong to the *Unassigned* category.

One way to place a macro in a category is to drag it from the Macros Pane to the Categories Pane and drop it into the target category. Click and hold the left mouse button down on the macro to be placed. Drag it over top of the category you are placing it into and then let go of the mouse button. It will disappear from the current macro list and appear in the macro list that it now belongs to. While you are dragging, the mouse cursor changes to a Drag icon. When you let it go, it changes back.

Moving a macro can also be done from a special dialog. Highlight the macro in the Macros Pane to be moved and then press the **Alt+M,M** shortcut. The *Move Macro(s) to Category* dialog pops up. Use it to select the target category. The same navigation keys used in the Categories Pane can also be used here. Select a category and then click **OK**. The macro will disappear from the current macro list and then appear in the macro list that it now belongs to.

Both methods can be used to move multiple macros at the same time. It is just a matter of selecting more than one macro in the Macros Pane and following the same steps.

A macro can only belong to one category at a time.

Macros Pane

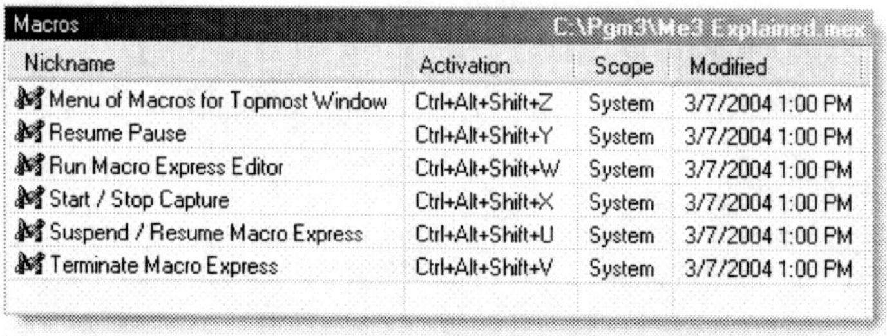

The Macros Pane contains your macros. The **Nickname** column holds the name of the macros and can display an icon as well. The macro nickname is covered in the *Properties Tab* section within the *Creating and Editing Macros* chapter. The **Activation** column displays the chosen activation method. The **Scope** column shows which program or window the macro is scoped to. Macro activation and scoping is detailed in the *Running and Activating Macros* chapter. The **Modified** column keeps track of when the macro was created, copied, and last changed.

Macros			C:\Pgm3\Me3 Explained.mex
Nickname	Activation	Scope	Modified
Menu of Macros for Topmost Window	Ctrl+Alt+Shift+Z	System	3/7/2004 1:00 PM
Resume Pause	Ctrl+Alt+Shift+Y	System	3/7/2004 1:00 PM
Run Macro Express Editor	Ctrl+Alt+Shift+W	System	3/7/2004 1:00 PM
Start / Stop Capture	Ctrl+Alt+Shift+X	System	3/7/2004 1:00 PM
Suspend / Resume Macro Express	Ctrl+Alt+Shift+U	System	3/7/2004 1:00 PM
Terminate Macro Express	Ctrl+Alt+Shift+V	System	3/7/2004 1:00 PM

Columns

Although you cannot change the order of the columns, you can change their widths by dragging the right column marker line in the header towards the left or right

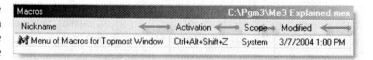

depending on your need to collapse or expand the column. This also lets you hide columns by dragging the right column marker line over to the right column marker line of the adjacent column. For example, to hide the **Modified** column, move the mouse over the right column marker line, click and hold the left mouse button down and then drag it all the way over to the right column marker line of the **Scope** column. This sets the width of the **Modified** column to zero. Reverse the steps to unhide the column. If you hide one or all the columns (why would you?), and for some reason cannot restore them, take the following steps:

> Choose (Options | Preferences) from the Main Menu. Or press **Alt+O,P**.
> Click on the **Restore Defaults** button.
> Answer **Yes** to the prompt.
> Click on the **Apply** button.

Also, double-clicking on any column marker line will expand or collapse the column width to suit the longest string within the column.

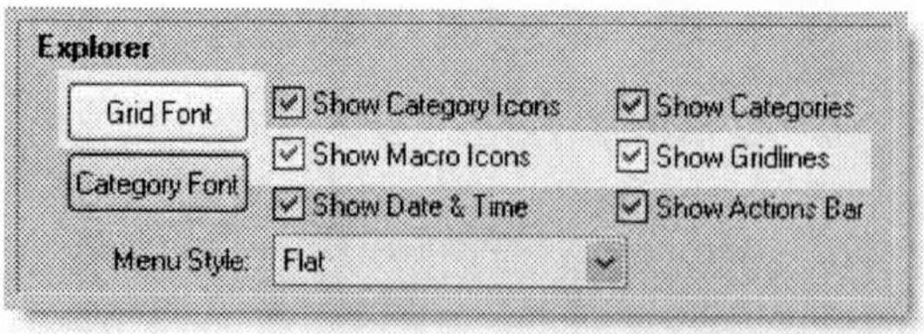

Each macro can be stamped with a different icon. The process of choosing an icon, where they are found, and how to add them, is described in the *Properties Tab* section within the *Creating and Editing Macros* chapter. You control whether to display them by setting the **Show Macro Icons** checkbox, which is found in the (Options | Preferences | Appearance) dialog. If checked, the icons are displayed with the nickname; otherwise, just the nickname is listed as shown here.

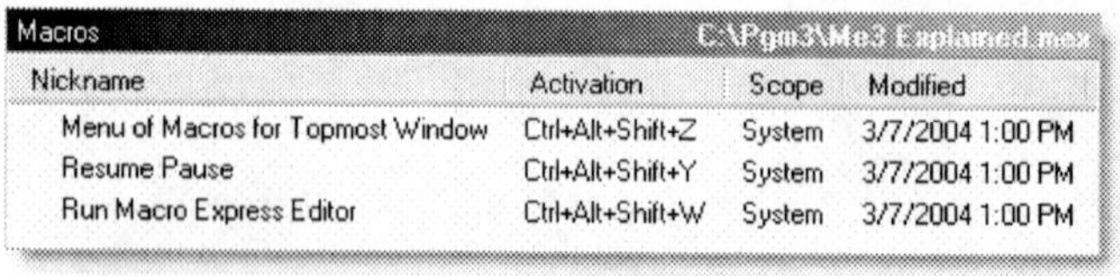

Explorer

Grid Font	☑ Show Category Icons	☑ Show Categories
Category Font	☑ Show Macro Icons	☑ Show Gridlines
	☑ Show Date & Time	☑ Show Actions Bar
Menu Style:	Flat	

Macros			C:\Pgm3\Me3 Explained.mex
Nickname	Activation	Scope	Modified
Menu of Macros for Topmost Window	Ctrl+Alt+Shift+Z	System	3/7/2004 1:00 PM
Resume Pause	Ctrl+Alt+Shift+Y	System	3/7/2004 1:00 PM
Run Macro Express Editor	Ctrl+Alt+Shift+W	System	3/7/2004 1:00 PM

The Macros Pane is displayed using spreadsheet-style gridlines by default. You can change this by unchecking the **Show Gridlines** checkbox, which is also found in the (Options | Preferences | Appearance) dialog highlighted on the previous page.

The **Grid Font** button allows you change the default font in the Macros Pane. Macro Express uses MS Sans Serif, Regular, 8 points, and Black as the default font. Refer to the previous section covering the *Categories Pane* for an example on changing fonts. Both the **Category Font** and **Grid Font** buttons work the same.

Views

You are not limited to viewing the Macros Pane as a detailed column list. This is just the default view (**Details**). There are three other views to choose from, **Large Icons**, **Small Icons**, and **List**. Choose (Options | View) from the Main Menu or press the **Alt+O,V** shortcut.

These views can also be accessed by right-clicking someplace in the Macros Pane where there is no macro. In the **Details** list, it would be after the end of the macros.

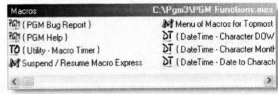

The three view pictures here are shown with the **Show Macro Icons** setting turned on (the checkbox is checked). When using the **Large Icons** view, it makes sense to leave it this way. However, for the **Small Icons** and **List** views it does not matter.

The **Show Gridlines** setting is ignored in any view other than the **Details** view. Also, if you make any changes to the *Preferences* dialog (Options | Preferences) and then apply them, the Macros Pane view will change back to the default **Details** view.

Sorting

Back to the default **Details** view. The columns can be sorted alphabetically in ascending or descending order and there are two different quick and easy ways to do it.

Macros			C:\Pgm3\PG
Nickname	Activation	Scope	M ed
Me3 Explained	No Activation	Global	3/25/2004
Suspend / Resume Macro Express	Ctrl+Alt+Shift+U	System	3/24/2004 11:11 PM
{ String - Parse }	No Activation	Global	10/6/2003 11:07 PM
{ PGM Bug Report }	Ctrl+Alt+Shift+B	Global	10/6/2003 4:53 PM

The first is to click on whichever column header you would like the macros sorted by. There is a small triangle-shaped icon that points up or down for ascending or descending respectively. To change the order, just click again on the same column header. Each time you click, the icon toggles between ascending and descending. It stays this way as you click from one column header to the next. Say, for example, you are viewing the macros by descending date and time (the **Modified** column). When you click on the **Nickname** column header, the macros are re-listed in descending nickname order. In other words, the ascending and descending sort is a "sticky" sort. It does not change unless you change it, no matter which column header you click on.

The other option is to use the Main Menu to choose which column to sort by. Choose (Options | Sort Macros) or press **Alt+0,0**. The same ascending or descending rule applies. It will stay the way it is until changed by you. However, you cannot change it from the Main Menu. It can only be changed by clicking on one of the column headers.

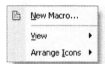 These sort options can also be accessed by right-clicking someplace in the Macros Pane where there is no macro. In the **Details** list, it would be after the end of the macros.

When using the menu, you may find it to be out of synch with the way that the macros are actually sorted. The column headers takes precedence over the checkmark in the menu. Also, it

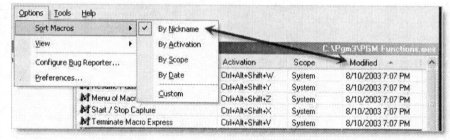

is the order of the column headers, or the custom sort setting, that control how the macros are sorted when the Macro Express Editor is first launched or when you open another macro library file.

If you need a more intricate sort, or if you want manually to move the macros in the list, choose (Options | Sort Macros | Custom) from the Main Menu or press **Alt+0,0,C**. This pops up the *Sort Options* dialog.

This dialog is easier to understand and to use than it looks. The reason for only two choices in the

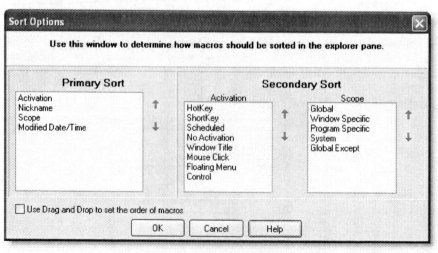

Secondary Sort section (**Activation** and **Scope**) is because **Nickname** is always alphabetical and **Modified Date/Time** is always, well … date+time, so there is no order to be set. The order of the **Activation** and **Scope**

windows are the order they will be used at the time they are accessed by the *Primary Sort*. In our case, the sort order for **Activation** will be **HotKey**, **ShortKey**, **Scheduled**, and so forth.

The actual **HotKey** combination is used for sorting, "Ctrl+A", "Ctrl+B", "Ctrl+C", and so forth. Only the word "ShortKey" is used by the **ShortKey** sorts. In the example "ShortKey: qwerty", "qwerty" is ignored. It is the same with the **Window Title** sort. Only the word "Window" is used and the name of the window is ignored. This is also true of the **Window Specific** and **Program Specific** scopes within the Scope sort.

There is an advanced feature that allows you to turn off the Activation and Scope prefixes. You can read about it in the *Advanced Options* section within the *Running and Activating Macros* chapter. However, this has no effect on sorting. Words like "Window", "ShortKey", and so forth, may not appear in the macro list, but they are still used for the sort.

To change the order of the keys inside the lists, select a key to move and then click on the **Up** or **Down** arrow in the column next to the window. You cannot move keys with you keyboard. Once they are set, click the **OK** button and your macros will be re-sorted.

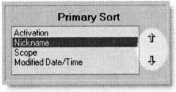

In my opinion, the macro listing that results from using the *Primary Sort* and *Secondary Sort* options is not always correct. However, other users and developers may find that I am not always correct.

If you do not want to use any particular sort, or if you want manually to sort the macros, put a checkmark in the **Use Drag and Drop to Set the Order of Macros** checkbox, or just press the "**D**" shortcut. This will

disable all other features within the *Set Options* dialog. Click **OK**.

Now you can drag the macros and place them in any order. Click and hold the left mouse button down anywhere on the macro line to be moved. Drag it up or down to the line that it will be inserted at and then let go of the mouse button. The other macros will be pushed down and the one you moved will be inserted. While you are dragging, the mouse cursor changes to a Drag icon. When you let it go, it changes back.

Multiple macros can be moved at the same time. It is just a matter of selecting more than one macro and following the same steps.

This drag and drop feature can be used in all macro views, **Large Icons**, **Small Icons**, or **List**. Also, whatever sort order is chosen or customized; it will be respected by every view.

The same steps are taken for any of the sort features when the Categories Pane is enabled (which displays only macros belonging to the current category). You can sort by the column headers, or choose the sort order from a menu, or customize a sort. You can even use the drag and drop feature.

Navigating

The keys used to navigate through the Macros Pane are basic keys that you are already familiar with. However, there is an optional setting called *incremental search* that makes navigating long lists easier. There is also a handy *Find* dialog.

Macros Pane	
Key	**Action**
Home	Move to the beginning of the macro list
End	Move to the end of the macro list
Page Up	Move up a full pane
Page Down	Move down a full pane
Up Arrow	Move to previous line in macro list
Down Arrow	Move to next line in macro list
Character(s)	Move to next line that begins with typed characters (will wrap at the end)
Shft+Home	Select to the beginning of the macro list
Shft+End	Select to the end of the macro list
Shft+Page Up	Select up a full pane
Shft+Page Down	Select down a full pane
Shft+Up Arrow	Select previous line
Shft+Down Arrow	Select next line
Ctrl+F or Alt+M H	Find dialog
F3 or Alt+M G	Find again
Tab	Move cursor from the Macros Pane to the Categories Pane
Enter	Edit selected macro (only if single line selected)
Delete or Alt+M R	Delete selected macro(s)

If more than one macro is selected when you hit the **Enter** key, an error message is displayed.

The "Character(s)" key in the chart is an option setting found in the *Preferences* dialog. Choose (Options | Preferences) from the Main Menu or press the **Alt+O,P** shortcut. When you navigate to the *Miscellaneous* panel, you will see the **Enable Incremental Search in Explorer** checkbox. It will need to be checked (the default) to use this feature.

When enabled, it works the same as when inside Windows Explorer. As you begin to type the name of a macro, the highlight bar is automatically moved to what you have typed so far. If you stop typing, or if you pause too long, the incremental search starts over when you begin typing again.

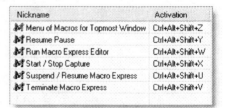

Let's say that we are using the macro list pictured here. If you type "S" and then stop, the highlight bar will be moved over the **Start / Stop Capture** macro. If instead, you type "Su" and then stop, then **Suspend / Resume Macro Express** is highlighted. Character case does not matter; "s" or "su" could have been typed with the same results.

The incremental search will wrap back to the top of the macro list if it does not find anything. Say, for example, the **Suspend / Resume Macro Express** macro is highlighted. Now type "Re", and the search will begin from the highlighted macro, search down through the end of the list, wrap back around to the top, and then continue the search stopping on the **Resume Pause** macro.

The macros *do not* have to be sorted by name. The incremental search feature will work no matter which sort option is used.

Macro Express also has a *Find* dialog to help navigate through a macro list. Press the **Ctrl+F** or **Alt+M,H** shortcut or choose (Macros | Search) from the Main Menu. Enter something to search for into the **Find What** field. In this case, we will search for a macro name containing the word "resume". The **Match Case** checkbox is not needed for this search so leave it unchecked and press the **Enter** key or click on the **Find Next** button. It will begin

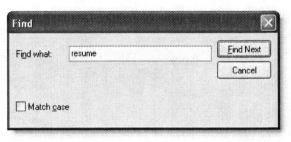

searching from wherever you are positioned within the macro list so, if you want to search the whole list, go to the beginning before using this tool.

If Macro Express can find what you are searching for, the macro will be highlighted. In our example, this is the **Resume Pause** macro. The *Find* dialog, however, will keep focus until you close it.

Press **Enter** or click **Find Next** if you want to search for the next case, which will be the **Suspend / Resume Macro Express** macro.

If you try to find another occurrence, the *End of List* message is displayed. This message is displayed anytime the search string cannot be found.

You could have closed the *Find* dialog and pressed the **F3** (find again) key as an alternative to pressing **Enter** the second time. The **F3** key will hold the last string searched for until you search for a different string or enter an empty string into the **Find What** field.

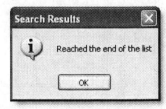

Notice that searching looks for a macro name *containing* the string in the **Find What** field. It does not matter if the string is at the beginning, middle, or end of the macro name.

The search can be limited to a case-sensitive search by checking the **Match Case** checkbox or by pressing the **Alt+C** shortcut when the *Find* dialog has focus.

Add Macros

Adding a macro to the Macros Pane can be done in several ways. But first, if you are using categories, be sure the category that you want to create the macro for is selected in the Categories Pane. If you forget, then you will have to move the macro after it is created. See the *Placing Macros* section.

Click on the Add Macro icon in the Menu Toolbar or choose (Macros | Add Macro) from the Main Menu (or press the **Alt+M,A** shortcut). Another option is to right-click an empty spot in the Macros Pane and then choose "New Macro" from the menu list (or press "**N**").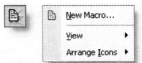

You could also double-click on an empty spot in the Macros Pane to pop up a dialog that asks if you want to create a new macro.

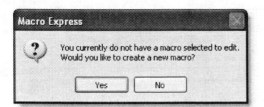

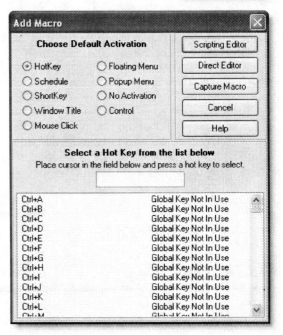

Regardless of which option you choose, the *Add Macro* dialog appears. The first task is to pick which activation to use for the new macro. There are nine choices. The bottom half of the dialog changes depending on which choice you make. In the picture, the dialog is ready to accept a HotKey because the **HotKey** option was picked. Read the *Running and Activating Macros* chapter to learn more about each type, but for now simply choose **No Activation**.

The final step is to tell Macro Express which tool you will use to create the macro. Your choices are the **Scripting Editor**, **Direct Editor**, or the **Capture Macro** button. All three are explained in the *Creating and Editing Macros* chapter. However, click on **Cancel** so we can continue learning about the Macros Pane.

Copy Macros

There are several methods available to copy a macro. Highlight the macro and then click on the Copy Macro icon in the Menu Toolbar or choose (Macros | Copy Macro) from the Main Menu (or press the **Alt+M,C** shortcut). Another option is to right-click on the macro and then choose "Copy Macro" from the menu list (or press "**C**").

Macros can only be copied one at a time. One reason to copy a macro is because there is no "Save As" feature in the editors. So, if you want to create a macro that is similar to another one, the best solution is to copy it first and then edit it.

Say that we want to copy one of the chapter macros. Highlight it and then click on the Copy Macro icon. The *Copy Macro* dialog pops up. It wants to know which activation option will be used for the new macro. Like the *Add Macro* dialog, the bottom half changes depending on which choice you make. The default choice is the activation method of the macro being copied. It is **No Activation** in our example. Read the *Running and Activating Macros* chapter to learn more about each type, but for now simply click **OK**.

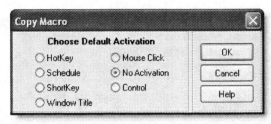

The macro will be copied and then named "Copy of" plus the original name. In our case it will be *Copy of Chapter M - Variables*. If you copy the copy it will have a "[2]" added to the name, *Copy of Chapter M - Variables [2]*, then a "[3]", "[4]", and so forth.

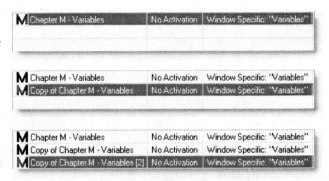

If you have a macro with a nickname that approaches the 50-character limit, and the copy exceeds the limit, the name will be truncated to 50 characters without warning.

If you copy the original macro in our example again, a warning message is displayed. This is because Macro Express wants to name it using "Copy of" again but there is already a macro named *Copy of Chapter M - Variables*. It is okay to have multiple macros with the same nickname. There is more information about this warning in the *Properties Tab* section within the *Creating and Editing Macros* chapter. But for now, click **No** so we can continue.

Rename Macros

Renaming a macro, or for that matter, naming one, is done through a macro's *Properties* dialog, which is discussed later in this chapter and in the *Properties Tab* section within the *Creating and Editing Macros* chapter.

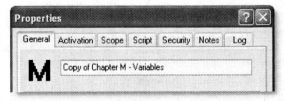

To rename the *Copy of Chapter M - Variables* macro created in the *Copy Macros* discussion, right-click on it and then choose "Properties" from the bottom of the menu list (or press "**P**"). The *Properties* dialog appears with the *General* Tag focused. Click on the nickname field and change the name to "Table of Contents". Click on the **OK** button at the bottom of the dialog (not shown). The macro is renamed and the Macros Pane is sorted to accommodate the new name. The macro, however, remains highlighted (selected).

Delete Macros

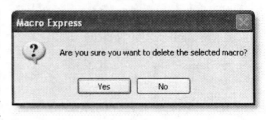

Deleting macros is perhaps the easiest task of all, and there are several ways to do it. Highlight the macro, or macros, to be deleted and then press the **Delete** key. This is the quickest way, however you can also click on the Delete Macro(s) icon in the Menu Toolbar or choose (Macros | Delete Macros) from the Main Menu (or press the **Alt+M,R** shortcut). Another option is to right-click on the selected macro, or macros, and then choose "Delete Macros" from the menu list (or press "**D**"). A confirmation message appears. If you click on **Yes**, the macros will be deleted, or more accurately, moved to the *Macro Recycle Bin* (refer to the *Macro Recycle Bin* section later in this chapter). Finally, the Macros Pane is sorted to account for the deleted macros.

Editing a Macro

The *Creating and Editing Macros* chapter explains all the following in greater detail. There are three built-in tools you can use to edit a macro. The Scripting Editor, Direct Editor, and External Editor. To edit a macro, double-click on it or highlight it and press the **Enter** key. The default editor will be launched.

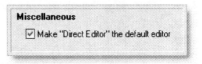

Only the Scripting Editor or Direct Editor can be set as the default. When Macro Express is first installed, the Scripting Editor is the default. You must tell Macro Express if you prefer this to be the Direct Editor by changing the setting in the *Preferences* dialog (Options | Preferences | Miscellaneous).

Any of the editors can be used to edit a macro no matter which one is set as the default. To use the Scripting Editor, highlight the macro and then choose one of several methods to launch the editor. Click on the Scripting Editor icon in the Menu Toolbar or Actions Toolbar. Or choose (Macros | Scripting Editor) from the Main Menu (or press **Alt+M,S**). You can also right-click and choose "Edit with Scripting Editor" from the menu list (or press "**S**").

To use the Direct Editor, highlight the macro and then click on the Direct Editor icon in the Menu Toolbar or Actions Toolbar. Or choose (Macros | Direct Editor) from the Main Menu (or press **Alt+M,D**). You can also right-click and choose "Edit with Direct Editor" from the menu list (or press "**E**").

To use the External Editor, it must first be set up. To learn how, read the *External Editor* section within the *Creating and Editing Macros* chapter. Once it is set up, highlight the macro, and then click on the External Editor icon in the Actions Toolbar. This is the only method available to access your external editor. The icon you see here is from my external editor, which is called **UltraEdit**. It is from IDM Computer Solutions, Inc. and can be downloaded from their web site at www.ultraedit.com.

Running a Macro

There are two methods available for running macros from the Macros Pane. Highlight a macro and then choose (Macros | Run Macro Now) from the Main Menu (or press **Alt+M,N**). You can also right-click and choose "Run Macro Now" from the menu list (or press "**R**"). For a detailed explanation about running macros read the *Running and Activating Macros* chapter. It covers other methods to run macros including from your Desktop, as a command line parameter, from the editors, and so forth.

Enable and Disable Macros

Enabling and disabling a macro is the mechanism Macro Express uses to turn it on and off. A disabled macro is listed in a grey italic font so it

Nickname	Activation	Scope	Modified
0 Chapter 0 - Clipboard	Win+Alt+F1	Window Specific: "Clipboard"	2/23/2004 8:05 AM
1 Chapter 1 - Installation	Win+Alt+F1	Window Specific: "Installation"	2/23/2004 4:11 PM
2 Chapter 2 - Variables	Win+Alt+F1	Window Specific: "Variables"	2/23/2004 3:42 PM
3 Chapter 3 - Programming	Win+Alt+F1	Window Specific: "Programming"	2/23/2004 3:43 PM

can be easily seen in the Macros Pane. It cannot be run with the *Macro Run* command or from a Popup or Floating Menu. However, a disabled macro can still be run from the Macros Pane by double-clicking on it, or by any other method explained above in the *Running a Macro* section.

Enabling and disabling macros is a "toggle" operation. If the macro you have selected is enabled, it will be disabled. If it is disabled then it will be enabled. This allows you to select multiple macros to enable one set at the same time you are disabling another set. The menu choices change between "Enable" and "Disable" depending on the state of the selected macro. The two pictures in the next paragraph show what this looks like.

There are a several different methods you can use to disable or enable macros in the Macros Pane. Highlight (select) the macro, or macros, to be disabled or enabled and then click on the Disabled/Enabled Macro icon in the Menu Toolbar. You could also choose (Macros | Disable/Enable Macro) from the Main Menu or press the **Alt+M,B** shortcut. A word of caution. If you have selected a Floating or Popup Menu, you may need to press **Alt+M,B,B** for the shortcut to get past the now-enabled "Menu Builder" choice in the same menu. Another option is to right-click on the selected macro, or macros, and then choose "Disable/Enable Macro" from the menu list (or press "**B**").

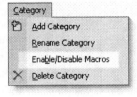

Another feature is the ability to disable or enable all macros belonging to the same category at the same time. Select the category from the Categories Pane. It is *not* necessary to select any macros in the Macros Pane. Now choose (Category | Enable/Disable Macros) or press the **Alt+C,B** shortcut. Any macros that were enabled are now disabled. Any macros that were disabled are now enabled. The change only affects the current category. Macros that belong to any subcategory are not changed.

Macro Properties

Each macro has its own *Properties* dialog that can be accessed by highlighting it and then clicking on the Properties icon in the Menu Toolbar. You can also choose (Macros | Properties) from the Main Menu (or press the **Alt+M,P** shortcut). Another option is to right-click on it and then choose "Properties" from the menu list (or press "**P**").

The *Properties* dialog has seven tabs. General, Activation, Scope, Script, Security, Notes, and Log. Each one holds a particular piece of information about the macro. There are also three common command buttons at the bottom named **OK, Cancel,** and **Apply**, which are accessible from any of the tabs.

The information in the *Properties* dialog is almost identical with that held in the tabs of the *Scripting Editor* and *Direct Editor* windows. You can see the Properties, Scope, Security, and Notes Tabs in the picture here of the *Scripting Editor* tabs. Most of the information in the following sections is more fully explained in the *Creating and Editing Macros* chapter.

To the right is a chart of the keyboard shortcut keys used in the *Properties* dialog.

Properties Dialog			
Shortcut	**Tab**	**Shortcut**	**Tab**
Alt+G	General	Alt+Y	Security
Alt+V	Activation	Alt+N	Notes
Alt+C	Scope	Alt+O	Log
Alt+I	Script	Alt+A	Apply
Escape	Cancel	Enter	OK

General Tab

When the *Properties* dialog is launched, this is the tab that first gains focus. This tab contains some information similar to the Properties Tab in the editors, but holds more basic information about the macro. Please read the *Properties Tab* section within the *Creating and Editing Macros* chapters for more detailed descriptions of the common fields.

General Tab	
Shortcut	**Field**
Tab	Nickname field
Alt+G T	Active checkbox
Alt+G H	Change Icon button

The untitled field at the top is the name (**Nickname**) of the macro, which can be up to 50 characters. The icon next to it is the chosen icon for the macro. The icon will always be displayed here regardless of the **Show Macro Icons** checkbox in the *Preferences* dialog.

How the macro is scoped in the Scope Tab, which category it belongs to, and the length of the macro are displayed in the next section. Details about scoping are found in the *Scope* section within the *Running and Activating Macros* chapter.

The next section shows how the macro's default activation is set in the Activation Tab, what the password for the macro is in the Security Tab, and the last time the macro was changed in any manner, including copying, editing, renaming, changing icons, and so forth. Details about macro activations are found in the *Activating Macros* section within the *Running and Activating Macros* chapter. Passwords are explained in the *Security Tab* section within the *Creating and Editing Macros* chapter.

The **Active** checkbox in the bottom section is used to enable or disable a macro from inside this tab. If the box is checked then the macro is enabled. The Change Icon button is used to pick a different icon for the macro.

Activation Tab

This tab is used to change macro activations. The *Activating Macros* section within the *Running and Activating Macros* chapter is where you will find details and instructions covering the macro activation features displayed here.

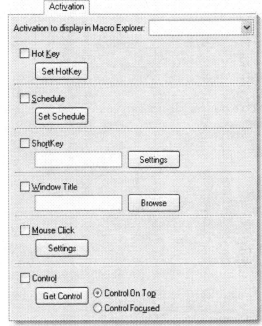

Activation Tab	
Shortcut	**Field**
Alt+V T	HotKey checkbox
Alt+V S	Schedule checkbox
Alt+V R	ShortKey checkbox
Alt+V W	Window Title checkbox
Alt+V M	Mouse Click checkbox
Alt+V L	Control checkbox
Alt+V P	Control on Top radio button
Alt+V U	Control Focused radio button

Activating a macro is simply a means to launch or invoke it manually or automatically. Macros can be invoked using a HotKey, ShortKey, or a Popup or Floating Menu. They can also be launched based on a schedule, window title, window object (control), program name, or the coordinates of a mouse click. More than one activation type can be set for a single macro. You could set a HotKey, Schedule, and a Mouse Click to activate a single macro.

Also, the *ability* to activate a macro can be scoped to a window title or program name. Macro activation and scoping are bound to each other in Macro Express. It is difficult to discuss one without the other so please read the *Scope* section within the *Running and Activating Macros* chapter to learn more about activating macros.

Scope Tab

This tab is used to change the scope of a macro and will display which windows or programs the macro can be launched with. It is identical with the Scope Tab in the editors.

Scope Tab	
Shortcut	**Field**
Alt+C L	Global radio button
Alt+C X	Global Except radio button
Alt+C W	Window Specific radio button
Alt+C P	Program Specific radio button
Alt+C S	Select button for any choice

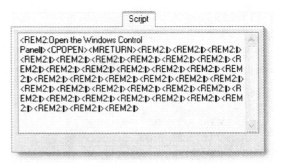

Please refer to the *Scope* section within the *Running and Activating Macros* chapter. It is where you will find details and instructions covering the macro scoping features displayed here.

Script Tab

This tab shows a read-only view of the macro as it would appear in the *Direct Editor* window. The Direct Editor is used to edit and display a macro in its natural state. Because this view is read-only, the text cannot be changed.

Security Tab

This tab is used to change macro passwords and is identical with the Security Tab in the editors.

Security Tab	
Shortcut	**Field**
Alt+Y U	Use Different Passwords radio button
Alt+Y W	Prompt for Password on Edit checkbox
Alt+Y H	Change Password button (for both the Use Different and Use Same choices)
Alt+Y M	Prompt for Password on run checkbox
Alt+Y A	Change Password button (for Prompt)
Alt+Y S	Use Same Passwords radio button

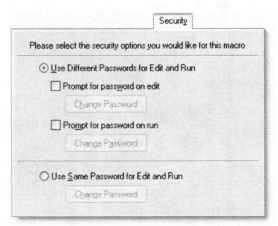

Please refer to the *Security Tab* section within the *Creating and Editing Macros* chapter. It is where you will find details and instructions covering both macro and system-wide password features.

Notes Tab

The Notes Tab contains any information that you want to keep about the macro and is identical with the Notes Tab in the editors, with one exception. This tab also displays the length of the notes at the bottom of the notes panel. Any changes made here can also be viewed, and changed, in the Notes Tab of either editor.

Please refer to the *Notes Tab* section within the *Creating and Editing Macros* chapter. It is where you will find details about editing the information in this tab.

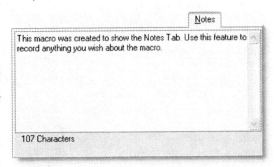

Log Tab

The Log Tab collects errors and messages you may want to track as your macro is running. This is a read-only tab, meaning that you cannot make any changes to the errors and messages collected.

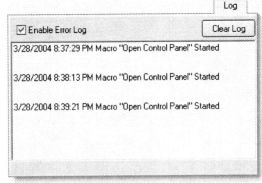

Log Tab	
Shortcut	**Field**
Alt+O E	Enable Error Log checkbox
Alt+O L	Clear Log button

If the **Enable Error Log** checkbox is checked, errors and messages will be collected for this macro. An error or message will be written to the default error text file named *ErrorLog.txt*. You can change the default name using the *Preferences* dialog. Choose (Options | Preferences | File Paths) from the Main Menu and then edit the **Default Error Log** field.

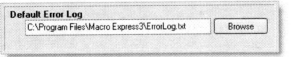

The **Enable Error Log** checkbox is identical with the **Use Log File** checkbox found within Properties Tab of the editors. The **Clear Log** button erases the log.

If you plan to log all errors and messages for all macros, there is a Macro Express feature that makes it easy to do. Choose (Options | Preferences | Playback) from the Main Menu and then check the **Log All Macro Information** checkbox.

Now errors and messages will be collected for every macro regardless of the **Enable Error Log** checkbox status.

As well as collecting errors and messages from all of your macros, there is a built-in feature that allows you to view what was collected. In the *Macro Explorer* window, choose (Tools | Error Log Viewer) from the Main Menu or press the **Alt+T,E** shortcut.

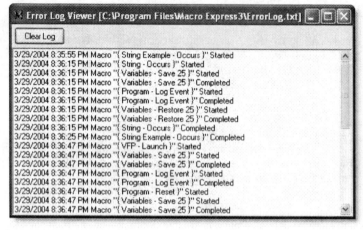

The read-only *Error Log Viewer* dialog pops up, which you can use to scroll through the errors and messages. They cannot be changed or deleted, but they can be copied to your clipboard by using standard select and copy editing keys. For example, **Ctrl+A**, **Ctrl+C**, and so forth.

Press the **Clear Log** button to erase the list. This actually deletes the file from your hard drive, which will be created again when needed.

System Macros

Macro Express provides six built-in system macros in every new macro library file you create. They cannot be copied, renamed, changed, or deleted, but they can be moved to a different category and their default HotKey activations can be changed. The HotKeys shown in the picture are the default HotKeys when Macro Express is first installed.

Nickname	Activation	Scope	Modified
Menu of Macros for Topmost Window	Ctrl+Alt+Shift+Z	System	3/7/2004 1:00 PM
Resume Pause	Ctrl+Alt+Shift+Y	System	3/7/2004 1:00 PM
Run Macro Express Editor	Ctrl+Alt+Shift+W	System	3/7/2004 1:00 PM
Start / Stop Capture	Ctrl+Alt+Shift+X	System	3/7/2004 1:00 PM
Suspend / Resume Macro Express	Ctrl+Alt+Shift+U	System	3/7/2004 1:00 PM
Terminate Macro Express	Ctrl+Alt+Shift+V	System	3/7/2004 1:00 PM

There is a single *Properties* dialog for all the system macros. Access it by highlighting any one of them and then clicking on the Properties icon in the Menu Toolbar. You can also choose (Macros | Properties) from the Main Menu (or press the **Alt+M,P** shortcut).
Another option is to right-click on it and then choose "Properties" from the menu list (or press "**P**").

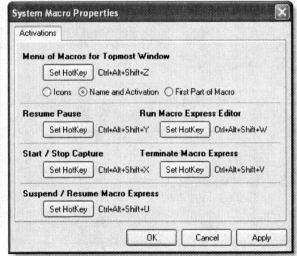

To change the default HotKey for any system macro, click on its **Set HotKey** button (there are no keyboard shortcuts in this dialog). The *Set HotKey Activation* dialog appears. Use it to choose a different HotKey. If you need help, read the *HotKey* section within the *Running and Activating Macros* chapter.

Menu of Macros for Topmost Window

When invoked, this macro will produce a Popup Menu of any macro in your library that is scoped to the currently focused window. On the next page, for example, is the Popup Menu produced as I am writing. The menu is built internally and uses partial matching of the window title to control which macros should be included.

Just because a macro is included, does not mean it can be invoked. In this case, the last line contains a macro named *[Book - Adjust Doc Map]*, which is scoped to use an exact window title match. In other words, I do not want this macro to run unless the window title says "Microsoft Word". Period. The window that is currently focused has "Microsoft Word" in the title; therefore the *[Book - Adjust Doc Map]* macro will be included in the Popup Menu, but it will not run if I try invoking it. This is because the macro is scoped to need an exact match of the window title. Disabled macros will also be included in the Popup Menu, but they cannot be invoked either.

Microsoft Word
☑ Run If On Top ☑ Exact Match

	Name	Activation
	Choose a Macro	
1	[Book - Format Clipboard]	Win+Alt+C
2	[Book - Format String]	Win+Alt+F
3	[Book - Open Advanced Dialog]	Win+Alt+6
4	[Book - Push Picture to Margin]	Win+Alt+4
5	[Book - Shrink Picture]	Win+Alt+2
6	[Book - Square Picture]	Win+Alt+3
7	[Book - Toggle Move w/Text]	Win+Alt+5
8	[Book - Type Decimal]	Win+Alt+D
9	[Book - Type Integer]	Win+Alt+I
A	[Book - Type Parameter]	Win+Alt+P
B	[Book - Type String]	Win+Alt+S
C	[Book - Adjust Doc Map]	Win+Alt+M
	Double Click or Press a Number or Letter	

This is the only system macro that has another feature that can be set in the *Properties* dialog. You pick the menu style that will be popped up. Your choices are **Icons**, **Name and Activation** (pictured), and **First Part of Macro**.

When set for **Icons**, Macro Express displays those in a single column (refer to the *Popup and Floating Menus* section within the *Running and Activating Macros* chapter). If there are more icons than can fit on the screen, they do *not* adjust themselves into multiple columns, but rather they drop off the bottom of the screen. This makes the "X" (close window) inaccessible at the top, which forces you to pick one of the icons. Also, there is no access to the icons that are now beyond the bottom of the screen.

When set for **Name and Activation** or **First Part of Macro**, the menu *will* allow for more than just the usual 36-macro limit. However, a lowercase "a" through "z" menu choice will not be recognized. Any character entered from the keyboard will always choose an uppercase "A" through "Z" menu choice.

Resume Pause

This system macro allows Macro Express to resume running when it has been temporarily stopped for a *Pause* command. You may find it more convenient to press the **Ctrl+Alt+Shft+Y** system HotKey (or whatever you have it set for) than clicking on the **Resume** button in the *Macro Paused* dialog.

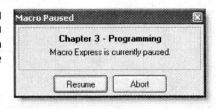

Macro Paused

Chapter 3 - Programming
Macro Express is currently paused.

[Resume] [Abort]

Run Macro Express Editor

Press the **Ctrl+Alt+Shft+W** system HotKey to launch the Macro Express Editor (*MacEdit.exe*). You will see the *Macro Explorer* window appear. Invoking this macro is identical with clicking on the Macro Express icon in your System Tray. Or right-clicking on it and then choosing "Open Editor" from the menu list. This is a nice keyboard shortcut that avoids having to click a Desktop icon link to start Macro Express. For all these choices to work, the Macro Express Player (*MacExp.exe*) must be running. Refer to the *Components* section within the *Running and Activating Macros* chapter.

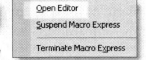

Open Editor
Suspend Macro Express
Terminate Macro Express

Start / Stop Capture

This system macro is used to start and stop the macro capturing process. Pressing the **Ctrl+Alt+Shft+X** system HotKey starts the process and pressing it again stops it. Please refer to the *Capture Macros* section within the *Creating and Editing Macros* chapter where you will find everything you need to know about capturing macros.

Suspend / Resume Macro Express

Use this system macro to suspend or resume the Macro Express Player program. Pressing the **Ctrl+Alt+Shft+U** system HotKey suspends the program. Pressing it again resumes the program. When suspended, the System Tray icon is crossed out.

Invoking this macro is identical with right-clicking the Macro Express icon in your System Tray and then choosing "Suspend Macro Express" from the menu list (or pressing "**S**"). If already suspended, the menu choice says "Resume Macro Express".

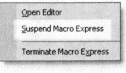

Suspending just means to temporarily stop the player from running any macros. However, the Macro Express Editor will remain running. Macros can be edited, deleted, moved, and so forth. But cannot be test-run or debugged. And all macro activations are ignored, including HotKeys, except for one, **Ctrl+Alt+Shft+U**, which resumes running the player program.

Terminate Macro Express

Pressing the **Ctrl+Alt+Shft+V** system HotKey terminates Macro Express by closing the Macro Express Editor program (*MacEdit.exe*) and the player program (*MacExp.exe*). Pressing this system HotKey is identical with pressing the **Alt+F,X** shortcut from within the *Macro Explorer* window or right-clicking the Macro Express icon in your System Tray and then choosing "Terminate Macro Express" from the menu list (or pressing "**X**").

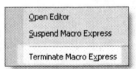

Macro Recycle Bin

This is where macros go to die. It is a dialog window with its own title and menu options that are separate from the *Macro Explorer* window, much like the *Scripting Editor* and *Direct Editor* windows are separate. Its purpose is to restore macros that you want to recover for any reason, including an accidental deletion. If you delete a macro in here, it is permanently removed and cannot be recovered.

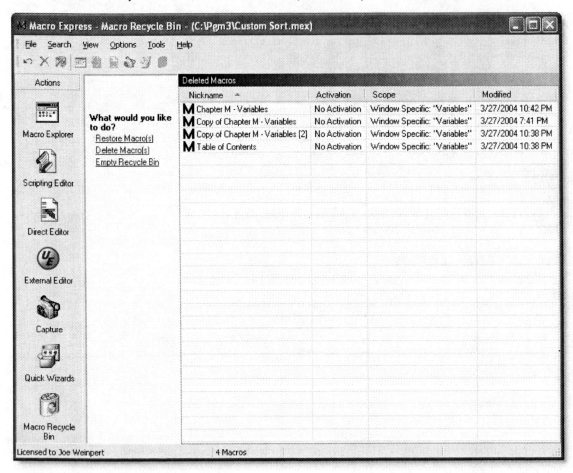

The *Macro Recycle Bin* is accessed from the *Macro Explorer* window by clicking on the Recycle Bin icon in the Menu Toolbar or Actions Toolbar. It can also be accessed by choosing (View | Recycle Bin) from the Main Menu (or press the **Alt+V,R** shortcut).

The *Macro Recycle Bin* window is separated into five sections:

1. Main Menu

   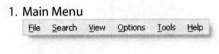

2. Menu Toolbar

3. Actions Toolbar

4. Options Pane

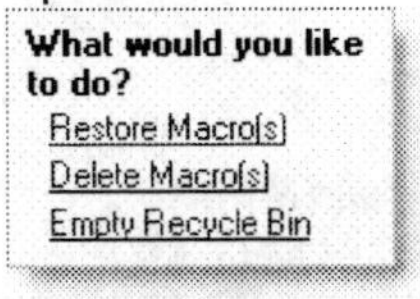

5. Deleted Macros Pane

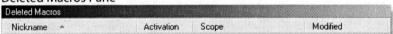

Most features of the *Macro Recycle Bin* window are identical with the *Macro Explorer* window. You may be asked to refer to the *Macro Explorer* window for more information as you read this section. The Scripting Editor, Direct Editor, and Recycle Bin menu choices and icons are marked as "(disabled)" or "(n/a) not applicable" in the charts below. They exist in the menus and toolbars, but cannot be accessed from the *Macro Recycle Bin* window.

Main Menu

The Main Menu takes its format style from the *Macro Explorer* window, which is **Flat**, **Standard**, or **Enhanced**. It can be moved to the bottom, left, or right side of the *Macro Recycle Bin* window or placed on your Desktop.

<table>
<tr><th colspan="3">File Menu</th></tr>
<tr><th>Shortcut</th><th>Action</th><th>Icon</th></tr>
<tr><td>Alt+F</td><td>File menu</td><td></td></tr>
<tr><td>Alt+F R</td><td>Restore Macro(s)</td><td></td></tr>
<tr><td>Alt+F D</td><td>Delete Macro(s)</td><td></td></tr>
<tr><td>Alt+F E</td><td>Empty Recycle Bin</td><td></td></tr>
<tr><td>Alt+F M</td><td>Return to Macro Explorer</td><td></td></tr>
<tr><td>Alt+F T</td><td>Terminate Macro Express Editor</td><td></td></tr>
<tr><td>Alt+F X
Ctrl+Alt+Shft+V</td><td>Terminate Macro Express Editor & Player</td><td></td></tr>
</table>

<table>
<tr><th colspan="2">Search Menu</th></tr>
<tr><th>Shortcut</th><th>Action</th></tr>
<tr><td>Alt+S</td><td>Search menu</td></tr>
<tr><td>Alt+S H or Ctrl+F</td><td>Search</td></tr>
<tr><td>Alt+S G or F3</td><td>Search Again</td></tr>
</table>

<table>
<tr><th>Tools Menu</th></tr>
<tr><td>Identical with Macro Explorer</td></tr>
</table>

<table>
<tr><th>Help Menu</th></tr>
<tr><td>Identical with Macro Explorer</td></tr>
</table>

<table>
<tr><th colspan="3">View Menu</th></tr>
<tr><th>Shortcut</th><th>Action</th><th>Icon</th></tr>
<tr><td>Alt+V</td><td>View menu</td><td></td></tr>
<tr><td>Alt+V E</td><td>Macro Explorer</td><td></td></tr>
<tr><td>Alt+V S
(n/a)</td><td>Scripting Editor
(disabled)</td><td></td></tr>
<tr><td>Alt+V D
(n/a)</td><td>Direct Editor
(disabled)</td><td></td></tr>
<tr><td>Alt+V Q</td><td>Quick Wizards</td><td></td></tr>
<tr><td>Alt+V R
(n/a)</td><td>Recycle Bin
(disabled)</td><td></td></tr>
</table>

<table>
<tr><th colspan="2">Options Menu</th></tr>
<tr><th>Shortcut</th><th>Action</th></tr>
<tr><td>Alt+O</td><td>Options menu</td></tr>
<tr><td>Alt+O O</td><td>Sort Macros</td></tr>
<tr><td>Alt+O O N</td><td>By Nickname</td></tr>
<tr><td>Alt+O O A</td><td>By Activation</td></tr>
<tr><td>Alt+O O S</td><td>By Scope</td></tr>
<tr><td>Alt+O O D</td><td>By Date</td></tr>
<tr><td>Alt+O O C</td><td>Custom</td></tr>
<tr><td>Alt+O B</td><td>Configure Bug Reporter</td></tr>
<tr><td>Alt+O P</td><td>Preferences</td></tr>
</table>

Menu Toolbar

The Menu Toolbar contains 9 icons, each matched with a choice within the Main Menu except the Capture icon. Refer to the chart below. Just  like the Main Menu, the Menu Toolbar can be moved to the bottom, left, or right side of the *Macro Recycle Bin* window. And it can be placed on your Desktop.

Icon	Action	Shortcut	Icon	Action	Shortcut
	Restore Macro(s)	Alt+F R		Direct Editor (disabled)	Alt+V D (n/a)
	Delete Macro(s)	Alt+F D		Capture	(none)
	Empty Recycle Bin	Alt+F E		Quick Wizards	Alt+V Q
	Macro Explorer	Alt+V E		Recycle Bin (disabled)	Alt+V R (n/a)
	Scripting Editor (disabled)	Alt+V S (n/a)			

Actions Toolbar

The Actions Toolbar is a system-wide toolbar; therefore it is the same in each of the Macro Express Editor's windows, *Macro Explorer*, *Scripting Editor*, *Direct Editor*, and *Macro Recycle Bin*. Refer to the *Actions Toolbar* section towards the beginning of this chapter for more information. If you click on any of the editor icons while in the *Macro Recycle Bin* window, an error message is displayed.

Options Pane

This contains a list of the three main tasks the *Macro Recycle Bin* window was designed to perform. They can only be accessed using your mouse. There are no keyboard shortcuts except those that exist for the matching entries in the File menu. They also match the first three icons in the Menu Toolbar. Refer to the *Menu Toolbar* section above.

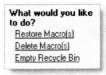

Deleted Macros Pane

The Deleted Macros Pane holds all the macros deleted from your library. It is identical with the Macros Pane in the *Macro Explorer* window with one exception, the only view is the default **Details** view. Other features are the same. Columns widths can be adjusted, and the macro list can be sorted using the same tools.

Nickname ▲	Activation	Scope	Modified
Chapter M - Variables	No Activation	Window Specific: "Variables"	3/27/2004 10:42 PM
Copy of Chapter M - Variables	No Activation	Window Specific: "Variables"	3/27/2004 7:41 PM
Copy of Chapter M - Variables [2]	No Activation	Window Specific: "Variables"	3/27/2004 10:38 PM
Table of Contents	No Activation	Window Specific: "Variables"	3/27/2004 10:38 PM

There are some minor differences in the navigation keys, which are shown by the chart. The rest of the keys are identical. You can scroll through the lines, use the incremental search, select lines, and so forth.

Deleted Macros Pane	
Key	**Action**
Ctrl+F or Alt+S H	Find dialog (Alt+M,H in *Macro Explorer*)
F3 or Alt+S G	Find again (Alt+M,G in *Macro Explorer*)
Tab	Not applicable (n/a). Key is ignored
Enter	Not applicable (n/a). Key is ignored
Delete or Alt+F D	Delete selected macro(s) (Alt+M,R in *Macro Explorer*)

Restore Macro(s)

There are several ways to restore macros. Highlight the macro, or macros, to be restored and then click on the "Restore Macro(s)" line in the Options Pane or the Restore Macro(s) icon in the Menu Toolbar. You can also choose (File | 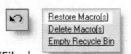 Restore Macros) from the Main Menu (or press the **Alt+F,R** shortcut). Another option is to right-click on the selected macro, or macros, and then choose "Restore Macros" from the menu list (or press "**R**"). The macros will be immediately restored. There is *no* confirmation message. And if you are using categories, they will be restored to whichever category they had belonged to before being deleted … if possible. You may have since deleted the category, if so, then they will be restored to the default *Unassigned* category.

Delete Macro(s)

There are also several methods to delete macros. Remember, however, the macros will be permanently deleted. Highlight the macro, or macros, to be deleted and then press the **Delete** key. This is the quickest way, however you can also click on the "Delete Macro(s)" line in the Options Pane or the Delete Macro(s) icon in the Menu Toolbar. You can also choose (File | Delete Macros) from the Main Menu (or press the **Alt+F,D** shortcut). Another option is to right-click on the selected macro, or macros, and then choose "Delete Macros" from the menu list (or press "**D**"). A confirmation message pops up. Click on the **Yes** button to delete them or the **No** button to cancel the operation.

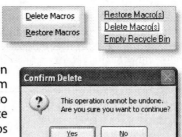

Empty Recycle Bin

This choice will permanently remove all the macros in the Deleted Macros Pane. There is no need to highlight the macros. Click on the  "Empty Recycle Bin" line in the Options Pane or the Empty Recycle Bin icon in the Menu Toolbar. You can also choose (File | Empty Recycle Bin) from the Main Menu (or press the **Alt+F,E** shortcut). A confirmation message appears. Click on the **Yes** button to complete the task.

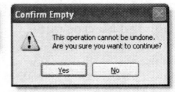

Summary

- The *Macro Explorer* window is the main window of the Macro Express Editor.
- Add, copy, rename, delete, run, enable, disable, and edit are all tasks that can be performed from the *Macro Explorer* window.
- Choose among three different menu styles.
- The menu bar can be moved to any edge inside the *Macro Explorer* window or to the Desktop.
- Choose among four different macro list views.
- The Actions Toolbar, gridlines, icons, and categories can be turned on or off.
- Macros can be categorized.
- There is a limit of 255 on all categories and subcategories.
- Macros can be sorted by any column, ascending or descending. There is also a custom sort feature.
- Macros cannot be "saved as". To create a similar macro, copy it first and then edit it.
- Set the macro name, icon, activation, scope, password, notes, and logging from the *Properties Tab* of each macro.
- There are always six built-in system macros in every macro library (*.mex*) file.
- The Macro Express Player can be suspended (and restarted) without terminating Macro Express.
- The *Macro Recycle Bin* window is similar to the Windows Recycle Bin on your computer.

Creating and Editing Macros

The purpose of course in using Macro Express is to create macros. This chapter will strengthen your understanding of how to do that. There are five ways to create and edit macros:

1. The Scripting Editor
2. The Direct Editor
3. Using an external text editor
4. Capturing keystrokes and mouse clicks
5. Running a Quick Wizards tool

We will examine each of them separately; however, they can be used together. You could create a macro by capturing keystrokes or by using a Quick Wizard and then tweak it using the Scripting and Direct Editors. Or just use the Scripting and Direct Editors for everything. And because a macro is just text, the ability to use an external text editor is a great feature. However, to be efficient with it, you will need to become familiar with Macro Express commands as they appear in the Direct Editor.

The Scripting Editor is my tool of choice for creating and editing macros. To be fair, I do switch back and forth with the Direct Editor depending on what I need to do, and how fast it needs to be done. Each of the two built-in editors has its own advantages.

The Scripting Editor is structured and easy to read. You can see what your macro is doing one line at a time. In the Direct Editor, your macro is a single unbroken line of mnemonic commands, which makes it difficult to read and almost impossible to determine the "flow" of the macro. The two examples on the right are the same macro as viewed from both editors.

Macro Script
- Activate or Launch: "Notepad" OR "notepad.exe"
- Wait For Window Title: "Notepad"
- **A** Text Type: The quick brown fox jumps over the lazy dog<ENTER>
- Window Close: Current Window
- Macro Return

When you view your macro from the Direct Editor, you are looking at it in its "natural" state. The Scripting Editor is just a convenience. Thank you Insight! The Direct Editor view, by the way, is the same view you see when using your own external text editor.

Macro Text
```
<LAUNCHYES3:0:0112Notepad<LAUNCH:notepad.exe>
<WAITWIN2:000010:000000:Notepad|><TEXTTYPE:The quick brown fox jumps over
the lazy dog<ENTER>|><WCLS:"CURRENT"><MRETURN>
```

Editing is also easier using the Scripting Editor. There are embedded tools in the editing pane columns that insert commands before or after the current command and also add them to the end of the macro. The tools in the right-hand column move commands up and down within the macro and copy the selected commands. You can change an existing command by double-clicking on it, which will pop up its editing dialog. There is none of this in the Direct Editor. Moving or inserting commands is a matter of cutting and pasting. Changing a command means to type the changes manually or delete it and choose its dialog again from the Commands Pane. If you are using an external text editor, your capabilities are limited to the features in your text editor.

There are no debugging features within the Direct Editor. You can run the macro but you cannot set breakpoints, step through it, review the state of variables, check syntax, and so forth. This is also true when using an external text editor.

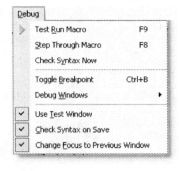

The Direct Editor does have some important features the Scripting Editor lacks, one of which is the ability to search for, and replace text. The Scripting Editor can only find text. Choose (Edit | Search and Replace) to access the *Replace* dialog. Refer to the Direct Editor section if you need help.

Another feature is the ability to "undo" the last editing action inside the Macro Text Pane. Either press the **Ctrl+Z** shortcut or right-click and choose "Undo" from the menu.

Another advantage of the Direct Editor is how it handles text that you want your macro to output. It has the **Text Type** command style toolbars built into the bottom of the editing pane. This means that you can enter text directly into the editing pane and it will be converted to a **Text Type** command automatically when

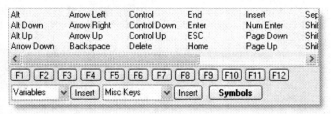

you switch back to the Scripting Editor. This may not be much faster than choosing the **Text Type** command from the Commands Pane, but it is more convenient if your macros use the **Text Type** command a lot.

The Scripting Editor is the default editor when you first install Macro Express. However, you can make the Direct Editor the default editor. Choose (Options | Preferences | Miscellaneous) from the Main Menu. Place a check in the **Make Direct Editor the Default Editor** checkbox and then save the settings. Now anytime you edit

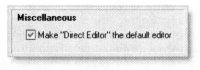

a macro, the Direct Editor will be used. Of course you can still switch back and forth between them as needed.

The Scripting Editor has five tabs and so does the Direct Editor. The Editor Tab in the Direct Editor is the equivalent of the Script Tab in the Scripting Editor. It is where creating and editing macros takes place.

Scripting Editor

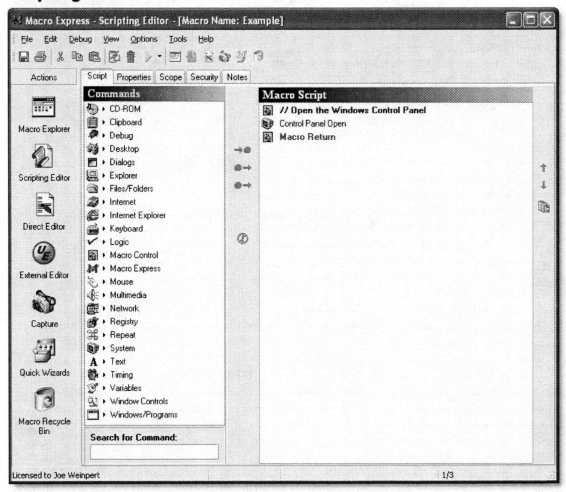

The Script Tab of the Scripting Editor contains three sections, Commands Pane (**Alt+Left Arrow**), Search Box (**Alt+Down Arrow**), and Macro Script Pane (**Alt+Right Arrow**). It is a menu-driven system. To create a macro pick commands from the Commands Pane to be moved to the Macro Script Pane. When you choose a command, it may, or may not, have an associated dialog. If it does, set the features you want, click **OK**, and the command will be placed into the Macro Script Pane.

The example is a simple macro that opens your Control Panel dialog. It is equal to choosing (Start | Control Panel) from the Taskbar or clicking on the My Computer Desktop icon and then clicking on "Control Panel". There are three commands involved:

Pick the *Remark* command from within the *Macro Control* category. A dialog appears. Type the remark into the **Comments** field. Click **OK**. The first line is added to the Macro Script Pane.

Choose the *Control Panel Open* command from within the *System* category. A dialog appears. Leave the **Open Main Control Panel** choice. Click **OK**. The second line is added to the Macro Script Pane.

Pick the *Macro Return* command from within the *Macro Control* category. There is no dialog; it is just added directly to the Macro Script Pane.

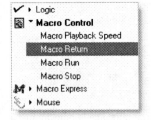

That is the basics of creating a macro using the Scripting Editor. You can now run the

 macro by pressing **F9** or by clicking on the green Run icon or by choosing (Debug | Test Run Macro) from the Main Menu.

Here is a list of navigation shortcuts for the Scripting Editor. The Commands Pane and Macro Script Pane each have their own shortcut charts. Note that there is no shortcut for the Security Tab.

Scripting Editor			
Shortcut	**Set focus to**	**Shortcut**	**Set focus to**
Alt+F	File Menu	Alt+Left Arrow	Commands Pane
Alt+E	Edit Menu	Alt+Right Arrow	Macro Script Pane
Alt+D	Debug Menu	Alt+Down Arrow	Search Box
Alt+V	View Menu	Alt+I	Script Tab
Alt+O	Options Menu	Alt+P	Properties Tab
Alt+T	Tools Menu	Alt+C	Scope Tab
Alt+H	Help Menu	(none)	Security Tab
F1	Help	Alt+N	Notes Tab

Commands Pane

This gives you access to all the Macro Express commands, of which there are over 260 separated into 24 categories. Some commands are listed under multiple categories for convenience.

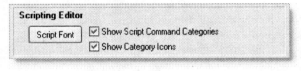

Do they need to be listed under multiple categories? No. You can change this using the (Options | Preferences | Appearances) dialog. If you uncheck the **Show Script Command Categories** checkbox then the commands will be listed alphabetically without categories. If this is your choice, then the **Show Category Icons** option is ignored, and the icons are not shown, not even in the Macro Script Pane.

The command category icons are normally shown. You can see them in the main example at the beginning of this chapter. If you prefer not to show them, but still want the commands separated into categories, then uncheck the **Show Category Icons** checkbox and leave the **Show Script Command Categories** checked.

The **Script Font** button allows you change the default font in the Commands Pane and the Macro Script Pane.

Macro Express uses a default font, MS Sans Serif, Regular, 8 points, and Black.

All three of these features, the **Show Script Command Categories** checkbox, the **Show Category Icons** checkbox, and the **Script Font** button change the Direct Editor window, too, even though they are listed in the **Scripting Editor** section of the dialog.

You are not limited to just the 24 command categories supplied by Macro Express. They are just the defaults. You can add and subtract categories, as well as change which commands are placed

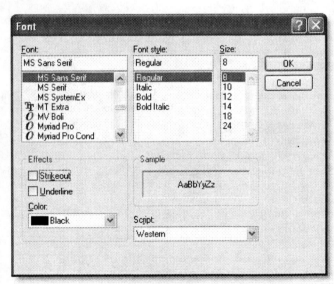

in what categories. On the next page is the *Customize Categories* dialog, which is accessed from the (Options | Customize Categories) menu. The changes made here also affect the Direct Editor even though the top section says "Customize Script Categories".

What is nice about this feature is that, no matter how you mess it up, it can be put back in place by simply choosing the **Use Default Categories** option. So feel free to experiment!

All the Macro Express commands are listed alphabetically in the right-hand field. The selected ones are those that belong to the category highlighted in the left-hand pane. The selection is done automatically; as you move the highlight from one category to the next in the left-hand pane, the commands associated with that particular category are selected in the right-hand pane.

To change the commands associated with a category, move the highlight in the left-hand pane to the category, then click on whichever commands to add, or remove, from the right-hand pane. Clicking once on a command selects it, clicking again deselects it.

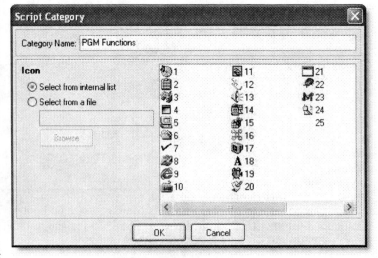

A command can belong to any number of categories. There is no limit. If you disassociate a command from a category by accident, it will be placed automatically into one named *Uncategorized* by Macro Express.

The **Add**, **Modify**, and **Delete** buttons are used to change the categories. Clicking on either **Add** or **Modify** brings forward the *Script Category* dialog. Use the **Category Name** field to add a new category or change the name of an existing one. You can even change the names of the default categories.

You are required to choose an icon for the category whether you display them or not (Options | Preferences | Appearances | Show Script Command Categories). Choose the **Select from Internal List** option and pick one of the 25 built-in icons by highlighting it. Or choose **Select from a File** and use the *Select an Icon File* dialog to choose one. You can pick from four different kinds of files to retrieve your icon or icon list. A standalone icon (*.ico*) file, an icon library (*.icl*) file, an executable (*.exe*) file, and a dynamic link library (*.dll*) file. The latter three may have more than one icon. If so, they will all be listed in the icon window for you to pick one.

To delete a category, click on the **Delete** button. You will be asked to confirm your choice. Nothing happens to the commands within the category. They will still belong to other categories. For those that belong only to the category just deleted, they will be placed automatically into a default category named *Uncategorized* by Macro Express.

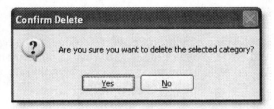

The Commands Pane has its own set of shortcuts. They work the same whether you are showing categories or just commands (Options | Preferences | Appearances | Show Script Command Categories).

	Commands Pane only
Shortcut	**Action**
Home	Move to beginning of command or category names
End	Move to end of command or category names
Page Up	Move up a full pane
Page Down	Move down a full pane
Up Arrow	Move to previous command or category name
Down Arrow	Move to next command or category name
Character	Move to next command or category starting with character
Enter (category)	Expand category list
Enter (command)	Invoke the command's dialog

The purpose of the Commands Pane is to place a command line into the Macro Script Pane, but where will it be placed? It is your choice. You set the default placement using the (Options | Command Insertion) menu. My choice is **Insert After Highlighted Command**. When you install Macro Express, the default is **Insert at End of Macro Script**. The other choice is **Insert Before Highlighted Command**. Of course the highlighted command being referenced is in the Macro Script Pane, not the Commands Pane. The choice you set is used by Macro Express only if it does not know what else to do.

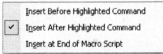

You can pick where to place the command before choosing it. Make sure you are where you want to be in the Macro Script Pane. Let's position ourselves on the *Control Panel Open* line in the Macro Script Pane.

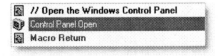

Highlight the command in the Commands Pane you want to insert into the Macro Script Pane. Let's use the *Clipboard Empty* command. Do not double-click … highlight only.

Now, if you want to insert it before your position in the Macro Script Pane, press **Ctrl+K** or click on the top arrow in the center column. This will place the command immediately before the *Control Panel Open* line in the

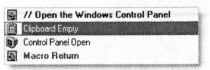

Macro Script Pane.

Ctrl+I, or the middle arrow, will insert it after the ***Control Panel Open*** line and **Ctrl+E**, or the bottom arrow, will add it to the end of the macro. You could have also picked the insert positions from the Edit menu.

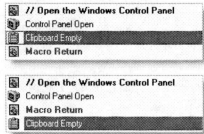

If you were simply to double-click on the ***Control Panel Open*** command in the Commands Pane, then it would be inserted at the default position named in the (Options | Command Insertion) menu. Why? Because clicking on it does not tell Macro Express where to place it, so it uses the default setting.

There is another convenience feature Macro Express has built in to the Commands Pane; the ability to switch focus to the Macro Script Pane after a command is picked. This means that subsequent keystrokes are immediately directed at the Macro Script Pane rather than the Commands Pane.

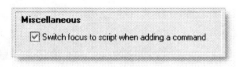

Choose (Options | Preferences | Miscellaneous) from the Main Menu and place a check in the **Switch Focus to Script When Adding a Command** checkbox. When Macro Express is first installed, the default is not to switch focus. Without this option you can click on the Macro Script Pane or press **Alt+Right Arrow** to focus on it after picking a command.

Search Box

Use the Search Box to find a command in the Commands Pane if you do not know in which category it belongs or to avoid having to search and pick it from a list. Access the Search Box by pressing **Alt+Down Arrow** or click on it.

The Commands Pane moves towards the matching command as you type each character in the name. The search is *not* case sensitive. The more characters you type, the closer to the command you get. What is nice is that each time you type another character, Macro Express searches the commands from the beginning, and so if you happen to be positioned beyond what you are searching for, you will still find it.

Let's say that you want to search for the ***If Mouse Cursor*** command. Type the letter "I" and the Commands Pane is positioned to ***If Clipboard*** because it is the first "I" that it found. Add an "f" and the Commands Pane remains positioned on "If Clipboard" because it is the first "If". Add a space and the Commands Pane remains the same because it is the first "If ". Add an "M" and the Commands Pane is repositioned to ***If Macro*** because it is the first "If M". Add an "o" and the Commands Pane is repositioned to ***If Mouse Cursor*** because it is the first "If Mo".

At any point as you are entering the command name to find, you can hit the **Up** or **Down Arrow** key to reposition the Commands Pane yourself, and then continue typing because the Search Box does not lose focus. Why would you want to do this? It is handy if there is a long series of commands that begin with the same letters. An example would be any command that begins with "Window". Say that you wanted the *Window Close* command. When you type "W" the Commands Pane is positioned to the *Window Activate* command. Now you add "indow C" and the *Window Close* command is highlighted. Or you could have simply pressed the **Down Arrow** key once.

Now that you have found the command, you can click on one of the Arrow icons in the center column to place the command in the Macro Script Pane. You could also use one of the shortcut keys, **Ctrl+K**, **Ctrl+I**, or **Ctrl+E**, or just press **Enter**, which will place the command using the default choice.

Macro Script Pane

The Macro Script Pane contains your macro. The other panes are tools used to support this one. Macro Express provides some nice editing tools that make your task easier, which we will examine in this section:

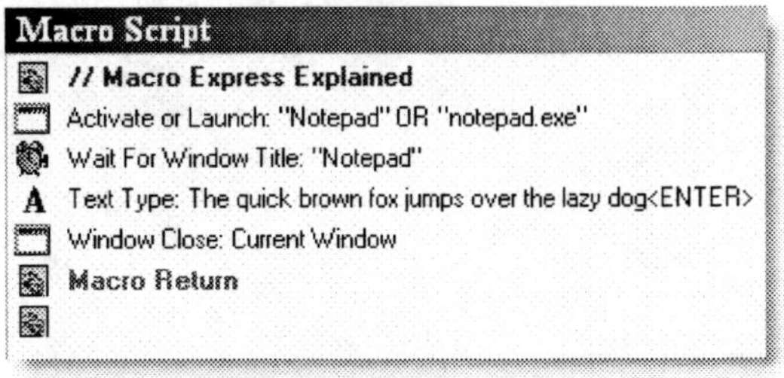

- Move lines
- Duplicate lines
- Insert lines
- Add lines
- Edit lines (dialogs)
- Go to a line
- Disable lines
- Search macro
- Print macro
- Run macro
- Step through macro
- Set breakpoints
- View variables
- Check syntax
- Use a test window

The charts on the right and on the next page show the Macro Script Pane editing tool shortcuts.

The chart on the right are those specific to Macro Express and the Macro Script Pane. Each of these shortcuts match an icon somewhere or a menu choice. I find them useful and they have become second nature when I am developing macros and not writing books.

Macro Script

> // Macro Express Explained
> Activate or Launch: "Notepad" OR "notepad.exe"
> Wait For Window Title: "Notepad"
> A Text Type: The quick brown fox jumps over the lazy dog<ENTER>
> Window Close: Current Window
> Macro Return

Macro Script Pane (special)	
Shortcut	**Action**
Enter	Invoke the command's dialog
Ctrl+B	Toggle breakpoint of current command
Ctrl+K	Insert command before selected command
Ctrl+I	Insert command after selected command
Ctrl+E	Add command to end of macro
Ctrl+N	Enable or disable selected commands
Ctrl+Up Arrow	Move selected commands up
Ctrl+Down Arrow	Move selected commands down
Ctrl+D	Duplicate selected commands
Ctrl+S	Save macro
Ctrl+P	Print dialog
Ctrl+G	Go To Line Number dialog
Ctrl+F	Find dialog
F3	Find again
F1	Macro Express context sensitive help
F8	Step through macro
F9	Run macro

The chart here shows standard editing tools (which you should already be familiar with) that work in the Macro Script Pane.

Macro Script Pane (editing)			
Shortcut	**Action**	**Shortcut**	**Action**
Ctrl+X	Cut selected commands	Up Arrow	Move to previous command
Ctrl+C	Copy selected commands	Down Arrow	Move to next command
Ctrl+V	Paste commands	Left Arrow	Scroll pane left
Ctrl+A	Select whole macro	Right Arrow	Scroll pane right
Delete	Delete selected commands	Shft+Home	Select to beginning of macro
Home	Move to beginning of macro	Shft+End	Select to end of macro
End	Move to end of macro	Shft+Page Up	Select up a full pane
Page Up	Move up a full pane	Shft+Page Down	Select down a full pane
Page Down	Move down a full pane	Shft+Up Arrow	Select previous command
Ctrl+Left Click	Select another command	Shft+Down Arrow	Select next command

Selecting Lines

Selecting lines to perform operations on, such as moving, duplicating, disabling, and so forth is straightforward. Moving through the macro with the **Up** and **Down Arrow** keys automatically selects the current line. To select multiple lines, hold the **Shift** key down as you move with the **Arrows**. Selecting multiple lines that are not concurrent is also easy. Simply use the **Ctrl+Left Click** shortcut.

Moving Lines

To move a line, select it and then click on the Up or Down Arrow icons in the right-hand column or press **Ctrl+Up Arrow** or **Ctrl+Down Arrow** shortcut. The example here shows moving the *Macro Return* line down, however, this same feature works with blocks of selected lines and selected lines that are not concurrent.

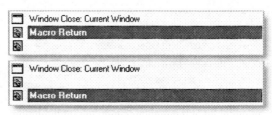

Duplicating Lines

To duplicate a line, select it and click on the Copy icon, which is the bottom icon in the right-hand column or press the **Ctrl+D** shortcut. The example here shows duplicating the *Macro Return* line, however, this same feature works with blocks of selected lines and selected lines that are not concurrent.

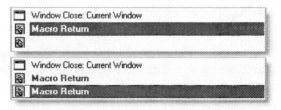

Inserting Lines

Inserting and adding lines is the same as that explained in the Commands Pane section. Move to the desired position and then click one of the icons in the center column to insert or add the command highlighted in the Commands Pane. You can also use the **Ctrl+K**, **Ctrl+I**, and **Ctrl+E** shortcut keys.

Deleting Lines

To delete a line, select it and press the **Delete** key. You can also click on the Trashcan icon in the toolbar or choose (Edit | Delete) from the Main Menu. This same feature works with blocks of selected lines and selected lines that are not concurrent. Be careful when deleting lines. There is no confirmation prompt and there is no "undo" **Ctrl+Z** like in the Direct Editor.

Changing Lines

To edit or change a line, select it and press **Enter**, or double-click on it, or click on the Notepad icon in the toolbar. Let's say that you want to change the **Remark** line at

the beginning of the macro. Highlight it and press **Enter** to pop up its dialog. Make your change (add the chapter name) and then click **OK**. The changed line is rewritten and saved.

Disabling Lines

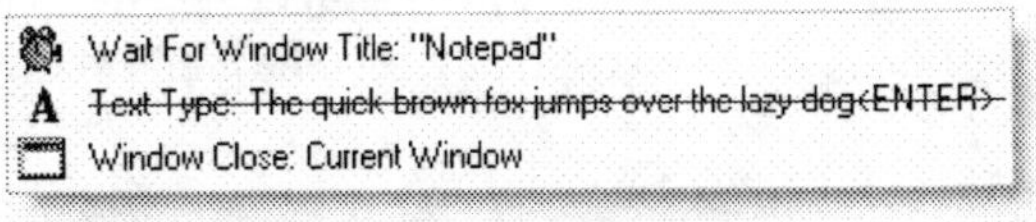

Sometimes when you are testing a macro you would like temporarily to disable a line so it is bypassed while you test other lines. Macro Express allows you to do this. In fact, you can disable

and enable blocks of selected lines and even selected lines that are not concurrent. Let's disable the **Text Type** line. Select it and then click on the antiexclamation Point icon in the center column, or press the **Ctrl+N** shortcut. The line is changed with a red strikeout running through it. And the icon is changed to a regular exclamation point. If you move off the line, the icon changes back to an antiexclamation point.

The icon is a toggle. If the line that you are positioned on is enabled, the icon will be an antiexclamation point, which means it can be disabled. A disabled line, one with a strikeout running through it, will be an exclamation point, which means that it can be enabled. But, because you could have more than a single line selected, some of which may be disabled and others enabled, there is a third icon shown here. It means that if you click on it or press the **Ctrl+N** shortcut, the enabled lines will be disabled and the disabled lines will be enabled. In other words, their status will be reversed.

Breakpoints

Maybe while testing a macro, you would like to run it to a certain point and then stop before continuing. This could be to examine variables, check for a file, and so forth. It is called a breakpoint, and Macro Express has this feature. Select the line that you want to break and then press the **Ctrl+B** shortcut or choose (Debug | Toggle Breakpoint) from the Main

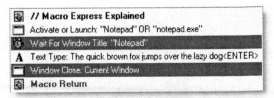

Menu. The line will be changed to a sort of green color. Multiple breakpoints are allowed but they have to be set one at a time.

The example shows the **Wait For Window** and **Window Close** lines are set to break when the program runs. When Macro Express gets to the first break, the line changes to red and the macro stops. It will wait until you click the green Run icon, then it will run to the next break and stop again. Click the icon to continue. The green Run icon is the only tool you can use to continue a macro between breakpoints. There is no "continue" option.

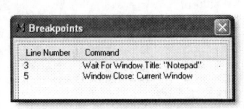

Because you can set many breakpoints in a macro during the development phase, Macro Express provides a window to display them outside the Macro Script Pane. This makes them easy to find and get to in long macros. Choose (Debug | Debug Windows | Breakpoints) from the Main Menu to pop up the *Breakpoints* dialog. When you double-click on any breakpoint in the list the Macro Script Pane is repositioned to the matching line number for you.

Breakpoints are saved with the macro. To remove a breakpoint, select the line then press the **Ctrl+B** shortcut or choose (Debug | Toggle Breakpoint) from the Main Menu. A trick you can use to clear them all at once is switch to the Direct Editor and then back again, then save the macro.

Stepping Through a Macro

During the development phase you may want to step through and test a macro one line at a time. Macro Express provides for this, too. Press the **F8** key or choose (Debug | Step Through Macro) from the Main Menu. It is similar to the breakpoint feature, in that every line is treated as a breakpoint.

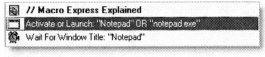

In the example you can see at which line the macro is positioned because it changes to red and the macro stops. *Remark* lines are ignored. Macro Express will wait until you click the green Run icon, then it will go to the next line and stop. Click the icon to continue, and so forth. The green Run icon is the only tool you can use to continue a macro when stepping through it.

If you have built a macro that calls another macro using the **Macro Run** command, then that macro will also be stepped through. On returning, your macro will continue stepping through one line at a time.

Running a Macro

Run a macro by pressing **F9**, or click the green Run icon, or choose (Debug | Test Run Macro) from the Main Menu. It will run until finding a breakpoint, or it finishes, or until stopped by clicking the red Stop icon, which does not appear until the macro is running.

Change Focus Automatically

There is another feature related to stepping through a macro, which is how Macro Express handles setting focus between the steps. For example, let's say that you have a macro which outputs text to the Notepad. If Change Focus Automatically (Debug | Change Focus to Previous Window) is turned off, then you will have manually to click

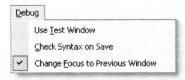

back on the Scripting Editor window each time to press the **F8** key again. If it is turned on (checked), then you will be automatically returned to the Scripting Editor window after processing each command line, and then switched back to the other window when the command line runs. You would *not* be able to step through the macro with this feature turned off. The editor has to have focus when you press the **F8** key. And with it turned off, will not switch focus back to the Notepad window before running the command meaning the *Text Type* command would attempt to type over your macro.

Test Window

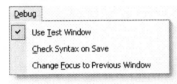

For those applications that you would like to test output for, such as text or variables, there is a test window built in to the debugging feature. You can set this window to pop up by default each time you test a macro by choosing (Debug | Use Test Window) from the Main Menu. Choose it again to disable it. This feature only works from inside the Scripting Editor window and can be used with both the **F8** (stepping) key and the **F9** (run) key.

You can choose to use, or not use, the default setting each time you retest a macro. Look closely at the green Run icon. There is a small black triangle next to it. If you click on it, a menu is displayed that allows you to use, or not use, the test window for this particular run, overriding the default setting.

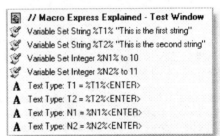

Whichever one you pick, the macro will immediately run. And because clicking on the green Run icon is the same as pressing the **F9** (run) key, this antidefault feature is not available for the **F8** (stepping) key.

An example of using this feature is shown on the right. The test window is launched automatically when the macro runs. The macro sets some variables and then outputs their values using the *Text Type* command. The *Macro Express Test Window* receives the output.

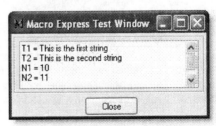

Viewing Variables

Let's examine another debugging feature of Macro Express, the *Variables* dialog. It is accessed by choosing (Debug | Debug Windows | Variable Values) from the Main Menu. You can use this feature to examine variables while sitting at a breakpoint, or stepping through a macro, or even after the macro is finished running. I cannot remember the last time that I did *not* use this feature when developing a macro application.

After running the above sample macro, you can see the values displayed in the *Variables* dialog. If you step through a macro then each variable is displayed as it is set by the current command line. All variable values are held by Macro Express until another macro is run, which is why you can view variables after the macro has finished.

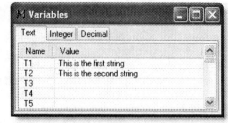

The dialog contains three tabs, **Text**, **Integer**, and **Decimal**. In other words, one for each variable type. Obviously I have compacted the dialog to save space in the book, but you can view all 99 variables in each tab by expanding it.

Syntax Checking

Knowing that you entered proper commands into a macro is an important feature of the editing and debugging process. Macro Express let's you check this at any time. Choose (Debug | Check Syntax Now) from the Main Menu and the macro will be checked. The example purposely leaves off the **End If** command so when the syntax is checked an error is displayed.

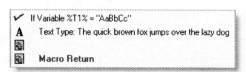

Macro Express gives you the ability to have the syntax checked automatically each time a macro is saved. This relieves you of having to remember it each time you make a change to a macro.

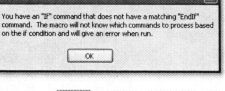

Choose (Debug | Check Syntax on Save) to enable this feature. Choose it again to turn it off. No matter what you decide, on or off, or whether you check syntax manually, an error message will be displayed at runtime if syntax is wrong.

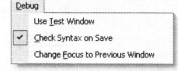

Go To Line

This feature is more important in long macros than short ones. However, during the editing process you may need the ability to go to a specific line in a macro. Macro Express displays the current line number, and the total number of lines in the macro, at the bottom of the Macro Script Pane.

Press the **Ctrl+G** shortcut or choose (Edit | Go To Line) from the Main Menu. Enter a target line number and click **OK**. The Macro Script Pane will be repositioned to the line number. If you enter a number larger than the number of lines in the macro then Macro Express will go to the last line.

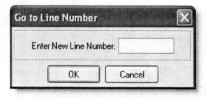

Finding Text

This feature is used to find text in a macro. It will begin searching from wherever you are positioned within the macro so, if you want to search the whole macro, go to the beginning before using this tool.

Press the **Ctrl+F** shortcut or choose (Edit | Find) from the Main Menu. Enter something to search for into the **Find What** field. In this case we will search for the line containing "lazy dog". The **Match Case** checkbox is not needed for this search so leave it unchecked and press the **Enter** key or click on the **Find Next** button.

If Macro Express can find what you are searching for, the Macro Script Pane will be repositioned to the line containing the string. The *Find* dialog, however, will keep focus until you close it.

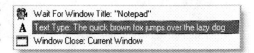

Press **Enter** or click **Find Next** if you want to search for the next case. In our case, there is not another instance of "lazy dog" so an *End of Script* message is displayed. This message is displayed anytime the search string cannot be found.

You could have closed the *Find* dialog and pressed the **F3** (find again) key as an alternative to pressing **Enter** the second time. The **F3** key will hold the last string you searched for until you edit a different macro or enter an empty string into the **Find What** field.

Saving a Macro

Click on the Save icon, or press the **Ctrl+S** shortcut, or choose (File | Save) from the Main Menu to save the changes to the macro. The macro will immediately be written to the Macro Express library file. There is no "Save As" feature; instead, copy the macro using the Macro Explorer.

Printing a Macro

Click on the Printer icon, or press the **Ctrl+P** shortcut, or choose (File | Print Script) from the Main Menu to print the macro. A Windows *Print* dialog will pop up. Choose your printer and click on the **OK** button.

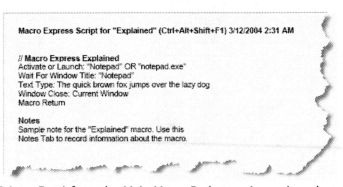

The macro is printed with a header containing the name of the macro in quotation marks, the activation key in parenthesis, and a date and time stamp. You can change the printer font by using the *Font* dialog. Choose (File | Printer Font) from the Main Menu. Each page is numbered on the bottom. The **Notes Tab** field is printed on the last page. See the *Notes Tab* section in this chapter. A sample printout is shown on the previous page.

Copy Command Text

This is a nice feature that let's you copy and paste lines from the Macro Script Pane as they appear, rather than their natural state as viewed in the Direct Editor window. Select the lines to copy and then choose (Edit | Copy Command Text) from the Main Menu. The lines are copied into your clipboard as they appear in the Macro Script Pane. Here, for example, is what the "Activate or Launch" line looks like copied and pasted with this feature:

> Activate or Launch: "Notepad" OR "notepad.exe"

You can also copy selected lines in their natural state by using the **Ctrl+C** shortcut, or (Edit | Copy) from the Main Menu. Here is the same line using **Ctrl+C**:

> <LAUNCHYES3:0:0112Notepad<LAUNCH:notepad.exe>

Direct Editor

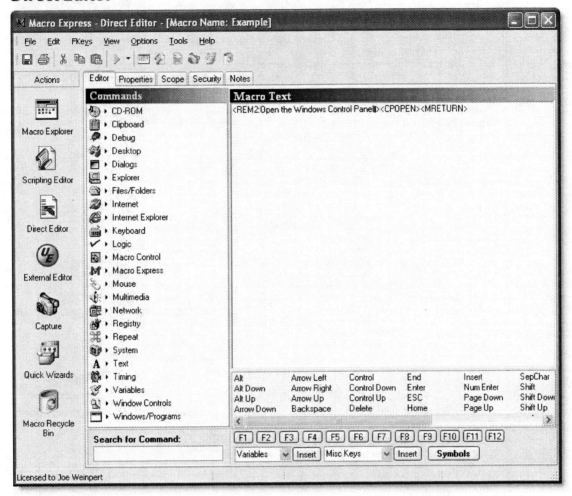

The **Editor Tab** of the Direct Editor contains three sections, Commands Pane (**Alt+Left Arrow**), Search Box (**Alt+Down Arrow**), and Macro Text Pane (**Alt+Right Arrow**). It is a menu-driven system. To create a macro, pick commands from the Commands Pane to be moved to the Macro Text Pane. When you choose a command, it may, or may not, have an associated dialog. If it does, set the features you want, click **OK**, and the command will be placed into the Macro Text Pane at wherever your cursor is positioned.

The example is a simple macro that opens your *Control Panel* dialog. It is equal to choosing (Start | Control Panel) from the Taskbar or clicking on the My Computer Desktop icon and then clicking on "Control Panel". There are three commands involved:

Pick the **Remark** command from within the *Macro Control* category. A dialog appears. Type the remark into the **Comments** field. Click **OK**. The first line is added to the Macro Text Pane.

Choose the **Control Panel Open** command from within the *System* category. A dialog appears. Leave the **Open Main Control Panel** choice. Click **OK**. The second line is added to the Macro Text Pane.

Pick the **Macro Return** command from within the *Macro Control* category. There is no dialog; it is just added directly to the Macro Text Pane.

That is the basics of creating a macro using the Direct Editor. You can now run the macro by clicking on the green Run icon.

Here is a list of navigation shortcuts for the Direct Editor. The Commands Pane and Macro Text Pane each have their own shortcut charts. Note that there is no shortcut for the Security Tab.

Direct Editor			
Shortcut	**Set focus to**	**Shortcut**	**Set focus to**
Alt+F	File Menu	Alt+Left Arrow	Commands Pane
Alt+E	Edit Menu	Alt+Right Arrow	Macro Text Pane
Alt+Y	FKeys Menu	Alt+Down Arrow	Search Box
Alt+V	View Menu	Alt+I	Editor Tab
Alt+O	Options Menu	Alt+P	Properties Tab
Alt+T	Tools Menu	Alt+C	Scope Tab
Alt+H	Help Menu	(none)	Security Tab
F1	Help	Alt+N	Notes Tab

Commands Pane

The Commands Pane, as used in the Direct Editor, is identical with the Scripting Editor except for one very important aspect; the chosen command will *always* be inserted at the cursor position in the Macro Text Pane. All text will be shifted to the right and the command will be inserted. There are no other options. The special insertion commands (**Insert Before**, **Insert After**, and **Insert at End**) used in the Scripting Editor are not applicable in the Direct Editor. Everything else works the same. Please refer to the Scripting Editor section in this chapter to learn more about options, settings, and using the Commands Pane.

Search Box

Just like the Commands Pane, the Search Box, as used in the Direct Editor, is identical with the Scripting Editor, except the chosen command will *always* be inserted at the cursor position in the Macro Text

Pane. Everything else works the same. Please refer to the Scripting Editor section in this chapter to learn more about using the Search Box.

Macro Text Pane

The Macro Text Pane contains your macro, but is completely different from the Macro Script Pane in the Scripting Editor. In this pane, the macro is displayed and edited in its natural state. The chart shows editing

> **Macro Text**
> ⟨REM2:Macro Express Explained⟩<LAUNCHYES3:0:0112Notepad
> <LAUNCH:notepad.exe><WAITWIN2:000010:000000:Notepad⟩<TEXTTYPE:The quick brown fox jumps over the lazy dog<ENTER>⟩<WCLS:"CURRENT">
> <MRETURN><REM2:⟩

shortcuts. It is not as overwhelming as it seems. The first eight rows deal with moving the cursor, the next eight rows deal with selecting text, and the last six rows cover other editing shortcut keys.

Macro Text Pane			
Shortcut	**Action**	**Shortcut**	**Action**
Up	Move to previous line	Ctrl+Up	Move to start of macro
Down	Move to next line	Ctrl+Down	Move to end of macro
Left	Move left	Ctrl+Left	Move left one word
Right	Move right	Ctrl+Right	Move right one word
Home	Move to start of line	Ctrl+Home	Move to start of macro
End	Move to end of line	Ctrl+End	Move to end of macro
Page Up	Move up a full pane	Ctrl+Page Up	Move to start of pane
Page Down	Move down a full pane	Ctrl+Page Down	Move to end of pane
Shft+Up	Select up one line	Ctrl+Shft+Up	Select to start of macro
Shft+Down	Select down one line	Ctrl+Shft+Down	Select to end of macro
Shft+Left	Select left one letter	Ctrl+Shft+Left	Select left one word
Shft+Right	Select right one letter	Ctrl+Shft+Right	Select right one word
Shft+Home	Select to start of line	Ctrl+Shft+Home	Select to start of macro
Shft+End	Select to end of line	Ctrl+Shft+End	Select to end of macro
Shft+Page Up	Select up one pane	Ctrl+Shft+Page Up	Select to start of pane
Shft+Page Down	Select down one pane	Ctrl+Shft+Page Dn	Select to end of pane
Ctrl+X	Cut selected text	Ctrl+S	Save macro
Ctrl+C	Copy selected text	Ctrl+P	Print dialog
Ctrl+V	Paste text	Ctrl+R	Search & Replace dialog
Ctrl+A	Select whole macro	Ctrl+F	Find dialog
Ctrl+Z	Undo	F3	Find again
Delete	Delete selected text	F1	Macro Express help

The **Ctrl+Z** "undo" shortcut only works while in the Macro Text Pane, and it only affects your last action. If you select some text and then delete it, you can bring it back by pressing **Ctrl+Z**, but it must be done before making any other changes. You can also right-click and choose "Undo" from the menu.

Separator Character

A macro is a single string of mnemonic commands. Some of them use a *Separator Character*, which is an ASCII 1, which in turn, is an SOH (Start of Heading) character. Refer to the *ASCII Values and Variables* and the *Special Characters* sections within the *Variables* chapter. It appears as a solid vertical bar in the Macro Text Pane and is used to mark the end of a command, but can also mark the end of sections inside a command. And to confuse the issue more, not all commands have this character, so it does not mark the end of every command. Here is how the macro would look if each command were on a separate line like the Scripting Editor:

<REM2:Macro Express Explained·>
<LAUNCHYES3:0:0112Notepad<LAUNCH:notepad.exe>
<WAITWIN2:000010:000000:Notepad·>
<TEXTTYPE:The quick brown fox jumps over the lazy dog<ENTER>·>
<WCLS:"CURRENT">
<MRETURN>
<REM2: ·>

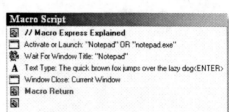

The font I am using in this book shows the *Separator Character* as a "dot" and not a solid vertical bar, however, you can see that four commands use it to mark the end while the others do not.

Text Type

The key to editing macros in the Macro Text Pane is to know where one command ends and another begins. It is easy to get confused. If you insert a command in the wrong place, say in the middle of another command, Macro Express will not know what to do and will convert your command, the command you inserted it into, and all following commands up to the next separator character, into a *Text Type* command. The advantage to this is that syntax integrity for the rest of the macro is saved.

The correct output from the above example is to type "The quick brown fox jumps over the lazy dog" into the Windows Notepad program as shown here.

File   Edit   Format   View   Help

The quick brown fox jumps over the lazy dog

Let's insert a command into the wrong place by putting a *Macro Return* command into the middle of the *Wait for Window* command and then save the change.

<REM2:Macro Express Explained|><LAUNCHYES3:0:0112Notepad
<LAUNCH:notepad.exe><WAIT<MRETURN>WIN2:000010:000000:Notepad|>
<TEXTTYPE:The quick brown fox jumps over the lazy dog<ENTER>|>
<WCLS:"CURRENT"><MRETURN><REM2:|>

When the macro is run again, the output is wrong. During the run, Macro Express automatically placed what it thinks were incomplete commands, or text, into a *Text Type* command to preserve the integrity of the macro.

File   Edit   Format   View   Help

<WAIT

You can see how this changed the macro by viewing it from the Scripting Editor. The inserted *Macro Return* command is now surrounded by two *Text Type* commands that Macro Express created. So the macro ran as directed, stopping after typing the word "<WAIT" into the Windows Notepad program.

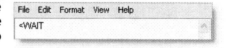

// Macro Express Explained
Activate or Launch: "Notepad" OR "notepad.exe"
Text Type: <WAIT
Macro Return
Text Type: WIN2:000010:000000:Notepad|>
Text Type: The quick brown fox jumps over the lazy dog<ENTER>
Window Close: Current Window
Macro Return

This same feature (changing errors into *Text Type* commands) is used by Macro Express to convert text that you enter directly into the Macro Text Pane into proper commands.

The Macro Text Pane is used like the *Text Type* command dialog. It contains the same fields and buttons for entering characters. Refer to the *Text Type* section within the *Keyboard* chapter for details on how to use these fields and buttons.

Let's create an example. Start with a macro that sets a string variable.

      Variable Set String %T10% "Aa"

Use the Macro Text Pane. Add two more lines and edit them. Change the variable and text for each.

      Variable Set String %T10% "Aa"
      Variable Set String %T11% "Bb"
      Variable Set String %T12% "Cc"

Now add text between each command that will type the value of the variables. Save the macro using the **Ctrl+S** shortcut and then switch to the Scripting Editor.

      Variable Set String %T10% "Aa"
      Text Type: T10 = %T10%<ENTER>
      Variable Set String %T11% "Bb"
      Text Type: T11 = %T11%<ENTER>
      Variable Set String %T12% "Cc"
      Text Type: T12 = %T12%<ENTER>

Looking at the macro listing above, you can see that Macro Express has changed the text that you entered between commands to *Text Type* commands. Switch back to the Direct Editor to see the changes.

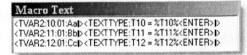

Running a Macro

There is no stepping through a macro in the Direct Editor. And there is no **F9** key. The only way to run a macro is to click on the green Run icon. It will run until it is finished, or until you click on the Running Man icon in the System Tray, or press the HotKey to stop a macro. See the *Stopping a Macro* section within the *Running and Activating Macros* chapter. Unlike the Scripting Editor, there are no breakpoints and there is no red Stop icon.

Test Window

For those applications that you would like to test output for, such as text or variables, the same test window found in the Scripting Editor is built into the Direct Editor. The difference is there is no default setting. You must choose to run it, or not run it, each time you test the macro.

Finding Text

Use this feature to find text in a macro. It is the same as in the Scripting Editor. Refer to the *Finding Text* section if you need help on its use.

Search and Replace Text

This feature is unique to the Direct Editor. Use it to find and replace text in a macro. Press the **Ctrl+R** shortcut or choose (Edit | Search and Replace) from the Main Menu.

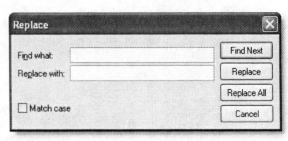

The **Find What** field contains what to search for and the **Replace With** field holds the substitution text. You can choose a case-sensitive search by checking the **Match Case** checkbox. Press the **Find Next** button to search for the next instance of the **Find What** string. The search begins from the position of the cursor, so if you want to search and replace from the beginning of the file, move the cursor before using the dialog.

If Macro Express finds what you are searching for, the Macro Text Pane will be repositioned to the string. The *Replace* dialog, however, will keep focus until you close it. If the string cannot be found, then an *End of Script* message is displayed. This message is displayed anytime the search string cannot be found.

Click on the **Replace** button to replace the text. To replace the next instance, click on the **Find Next** button again and then the **Replace** button. If your goal is to replace every instance of the search string, then simply click on the **Replace All** button.

Saving a Macro

Click on the Save icon, or press the **Ctrl+S** shortcut, or choose (File | Save) from the Main Menu to save the changes to the macro. They will immediately be written to the Macro Express library file. There is no "Save As" feature; instead, you copy the macro using the Macro Explorer.

Printing a Macro

Use this feature to print a macro script. It is the same as in the Scripting Editor. Refer to the *Printing a Macro* section if you need help on its use.

Properties Tab

The Properties Tab, as viewed from either editor, consists of two sections, **General** and **Activation**. The **Activation** section is detailed in the *Running and Activating Macros* chapter and will not be repeated here. And there is a *Properties* dialog accessed from the *Macro Explorer* window, which contains many of the same settings as this Properties Tab. See the *Macro Express Editor* chapter for more information.

Nickname

The **Nickname** field is the name of the macro and can be up to 50 characters. There are two system-wide preference settings that affect this field. They are found in the (Options | Preferences | Dialogs) dialog.

If checked, the **Warn the User About Macros with no Nicknames** checkbox will pop up a warning if this field is empty. The warning is displayed

only when accessing the *Macro Commands* dialog (Macro Control category), which contains four different commands that can be added to a macro. The **Don't Tell Me This Again** checkbox in the *Warning* dialog will, if checked, clear the **Warn the User About Macros with no Nicknames** checkbox in the *Preferences* dialog. The default is the checkbox is checked.

If checked, the **Warn About Duplicate Nicknames when Saving** checkbox will pop up a warning if the name in this field matches another macro. The warning is displayed *only* when you try to create a new macro or save changes to an existing one.

The **Don't Ask Me This Again** checkbox in the *Duplicate Name Warning* dialog will, if checked, clear the **Warn About Duplicate Nicknames when Saving** checkbox in the *Preferences* dialog. The default is the checkbox is *not* checked.

Icon

Each macro can have its own icon. Whether or not they are

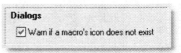

displayed in the *Macro Explorer* window depends on the (Options | Preferences | Appearance | Show Macro Icons) checkbox. If it is checked (the default setting) they will be displayed. But there is another system-wide preference setting that affects this feature, the **Warn if Macro's Icon does not Exist** checkbox and it is found in the (Options | Preferences | Dialogs) dialog. If checked, it will pop up a warning when the chosen icon is missing from your system. Maybe it was deleted, moved, or renamed.

If Macro Express cannot find an icon when it is launched, the default system icon is displayed, but no warning is given. The warning is displayed *only* when you click on the **Change** button. Then you are given an opportunity to find or change it.

Clicking on the **Change** button pops up the *Select an Icon* dialog. The **Filename** field contains the full path name of the current icon file. The **Current Icon** field may contain multiple icons depending on the file chosen in the **Filename** field. If it does (like the example here), the current chosen icon will be highlighted.

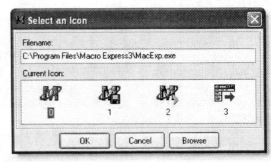

You can pick another icon from the same file or click on the **Browse** button to pop up the system-wide *Select an Icon File* dialog to choose one.

There are four different kinds of files that contain an icon or icon list. A standalone icon (*.ico*) file, an icon library (*.icl*) file, an executable (*.exe*) file, and a dynamic link library (*.dll*) file.

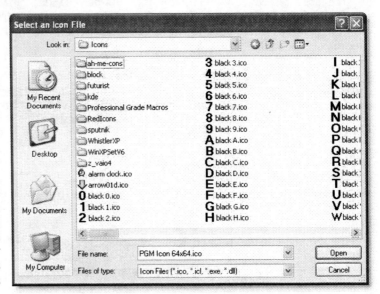

When Macro Express is installed an **Icons** folder is created containing over 400 icons. You may pick anything from the folder or choose your own icon location. Icons for the PGM Functions™ Library that we market, are kept in a subfolder called Professional Grade Macros, which provides a common location with other icons. Macro Express always knows where its **Icons** folder is located.

Active

The **Active** checkbox is used to enable or disable a macro from inside the Properties Tab. If the box is checked then the macro is enabled. Enabling and disabling a macro is the

mechanism used to turn it on or off. A disabled macro cannot be run with the *Macro Run* command or from a Popup or Floating Menu. However, it can be run by clicking on it in the *Macro Explorer* window. This checkbox can also be controlled programmatically from a macro by using the *Macro Enable* and *Macro Disable* commands. In the *Macro Explorer* window, a disabled macro is listed in a grey italic font so it can be seen as being disabled.

Use Log File

The **Use Log File** checkbox in this Properties Tab matches the **Enable Error Log** checkbox found in the Log Tab accessed from the *Properties* dialog in the *Macro Explorer* window. Its purpose is to turn the

logging of macro errors on and off. See the *Macro Express Editor* chapter for more information on logging.

Scope Tab

The settings inside the Scope Tab of either editor are detailed in the *Running and Activating Macros* chapter and will not be repeated here. And there is a *Properties* dialog accessed from the *Macro Explorer* window, which contains many of the same settings as this Scope Tab. See the *Macro Express Editor* chapter for more information.

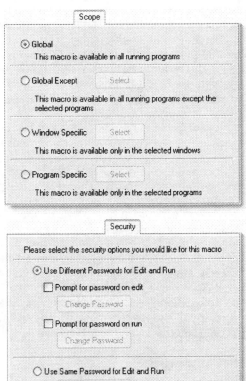

Security Tab

The Security Tab is all about passwords and preventing others from viewing or running your macros or both. There is a *Properties* dialog with a Security Tab that is accessed from the *Macro Explorer* window. It contains the same settings as this one. See the *Macro Express Editor* chapter for more information.

Passwords can contain letters, numbers, symbols, and spaces. They are case sensitive and the longest password allowed is eight characters.

All the password entry dialogs look and work the same. The only difference is the window title. There is an **Old Password**, **New Password**, and **Confirm New Password** field in each.

When creating or changing passwords, if the old password is not correct or the new and confirmation passwords do not match, an error message is displayed similar to this one. You must fix the problem before you will be allowed to continue. Please note that all three fields could remain blank. If this is the case, then that particular password is ignored, even though it is enabled.

The **Use Different Passwords for Edit and Run** choice enables users to run macros without the ability to edit or change them. The opposite is also true. A user can be allowed to edit a macro but not run it, except from within one of the editors. I am not sure under what circumstance this would be used, but it is available.

Check the **Prompt for Password on Edit** checkbox to set a password for editing. The **Change Password** button will be enabled. Click on it to use the *Enter Edit Password* dialog.

Enter the existing password into the **Old Password** field. If this is the first time, leave it blank and tab to the **New Password** field and enter the password. Dots will be displayed as you type. Tab to the **Confirm New Password** field and enter the same password, then click the **OK** button.

Take the same steps for the **Prompt for Password on Run** checkbox if a user must enter a password to run a macro. This includes running a macro with the *Macro Run* command, or from a Floating or Popup Menu. However, the **Prompt for Password on Run** checkbox is ignored when running a macro from inside one of the editors. For example, using the **F9** or **F8** shortcut key.

Choose the **Use Same Password for Edit and Run** radio button if a user must enter the same password to edit as well as run a macro. Follow the same steps as the other passwords.

Once entered, exit out of the editor and to the *Macro Explorer* window. Depending on which passwords you set, if a user tries to edit, run, delete, or export the macro, they will be prompted to enter the correct password. A user needs to know the editing password to delete or export a macro.

Removing passwords for the **Use Different Passwords for Edit and Run** choice is a matter of unchecking both boxes and then saving the macro. To remove the password for the **Use Same Password for Edit and Run** choice, change to **Use Different Passwords for Edit and Run** and save the macro. If you choose to use passwords again, it is identical with the first time where you left the **Old Password** field blank.

Main File Passwords

The passwords in the Security Tab affect only a single macro. There is another set of passwords that will protect access to the Macro library (*.mex*) file. They are accessed from the (Options | Preferences | Passwords) dialog.

The **Password on Edit** and **Password on Run** checkboxes work, and are set, in the same manner as the passwords explained above. There is an **Old Password**, **New Password**, and **Confirm New Password** field in each. The only difference is the window title in each dialog.

Well almost!

This is important to remember; if you have already set up a password for the **Password on Edit** or **Password on Run** options, and you want to remove one or both of them then you must do more than just uncheck the boxes. You must first change the **Old Password**, **New Password**, and **Confirm New Password** fields to blanks (empty). If you do not, Macro Express will forever remember the last password used and the fields will be "blanked" after unchecking the boxes. You, however, may forget a few months down the road what those passwords were. So, if *you* empty the fields then you do not have to remember anything. By the way, this is *not* true of the passwords in the Security Tab of the individual macros. They are emptied automatically so you do not have to do it.

Back to the task at hand -

You are prompted for the **Password on Edit** password when the library file is protected
-AND-
you click on the Macro Express icon in your System Tray
-OR-
you use the "Run Macro Express Editor" HotKey **Ctrl+Alt+Shft+W**
-OR-
you choose (File | Open Macro File) from the Main Menu to load a different library file.

It will prevent the *Macro Explorer* window from being launched if the password is entered wrong. You are given three choices when this happens. The **Try Again** button gives you an unlimited number of tries at the correct password. The **New File** button will pop up the *Please Select New File* dialog, which allows you to pick a different library. And the **Cancel** button will cancel the operation.

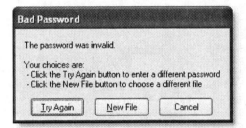

Whether the password is entered correctly or wrongly, HotKeys, ShortKeys, Floating Menu, Desktop macros, and so forth, are all available because the player program (*MacExp.exe*) is already launched. This is not so when using the **Password on Run** password and Macro Express is not yet been launched.

When you launch Macro Express, you are prompted for the password, but since this prompt occurs before the player is loaded, there is no access to anything. If you enter the correct password, Macro Express continues to load as expected. In case of a wrong password, the same *Bad Password* dialog is displayed as with **Password on Edit**, giving you the opportunity to correct it.

When using both password features with Macro Express not yet launched, you will be prompted for the **Password on Run** password. Macro Express then launches the player program. When you try to open the *Macro Explorer* window, you will be prompted for the **Password on Edit** password.

If you are in the *Macro Explorer* window and you try to load a macro file containing both passwords, you will be prompted for the **Password on Edit** password first, then the **Password on Run** password immediately afterwards.

Notes Tab

The Notes Tab contains any information that you want to keep about the macro. There is a *Properties* dialog with a Notes Tab that is accessed from the *Macro Explorer* window. It contains the same settings as this one. See the *Macro Express Editor* chapter for more information.

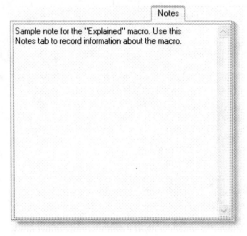

This is a freeform text field with some editing abilities (see the chart below). A length limit on the field could not be determined. I have tested it beyond 256k without trouble, which I am sure is way beyond any practical limit.

The information that you place in here is printed at the end of the macro listing when you print a macro. Refer to the *Printing a Macro* section in this chapter for an example printout.

Notes Tab Editing			
Shortcut	**Action**	**Shortcut**	**Action**
Up	Move to previous line	Ctrl+Left	Move left one word
Down	Move to next line	Ctrl+Right	Move right one word
Left	Move left	Ctrl+Home	Move to start of notes
Right	Move right	Ctrl+End	Move to end of notes
Home	Move to start of line	Ctrl+Shft+Left	Select left one word
End	Move to end of line	Ctrl+Shft+Right	Select right one word
Page Up	Move up a full pane	Ctrl+Shft+Home	Select to start of notes
Page Down	Move down a full pane	Ctrl+Shft+End	Select to end of notes
Shft+Up	Select up one line	Ctrl+X	Cut selected text
Shft+Down	Select down one line	Ctrl+C	Copy selected text
Shft+Left	Select left one letter	Ctrl+V	Paste text
Shft+Right	Select right one letter	Ctrl+Z	Undo
Shft+Home	Select to start of line	Delete	Delete selected text
Shft+End	Select to end of line	Ctrl+S	Save macro
Shft+Page Up	Select up one pane	Ctrl+P	Print dialog
Shft+Page Down	Select down one pane	F1	Macro Express help

External Editor

An external text editor of your choice can be used to edit macros. I use an editor called **UltraEdit** from IDM Computer Solutions, Inc. and can be downloaded from their web site at www.ultraedit.com.

Setting this feature is easy. Choose the (Options | Preferences | File Paths) dialog. Enter the full path name of the text editor program into the **External Editor** field or click on the **Browse** button to find the it. It *must* be a full path name. When you click the **Apply** button, the editor's icon is immediately displayed in the Actions Toolbar signaling that it is ready to use.

Your External Editor can be used only when you are in the *Macro Explorer* window. An error is displayed if you click on the icon in the Actions Toolbar while in one of the editors.

Highlight the macro to edit in the right-hand pane and then click on your editor's icon in the Actions Toolbar.

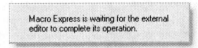

Macro Express immediately displays a message, launches your editor, and stuffs the macro into it. The macro is a playable file named *macro.mxe*. Refer to the *Running and Activating Macros* chapter to learn about playable macro files.

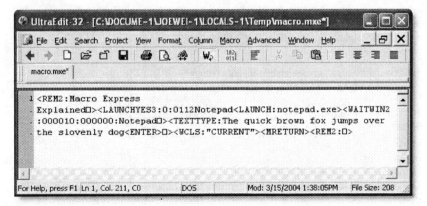

The macro presented to your editor is in its natural state. This is the same view as presented within the Direct Editor. Save the file after making your changes. When you close your editor, the changes will be read back into the library file.

Capturing Macros

Capturing a macro can be as simple as pressing **Ctrl+Alt+Shft+X**, running through your keys and mouse clicks, and then pressing **Ctrl+Alt+Shft+X** again to stop recording. This is the default HotKey for capturing macros. It can be changed at any time, as can any of the other default HotKeys. "Capturing" is just one-way to create a macro. And like any other macro, once created, it can be edited and changed.

Capture Settings

Macro Express has a sophisticated built-in recorder for capturing keyboard strokes, and mouse activity. The foundation settings for this feature are stored in three different *Preferences* dialogs. The main settings are stored in the (Options | Preferences | Capture) dialog shown on the right.

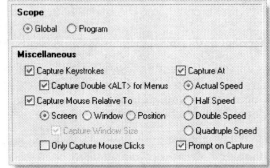

There is also a setting to show, or not show, the Recording icon in your System Tray. This is found in the (Options | Preferences | Appearance) dialog shown above. If the **Show Recording Icon** checkbox is checked a Recording icon will appear in your System Tray as you begin capturing the macro. This icon can be used to stop the recording by right-clicking on it.

Another setting is found in the (Options | Preferences | Dialogs) dialog. If the **Show Double Alt Message when Recording** checkbox is checked when you begin capturing a macro, one of two warnings will pop up before anything else happens. You can avoid them by unchecking the box here, or by checking the **Don't Show this Message Again** checkbox in either warning dialog.

The **Capture Double <ALT> for Menus** checkbox in the **Miscellaneous** section of the (Options | Preferences | Capture) dialog (top of the page) controls which warning appears. If the box is checked, you will be warned about capturing two <ALT><ALT> keys every time you press the <ALT> key. If the box is unchecked you will be warned about *not* capturing them. Clicking on the **Help** button will present you with even more information, but I do not recall needing to use <ALT><ALT> lately in a macro to access menus. A single <ALT> is enough. However, it does not hurt to use it. These options give us a choice.

Back to the main default settings dialog. The **Prompt on Capture** checkbox tells Macro Express to display a dialog (after the <ALT><ALT> warning) before beginning the capture process. It is informational only. Once you press **Ctrl+Alt+Shft+X** there is no way to start or stop the capture process without clicking on this **OK** button. Once the process starts you can stop it by pressing the HotKey again. Uncheck the **Prompt on Capture** checkbox if you do not want this dialog. If this, and the <ALT><ALT> warning, are disabled capturing begins immediately.

The **Scope** setting can be **Global** or **Program**. The default is **Global** when Macro Express is installed. Every macro has a scope. The macro you are capturing is no different. This setting sets the scope for you. If you choose **Global**, the macro will be recorded and saved as Global. If you choose **Program**, it will be scoped to the program that has focus when the capturing process *ends*. Yes, ends. You may start off in one program and finish in another. Let's say you are copying data from Excel to Word and Excel has focus when capturing begins. If you select some cells, click on Word, paste the cells, and then stop capturing, the macro will be scoped to "*winword.exe*", even though capturing started when Excel had focus. If this is what your macro is intended to do, then click back on Excel before you stop capturing to be sure it is scoped properly. If you end the capture process on your Desktop the macro will be scoped to "*explorer.exe*". Like everything else related to capturing a macro, the scoped program name can be changed later. Refer to the *Running and Activating Macros* chapter to learn more about scoping.

The **Capture Keystrokes** checkbox controls if keyboard strokes are recorded during the capture process. If the box is checked (the default) they are recorded. If unchecked, they are ignored and only mouse activity will be recorded. The **Ctrl+Alt+Shft+X** start and stop HotKeys are never recorded. The *Text Type* command is used to store the keyboard strokes. The **Capture Double <ALT> for Menus** checkbox controls whether <ALT> or <ALT><ALT> is recorded when pressing the **Alt** key as explained at the beginning of this section.

The **Capture Mouse Relative To** checkbox controls whether you record or ignore mouse activity. If checked then mouse activity is recorded. If unchecked, mouse activity is ignored and only keyboard input is recorded. When capturing mouse activity, Macro Express needs to know what the mouse coordinates are related to. There are three choices, **Screen**, **Window**, and **Position**.

If you choose **Screen** then all mouse coordinates are relative to your display. The *Mouse Move Screen* command is used to record the mouse coordinates as you move the mouse.

Choose **Window**, and all mouse coordinates are relative to the program window that currently has focus. When you switch to another window then coordinates will be relative to it. In other words, coordinates are not relative to only the first window, but rather whichever window currently has focus. It does not matter how many windows you switch to during the recording process. The *Mouse Move Window* command is used to record the mouse coordinates as you move the mouse.

Choosing the **Window** option enables another choice. The **Capture Window Size** checkbox, if checked, will place a *Window Resize* command at the beginning of the captured macro. The effect is that, whenever the macro is run, the window will be reconfigured to the same size it was when the macro was captured, which may help the macro to perform the same way each time. This option does not, however, place a *Window Resize* command between multiple windows. In other words, if you are capturing a macro that switches between windows, only a single **Window Resize** command is placed at the beginning of the macro. Here is an example from capturing mouse movements inside a test Notepad window with the **Capture Window Size** checkbox checked.

> **Window Resize: Current Win - (Width: 260, Height: 260)**
> **Mouse Move Window 71, 141**
> **Mouse Left Button Down**
> **Mouse Left Button Up**

If you choose the **Position** option, the coordinates are recorded based on the current location of the mouse. The coordinates are not related to your screen or a window. Moving the mouse towards the right and bottom of your display will record positive numbers. Moving the mouse towards the left and top of your display will record negative numbers. The slower you move the mouse the more **Mouse Move Position** commands are recorded in the macro.

The **Capture At** checkbox controls two commands that may be placed in your macro by the capture process. **Macro Playback Speed** and **Delay**. If this box is left unchecked then neither command is used and your recorded macro will play back at its maximum speed without any delays. There is a difference between the "real" time it takes to capture a macro and the maximum speed at which it can be played back. If the **Capture At** checkbox is checked, delays are inserted between commands during the capture process to force the macro to play back at the same speed it was recorded.

Below are two captured macros. The one on the left was captured with the **Capture At** checkbox checked and the **Actual Speed** choice picked. The one on the right was captured with the **Capture At** checkbox unchecked so the **Macro Playback Speed** and **Delay** commands would not be inserted. I added the comments to make comparing the macros easier.

// Calculator with delays	// Calculator without delays
Macro Playback Speed: Normal Speed	
Window Resize: Current Win - (Width: 260, Height: 260)	**Window Resize: Current Win - (Width: 260, Height: 260)**
Delay 1015 Milliseconds	
// Move to "6"	// Move to "6"
Mouse Move Window 153, 161	**Mouse Move Window 153, 161**
Mouse Left Button Down	**Mouse Left Button Down**
Mouse Left Button Up	**Mouse Left Button Up**
Delay 702 Milliseconds	
// Move to "*"	// Move to "*"
Mouse Move Window 190, 168	**Mouse Move Window 190, 168**
Mouse Left Button Down	**Mouse Left Button Down**
Mouse Left Button Up	**Mouse Left Button Up**
Delay 828 Milliseconds	
// Move to "5"	// Move to "5"
Mouse Move Window 106, 169	**Mouse Move Window 106, 169**
Mouse Left Button Down	**Mouse Left Button Down**
Mouse Left Button Up	**Mouse Left Button Up**
Delay 983 Milliseconds	
// Move to "="	// Move to "="
Mouse Move Window 225, 233	**Mouse Move Window 225, 233**
Mouse Left Button Down	**Mouse Left Button Down**
Mouse Left Button Up	**Mouse Left Button Up**

The macro on the left takes about 3-1/2 seconds to run, and mirrors the real time it took to capture it. The one on the right takes less than 1/3 of a second to run, which may be too fast. A macro can appear to skip steps but it does not. The computer may not be able to keep up with a macro. This is more noticeable when using the *Text Type* command. A macro can send keystrokes to the buffer faster than the computer can process them, which overflows the buffer making it look like characters have been skipped. So, be careful when capturing macros with the **Capture At** checkbox unchecked. And be aware that those macros will probably need to be edited to slow them down at certain critical points.

With the **Capture At** option unchecked (disabled), and the **Only Capture Mouse Clicks** option checked (enabled), the macros captured will be the shortest possible while still being able to capture both keyboard and mouse activity. This makes it easier to edit.

All macros are captured and recorded at the same speed so the term "Capture At" is inaccurate. What changes is the playback speed. You have four playback speed choices, **Actual**, **Half**, **Double**, and **Quadruple**. Macro Express inserts a *Macro Playback Speed* command at the beginning of the macro when recording it. The speed attached to it depends on your choice:

Macro Playback Speed: Normal Speed	// Actual
Macro Playback Speed: 2 Times Slower than Normal	// Half
Macro Playback Speed: 2 Times Faster than Normal	// Double
Macro Playback Speed: 4 Times Faster than Normal	// Quadruple

Picking the **Actual** choice will set the captured macro to playback at the same speed it was captured. **Half** will play it back at half the speed (twice as slow). **Double** plays it twice as fast as it was captured. And **Quadruple** four times as fast. Of course, you can edit the macro and change the speed after it is recorded.

The *Delay* commands that are inserted into the macro are the same for each speed choice. During the capture process, if it takes two seconds to do something then a *Delay 2000 Milliseconds* command is inserted into the macro no matter which speed choice you have picked. What makes the macro play back faster or slower is the *Macro Playback Speed*. If you delete this command from the macro, the macro will play back at the same speed it was captured.

Capture Options

There are four ways to begin capturing a macro.

1. Using the system **Ctrl+Alt+Shft+X** HotKey.
2. Clicking on the Capture icon in the Actions Toolbar.
3. Choosing (Macros | Recapture Macro) from the Main Menu.
4. Choosing (Wizards | Macro) from the Main Menu.

System HotKey

This method uses the *Preferences* dialog settings explained in the previous section and assumes you are where you want to be (window focused, mouse positioned, and so forth) when recording begins. When finished, you are prompted for macro name, activation, and scope information. The steps for this method are as follows:

1. Switch to the *Macro Explorer* window.
2. Set the (Options | Preferences | Capture) dialog settings.

3. Prepare to start capturing. Set focus to the target window, move the mouse to its starting position, and so forth.
4. Press the **Ctrl+Alt+Shft+X** HotKey to start recording.
5. Record your keystrokes and mouse activity.
6. Press the **Ctrl+Alt+Shft+X** HotKey to stop recording.
7. The *Capture Complete* dialog appears. Fill in the macro name, set the activation method, and choose a scope. Click on the **Save** button.

The *Capture Complete* dialog is necessary because all macros need a name, activation, and scope. And using the system HotKey to produce a macro means that Macro Express must get the information from you *after* the keyboard and mouse activity is recorded, but before the macro is produced.

Enter a name for the macro into the **Nickname** field up to 50 characters. If you enter the name of an existing macro, the *Duplicate Name Warning* dialog will pop up. This, and other information about a macro's nickname, can be found in the *Nickname* section within *Properties Tab* section discussed earlier in this chapter.

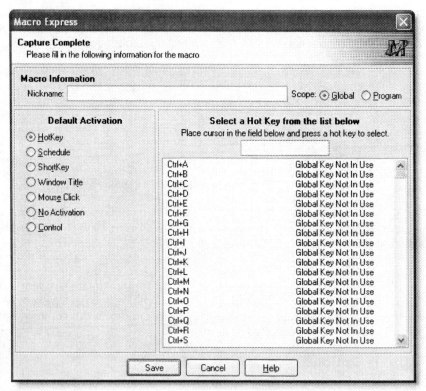

Pick a **Scope** for the macro, **Global** or **Program**. The default choice here is taken from the *Preferences* dialog setting. You can change it for this macro and it will *not* affect the *Preferences* default. If you choose **Program**, it will be scoped to the program that has focus when the capturing process *ends*. See the discussion about the **Scope** setting in the *Capture Settings* section a few pages back.

Finally, choose a **Default Activation** from the left-hand pane. There are seven choices with the default being **HotKey**. The right-hand pane will change depending on which activation you choose.

On the next page are couple of examples showing the right-hand pane when the **Mouse Click** and **Schedule** activations are picked. The macro activation options are detailed in the *Running and Activating Macros* chapter so they will not be discussed here.

Once the macro name, scope, and activation information has been entered, click on the **Save** button to produce the macro. The *Macro Explorer* window will be reactivated and the new macro will be highlighted in the right-hand pane.

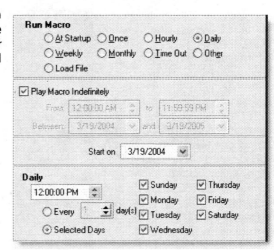

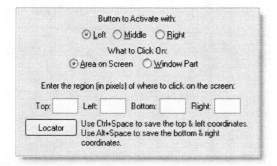

Capture Icon

This method lets you set all the information about a macro before you begin capturing it, which is opposite of what you have read so far in this section. The steps for this method are as follows:

1. Switch to the *Macro Explorer* window.
2. Click on the Capture icon in the Actions Toolbar, or in the Menu Toolbar. You can also choose (Macros | Add Macro) from the Main Menu.
3. The *Add Macro* dialog pops up. Choose an activation method and then click on the **Capture Macro** button.
4. The *Capture Window* dialog appears. Adjust the capture settings. Choose a macro name, scope, and the program or window to set focus to for recording. Click on the **Start Capture** button.
5. Record your keystrokes and mouse activity.
6. Press the **Ctrl+Alt+Shft+X** system HotKey to stop recording or, if you have picked a HotKey to activate the macro, you can use it to stop recording.
7. A message pops up. Click the **OK** button.

The *Add Macro* dialog in Step 3 is necessary to set the activation method for the macro you are about to capture. The seven enabled choices are identical with those available when using the system HotKey to capture a macro. Note, however, that if you chose (Macros | Add Macro) from the Main Menu to get to Step 3 instead of clicking the Capture icon, other choices are made available that are not related to capturing macros. Macro activation options are detailed in the *Running and Activating Macros* chapter.

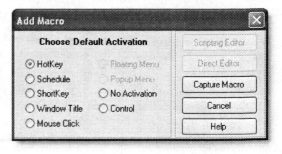

The *Capture Macro* dialog in Step 4 pops up to allow you to fill in the rest of the information before capturing the macro.

Enter a name for the macro into the **Nickname** field up to 50 characters. If you enter the name of an existing macro, the *Duplicate Name Warning* dialog will pop up. This, and other information about a macro's nickname, can be found in the *Nickname* section within *Properties Tab* section discussed earlier in this chapter.

Pick a **Scope** for the macro, **Global** or **Program**. The default choice here is taken from the *Preferences* dialog setting. You can change it for this macro and it will *not* affect the *Preferences* default. If you choose **Program**, it

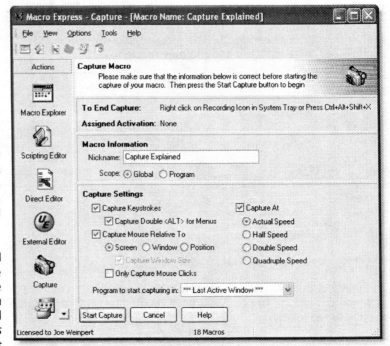

will be scoped to the program that has focus when the capturing process *ends*. See the discussion about the **Scope** setting in the *Capture Settings* section a few pages back.

The fields within the **Capture Settings** section are also taken from the *Preferences* dialog. And, like **Scope**, they can be changed without affecting the defaults. There is a unique feature here, the **Program to Start Capturing In** drop-down list. It is a list of the window titles of all applications currently running on your computer. Included in this list is the default choice "*** Last Active Window ***". Whichever window you pick, Macro Express will set focus to it just before the start of the capture process. This avoids *you* having to set focus to the target window like what is needed when using the system HotKey to start a macro. The "*** Last Active Window ***" choice will set focus to whichever window last had focus (excluding the Macro Express window) before clicking on the Capture icon.

When you are finished capturing a macro (Step 7) a message is displayed, and when you click **OK**, the *Macro Explorer* window will be reactivated with the new macro highlighted in the right-hand pane.

Recapture Macro

Recapturing a macro is the process of overwriting an existing macro. You are, in effect, creating a new macro. If you have edited the macro that you are recapturing, those changes will be overwritten. This method can only be run by choosing (Macros | Recapture Macro) from the Main Menu. The steps involved are almost identical with those in the previous section.

1. Switch to the *Macro Explorer* window.
2. Highlight the macro to recapture in the right-hand pane.
3. Choose (Macros | Recapture Macro) from the Main Menu.

4. The *Capture Window* dialog appears. Adjust the capture settings, change the scope, and anything else that you want, including the name. Click on the **Start Capture** button.
5. Record your keystrokes and mouse activity.
6. Press the **Ctrl+Alt+Shft+X** system HotKey to stop recording or, if you have picked a HotKey to activate the macro, you can use it to stop recording.
7. A message pops up. Click the **OK** button.

The *Capture Macro* dialog in Step 4 is the same as shown in the previous section. Change the **Nickname** field if you want to change the name of the macro. The **Scope** choice is taken from the *Preferences* dialog and *not* the current scope of the macro. The fields within the **Capture Settings** section are also taken from the *Preferences* dialog in their current state.

When you are finished capturing a macro (Step 7) a message is displayed, and when you click **OK**, the *Macro Explorer* window will be reactivated with the changed macro highlighted in the right-hand pane.

Capture Wizard

This is a menu-driven method for capturing a macro. Choose (Wizards | Macro) from the Main Menu, or click on the Quick Wizards icon in the Actions Toolbar (or in the Menu Toolbar) then pick "Macro". Let's step through capturing a macro using this method.

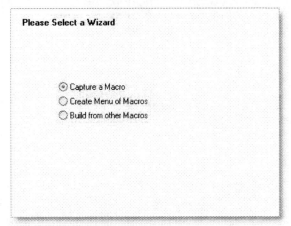

The *Please Select a Wizard* is the first dialog to appear. Choose **Capture a Macro** and then click the **Next** button, which is in every dialog.

The next dialog is a short review of what this particular wizard can produce. The rest of the dialogs will prompt for how to set features that match those found within the *Capture Macro* dialog shown in Step 4 of the *Capture Icon* section above.

The *Do You Wish to Capture Keystrokes?* dialog prompts whether to record keystrokes. It will also capture double <ALT><ALT> keys when the box is checked.

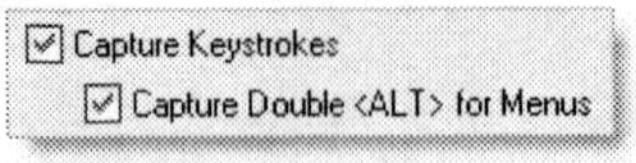

> ☑ Capture Keystrokes
>   ☑ Capture Double <ALT> for Menus

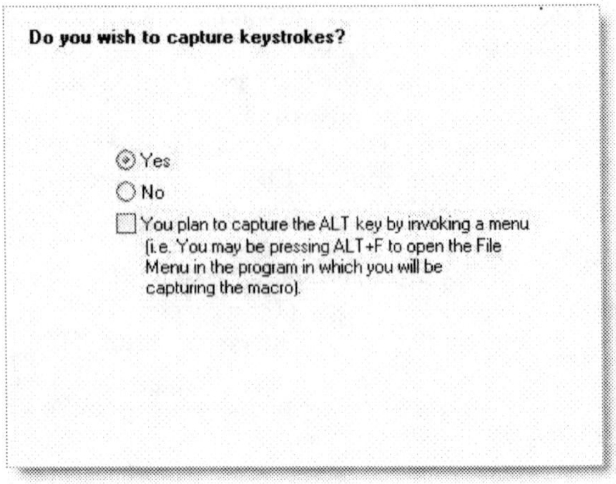

Do you wish to capture keystrokes?

◉ Yes
○ No
☐ You plan to capture the ALT key by invoking a menu (i.e. You may be pressing ALT+F to open the File Menu in the program in which you will be capturing the macro).

The *Do You Wish to Capture Mouse Movements and Clicks?* dialog sets which mouse activities to record and the coordinate system to use.

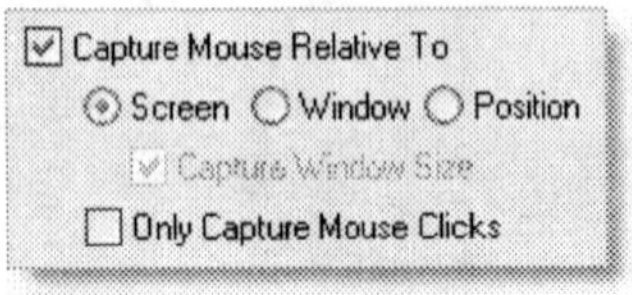

> ☑ Capture Mouse Relative To
>   ◉ Screen ○ Window ○ Position
>   ☑ Capture Window Size
>   ☐ Only Capture Mouse Clicks

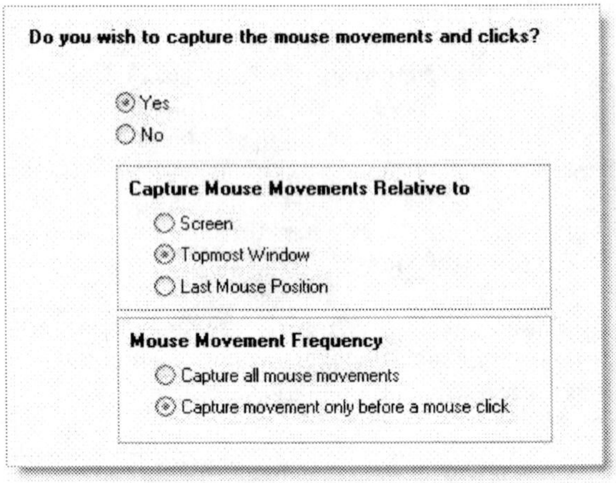

Do you wish to capture the mouse movements and clicks?

◉ Yes
○ No

Capture Mouse Movements Relative to
○ Screen
◉ Topmost Window
○ Last Mouse Position

Mouse Movement Frequency
○ Capture all mouse movements
◉ Capture movement only before a mouse click

The *Do You Wish the Macro to Play Back* dialog sets the playback speed. The **At Ten Times the Speed as Recorded** option is not available in the *Capture Macro* dialog.

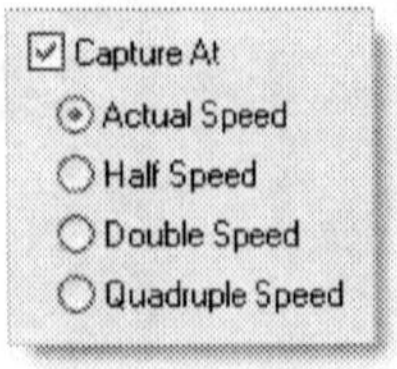

> ☑ Capture At
>   ◉ Actual Speed
>   ○ Half Speed
>   ○ Double Speed
>   ○ Quadruple Speed

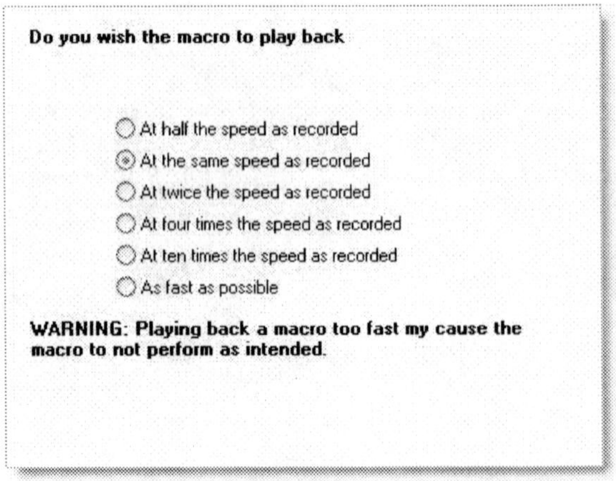

Do you wish the macro to play back

○ At half the speed as recorded
◉ At the same speed as recorded
○ At twice the speed as recorded
○ At four times the speed as recorded
○ At ten times the speed as recorded
○ As fast as possible

WARNING: Playing back a macro too fast my cause the macro to not perform as intended.

This dialog asks for which window should be focused for recording. Macro Express will set focus to it. The **Make the Macro Specific to this Window Only** checkbox sets the captured macro scope to the selected window title. The **Minimize the Macro Explorer** checkbox will minimize Macro Express to your Taskbar when recording begins. These two checkbox features are not available in the *Capture Macro* dialog, which allows for scoping only to program names and not window titles.

the following is a list of all of the window titles of the windows that are running on your computer. Choose the one you would like to start your recording in.

> [Book - Floating Menu]
> Macro Express - Quick Wizards
> Macro Express
> SnagIt
> Macro Express
> Calculator

☑ Make the macro specific to this window only
☑ Minimize the Macro Explorer

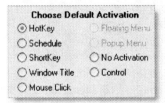

Scope: ⦿ Global ○ Program

Program to start capturing in: `*** Last Active Window ***` ⌄

The *Choose an Activation for the Macro* dialog is next. This is the first of two dialogs containing activation options. Choosing **Other** and then clicking on the **Next** button will pop up the second dialog. These choices are found in the *Capture Complete* and *Add Macro* dialogs.

Choose an activation for the macro

⦿ HotKey
   A key combination such as CTRL+ALT+A, ALT+F2, CTRL+Right Mouse Click, etc.

○ ShortKey
   A set of characters such as abc, myname, etc.

○ Schedule
   On a specific timed event such as a given time each day, once a week, every 5 minutes, after 2 minutes of computer inactivity, etc.

○ Other
   Based on a Window Title (i.e. a program gets focus), based on a Mouse Click or no macro activation.

Choose Default Activation

⦿ HotKey   ○ Floating Menu
○ Schedule   ○ Popup Menu
○ ShortKey   ○ No Activation
○ Window Title   ○ Control
○ Mouse Click

This is the second *Choose an Activation for the Macro* dialog, which is accessed by choosing **Other** in the first dialog. There are six activation choices between the two dialogs. **Window Control** activation is not available using this wizard.

Choose an activation for the macro

○ Window Title Appears
   A macro launches when a specific window gains focus.

○ Mouse Click
   Click on a Window Border, Title Bar, Menu Bar, Maximize Button, etc. or click on a specific area on the screen.

⦿ No Activation
   Use this later inside another macro or place it in a popup menu of macros.

This dialog, or something like it, will pop up next if you have chosen an activation. Here I have chosen a HotKey activation, so it is prompting me for which HotKey. If I had chosen a ShortKey, it would prompt for a ShortKey string, and so forth.

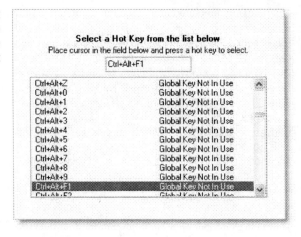

The *Would You Like the Macro to* dialog scopes the captured macro to any of the four available scope options in Macro Express. This feature is not available in the *Capture Macro* dialog, which allows for scoping to only a single program name. Here you can scope the macro to multiple programs, windows, and so forth. For our example, I chose **Play Back in Specific Window**.

Would you like this macro to

- ○ Play back in all programs
- ○ Play back in specific programs
- ● Play back in specific windows
- ○ Play back in all programs except those specified

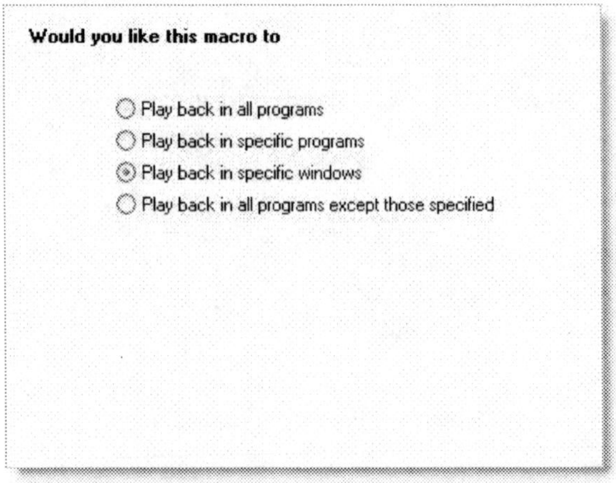

The *Play Back Macro in Specific Windows* dialog appears because it was chosen in the previous dialog. If either of the "program" choices were to have been picked then a matching dialog would have popped up. Click on the **Select** button to add to the list of windows the captured macro will be able to run with.

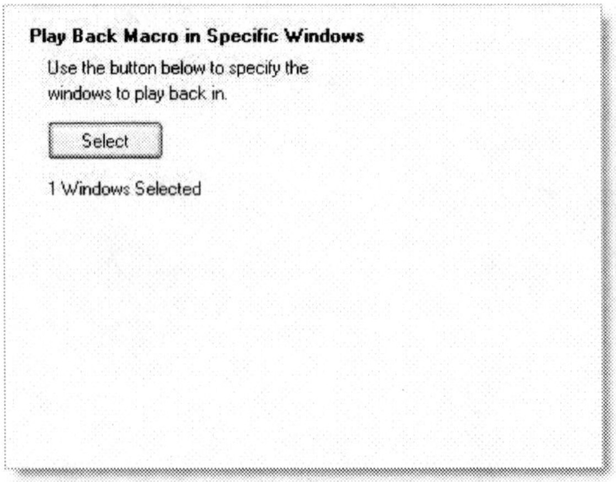

Play Back Macro in Specific Windows

Use the button below to specify the windows to play back in.

Select

1 Windows Selected

The *Select Window(s)* dialog pops up. Use it to select the window titles. When finished, click the **OK** button and you will be taken back to the *Play Back Macro in Specific Windows* dialog above. If you need help with this dialog then please refer to the *Scope* section within the *Running and Activating Macros* chapter.

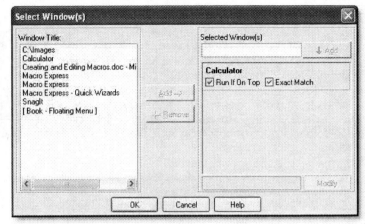

The *Macro Nickname* is the last dialog. This one has an option that is not available in the *Capture Macro* dialog. The **Change Icon** button will enable you to select a different macro icon before capturing the macro. Refer to the *Icon* section within the *Properties Tab* section earlier in this chapter for more information on using this feature.

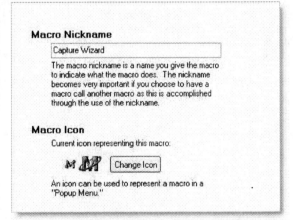

Clicking on the **Finish** button will begin the recording process. A message is displayed with instructions on how to stop recording regardless of how the **Prompt on Capture** feature is set in the *Preferences* dialog. If you have chosen a HotKey activation, it too will be a way to stop recording. And you can always right-click on the Recording icon in your Taskbar.

Notes on Capturing Macros

Unless you look in your System Tray, it may be difficult to tell that you are capturing a macro. If you press the **Ctrl+Alt+Shft+X** system HotKey while another macro is recording, you will receive and error message.

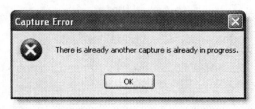

Besides pressing the **Ctrl+Alt+Shft+X** system HotKey again to stop the recording process, you can also right-click the Recording icon in your System Tray. This is similar to right-clicking on the Running Man icon to stop a macro.

If the **Capture Keystrokes**, **Capture Mouse Relative To**, and **Capture At** checkboxes are all unchecked then no keyboard or mouse activity is captured. You will be going through the motions, but nothing will get recorded. This also affects recapturing a macro because without the ability to capture something, nothing can be overwritten.

The Capture Wizard has features that are not available when using any of the other three capture methods. For example, scoping the captured macro to a window title, or multiple window titles, instead of just a single program name.

Quick Wizards

Macro Express provides a menu-driven method for creating several different macros to perform various tasks. Click on the Quick Wizards icon in the Actions Toolbar or in the Menu Toolbar to engage the *Quick Wizards* main dialog.

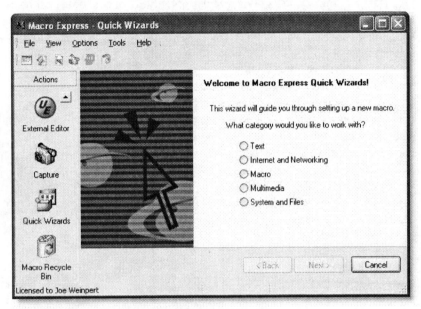

Or choose "Wizards" from the Main Menu to get the wizard drop-down list shown here.

There are 28 wizards separated into the five categories shown above. Pick one of the categories and then click the **Next** button to pop up a list of available wizards for the category. The picture on the right is from the **System and Files** category.

An example of using a wizard is given in the *Capture Wizard* section inside the *Capturing Macros* section. Although there are different dialogs and prompts to be answered, they all work similar to each

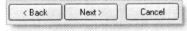

other. The next dialog is popped up; you set the features within it, click the **Next** button, the next dialog is popped up, and so forth. Each dialog has a **Back**, **Next**, and **Cancel** button. The last dialog has a **Finish** button.

A macro produced by any of the wizards can be edited and changed like any other macro. In fact, using a wizard is a great way to learn how Macro Express commands are strung together to form useful functions.

The table on the next page lists the 28 wizards with a short description of each, which are taken from the Macro Express help system.

Text Wizards

Create a Reminder	Create a reminder to be displayed at a specific time.
Paste Text and Graphics	Have Text or Graphic images pasted into your programs automatically.
Type Date or Time	Type the current, future, or past date or time into your programs.
Type a Symbol	Place an international character or a symbol in your programs.
Type Text or Keystrokes	Have Text, Keystrokes, and Symbols typed into your programs automatically.

Internet and Networking Wizards

Send Email	Send Email and attachments to one or more recipients.
Go to a Web Page	Go to a web site or initiate an ftp download.
Connect Network	Connect, Disconnect or Toggle Network drives.
Web Sweepstakes	Enter sweepstakes on the Internet.
Dial-Up Networking	Connect and Disconnect to the Internet and other computers using Dial-Up Networking.

Macro Wizards

Capture a Macro	Capture all mouse clicks, movements, and key presses into a macro.
Create Menu of Macros	Build a Popup Menu of macros.
Build from Other Macros	Build a macro from other macros.

Multimedia Wizards

Play Audio CD-ROM	Play an Audio CD.
Play a Video Clip	Play a Video Clip.
Sounds and Volume	Play a sound or set audio volume, treble and bass controls.

System and Files Wizard

Launch or Activate Programs	Launch a program or a document. Or switch to a program that is already running.
Reboot or Shut Down	Logoff, Reboot, or Shut Down your computer.
Copy, Delete, Rename	Copy, Delete, Rename Files. Change current folder.
Set Display Resolution	Change the display resolution.
Choose a Printer	Choose a Default Printer.
Change Desktop Wallpaper	Change the Desktop wallpaper.
Move or Size a Window	Resize or Position a Window.
Maximize, Minimize Windows	Maximize, Minimize, Restore, Hide, Close Windows.
Open an Explorer Folder	Open up an Explorer Folder.
Desktop Goodies	Cascade, Tile, Minimize, or Restore All Windows. Undock and suspend computer.
Screen Saver Options	Set Screen Saver Settings.
Run Control Panel	Open up the Control Panel or run a Control Panel applet.

Summary

- There are five ways to create a macro, Scripting Editor, Direct Editor, External Editor, capturing keyboard and mouse activity, and using a Quick Wizard.
- The Scripting Editor is menu-driven, structured, and easy to read.
- The Direct Editor is a text editor and the macro is a single unbroken line of mnemonic commands, which is its natural state.
- The Direct Editor has a text search and replace function.
- Change the look and feel of the editors by changing fonts, categories, and icons.
- All macros can be edited regardless of which tool was used to create them.
- There are over 260 Macro Express commands.
- A single command can belong to multiple categories.
- A macro name can be 50 characters long.
- Each macro can have its own icon.
- You can step through a macro and set breakpoints during development for debugging.
- Variables can be viewed while a macro is running or after it is finished when debugging.
- Running and editing a macro can have separate passwords.
- Unlimited notes can be stored with a macro.
- Without delays, a macro may overrun an application.
- There are 28 built-in macro builder wizards.

Running and Activating Macros

When I first sat down to write this chapter I thought that I could explain running a macro by simply explaining HotKeys, ShortKeys, and a couple of other features. However, there are many other ways to run and activate macros. Let's cover running them first.

Running Macros

Running a macro is slightly different from activating a macro. Both activities launch or invoke macros, but "running" is something that is done from a command line, Windows Explorer, the Macro Express Explorer, Scripting Editor, and Direct Editor. For running macros, it is important to understand the different components that make up Macros Express.

Components

Macro Express consists of many different components such as the editor program, player programs, macro library files, playable macro files, help files, and so forth. The editor program (*MacEdit.exe*) is used to create, change, export, and import macros. It is the program used to generate and control your macro library (*.mex*) files. It does not, however, run macros although it appears so when you are developing and testing them within one of the editors. The *MacExp.exe* and *MeProc.exe* programs run macros. In fact, if you examine the properties of the Macro Express icon on your Desktop you will see that it is the *MacExp.exe* player program which is launched and not the *MacEdit.exe* editor program. If you attempt to run *MacEdit.exe* without *MacExp.exe* already running you will receive an error message

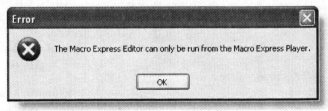

because the editor cannot be run without the player. The *MeProc.exe* program launches macros faster than the *MacExp.exe* player program if *MacExp.exe* is already running. If it is not running, *MeProc.exe* will need to launch it.

There are two types of macro files that can be "run", those that are invoked from within a library (*.mex*) file and those that are

playable (*.mxe*) macros. The latter being external, standalone, text files. The *.mex* library is a collection of *.mxe* files, which can be edited from within the library itself with either the Scripting Editor or the Direct Editor. And also, an external editor of your choice. As you can see, I use an editor called **UltraEdit** from IDM Computer Solutions, Inc. (www.ultraedit.com). The external editor is named in the (Options | Preferences | File Paths) dialog. Once entered, the editor's icon is displayed in the Actions Toolbar, which is on the left-hand side of the Macro Express *Explorer* window.

Command Line Parameters

Both types of macros, *.mex* and *.mxe*, can be run from a Desktop icon or from the *Run Window* dialog using command line options and either the *MacExp.exe* or *MeProc.exe* player programs. There are 15 different command line parameters that can be used with *MacExp.exe* and *MeProc.exe*. All parameters can be in uppercase, lowercase, or mixed case but must begin with a forward slash ("/") and then the letter without any spaces between. For parameters that accept additional options like <nickname>, <filename>, and so forth, there can usually be no spaces between the parameter and the option, but see the individual descriptions for exceptions.

Even though multiple parameters are acceptable, it may be that certain combinations do not work properly together. Since **/IC** loads the preferences and since the preferences contain the name and path to the macro file, it makes sense that **/IC** and **/F** do not work together. Also, Windows limits the command line. On my XP system the length is 256 characters.

Macro Express will run only a single instance of itself no matter how many times you click its icon. So, if you have multiple icons, or batch files, setup to run different parameters, you *may not* need to terminate Macro Express each time. It depends, of course, on which parameters you are invoking. The individual descriptions will tell you if Macro Express can already be running when the command line is launched. The parameter portion of the command line will always be run.

/A<nickname>

Activate (run) a macro in the current *.mex* library file when Macro Express launches or is already launched. The <nickname> option contains the name of the macro to run. To run a macro named "Me3 Explained Chapter Four" use the syntax "/AMe3 Explained Chapter Four" without the quotes. Spaces are allowed in the nickname but not between the parameter ("/A") and the option ("<nickname>").

> **"c:\Program Files\Macro Express3\MeProc.exe" /AMe3 Explained Chapter Four**

/MXE<\path\filename>

Run an external, playable *.mxe* macro file. The <\path\filename> option contains the full path name of the file to run. For example, to run a file named "Me3 Explained Chapter Four.mxe", use the syntax "/MXEc:\PGM\Book\Me3 Explained Chapter Four.mxe" without the quotes. You must use a fully qualified path name even if you are located in the same folder as the playable macro file. The ".mxe" file extension is required, but the drive designator ("c:") is not strictly needed unless, of course, your macro files are located on a different drive. Spaces are allowed in the filename and between the parameter ("/MXE") and the option ("<\path\filename>").

> **"c:\Program Files\Macro Express3\ MeProc.exe" /MXEc:\PGM\Book\Me3 Explained Chapter Four.mxe**

When run, this parameter does not change, or affect in any manner, the currently loaded Macro Express library file.

/V<variable:value>

This parameter is used to preset variables with values before calling a macro. It stuffs values into the Macro Express variable memory space to be accessed with one of the *Variable Restore* commands the next time you run a macro. For example, to place "Macro Express Explained" into the **T1** string variable, use the syntax "/VT1:Macro Express Explained" without the quotes. Place the target variable ("T1") immediately after the "/V" without any spaces between. Then use a colon (":") to separate the variable from the value. Spaces are allowed in the string values. Here are some examples:

/VT98:The quick	- Preset T98 to a string
/VT99: brown fox	- Preset T99 to a string with a leading space (will be stripped)
/VN22:65535	- Preset N22 to an integer value
/VN23:-65535	- Preset N23 to a negative integer value
/VD65:3.14159	- Preset D65 to a decimal value
/VD66:-89.99	- Preset D66 to a negative decimal value

When the next *Variable Restore* command is run from a macro, **T98** will be set to "The quick", **T99** will be set to "brown fox", **N22** to 65535, **N23** to -65535, **D65** to 3.14159, and **D66** to -89.99. Note that leading and trailing spaces are stripped from the values even though spaces are allowed after the colon (":"). On the other hand, spaces between multiple "/V" parameters are not required. You could enter a parameter string such as this (without the quotes): "/VT1:Aa/VT2:Bb/VT3:Cc". Any variable number outside the range of 1 through 99 will simply be ignored.

"c:\Program Files\Macro Express3\ MeProc.exe" /VT98:The quick /VT99: brown fox /VN22:65535 /VD65:3.14159

/F<\path\filename>

Load a new Macro Express (*.mex*) library file when Macro Express launches or is already launched. The <\path\filename> option contains the full path name of the file to load. This is the same as choosing (File | Open Macro File) from the *Macro Explorer* window.

To load a file named "Me3 Explained Chapter Four.mex", use the syntax "/Fc:\PGM\Book\Me3 Explained Chapter Four.mex" without the quotes. You must use a fully qualified path name even if you are located in the same folder as the library file. The ".mex" file extension is required, but the drive designator ("c:") is not strictly needed unless, of course, your library files are located on a different drive. Spaces are allowed in the filename and between the parameter ("/F") and the option ("<\path\filename>").

"c:\Program Files\Macro Express3\MacExp.exe" /Fc:\PGM\Book\Me3 Explained Chapter Four.mex

/IC<filename>

Import a configuration (*.mcf*) file when Macro Express launches or is already launched. The <filename> option contains the name of the configuration file to import. This is identical with choosing (Tools | Import Program Configuration) from the *Macro Explorer* window.

To import a configuration file named "Explained.mcf", use the syntax "/ICc:\PGM\Book\Explained.mcf" or "/ICExplained.mcf" without the quotes. You must use a path name if the configuration file is located in a different folder than where you are launching Macro Express. The ".mcf" file extension is required. Spaces are allowed in the filename and between the parameter ("/IC") and the option ("<filename>").

"c:\Program Files\Macro Express3\MacExp.exe" /ICc:\PGM\Book\Explained.mcf

If all users that log on and use Macro Express use the same settings (Options | Preferences | Miscellaneous) then all users use the same preferences. If one user changes a preference, then all users will see and use that same change  the next time they launch Macro Express unless you add this parameter to the command line. Then, when Macro Express starts, the settings will be reset to what is in this *.mcf* configuration file, essential making any changes by individual users temporary.

/delay:<seconds>

This forces Macro Express to delay the number of specified seconds before performing its internal startup procedures such as establishing the hooks and shared memory. Note that "/delay" *must* be lowercase. If you are having trouble launching Macro Express, then use this parameter. The <seconds> option contains the time to delay and may be between 1 and … whatever. I have tested up to 1200 seconds (20 minutes) without error. When used, this parameter is recognized whenever Macro Express is launched. On the other hand, the delay setting in the **Run on Windows Startup** field (Options | Preferences | Startup) is only recognized when Macro Express is launched with Windows.

/N

This parameter means "network". With the next two parameters (**/S** and **/SM**), it affects how, or if, Macro Express locks and updates macros in a *.mex* library while editing them over a network. It must be invoked when Macro Express is first launched or it will have no effect. If Macro Express is already running then terminate it before invoking this parameter.

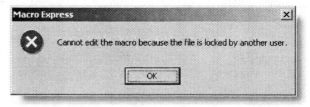

Its purpose is to set the Macro Express network mode on, which it must be for the other two parameters to work. If you are not running macros over a network, then you will not need this parameter, although no harm is done if it is used. It is identical with checking the (Options | Preferences | Network | File Locking of Macro Files) checkbox. There is no "reversing" parameter. In other words, the only way to turn the network mode off again is from within the *Preferences* dialog.

Although two or more users may have the same *.mex* library file open, they cannot have the same macro open for editing at the same time. If a user attempts to open an already opened macro an error message is immediately displayed.

/S

This parameter means "synchronize" and must be invoked when Macro Express is first launched or it will have no effect. See the **/SM** description parameter below for an explanation.

If Macro Express is already running then terminate it before invoking this parameter. It is the same as checking the (Options | Preferences | Network | Automatic Synchronization Update checkbox). See the picture displayed in the **/N** description. There is no "reversing" parameter. In other words, the only way to turn synchronization off again is to uncheck the box from within the *Preferences* dialog.

If networking is turned off (**File Locking of Macro Files** field), and the **/N** parameter is not invoked, it will still check the preference box but will not go into effect until networking is turned on.

/SM<minutes>

This parameter means "synchronize minutes" and must be invoked when Macro Express is first launched or it will have no effect. If Macro Express is already running then terminate it before invoking this parameter. Its purpose is to place a value into the (Options | Preferences | Network | Synchronization Minutes) field. See the picture displayed in the **/N** description. The <minutes> option contains the number of minutes between synchronizations and may be between 1 and 999.

So, what gets synchronized? Let's say that you have a common macro library on your server and you have several users running macros from within that library. When they launch Macro Express, the library is stuffed into the Macro Express cache memory on their workstation, if caching is enabled (Options | Preferences | Caching). While the library is in their cache, you make changes to one of the macros in the library and then save it. Their cache copy does not know of the change until the next synchronization occurs, which reloads their cache memory with the changed library. If nothing is changed, then nothing happens.

To synchronize the network every 10 minutes, use the syntax "/SM10" without the quotes. Place the value ("10") immediately after the "/SM" without any spaces between. If networking is turned off (**File Locking of Macro Files** field), and the **/N** or **/S** parameters are not invoked, it will still place the value inside the minutes field but will not go into effect until networking and synchronization are turned on.

"c:\Program Files\Macro Express3\MacExp.exe" /N /S /SM8

The command line says to launch Macro Express in the network mode, activate synchronization, and synchronize the network every 8 minutes.

/T

This parameter means "System Tray" and is the reverse of **/H** below. It must be invoked when Macro Express is first launched or it will have no effect. If Macro Express is already running then terminate it before invoking this parameter. This is identical with choosing the (Options | Preferences | Appearance | Show in System Tray) radio button. The purpose is to

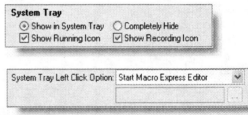

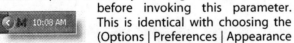

display the Macro Express icon in your System Tray so the editor can be run by clicking on it. If you want to left-click on it, then be sure the (Options | Preferences | Miscellaneous | System Tray Left Click Option) field is set correctly as shown above, which is the default. If this option is set for something else, say "Do Nothing", then right-click on the icon and choose "Open Editor" from the menu list to invoke the Macro Express editor.

/H

This parameter means, "hide program" and is the reverse of **/T** above. It must be invoked when Macro Express is first launched or it will have no effect. If Macro Express is already running then terminate it before invoking this parameter. It is the same as choosing the (Options | Preferences | Appearance | Completely Hide) radio button. See the picture displayed in the **/T** description. It *does not* put the Macro Express icon in the System Tray. The editor can still be opened using the built-in "Run Macro Express

Editor" HotKey, which was set to **Ctrl+Alt+Shift+W** when Macro Express was first installed. Also, it can be shutdown using the "Terminate Macro Express" HotKey, which was set to **Ctrl+Alt+Shift+V**.

/B

This parameter means, "browse mode". Invoking it means the Macro Express editor cannot be run and any attempt to do so will generate a message. Macros however, can still be run. You can use this feature to help prevent others from making unwanted changes to macros. I am not sure where the term "browse mode" came from because there is nothing to browse without the editor.

/EY

This parameter means, "run editor" and is the reverse of **/EN** below. Its purpose is to invoke the editor automatically when Macro Express launches and is identical with checking the (Options | Preferences | Startup | Start Editor on Startup of Macro Express) checkbox.

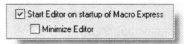

/EN

This parameter means "do not run editor" and is the reverse of **/EY** above. Its purpose is to prevent the editor from starting when Macro Express launches and is identical with clearing the (Options | Preferences | Startup | Start Editor on Startup of Macro Express) checkbox. See the picture displayed in the **/EY** description above.

/NQS

This parameter means "no Quick Start" and will prevent the Quick Start program from running when Macro Express is launched. It is the same as checking the (Options | Preferences | Startup | Show Quick Start Guide on Startup) checkbox. There is no "reversing" parameter. In other words, the only way to turn the feature off again is from within the *Preferences* dialog.

Windows Explorer

When you install a software program on your computer, the file extensions associated with that program are registered in Windows. And so it is with Macro Express. The *.mex* and *.mxe* file extensions are both associated with Macro Express, which means they will run when you click on them in Windows Explorer, or run them from the system *Run* dialog.

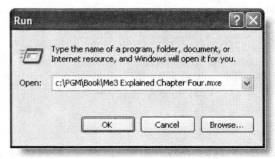

Let's say for example that you have a file named "c:\PGM\Book\Me3 Explained Chapter Four.mxe" on your hard drive. You could navigate to it using Windows Explorer then double-click on it. Or right-click on it and choose (Open With | MeProc) from the menu. As an alternative, you could also enter the name into the system *Run* dialog.

A macro inside a *.mex* library can also be run from Windows Explorer, but you must do some setup first. Macro Express gives you the ability to schedule a macro to run at a certain time. In this case, you would want to choose "Load File", which tells Macro Express to run this macro every time that this particular library is loaded into the player/editor.

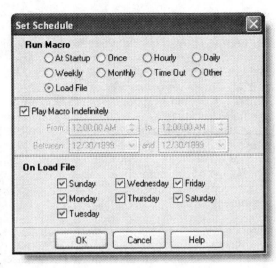

Let's say that you have a library named "c:\PGM\Book\Me3 Explained.mex" and inside it there is a macro called "Chapter One". Go to the *Macro Explorer* window and highlight the "Chapter One" macro in the right-hand pane. From the *Set Schedule* dialog (Macros | Properties | Activation | Set Schedule) dialog, choose **Load File** from the **Run Macro** section. Also check the **Play Macro Indefinitely** checkbox as well as checking all the day-of-week checkboxes in the **On Load File** section. Now save it by clicking **OK** and then terminate Macro Express.

Now, just like the *.mxe* example, you can navigate to the "c:\PGM\Book\Me3 Explained.mex" library file using Windows Explorer then double-click on it and the "Chapter One" macro will run. Or right-click on it and choose (Open With | MeProc) from the menu. Or enter the name into the system *Run* dialog.

Desktop

Any macro can be run from your Desktop, too! Macro Express will create a Desktop shortcut for you from the *Macro Explorer* window. Simply highlight the macro in the right-hand pane that you want to place on the Desktop and then choose (Macros | Place on Desktop) from the Main Menu. A shortcut will be generated using the icon associated with the macro, and will give it the name of the macro. The **Target** field in the Shortcut Tab of the *Properties* dialog will contain the /A command line argument as explained in the above *Command Line* section.

Macro Express Explorer and Editors

From the *Macro Explorer* window, highlight the macro in the right-hand pane that you want to run and then choose (Macros | Run Macro Now) from the Main Menu, or right-click and then choose "Run Macro Now". If you are in the Scripting Editor you can click on the green Run icon in the toolbar below the Main Menu, or choose (Debug | Test Run Macro), or hit the **F9** key. You can also step through each line in the macro by hitting the **F8** key. Within the Direct Editor, you can click on the green Run icon in the toolbar below the Main Menu.

Activating Macros

Activating macros is different from running macros. Both activities launch or invoke macros, but "activating" is something that is done to macros from inside a *.mex* library with a HotKey, ShortKey, schedule, or a Popup or Floating Menu. External *.mxe* playable macros cannot be activated using these features. Macros can also be automatically activated based on a window title, window object (control), program name, or the coordinates of a mouse click. Also, the *ability* to activate a macro can be scoped to a window title or program name.

When creating a new macro, activation can be set from the *Add Macro* dialog, however, it can also be set after a macro is created from the Activation Tab of its *Properties* dialog.

To invoke the *Add Macro* dialog from the *Macro Explorer* window, choose (Macros | Add Macro) from the Main Menu or right-clicking anywhere in the right-hand pane and choose "New Macro" from the list. By default the **HotKey** option is chosen when this dialog is invoked, however, you can chose any other option. In this case, I have chosen **No Activation**, which means that none of the activation types will be used to invoke the macro.

If the macro is already created you can get to the *Properties* dialog from the *Macro Explorer* window by selecting the target macro in the right-hand pane. Click on the Properties icon in the toolbar, or choose (Macros | Properties) from the Main Menu, or right-click and choose Properties from the menu list. And it can be chosen from either editor by simply clicking on the Properties Tab. To set a macro for **No Activation** from the Properties Tab, simply uncheck, or clear, each of the activation checkboxes, and then choose **Apply**.

More than one activation type can be setup for a single macro. You could set a HotKey, Schedule, and a Mouse Click all to activate one macro. The **Activation to Display in Macro Explorer** drop-down list at the top of the Activation Tab becomes available to use if you pick more than one activation type. Use it to tell Macro Express which one to display in the Activation column of the *Macro Explorer* window. If you choose only a single activation type the drop-down list cannot be accessed but your choice will automatically be displayed in the Activation column.

Macro activation and scope are bound to each other in Macro Express. It is difficult to discuss one without the other so you will see references to "scope" throughout this section. See individual descriptions to learn how the scope of a macro is affected by your choice of activations. And to learn about scoping, please review the *Scope* section that follows the activation descriptions.

HotKey

A HotKey is a combination of keys that when pressed together, and then released, will activate a macro. You are familiar with the preset **Ctrl+Alt+Delete** (Task Manager), **Ctrl+P** (print), **Ctrl+C** (copy), **Ctrl+X** (cut), and **Ctrl+V** (paste) combinations in Windows. These are all HotKeys that perform a task.

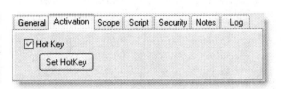

Macro Express recognizes 725 different HotKey combinations for activating macros. Each can be one to four keys in length. Checking the **Hot Key** checkbox and then clicking on the **Set HotKey** button from the macro's Properties Tab will invoke the *Set HotKey Activation* dialog.

Place the cursor in the top field and then using your keyboard enter the key combination you desire. The list will be moved to your choice and the combination will be placed in the top field. If it is correct then click **OK**. You may also scroll through the list to find your HotKey but click on the list first or else the dialog will think the key you just pressed is the HotKey that you want. The HotKeys are automatically placed in the top field as you scroll.

The list displays all the HotKeys that Macro Express recognizes. The ones that are dimmed or greyed-out are already in use and should not be picked. This is to prevent duplication. The ones listed in red are those that might interfere with reserved Windows HotKeys. There are 14 of them and are listed in the chart on the right. A "Y" means the key is reserved.

The left, middle, and right mouse buttons can also be included as HotKeys. On the next page is a list of all the available HotKey combinations, including the mouse, and those that are reserved for Windows. The *Legend* chart explains the meaning of the key names in the left-hand column of the *HotKeys* chart.

Reserved HotKeys				
	Win	Alt	Ctrl+Alt	Ctrl+Win
F1	Y			
F6		Y	Y	
B	Y			
C	Y			
D	Y			
E	Y			Y
F	Y			
K	Y			
L	Y			
M	Y			
R	Y			
V	Y			

Legend		
Keys	**Qty**	**Description**
F1 - F12	12	Function keys
A - Z	26	Character keys
0 - 9	10	Number keys in top row of keyboard
Punct'n	11	The \ , . / ; ' [ ] - = ` punctuation keys
Navigation	8	Home, End, PageUp, PageDn, and Up, Down, Left, and Right arrows
Keypad /-*+	4	Arithmetic operation keys on the keypad
Keypad 0-9	10	Number keys on the keypad
Mouse Click	3	The Left, Middle, and Right mouse buttons (single-click)

HotKeys											
	Alone	Shft	Win	Ctrl	Alt	Ctrl+ Shft	Ctrl+ Alt	Ctrl+ Win	Alt+ Shft	Alt+ Win	Ctrl+ Alt+ Shft
F1 - F12	Y	Y	Y	Y	Y	Y	Y	Y	Y	Y	Y
A - Z			Y	Y	Y	Y	Y	Y	Y	Y	Y
0 - 9 (toprow)			Y	Y	Y	Y	Y	Y	Y	Y	Y
Punct'n				Y	Y	Y	Y		Y		Y
Space	Y	Y	Y	Y	Y	Y	Y		Y		Y
Enter		Y		Y	Y	Y	Y		Y		Y
Tab		Y		Y		Y	Y				Y
Back- space		Y		Y	Y	Y	Y		Y		Y
Insert	Y	Y		Y	Y	Y	Y		Y		
Delete	Y	Y		Y	Y	Y			Y		
Escape	Y										
Navi- gation	Y	Y		Y	Y	Y	Y		Y		Y
Keypad /-*+	Y	Y		Y	Y	Y	Y		Y		Y
Keypad 0-9	Y			Y	Y		Y				
Mouse Click	Y	Y		Y	Y	Y	Y		Y		Y

When using HotKeys to invoke macros (or Popup Menus), the scope setting is always checked. There are two different warning messages that may appear if you attempt to choose a global HotKey that is already in use. Both of them will let you continue, but you must be careful not to duplicate HotKeys and scopes.

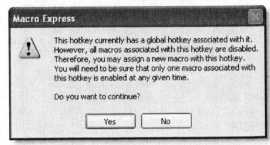

Both messages reference a global HotKey, but what is it? The word "global" refers to the scope of a macro. When you first create a macro it is scoped as being global by default, meaning that it can be activated anywhere at anytime (refer to the *Scope* section in this chapter). By the way, if you are unsure of how your macro is scoped, look at the Scope column in the *Macro Explorer* window.

The warning messages are telling you that a globally scoped macro is already using this HotKey. The top message is displayed if the other macro is enabled and the bottom one is displayed if the other macro is disabled. Choosing to continue will mean that two macros will both have the same HotKey, and at least one of them is global in scope. This is not good, however, Macro Express allows you to continue because it assumes that you will change the scope of the global macro. The warning message on the left says that your macro's scope will be set to Program Specific if you continue. Ignore that sentence. It is not true. You must change the scope yourself.

It is possible to duplicate HotKeys and scopes either by accident or by simply ignoring the warning messages. The example shows two macros with the same HotKeys and the same

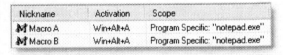

scope. If the "notepad.exe" program has focus and you invoke the **Win+Alt+A** HotKey, one of them will run and the other will not. But which one? Usually the one that was created first will run, although there is no guarantee. That is why it is best not to have duplicates such as these.

Getting back to the *Set HotKey Activation* dialog. As mentioned before, the HotKeys in the list that are colored red might interfere with the reserved Windows HotKeys. If you attempt to use one of them, then a warning message is displayed. Again, it is your choice to continue or change the HotKey. With over 700 to choose from I would change it.

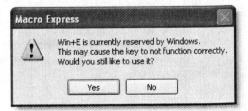

Schedule

This option enables you to schedule a macro to run at certain days and times, intervals, when a particular event occurs, or when your computer is inactive for some time. Checking the **Schedule** checkbox and then clicking on the **Set Schedule** button from the macro's

Properties Tab will invoke the *Set Schedule* dialog.

Only the top portion of the *Set Schedule* dialog is shown here because the rest of it changes based on which schedule you choose. There are nine different scheduling choices to pick from and the individual descriptions contain the relevant dialog sections. In general, the middle sections contain time frame and date range fields to further control a macro.

Although they differ slightly by choice of schedule, they are all used in the same manner. The bottom section usually contains options centered around a day of week, day of month, hour of the day, and so forth, to further control a macro's schedule.

All fields and options are inclusive to each other rather than exclusive. In other words, they all work together to pinpoint when a macro should, or should not, run. For example you can set a macro to run daily, but only between this date -AND- that date -AND- only if it is noon -AND- only on Sunday -AND- Tuesday.

When it is time for a scheduled macro to run, its scoped is checked. If the macro is in scope then it will run, otherwise, the macro will be ignored.

Preferences

The system-wide preferences dialog (Options | Preferences | Scheduler), tells Macro Express three things about running scheduled macros:

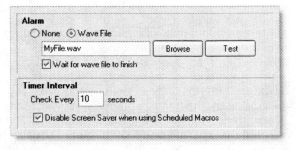

1. To play a .wav file when a scheduled macro runs.
2. How often to check the scheduled times.
3. Whether to disable your screen saver for scheduled macros.

Except for the **At Startup** and **Load File** schedules, a wave (.*wav*) file can be played when a scheduled macro runs. Choose the **Wave File** option, and then enter its path and name into the field, or click on the **Browse** button and, using a file-picker dialog, find one. If the file cannot be found at runtime, then nothing will play and there is no error message generated. The **Wait for Wave File to Finish** checkbox, if checked, instructs Macro Express to not run the macro until after the file finishes playing. If you are unsure of which wave file you have picked, click on the **Test** button to play it.

The **Check Every** XX **Seconds** field is the interval that Macro Express waits between checks to determine if it is time to run a macro. The allowable range is 1 through 99 seconds. If you enter a zero by accident, it will be changed to a "1" after you exit the dialog. The interval entered here overrides the interval in your scheduled macro. For example, if you have scheduled a macro to run every minute, and you set this interval field for 90 seconds, then your macro will run every 90 seconds instead of every minute.

If you have scheduled a macro to run every 60 seconds, it may not do so, depending on how long it takes the macro to run. The 60 seconds does not begin until after the macro stops. Let's assume the

Check Every XX **Seconds** field is set to its default value of 10 seconds and you have scheduled a macro to run every 60 seconds, but the macro takes anywhere from 10 to 15 seconds to run:

    00:00 - Macro runs
    00:15 - Macro finishes after 15 seconds
    01:15 - Macro begins after 60 seconds
    01:25 - Macro finishes after 10 seconds
    02:25 - Macro begins after 60 seconds
    02:40 - Macro finishes after 15 seconds

As you can see, the macro will run at 00:00, then 75 seconds later at 01:15, then 70 seconds beyond that at 02:25, and so forth. But even this is not exact, because it does not consider the **Check Every** XX **Seconds** field and the possibility of missing a beat and having to wait another 10 seconds, each time.

Macro Express can only run one macro at a time. But, if you have more than one macro scheduled to run, and it so happens they will launch about the same time, the second macro will be placed into a queue and run after the first one finishes.

With the **Disable Screen Saver When Using Scheduled Macros** checkbox checked, as long as Macro Express is running and the current library (*.mex*) file contains at least one scheduled macro, the screen saver will never see the light of day. If you leave this box unchecked, remember that a scheduled macro may not run if the screen saver is engaged.

Common Fields

Common to all schedule choices are time frame and date range fields. Time frame fields hold time in a "HH:MM:SS ?M" format and are named **From**, **To**, **Start At**, and so forth. Date range fields hold dates in a "MM/DD/YYYY" format and are named **Between**, **And**, **Start On**, and so forth. Both field types are edited the same way by changing the individual "sections" inside the field like "HH", "MM", "SS", and so forth.

Using the **Left** and **Right** arrow keys moves the cursor from one section to the next. To change the current section enter a new value. Or hit the **Up Arrow** or **Plus** (+) key on the keypad to increment the value by one. Or hit the **Down Arrow** or **Minus** (-) key on the keypad to decrement the value by one. For the time frame fields you can also increment or decrement a value by clicking on the attached button on the right-side of the field.

Specific to the date range field is a popup calendar that you access by clicking on the attached button on the right-side of the field. Initially the calendar displays whichever date is in the field. Clicking on any other date will close the calendar and place your choice into the field for you. Clicking on either of the two buttons found in the upper corners of the calendar will navigate through the months and years. Clicking on the red box found in the lower-left corner will choose today's date.

At Startup

This schedule instructs the macro to run when Macro Express first launches. You further control this by using the time frame (**From** and **To**) and date range (**Between** and **And**) fields, which are accessible if the **Play Macro Indefinitely** checkbox is *not* checked, as shown here. Checking the box turns the time frame and date range fields off so they are ignored. This states that you want the macro to run whenever Macro Express launches no matter what the date or time is, as long as you have all the day of week checkboxes checked.

The **From** and **To** fields set a range during a 24-hour period the macro will be allowed to run when Macro Express starts up. The **Between** and **And** fields set the range of allowable dates. The example is set for midnight to one second before midnight (all day) for all of February, 2004. If the time in the **From** field is set later than the **To** field, or if the current time is not within the **From** and **To** range, or today is not between the **Between** and **And** range, the macro will not run.

The day of week checkboxes, **Sunday**, **Monday**, **Tuesday**, and so forth, further control when the macro can run. The example is set to run every day of the week as long as the time and date are within the correct ranges. If only the **Monday**, **Wednesday**, and **Friday** boxes were checked, then those are the days the macro will be allowed to run when Macro Express starts up. If none day of week boxes are checked, the macro will never run.

Once

This schedule instructs the macro to run once at a specific time and day. Use the **Run At** time frame field to set the time and the **On** date range field to set the date. When this is reached, the macro will run. The example says to run the macro at 2:00 PM on March 10th, 2004.

Hourly

This schedule instructs the macro to run every hour or a frequency of hours. The **Play Macro Indefinitely** checkbox toggles between a fixed range of time and days, and an infinite range that begins at a specific time using the **Start At** time frame field.

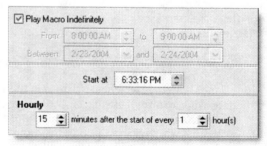

The **Hourly** section at the bottom sets the number of minutes past the hour the macro runs and how many hours should be skipped between runs, if any. In other words, the top sections tells Macro Express when it is okay to run what is further defined by the **Hourly** section.

Use the **Minutes After the Start** field to set the number of minutes past the top of each hour to run the macro. It accepts any value between 0 and 60, although the top end should only be 59 minutes. If, for example, you want to run a macro at the bottom of every hour set this value to 30. The **every** XX **Hour(s)** field sets how many hours to skip between runs. It accepts any value between 1 and 720 (30 days). A value of 1 means not to skip anything and run the macro every hour, 2 is every other hour, and so forth.

Let's look at the example (previous page). The **Start At** time frame field is set for 6:33:16 PM, the **Minutes After the Start** field is 15, and the **every** XX **Hour(s)** field is 1. The macro will run at 7:15 PM, then at 8:15 PM, 9:15 PM, and so forth. If the **every** XX **Hour(s)** field is changed to 2, it will run at 8:15 PM, then 10:15 PM, 12:15 AM, and so forth.

You can use the **Hourly** schedule to have a macro run only during normal business hours, say 8:00 AM through 5:00 PM. Use the time frame (**From** and **To**) and date range (**Between** and **And**) fields, which are accessible if the **Play Macro Indefinitely** checkbox is *not* checked. Set the fields as shown. The **From** time frame field starts one minute before 8:00 AM, and the **To** time frame field is set to one minute after 5:00 PM

because I want the macro to begin at 8:00:00 AM. The **Check Every** XX **Seconds** field in the *Preferences* dialog is set to 10 seconds. If the **From** time frame field were set to 8:00:00 AM then the scheduler may not check the time until 8:00:10 AM, which means that it would miss running by 10 seconds and will not run again until 9:00:00 AM. Also, notice how the **And** date range field is set to 100 years in the future. Almost as good as infinity.

Daily

This schedule instructs the macro to run at a specific time every day, a frequency of days, or just certain days. The **Play Macro Indefinitely** checkbox toggles between a fixed range of days and an infinite range that begins at a specific day using the **Start On** date range field. Even though they are shown in this dialog, the **From** and **To** time frame fields are never available because they are meaningless to the **Daily** schedule.

The **Daily** section at the bottom sets the time of day to run the macro and how many days should be skipped between runs (if any), or optionally, which days of the week to run. In other words, the top sections tells Macro Express when it is okay to run what is further defined by the **Daily** section.

Set the time of day to run the macro using the **Daily** time frame field. The **Every** XX **Day(s)** field sets how many days to skip between runs. It accepts any value between 1 and 1,000 (almost 3 years). A value of 1 means not to skip anything and run the macro every day, 2 is every other day, and so forth.

Let's look at the example. The **Start On** date range field is set for 2/27/2004, the **Daily** time frame field is set for 9:00 AM, and the **Every** XX **Day(s)** field is 1. The macro will run at 9:00 AM on February 27th, 2004, then at the same time on the 28th, the 29th, and so forth. If the **Every** XX **Day(s)** field is changed to 2, it will run at 9:00 AM on the 27th, 29th, March 2nd, and so forth. In other words, every other day.

You could choose instead to run the macro on selected days of the week by clicking the **Selected Days** choice. This will turn off the **Every** XX **Day(s)** field and turn on the day of week checkboxes, **Sunday, Monday,**

Tuesday, and so forth. Putting a checkmark in every box is identical with placing a 1 in the **Every** XX **Day(s)** field. If you do not put a checkmark in any of the boxes, the macro will never run.

You can use the **Daily** schedule to have a macro run once a day, say at 8:00 AM, during normal business days on Monday through Friday, but only for March, 2004. Set the fields as shown. Uncheck the **Play Macro Indefinitely** checkbox. Set the **Between** date range field to 3/1/2004, and the **And** date range field to 3/31/2004. Set the **Daily** time frame field to 8:00:00 AM. Now click on the **Selected Days** option, and check **Monday, Tuesday, Wednesday, Thursday**, and **Friday**.

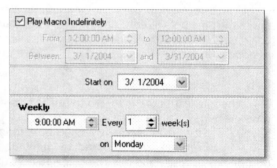

Weekly

This schedule instructs the macro to run at a specific time on a specific day every week or a frequency of weeks. It is similar to the **Daily** schedule except you are working with weeks instead of days. The **Play Macro Indefinitely** checkbox toggles between a fixed range of days and an infinite range that begins at a specific day using the **Start On** date range field. Even though they are shown in this dialog, the **From** and **To** time frame fields are never available because they are meaningless to the **Weekly** schedule.

The **Weekly** section at the bottom sets the time of day, and the day of week to run the macro, and how many weeks should be skipped between runs, if any. In other words, the top sections tells Macro Express when it is okay to run what is further defined by the **Weekly** section.

Set the time of day to run the macro using the **Weekly** time frame field and the day of week using the **On** drop-down list. The **Every** XX **Week(s)** field sets how many weeks to skip between runs. It accepts any value between 1 and 1,000 (over 19 years). A value of 1 means not to skip anything and run the macro every week, 2 is every other week, and so forth.

Let's look at the example. The **Start On** date range field is set for 3/1/2004, the **Weekly** time frame field is set for 9:00 AM, the **On** field (day of week) is "Monday", and the **Every** XX **week(s)** field is 1. The macro will run at 9:00 AM on March 1st (Monday), then again on March 8th, March 15th, and so forth. If the **Every** XX **Day(s)** field is changed to 2, it will run at 9:00 AM on March 1st, March 15th, March 29th, and so forth. In other words, every other week.

You can use the **Weekly** schedule to have a macro run all year, but just on Monday mornings at 9:00 AM. Set the fields as shown. Uncheck the **Play Macro Indefinitely** checkbox. Set the **Between** date range field to 1/1/2004, and the **And** date range field to 12/31/2004. Set the **Weekly** time frame field to 9:00:00 AM. Set the **Every** XX **week(s)** field to 1, and finally, choose

"Monday" from the **On** field (day of week) drop-down list.

Monthly

This schedule instructs the macro to run at a specific time on a specific day on a specific month or a frequency of months like quarterly or semi-annually. It is similar to the **Daily** and **Weekly** schedules except you are working with months. The **Play Macro Indefinitely** checkbox toggles between a fixed range of days and an infinite range that begins at a specific day using the **Start On** date range field. Even though they are shown in this dialog, the **From** and **To** time frame fields are never available because they are meaningless to the **Monthly** schedule.

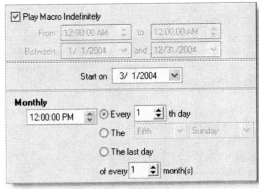

The **Monthly** section at the bottom sets the time of day, and a day of the month to run the macro, and how many months should be skipped between runs, if any. In other words, the top sections tells Macro Express when it is okay to run what is further defined by the **Monthly** section.

Set the time of day to run the macro using the **Monthly** time frame field. The day of the month is set using one of three fields. The **Every** XX **th Day** drop-down list contains the day of the month from 1 through 31. The **The** drop-down lists contain words like First, Second, Third, Sunday, Monday, and so forth. And finally, the **The Last Day** radio button, which means the last day of the month. The **Every** XX **Month(s)**

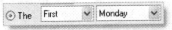

field sets how many months to skip between runs. It accepts any value between 1 and 1,000 (over 83 years). A value of 1 means not to skip any month, 2 is every other month, and so forth.

Let's look at the example above. The **Start On** date range field is set for 3/1/2004 and the **Monthly** time frame field is set for noon. The day of the month is set to "1" by using the **Every** XX **th Day** drop-down list and the **Every** XX **Month(s)** field is 1. The macro will run at noon on March 1st, then again on April 1st, May 1st, and so forth. If the **Every** XX **Month(s)** field is changed to 2, it will run at noon on March 1st, May 1st, July 1st, and so forth. In other words, at noon on the 1st of every other month.

If a day of month is chosen that is not contained in a month, then the macro will not run. If, for example, you choose 31 from the **Every** XX **th Day** drop-down list. The macro will *not* run in February, April, June, September, or November. To resolve this issue, choose instead, the **The Last Day** radio button option.

Here is another example. Uncheck the **Play Macro Indefinitely** checkbox. Set the **Between** date range field to 1/1/2004, and the **And** date range field to 12/31/2004. Set the Monthly time frame field to noon and use the **The** drop-down lists to choose the fifth Sunday of every month. Finally, set the **Every** XX **Month(s)** field to 1. This will run a macro at noon in February, May, August, and October.

Time Out

This schedule instructs the macro to run whenever there has been no keyboard or mouse activity for a specified amount of time. You further control this by using the time frame (**From** and **To**) and date range (**Between** and **And**) fields, which are accessible if the **Play Macro Indefinitely** checkbox is *not* checked, as shown here. Checking the box turns the time frame and date range fields off so they are ignored.

The **From** and **To** fields set a range during a 24-hour period the macro will be allowed to run. The **Between** and **And** fields set the range of allowable dates. The example is set for midnight to one second before midnight (all day) for the whole year of 2004. If the time in the **From** field is set later than the **To** field, or if the current time is not within the **From** and **To** range, or today is not between the **Between** and **And** range, the macro will not run.

The **Every** XX **Minutes** field sets the interval the macro will run until Macro Express senses some keyboard or mouse activity. The example says to run once every 15 minutes until activity is recognized. The **After** XX **Minutes of Idle Time** determines how long there can be no activity before the **Every** XX **Minutes** field interval timer begins running. The example will wait for inactivity to occur for 5 consecutive minutes. Both fields will accept values between 0 and 720 minutes (12 hours). To run a macro immediately after 1-hour of keyboard and mouse inactivity, set the fields as shown here. To wait 1-minute after 1-hour of inactivity, change the **Every** XX **Minutes** field to 1. If you set both fields to zero, Macro Express will still wait 1-minute before running the macro.

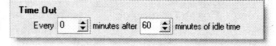

Other

This schedule runs a macro at the interval specified. The **Play Macro Indefinitely** checkbox, time frame (**From** and **To**) fields, and date range (**Between** and **And**) fields work identical with those in the **Time Out** schedule.

The **Every** XX **minutes and** XX **seconds** fields work together to set the interval of time the macro will run. The minimum time that can be set is 1-second. The maximum number of minutes allowed is 99,999 (over 69 days). The maximum allowable seconds is 60. Be careful not to set a time that is less than what it takes for the macro to run.

Load File

This schedule instructs the macro to run when the library (*.mex*) file containing the macro first loads. All the fields in this schedule work identically with those in the **At Startup** schedule.

ShortKey

A ShortKey is a sequence of up to 10 keys that, when typed, will activate a macro.

It is best to look at the *Preferences* dialog (Options | Preferences | ShortKeys) to set up the ShortKeys before using them. What you see here are the factory default settings. The dialog is split into two sections. The top section are settings that apply to any ShortKey you use in your library (*.mex*) file. The bottom section are settings that each ShortKey is initialized with, but can be changed without affecting any other ShortKey.

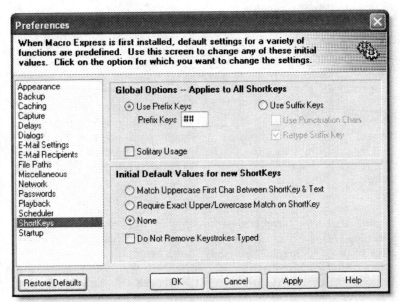

The idea behind ShortKeys is to type a word or phrase on your keyboard to invoke a macro. For obvious reasons it cannot be a common word like "the", "is", or "and", else your macro will invoke itself practically every time you type a sentence. There are features and rules that Macro Express has built in to the ShortKeys that resolve this issue.

There are three distinct features that make up a ShortKey. The Name, Prefix, and Suffix. Prefix and Suffix are exclusive of each other, you cannot use both at the same time. The chart on the next page shows the default allowable character keys for each feature. The Prefix and Name keys are almost identical. The difference is the Prefix is optional and therefore can be **Empty**, but it can also contain **Spaces**, whereas the Name cannot. The **Space** and **Enter** keys are always used for a Suffix. This is not an option and it cannot be changed.

You also see some punctuation keys that cannot be used in a Name, Prefix, or Suffix. They are listed because they round out the remaining punctuation characters, of which there are 32.

You can change any of the keys in the chart, but not through the (Options | Preferences) dialog. Insight Software Solutions has a free utility macro named *TweakMe3* that is available from their web site. Refer to the *Advanced Options* section in this chapter for more information. But for now, let's stick with the defaults.

Let's create a small example macro that opens the Windows Control Panel:

> **Delay 100 Milliseconds**
> **Control Panel Open**
> **Macro Return**

To give a ShortKey a name, check the **ShortKey** checkbox and the name field will be enabled.

We will name it "OpenCP". This is not the macro name; it is the name of the ShortKey, or more to the point, what you type on your keyboard to invoke the macro. The name can be up to 10 characters, and the **Name** column in the chart shows what characters you can use.

We will examine the **Settings** button later, but for now let's assume that you have not yet made any changes to the ShortKey *Preferences* on the previous page. At this point, if you were to type "##OpenCP" from anywhere, even your Desktop, your *Control Panel* would launch. The string you typed is a combination of what is contained in the **Prefix Keys** field and the ShortKey **Name** field.

The **Prefix Keys** field enables you to use a common, easy-to-remember ShortKey Name that will not accidentally invoke a macro. "OpenCP" may not be common, but what if it were just "Open"? Using the Prefix feature, you need to type "##Open" to invoke the macro, which is not common. The **Prefix Keys** field can be up to 3 characters, and the **Prefix** column in the chart shows what characters you can use. A prefix key is case sensitive. If you were to set the prefix key to "aaa", that is what you must type. "AAA" would be ignored. The **Prefix Keys** field can also be blank, making it optional. Using an empty **Prefix Keys** field in our example, you would simply type "OpenCP" to invoke the macro.

In Macro Express, the ShortKey **Name** field is always appended to the **Prefix Keys** field to form a ShortKey Name. The prefix is a convenience if you want each of your ShortKeys to begin with the same set of characters, especially if you want to change the characters later. You can make the change in one place rather than in every macro. Another advantage to using the **Prefix Keys** field is that it can contain spaces, unlike the **Name** field. An example then would be " OpenCP" (two spaces for prefix).

The **Solitary Usage** checkbox determines when Macro Express recognizes that a ShortKey should be invoked. The default is to leave the box unchecked (nonsolitary usage). This means that your ShortKey and prefix will be recognized even if it is buried in the middle of

Key	Prefix	Name	Suffix
A-Z	Y	Y	
a-z	Y	Y	
0-9	Y	Y	
!	Y	Y	Y
@	Y	Y	
#	Y	Y	
$	Y	Y	
%	Y	Y	
^	Y	Y	
&	Y	Y	
_	Y	Y	
=	Y	Y	
<	Y	Y	
>	Y	Y	
?	Y	Y	Y
.	Y	Y	Y
;	Y	Y	Y
,	Y	Y	Y
*	Y	Y	
-	Y	Y	Y
/	Y	Y	
+	Y	Y	
~			
:			Y
`	Y	Y	Y
'	Y	Y	Y
"	Y	Y	Y
(			
)	Y	Y	Y
{			
}			
[			
]	Y	Y	Y
\	Y	Y	
|			
Space	Y		Y
Enter			Y
Empty	Y		

another word. This is the easiest way to use ShortKeys because you never have to be concerned with what precedes your ShortKey name. You can type it anywhere at anytime and it will be recognized.

Check the box to turn on **Solitary Usage**. The ShortKey will be recognized only if the character preceding it *cannot* be used in a ShortKey Name (refer to the chart). So if you were to type "_##OpenCp" the macro would not run, however, type "~##OpenCp" and it will. If you are using a text editor like *notepad.exe*, typing the ShortKey name as the first thing in a new line will invoke the macro because it is preceded by either nothing, or an **Enter** key from the previous line.

The third feature that makes up a ShortKey is **Use Suffix Keys**. When using this feature, **Use Prefix Keys** is turned off and Macro Express is set to recognize ShortKeys based on a **Space** or **Enter** (CR/LF) key and optionally, certain punctuation keys. The **Suffix** column in the chart contains the recognized keys. Typing "OpenCP**<space>**" or "OpenCP**<enter>**" will invoke the macro, however, typing just "OpenCP" will not.

If you want to invoke the macro using more than just the **Space** or **Enter** keys, then check the **Use Punctuation Chars** checkbox and refer to the chart. Typing "OpenCP!" or "OpenCP?" will invoke the macro, however, typing just "OpenCP" will not and neither will "OpenCP~" because "~" is not a recognized suffix key.

The **Use Suffix Keys** feature depends on the preceding character to invoke a macro. In other words, it has its own built-in solitary usage rules identical with those found using the **Solitary Usage** option and the **Prefix Keys**. Typing "@OpenCP**<space>**" or "$OpenCP**<enter>**" will *not* invoke the macro because the "@" and "$" characters can be part of a macro name. However, typing "~OpenCP**<space>**" or "{OpenCP**<enter>**" will invoke the macro.

The **Retype Suffix Key** checkbox tells Macro Express to replace the **Suffix Key** after the macro has been run including the **Space** and **Enter** keys. The suffix key is erased before the macro is invoked unless you check this field. You cannot see this happening unless you are invoking a macro from inside a program or field that accepts text as input. In other words, if you type a ShortKey while on your Desktop, you do not see anything occurring because the Desktop is not a text input field. If you type a ShortKey from inside the Notepad program, you will see the suffix key, and probably the ShortKey name, erased before the macro invokes. So, unless you are creating macros where you want the suffix key put back after the macro runs, leave this field unchecked. Also refer to the **Do Not Remove Keystrokes Typed** checkbox below.

Macro Express uses ShortKeys to invoke macros. There is another product from Insight Software Solutions called *ShortKeys* and some of the ShortKey features found in Macro Express come from this product. It is used to substitute a ShortKey name with replacement text as you are typing away in a text editor or word processor program. For example, typing "Mex" could automatically be replaced with "Macro Express". In the example that we have been using the ShortKey invokes a macro that launches the Windows *Control Panel*. There is no reason to substitute any characters, or for that matter put the suffix key back after the macro runs.

The **Use Prefix Keys** and **Use Suffix Keys** settings affect every ShortKey macro. All of your ShortKey macros are invoked using the prefix or they are all invoked using the suffix. This cannot be changed for individual macros. However, the settings in the **Initial Default Values for New ShortKeys**

Initial Default Values for new ShortKeys
- ○ Match Uppercase First Char Between ShortKey & Text
- ○ Require Exact Upper/Lowercase Match on ShortKey
- ⦿ None
- ☐ Do Not Remove Keystrokes Typed

section of the *Preference* dialog can be individually set by clicking on the **Settings** button in the Activation Tab of the individual macro. This pops up the *ShortKey Settings* dialog. If you click on the **Use Global Settings** choice in the *ShortKey Settings* dialog (the default choice), the macro will use the global settings in the *Preference* dialog. Choosing the **Customize Macro Settings** instead, will enable you to change the settings just for this macro.

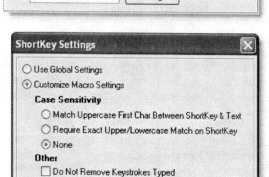

Match Uppercase First Char Between ShortKey & Text gives you a shortcut way to capitalize the first character of a sentence when using ShortKey activated macros to substitute text, without having to create separate macros. If the first character that you type to invoke the ShortKey macro is uppercase, then the first character of the replacement text will be uppercase, and conversely for lowercase.

Let's create an example. Say that you are writing a software manual that uses the phrase "command line argument" a lot. Create a single line macro with the following command:

> **Text Type: command line argument**

Now give it a ShortKey activation name of "cmd" without the quotation marks. Click the **Settings** button and pick this option. From within your word processor, type "##cmd". The phrase "command line argument" will automatically be substituted. If, however, you type "##Cmd" (uppercase "C") then "Command line argument" (uppercase "C") will be substituted.

The **Require Exact Upper/Lowercase Match on ShortKey** requires that a ShortKey be typed exactly as it is named, letter for letter, and case for case. In all of our examples, we could have typed "opencp", "oPeNcP", or "OPENCP" and the ShortKey would be invoked. However, with this option, only typing the name exactly as "OpenCP" would invoke the macro.

The **None** setting tells Macro Express to not use either setting.

The **Do Not Remove Keystrokes Typed** checkbox instructs Macro Express to not erase the **Prefix Keys** or the ShortKey **Name** before running the macro. As mentioned before, you cannot see this happening unless you are invoking a macro from inside a program or field that accepts text as input. The Desktop is not a text input field so you see nothing. However, in the Notepad program, you will see the **Prefix Keys** and ShortKey **Name** erased before the macro invokes. Unless you are creating macros where you want the keys to remain, then leave this field unchecked. Also refer to the **Retype Suffix Key** checkbox above.

Window Title

This option enables you to run a macro when a specific window gains focus, which means that it must be more than just "running" in the background. It has to have focus before the macro will invoke. Since the macro will run each time the window gains focus, then clicking back and forth 3 times between the window and your Desktop will invoke the macro 3 times.

Checking the **Window Title** checkbox will enable you to enter a window name into the field. It can be a partial name and is *never* case-sensitive. "NOTEPAD" will work as well as "notepad", "NOTEpad", or "NoTePaD". The name in the field is treated by Macro Express as a *partial* name. In other words,

Macro Express searches through the list of running applications until it finds a window title that *contains* whatever is in this field.

If you do not want manually to enter a window name into the **Window Title** field, then you can pick one from the *Running Windows* dialog by clicking on the **Browse** button.

There are two Tabs in this dialog. Visible and Hidden. The application windows listed in the Visible Tab are the ones that you can see on your Desktop … the ones that you normally work with. The Hidden Tab contains behind-the-

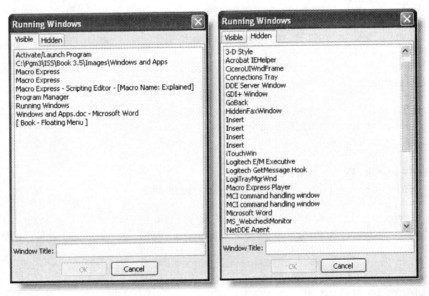

scene windows. These are applications that are running, but are marked as *hidden*. Since **Window Title** activation requires the program that is running has focus, the macro will never be activated if you choose a window title from the list of hidden windows.

When you have chosen a window by either picking it from the list, or typing it in manually, click **OK** and the dialog will disappear. The name will be placed into the **Window Title** field for you where it can be further edited to your liking.

There is a preference setting that affects this, and the Window Control activation. **Window Activation Caching** is found in the (Options | Preferences | Caching) dialog. If checked, it queues any macro that is automatically activated by its Window Title or Control.

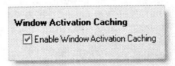

You may have multiple macros in your library that are activated when a window gains focus. If you happen to be running a macro that launches one of these windows, the macro tied to it will not run if the first macro still has commands to process. Two macros cannot run at the same time so the second macro is ignored. The **Window Activation Caching** feature resolves this issue. If it is checked (the default), it will queue the second macro and launch it when the first one finishes. If you do not want this to happen then leave the feature unchecked.

Mouse Click

This option enables you to use your mouse to invoke a macro. Checking the **Mouse Click** checkbox and then clicking on the **Settings** button from the macro's Properties Tab will invoke the *Select Mouse Activation* dialog.

Only the top portion of the *Select Mouse Activation* dialog is shown here because the rest of it changes based on which feature you want to click on, your display screen, or part of an application window.

Choose the **Left**, **Middle**, or **Right** mouse button from the **Button to Activate With** section. A single-click from any of them will invoke the macro. When a mouse click occurs that may invoke a macro, its scope is checked. If the macro is in scope then it will run, otherwise, the macro will be ignored.

Area on Screen

This is nice! You can define areas on the screen that, when you click with your mouse, will activate a macro. Refer to the *Literal Coordinates* section within the *Variables* chapter if you are unfamiliar with screen coordinates. Describe the area of the screen using the **Left**, **Top**, **Right**, and **Bottom** coordinate fields. Type the values manually or click on the **Locator** button to engage the Mouse Locator tool. This is the same tool that is explained in the *Mouse* chapter. Use it to determine which coordinates to use. It will also place coordinates for you. When the mouse cursor is located at the upper-left corner of your target area press the **Ctlr+Space** HotKey. The coordinates will be written to the **Left** and **Top** fields. Move the mouse cursor to the lower-right corner and press **Alt+Space** to write those coordinates to the **Right** and **Bottom** fields.

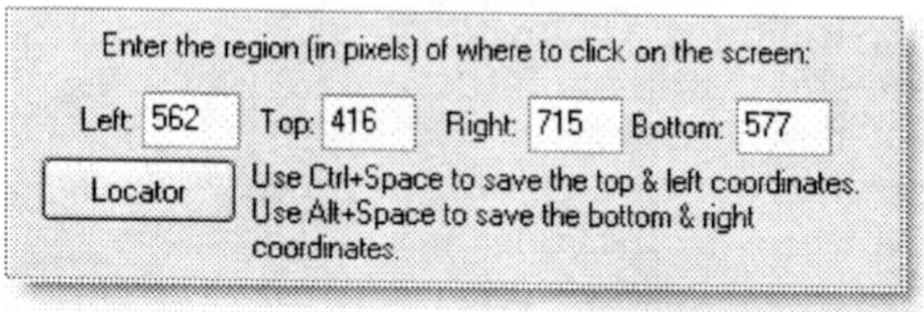

Once the area is defined, and you have chosen which mouse button to use, whenever you click on it, the macro will run. Be careful not to let areas overlap between two different macros. There is no guarantee which will run.

Window Part

You can set specific objects in an application window to click on and invoke a macro. There are eight objects. The first two, **Maximize Button** and **Minimize Button** are unavailable if you have chosen to use the **Left** mouse button as shown here.

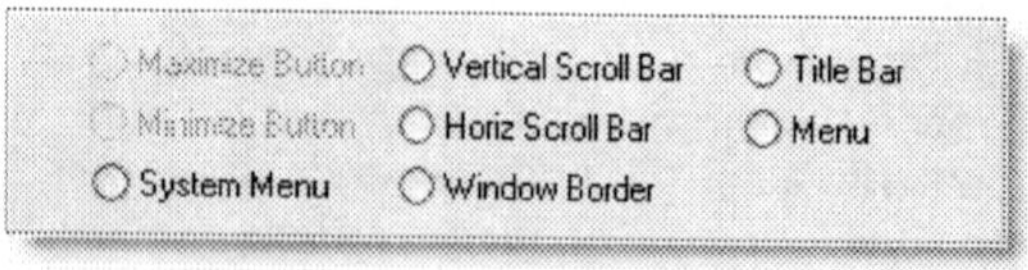

All objects are available for the other two mouse buttons. The table shows all but the **Window Border** choice which is simply the first few pixels that make up the perimeter of the window. As you pass your mouse over the window and it changes to a double arrow, you are on the Window border. See the *Window Sizing Border* command within the *Windows and Programs* chapter for more information.

Maximize Button	
Minimize Button	
System Menu	
Vertical Scroll Bar	
Horizontal Scroll Bar	
Title Bar	Macro Express – Scripting Editor
Menu	File Macros Category Wizards View Options Tools Help

Notice that these objects are not tied to any particular window, but rather *any* window. Once the object and mouse button have been chosen, whenever you click on it, the macro will run.

Window Control

This option enables activation of a macro when the window containing a **Control** gains focus. This is explained in the *Window Control Activation* section within the *Window Controls* chapter. Please examine this section to learn how to use this feature.

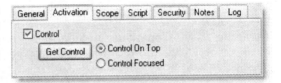

Scope

It is important to understand "scope" when activating macros. It prevents activating a particular macro unless a certain window or program is running or is active.

Let's say that you have created a series of macros designed specifically to run with your Microsoft Excel projects and have assigned HotKeys to each of them. Furthermore, you want to be sure that these HotKeys can be invoked only if Excel is running. This is where you want to use the scope feature.

The picture on the right shows the types of scoping that you can do with Macro Express. This dialog can be accessed from the *Macro Explorer* window by selecting the target macro in the right-hand pane. Click on the Properties icon in the toolbar, or choose (Macros |

Properties) from the Main Menu, or right-click and choose Properties from the menu list. And it can be chosen from either editor by simply clicking on the Scope Tab. To pick a scope, choose the appropriate radio button then click on the **Select** button. The scope setting for any macro is listed in the Scope column within the *Macro Explorer* window.

Activating a macro is tied directly to its scope. You can have a single HotKey combination, say **Win+Alt+F1**, for several different macros as long as each macro has a unique scope.

Nickname ▲	Activation	Scope	Modified
1 Chapter 1 - Installation	Win+Alt+F1	Window Specific: "Installation"	2/21/2004 9:54 AM
2 Chapter 2 - Variables	Win+Alt+F1	Window Specific: "Variables"	2/21/2004 9:54 AM
3 Chapter 3 - Programming	Win+Alt+F1	Window Specific: "Programming"	2/21/2004 9:55 AM
4 Chapter 4 - Controls	Win+Alt+F1	Window Specific: "Controls"	2/21/2004 9:55 AM
5 Chapter 5 - Registry	Win+Alt+F1	Window Specific: "Registry"	2/21/2004 9:55 AM
6 Chapter 6 - Files and Folders	Win+Alt+F1	Window Specific: "Files and Folders"	2/21/2004 9:55 AM

The macros shown above have the same activation HotKey, but each is scoped to a different window. The way to set the same activation HotKey to different macros is to set the macro scopes first. This same feature works for other activation types such as ShortKeys, scheduling (except "Load File"), mouse click location, and so forth. You will only be able to assign one globally scoped macro to a given HotKey. Scoping is ignored when "running" a macro from the *Macro Explorer* window, or either of the editors.

Scope only affects activating, or starting a macro. If a macro starts running and it has commands to focus on other windows, the macro still continues to run.

Global

This is the default scope. It means there are no restrictions on when or where a macro can be activated. It will run regardless of which window or program is active at the time the macro is invoked. There are no additional dialogs for this choice.

Global Except

This scope means there are no restrictions on when or where a macro can be activated except for your application choices. In other words, the macro will be invoked any time *except* when your choice of applications have been launched and at least one of them has focus. What the example dialog here does is to allow the macro to be invoked *except* if any one of the following applications has focus: Explorer.exe, MacEdit.exe, MacExp.exe, or GbTtray.exe.

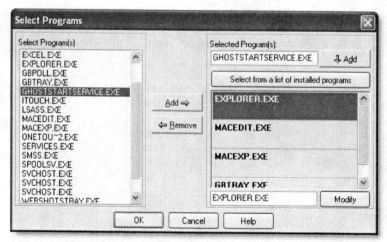

Clicking **Select** activates the *Select Programs* dialog for this scope, which is used to pick the exception applications. The idea is to copy the name of the target applications in the left-hand pane (**Select Programs**

list) over to the right-hand pane, which contains your choices. There are two buttons in the middle column, **Add** and **Remove**. The **Add** button copies them to the right-hand pane and the **Remove** button deletes them if you change your mind.

To copy an application name over to the right-hand pane, highlight it in the **Select Programs** list and then click on the **Add** button in the middle column. Double-clicking on the application name will move it directly to the right-hand pane, bypassing the need to use the **Add** button.

To remove an application name from the right-hand pane, highlight the name by clicking on it once, and then click the **Remove** button in the middle column. You can remove more than one application name at a time by clicking once on each of them and then clicking the **Remove** button. Clicking once on an application name in the right-hand pane highlights it. Clicking once more removes the highlight.

This same dialog is used for the **Windows Specific** and **Program Specific** scopes. Macro Express provides two ways to edit the names in the right-hand column, although you will probably only use them with the **Windows Specific** scope unless you have a need to change the name of an executable file.

Edit a name *before* placing it into the right-hand pane by highlighting it in the **Select Programs** list. As you move through the **Select Programs** list, each application name is automatically displayed in the **Selected Programs** field above the right-hand pane (the field with the **Add** button on its right side). Click on this field, edit the name, and then hit **Enter** or click the **Add** button on the right side.

Edit a name *after* it has been placed into the right-hand pane by using the **Modify** field below the right-hand pane. Each time you highlight a single application name in the right-hand pane, it is automatically displayed in the **Modify** field. Click on this field, edit the name, and then hit **Enter** or click the **Modify** button on the right side and the name will be changed.

The **Select Programs** list only displays application programs that are running on your computer. To choose an application that is not running, click on the **Select from a List of Installed Programs** button found above the right-hand pane. You will be presented with the *List of Installed Programs* dialog. When you pick something from this list it will be directly added to the right-hand pane.

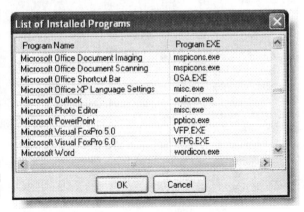

Another option to enter exception application names is to type them directly into the **Selected Programs** field and then hit **Enter** or click the **Add** button on its right-hand side.

Windows Specific

This scope means that a macro can be invoked only if specified windows are running and/or have focus (are active). What the example here does is to allow the macro to be invoked if a window with the word "Notepad" in it is running -OR- if a window with the words "Microsoft Excel" is running -AND- it has focus.

Clicking **Select** activates the *Select Window(s)* dialog for this scope, which is used to pick application window names. This is the same basic dialog as explained in the **Global Except** description above. It works the same way in that you copy names from the left-hand pane to the right-hand pane, edit names, add more than a single name, and so forth. The difference is the two checkboxes added to each application window title in the right-hand pane.

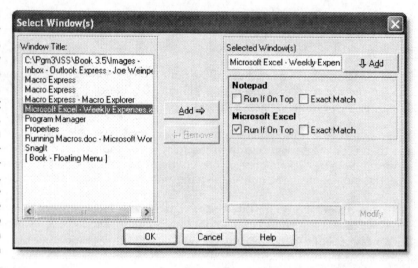

The **Run if On Top** checkbox controls whether the macro can be invoked *only* if the window has focus (the checkbox is checked), or if the window just needs to have been launched. The **Exact Match** checkbox controls whether the window title has to match exactly (the checkbox is checked), or just partially when Macro Express searches through the running windows before deciding if a macro can be invoked. Whichever you choose, it is *never* case-sensitive. "NOTEPAD", "notepad", and "NOTEpad" will all work.

Program Specific

This scope means that a macro can be invoked only if the specified program has been launched and/or has focus. The example here allows the macro to be invoked if a program named Notepad.exe is running -AND- it has focus -OR- if a program named Wordpad.exe is running -OR- if a program named Excel.exe is running.

Clicking **Select** activates the *Select Programs* dialog for this scope, which is used to pick applications. This is the same basic dialog as explained in the **Global Except** description above. It works the same way in that you copy application program names from the left-hand pane to the right-hand pane, edit names, add more than a single name, and so forth. The difference is the **Run if On Top** checkbox added to each chosen application program name in the right-hand pane. It controls whether the macro can be invoked *only* if the named program has focus (the checkbox is checked), or if it just needs to have been launched and is running.

Popup and Floating Menus

Macros can be run from two different types of menus, those that popup and those that float. These menus are specialty-type macros generated from the *Macro Explorer* window by choosing (Macros | Add Macro) from the Main Menu or right-clicking anywhere in the right-hand pane and choosing "New Macro" from the list.

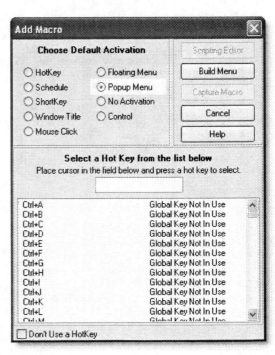

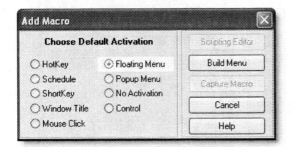

The *Add Macro* dialog on the right is what you see when the **Popup Menu** option is picked. The one above is displayed when choosing the **Floating Menu** option. The difference is that a Popup Menu can be invoked from a HotKey, but a Floating Menu cannot. If you do not want immediately to set a HotKey for a Popup Menu, then check the **Don't Use a HotKey** checkbox in the lower-left corner of the *Add Macro* dialog. You can always change it later.

There are many other differences between the two menu types. As you can see, the Floating Menu has fewer features than the Popup Menu.

The concept behind a Floating Menu is similar to that of a floating toolbar. A Floating Menu remains active after picking something from it, but a Popup Menu will disappear until it is reactivated from either a macro, the System Tray, or a HotKey. And since a Floating Menu remains active and showing, there is no reason to place it in the System Tray or even to display its list in the Windows default style. It is globally available so it cannot be scoped to a particular window or program. And since it floats on top of every other window on the Desktop, and can be dragged around, there are no placement coordinates for it.

Feature	Popup	Floating
Activate with a Hotkey	Y	
Change attached icon	Y	Y
Place menu in System Tray	Y	
Place menu at definable coordinates	Y	
List menu by icons (toolbar style)	Y	Y
List menu by first part of macro	Y	Y
List menu by name and scope	Y	Y
List menu using Windows default style	Y	
Scope menu globally	Y	Y
Scope menu to a window	Y	
Scope menu to a program	Y	

For all the differences in features, they look the same when activated. The menu on the left is a Popup Menu and the one on the right is a Floating Menu. Both menu lists are displayed by the macro name and scope.

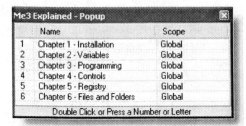

Building a Menu

Building a menu simply means to add, remove, or arrange macros within it. Both menu types are built in the same manner. Once you choose which type to build from the *Add Menu* dialog, you will see the *Menu Builder* dialog. It contains three or four Tabs named Editor, Properties, Scope (if a Popup Menu), and Notes. Building a menu is done from the Editor Tab.

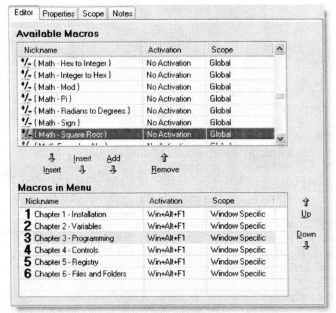

The **Available Macros** list at the top of the dialog is a list of all the macros in the library that have not yet been added to the menu, which is the **Macros in Menu** list on the bottom. There is a limit of 36 macros that can be placed into a menu. A design time error will be displayed if an attempt is made to go beyond the limit.

Macros marked as disabled in the top list, are *not* marked as such in the bottom list when building a menu, but they will be displayed properly when the menu is activated. You cannot run a disabled macro from a menu. Once a menu is created, feel free to enable or disable macros at will. Their status is always checked and displayed properly even if a menu is already activated.

To add a macro to the menu, move it from the top list to the bottom list. There are three positions in the bottom list that a macro can be moved to:

Before the highlighted macro. Say for example that you want to insert the *{ Math - Square Root }* macro between the *Chapter 2 - Variables* macro and the *Chapter 3 - Programming* macro. First highlight the *Chapter 3 - Programming* macro in the bottom list and then the *{ Math - Square Root }* macro in the top list. Now click on the first **Insert** button in the middle row of the dialog and the macro will be placed *before* the *Chapter 3 - Programming* macro.

 After the highlighted macro. Same example except that you want to insert the *{ Math - Square Root }* macro between the *Chapter 3 - Programming* macro and the *Chapter 4 - Controls* macro. First highlight the *Chapter 3 - Programming* macro and then the *{ Math - Square Root }* macro as before. Now click on the second **Insert** button and the macro will be placed *after* the *Chapter 3 - Programming* macro.

 Append to the end of the list. For this example you want to add the *{ Math - Square Root }* macro to the end of the menu list in the bottom pane. Highlight the *{ Math - Square Root }* macro and then click on the **Add** button. It will be appended to the end of the list immediately following the *Chapter 6 - Files and Folders* macro.

 Remove a macro from the list. This one is easy, too. Simply highlight the macro in the bottom list that you want to remove from the menu, say *Chapter 6 - Files and Folders* and then click on the **Remove** button. It will placed back into the list on top.

The **Up** and **Down** buttons in the right-hand column of the dialog enable you to arrange, or reorder the macro list in the bottom **Macros in Menu** list. This is done by highlighting a macro and then moving it up or down in the list by clicking on the appropriate button. Macro positions here will be the final position in the menu when it is activated.

Setting Menu Features

The next step in creating a menu is to define its features. Once you choose which menu to build from the *Add Menu* dialog, you will see the *Menu Builder* dialog, which contains a Tab named Properties. Features are set from this tab. The Properties Tab shown here is for a Popup Menu so some of the features are invalid for Floating Menus (refer to the chart at the top of this section). These fields will be pointed out in the descriptions below.

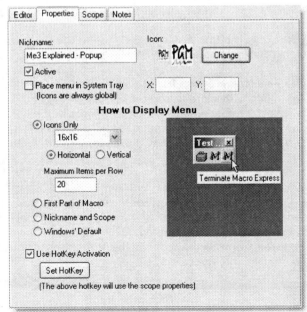

The first three fields, **Nickname**, **Active**, and **Icon** are common to all macros. The **Nickname** field contains the name of the menu and will be shown in its titlebar when it is activated. Each name can be up to 50 characters and should be unique. Even though a menu is a special macro, it is still a macro and needs a name to control it. It is your choice. You may have a good reason not to give it a name.

The **Active** checkbox is used to enable or disable a menu from inside the Properties Tab. If the box is checked then the menu is enabled. Enabling and disabling a Floating Menu is the mechanism used to turn it on or off. If it is enabled, it will automatically be displayed on the screen (not true for a Popup Menu). If it is disabled, it will not be displayed. The *Macro Run* command will *NOT* run a disabled Floating Menu. It will, however, run a Popup Menu.

The *Macro Run* command ignores the active status of a macro, and since a Popup Menu is just another form of a macro, its status is also ignored and will always be run using this command. Say for example that you have created a Popup Menu named "My Popup Menu" and have disabled it. If you create and run the following single-line macro, the menu will display itself on your screen, even though it is still disabled.

Macro Run: My Popup Menu

Because it is a Popup Menu it will remain on your screen until you make a choice. Either menu type, Floating or Popup, can be closed by clicking on the "X" in the upper-right-hand corner of its titlebar. For a System Tray Popup Menu, closing it is the same as making a choice from the menu. It will disappear from your screen but will remain active in the System Tray. It must be disabled permanently to close it.

The **Icon** is for the menu itself. If you are generating a Popup Menu to be placed in the System Tray, then this is the icon that will be used, and clicking on it will pop up the menu. Neither menu type uses the icon in its titlebar when the menu is activated, but like any other macro, the icon is displayed in the Nickname column within the *Macro Explorer* window. This assumes your preferences are set for it (Options | Preferences | Appearance | Show Macro Icons).

The **Change** button displays the system-wide *Select an Icon* dialog, which you are already familiar with.

The **Place Menu in System Tray** checkbox is only available for Popup Menus. If checked, it will place the Popup Menu **Icon** into the System Tray. This forces the menu to always be available for any window or program. In other words, the menu will act as if it is scoped globally, even though it may not be. This does not affect in any manner the scope of the individual macros listed in the menu. Their scopes remain unchanged. The menu must be disabled (inactivated) to remove the icon from the System Tray.

The **X and Y** fields contain the coordinates where the Popup Menu will appear. These fields are not available for Floating Menus, and neither are they available when you have chosen the **Windows Default** listing style explained below. For the other listing styles, **Icons Only**, **First Part of Macro**, and **Nickname and Scope**, the Popup Menu will appear at the coordinates in these two fields with one exception. If the **Place Menu in System Tray** checkbox is checked -AND- if the **X and Y** fields are blank -AND- if you click on the System Tray icon, the menus will appear at the bottom-right corner of your screen, as if you had placed those coordinates into the **X and Y** fields. On the other hand, if you invoke the menu with a HotKey or by using the *Run Macro* command, it pops up at the upper-left corner of your screen. This is because the **X and Y** fields have been treated as 0,0.

The **X and Y** fields will accept only literal integer values and you can enter some huge ones (positive or negative) without Macro Express giving you and error either at design time or runtime. If you need an explanation of the coordinate positioning system, then please review the *Literal Coordinates* section within the *Variables* chapter.

The **How to Display Menu** section contains four different macro list styles for a Popup Menu but only three for a Floating Menu. The **Windows Default** style is not available for Floating Menus. Choose from **Icons Only**, **First Part of Macro**, **Nickname and Scope**, or **Windows Default**.

The **Icons Only** list style is where all those icons you have attached to the macros included in the menu list are used. This option will display them in a "toolbar" fashion either horizontally or vertically. The drop-down list presents you with five different choices of display sizes. You will want to use the size the icons were originally created or they may look strange. An icon is a bit-mapped file that does not expand or contract well.

Me3 Explained - Popup
0 1 2 3 4 5 6 7 8 9 A B C D E F G H I J K L M N O P Q R S T U V W X Y Z

The **Horizontal** and **Vertical** choices are only available if you have picked the **Icons Only** listing style. As you can see from the two examples, the menu has the maximum 36 macros, one is set horizontally and the other vertically. Instead of displaying them all in a single row or column, use the **Maximum Items per Row** field to set the number of icons that can be placed into a row or column. The menus on the right were generated with a value of "9" placed into the field. The first is horizontal, so it means a maximum of 9 icons per row. Next to it is a vertical menu, so there are a maximum of 9 icons per column.

Macro Express does not tend this field well at design time. A developer should only be allowed to enter a value between 1 and 36; however, it will accept anything (except a zero) between -9 and 99. Entering a zero will display an error when you attempt to save the menu, but entering a negative value will cause the menu to display only 1 icon per row or column, and will reverse the horizontal or vertical choice. If you choose **Horizontal**, the menu will be displayed vertically and the converse is true. Entering a value beyond 36 is ignored.

Macro Express

Invalid number of items per row entered.
Please enter a number greater than zero.
The menu will not be saved.

[OK]

The **First Part of Macro** style choice will display a menu showing the first 50 characters of any macro within the menu, as would be displayed by the *Direct Editor*. The example shows the first 50 characters are a *Remark* command in each of the six macros. If you know that your menus will be listed using this option, you may want to place a *Remark* command at the start of each macro explaining what the macro does.

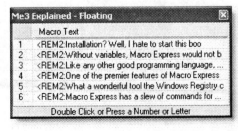

The **Nickname and Scope** style choice will display a menu showing the name of each macro and how it is scoped, Global, Global Except, Window, or Program. Refer to the *Scope* section earlier in this chapter. As you can see from the example, each macro is scoped to a window. The menu does not show which window, just the scope.

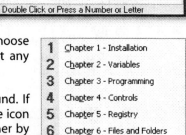

The final style choice is **Windows Default** and is available only for Popup Menus. It displays the name of the macros and their associated icons in a style similar to a Windows menu. If you choose this style, the **X and Y** fields are made "unavailable" meaning that any values they may contain are ignored.

When invoked, the menu will appear wherever your mouse is found. If you are using the **Place Menu in System Tray** checkbox, and click on the icon in the System Tray, the menu will appear at the bottom-right corner by the tray because that is where your mouse is. If your mouse is in the middle of the screen, invoking the menu with a HotKey or the *Macro Run* command will place it near the center of your display.

The **Use HotKey Activation** checkbox is only available for Popup Menus. If you want to invoke a Popup Menu using a HotKey, check this box and choose one by clicking on the **Set HotKey** button, which will display the system-wide *Set HotKey Activation* dialog. Refer to the *HotKey* section in this chapter if you need instructions on using this dialog. Your HotKey choice for the menu is displayed in the Activation column within the *Macro Explorer* window.

The Popup Menu HotKey is tied directly to the menu's scope, which defaults to Global. In other words, only when using a HotKey to invoke a Popup Menu will the scope setting be checked. See *Scoping a Menu* below for further details.

Scoping a Menu

You have the option to scope Popup Menus to a window or program the same as any other macro. The scope is set from the Scope Tab. The four choices are identical with those available to other macro types, and are explained in the *Scope* section of this chapter. Please refer to it for the meaning of each scope.

The scope setting for Popup Menus is listed in the Scope column within the *Macro Explorer* window.

Only when using a HotKey to invoke a Popup Menu will the scope setting be checked. The menu will be treated as if it were scoped to Global if you use any other form of invoking, such as calling it with the **Macro Run** command, or clicking the icon in the System Tray.

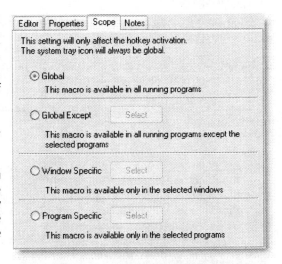

Switching Menu Types

You may change a Popup Menu to a Floating Menu and conversely from a Floating Menu to a Popup Menu. Do this from the General Tab of the main *Properties* dialog, which, for menus, can only be accessed from the *Macro Explorer* window.

Select the target menu from the right-hand pane, then click on the Properties icon in the toolbar, or choose (Macros | Properties) from the Main Menu, or right-click and choose Properties from the menu list.

Choose either the **Popup Menu** or the **Floating Menu** option. If you are changing a Popup Menu to a Floating Menu, the settings that are specific to only Popup Menus will be preserved internally so you may switch back without needing to reset them.

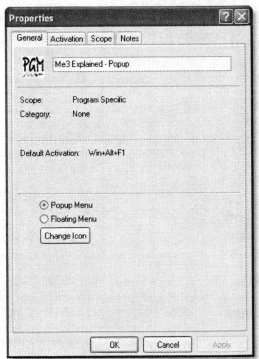

Stopping Macros

Knowing how to stop a runaway macro is important. I strongly suggest that you learn how … and practice before you need to do it.

When any method is used to stop a macro a message is displayed informing you the macro has been stopped. You can prevent this message from being displayed by using the free Macro Express *TweakMe3* macro available from Insight Software Solution's web site. Refer to the *Advanced Options* section in this chapter for more information.

The most common way to stop a macro is to right-click on the Running Man icon in the System Tray. The Running Man icon is enabled by putting a check in the **Show Running Icon** checkbox found inside the (Options | Preferences | Appearance) dialog. This is the default setting.

Another way is to press the abort HotKey. The default is **Scroll Lock+Pause** because they are conveniently found next to each other on the keyboard and can be pressed at the same time.

You can change the HotKey from inside the (Options | Preferences | Playback) dialog. The **Abort Macro HotKey** drop-down list contains four choices, **Scroll Lock+Pause**, **Win+`**, **Pause**, and **Break**.

If you choose **Break** (like what is shown in the example), you will need to press **Ctrl+Break** to abort a macro. This is not a function of Windows or Macro Express; it is how most keyboards work that have a "Pause/Break" key. Because "Pause" is printed on the top and "Break" is printed on the bottom, it seems that to choose "Pause" you would need to press **Shift+Pause**. Not true! **Shift** is not recognized with this key. So, if you want pause, press the **Pause** key. If you want break, press **Ctrl+Break**.

 If you are testing a macro from the Scripting Editor, then you can click on the red Stop icon that appears in the toolbar when a macro is running.

Stopping a macro can also be done using the *Macro Stop* command. Place it anywhere in your macro and when it is encountered your macro will immediately stop.

HOWEVER … it may happen that nothing you do will stop a macro. Sometimes, when Windows is too busy (perhaps another program is not responding or is locked up) Windows either stops processing its own messages, or they are processed very slowly.

If something in Windows is causing the keystroke messages to not be serviced or to be serviced slowly, it can keep your chosen HotKey from stopping the macro. Similarly, if something is affecting the mouse messages, then clicking on the Running Man icon may not stop the macro.

This behavior is one reason there are two different ways to stop a macro: a keystroke or a mouse click. If one method fails to stop the macro, the other method may work. Of course, if Windows is frozen, then nothing will stop the macro.

Dynamic Macros

Macros are usually static, but they can be *dynamic*. Dynamic macros adjust themselves to the current environment because as the designer, you cannot. For example, how are you to know what software a user has currently running on their computer? How is the display resolution currently set? It is impossible to know. This is where dynamic macros can help. They can be set for a particular need *before* the macro runs.

Macro Express provides two commands that can be used to create dynamic macros. One is the *Load Macro Text File* command and the other is *Run Macro in Variable*.

Load Macro Text File

This section will examine *Load Macro Text File*. Let's first look at a basic use for the *Load Macro Text File* command before learning how it is used to create a dynamic macro.

The macro on the right shows the *Load Macro Text File* command. The Notepad window below contains the referenced file named "*Load Cmd.txt*".

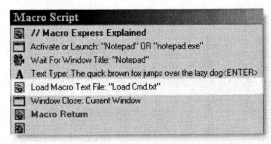

Understanding the *Load Macro Text File* command is just a matter of knowing that the highlighted command line (on the right) will be replaced with the executable text in the referenced file (on the left) when the macro runs. It is that simple. But where does the referenced file come from? You create and edit it external to Macro Express or from inside Macro Express. Since it is a text file you can do both, but let's just look at working from inside Macro Express.

Clicking on the *Load Macro Text File* line will pop up the command's dialog. The **File Name/Path** field contains the full path name of the referenced text file, which will accept a literal string or text variable (refer to the *Variables* chapter if you need help). If you do not want manually to enter the file name, use the **Browse** button to pick a

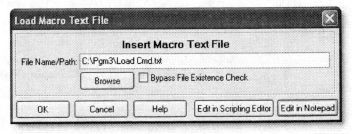

file. The **Browse** button and the **Bypass File Existence Check** checkbox are both explained in the *Variables* chapter.

Once the file name is entered, you can create or edit it by clicking on the **Edit in Scripting Editor** button or **Edit in Notepad** button. The latter is what you see in the above Notepad picture. When editing a macro external to Macro Express, you are editing the natural state of the commands as they appear in the Direct Editor window. Once you have saved the file, you are returned to the *Load Macro Text File* dialog.

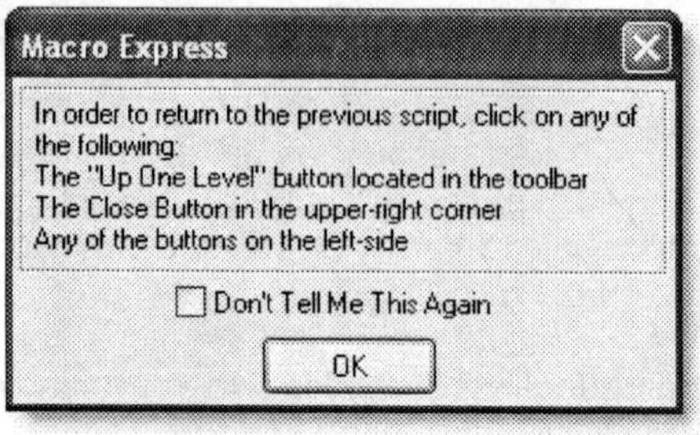

If you are unfamiliar with editing commands in their natural state, you can click on the **Edit in Scripting Editor** button, which will allow you to create or edit the referenced file using another instance of the Scripting Editor. A message appears with instructions on how to return to the *Load Macro Text File* dialog when finished.

You can prevent this message from appearing by checking the **Don't Tell Me This Again** checkbox. Or uncheck the **Show Instructions on Returning to Script Editor when Editing a File** setting found in the *Preferences* dialog (Options | Preferences | Dialogs).

The message is giving you three different ways to get back to the *Load Macro Text File* dialog when you are finished creating or editing the referenced file. The "Up One Level" button the message is referring to appears on the left-hand side of the green Run icon in the Scripting Editor toolbar. The "Close Button" is the standard Windows "X" button in the upper-right-hand corner of the Scripting Editor window. "Any of the buttons on the left side" refers to any icon in the Actions Toolbar in the Scripting Editor except for the External Editor icon.

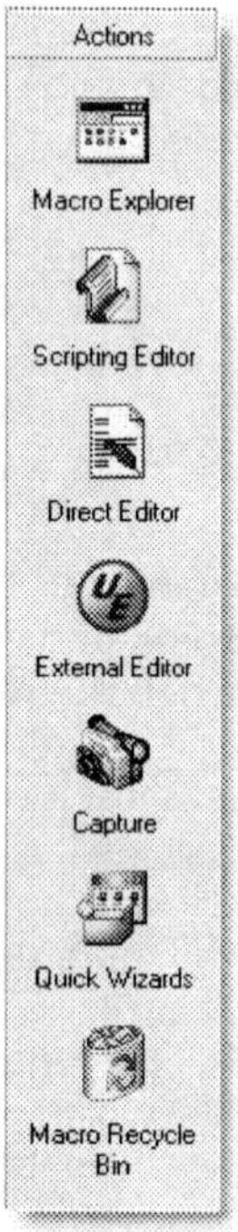

When you click the **OK** button in the message, a new Scripting Editor will appear with the referenced file ready to be edited as shown here. This of course is the same file as you see in the Notepad window on the previous page. Make your changes and then pick one of the three ways to get back. The changes are written to the referenced file on disk and you are returned to the previous *Load Macro Text File* dialog.

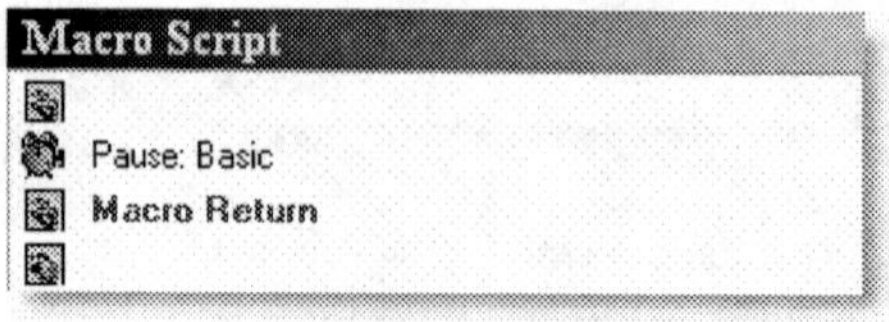

I say "previous" because the ***Load Macro Text File*** command can be cascaded. If, for example, this macro had a ***Load Macro Text File*** command in it, you would take the same exact steps to edit it as you did to edit this one. There is no practical limit to the number of levels.

Now that you know how the command works, let's use it to generate a dynamic macro. We will create one that centers whichever window is chosen from a menu. The menu will be generated from a list of currently running windows.

```
01
02  // Initialize the CRLF and SOH variables.
03  Delay 500 Milliseconds
04  Variable Set %T13% to ASCII Char of 013
05  Variable Set %T1% to ASCII Char of 010
06  Variable Modify String: Append %T1% to %T13%
07  Variable Set %T14% to ASCII Char of 001
08
09  // Loop through running windows to build list of applications.
10  // Ignore apps containing "Macro Express" or "Program Manager".
11  // If nothing found then tell the user and exit the macro.
```

```
12  Variable Set String %T2% ""
13  Repeat with Windows: Place title in %T1%
14   If Variable %T1% does not contain "Macro Express"
15     AND
16   If Variable %T1% does not contain "Program Manager"
17     Variable Modify String: Append %T1% to %T2%
18     Variable Modify String: Append %T13% to %T2%
19   End If
20  Repeat End
21  If Variable %T2% = ""
22   Text Box Display: Dynamic Macro
23   Macro Return
24  End If
25
26  // Build the applications menu and write it to a temp file.
27  // Run it using the "Load Macro Text File" command.
28  Variable Set String %T20% "<MENU2:1:T:19:CenterCenter: Dynamic Macro%T14%%T13%Below is a list of currently running
    applications on your computer. You are being asked to choose the one that you would like centered on your
    display.%T13%%T14%%T2%%T14%T>"
29  Variable Modify String: Save %T20% to Text File
30  Wait for File Ready: "Dynamic Macro.txt"
31
32  Repeat Until %N1% <> %N1%
33   Variable Set String %T19% ""
34   Load Macro Text File: "Dynamic Macro.txt"
35   If Variable %T19% = ""
36     OR
37   If Variable %T19% = "CANCEL"
38     If Message: "Cancel?"
39       Macro Return
40     End If
41   Else
42     Repeat Exit
43   End If
44  Repeat End
45
46  // Center the chosen window.
47  Activate Window: "%T19%"
48  Wait For Window Title: "%T19%"
49  Window Reposition: Center - %T19%
50  Macro Return
51
```

Line 03 is a delay to allow the user time to let go of the keyboard.

Lines 04 through 07 creates a CR/LF string variable and a "Separator Character" string variable to be inserted into the dynamic menu string. Refer to the *Running Macros from Variables* section within the *Variables* chapter to learn more about these special characters.

Line 12 makes sure the **%T2%** dynamic menu string is blank to start with.

Lines 13 through 20 builds a dynamic string of window names that are running. Line 18 adds a CR/LF after each window name, which separates the names inside the *Multiple Choice Menu* command. Any window containing the phrases "Macro Express" or "Program Manager" are skipped.

Lines 21 through 24 stops the macro if there are no applications running and displays a message.

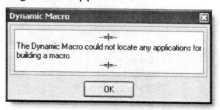

Line 28 generates the complete dynamic menu string that includes the string of window names created by lines 13 through 20. You need to be familiar with how the *Multiple Choice Menu* command is structured:

Section	Description
<MENU2:	*Multiple Choice Menu* command mnemonic
1:	1 = Save pick as menu line, 2 = Save pick as menu letter
T:	T = Single choice (radio button), F = Multiple choice (checkbox)
19:	String variable to hold menu pick
Position:	X and Y runtime coordinates
Title/s	Menu title + Separator Character
Instructions/s	Description/Prompt/Instructions + Separator Character
Menu choices/s	Menu choices (each ending in a CR/LF) + Separator Character
T	T = Set variable to "CANCEL" if Cancel is pressed, blank = Do not
>	End of command mnemonic

Note that Macro Express replaces the **%T2%**, **%T13%**, and **%T14%** variables in the string with actual values when generating the **%T20%** string. Refer to the *Variables* chapter for more information on how Macro Express handles variables.

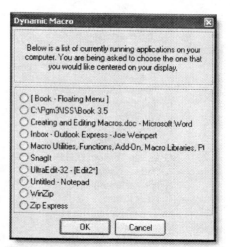

Lines 29 and 30 saves the generated dynamic menu string to a text file.

Lines 32 through 44 is an infinite loop that runs until the user chooses a window or cancels the macro. Line 33 makes sure the **%T19%** results string is blank before the menu is loaded. Line 34 is the key. It loads the saved dynamic *Multiple Choice Menu* command line that lets the user choose the window.

Lines 47 and 48 activate the chosen window.

Line 49 centers it.

Line 50 ends the macro.

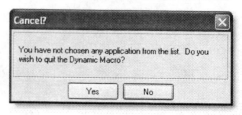

From the above example, lines 28, 29, and 30 generates and saves a dynamic *Multiple Choice Menu* command string to a text file named "c:\temp\Dynamic Menu.txt". The file is loaded by the *Load Macro Text File* command in line 34.

You can access the referenced file after running the macro once because, after all, it is the macro that generates and saves the dynamic string to the file. Run the macro and then click on the **Load Macro Text File** command line.

The view on the right is how the referenced file looks when clicking on the **Edit in Scripting Editor** button. The view below is what it looks like when clicking on the **Edit in Notepad** button.

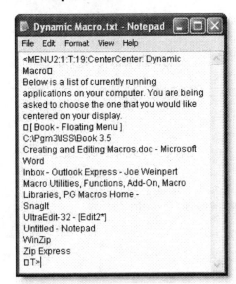

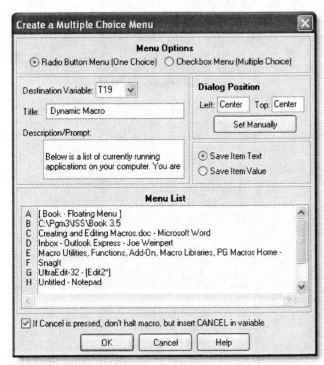

There is another useful aspect to the **Load Macro Text File** command to consider. Line 34 simply loads a generated text file. Macro Express does not care where it came from, or how it was created, or even what created it. Only its location and name is important. Therefore, you can have other programs generate text files to do whatever tasks suit your needs, big or small, dynamic or static. Then have a "generic" Macro Express function that simply uses the **Load Macro Text File** command to run them.

Run Macro in Variable

Now that you know how the **Load Macro Text File** command works, let's examine its companion **Run Macro in Variable** command as it is related to dynamic macros. If you are unfamiliar, please review the *Running Macros from Variables* section within the *Variables* chapter to learn more about the basics of the **Run Macro in Variable** command. Essentially it is used in the same manner as the **Load Macro Text File** command except all the work is done with a variable rather than a referenced file.

We will create another example macro that mirrors the functionality of the one just created for the *Load Macro Text File* command.

```
01
02 // Loop through running windows to build list of applications.
03 // Ignore apps containing "Macro Express" or "Program Manager".
04 // If nothing found then tell the user and exit the macro.
05 Delay 500 Milliseconds
06 Variable Set String %T2% ""
07 Repeat with Windows: Place title in %T1%
08  If Variable %T1% does not contain "Macro Express"
09   AND
10  If Variable %T1% does not contain "Program Manager"
11    Variable Modify String: Append %T1% to %T2%
12    Variable Modify String: Append "\r\n" to %T2%
13  End If
14 Repeat End
15 If Variable %T2% = ""
16  Text Box Display:  Dynamic Macro
17   Macro Return
18 End If
19
20 // Build the applications menu and save it to a variable.
21 // Run it using the "Run Macro in Variable" command.
22 Variable Set String %T20% "<MENU2:1:T:19:CenterCenter: Dynamic Macro\s\r\nBelow is a list of currently running
   applications on your computer. You are being asked to choose the one that you would like centered on your
   display.\r\n\s%T2%\sT>"
23
24 Repeat Until %N1% <> %N1%
25  Variable Set String %T19% ""
26  Run Macro in Variable %T20%
27  If Variable %T19% = ""
28   OR
29  If Variable %T19% = "CANCEL"
30    If Message: "Cancel?"
31     Macro Return
32    End If
33  Else
34   Repeat Exit
35  End If
36 Repeat End
37
38 // Center the chosen window.
39 Activate Window: "%T19%"
40 Wait For Window Title: "%T19%"
41 Window Reposition: Center - %T19%
42 Macro Return
43
```

Line 05 is a delay to allow the user time to let go of the keyboard.

Line 06 makes sure the **%T2%** dynamic menu string is blank to start with.

Lines 07 through 14 builds a dynamic string of window names that are running. Line 12 adds a "\r\n" string after each window name, which separates the names inside the **Multiple Choice Menu** command. Any window containing the phrases "Macro Express" or "Program Manager" are skipped.

Lines 14 through 18 stops the macro if there are no applications running and displays a message.

Line 22 generates the complete dynamic menu string that includes the string of window names created by lines 07 through 14. Macro Express replaces the **%T2%** variable in the string with actual value when generating the **%T20%** string. Refer to the *Variables* chapter for more information on how Macro Express handles variables.

Lines 24 through 36 is an infinite loop that runs until the user chooses a window or cancels the macro. Line 25 makes sure the **%T19%** results string is blank before the menu is run. Line 26 is the key. It runs the dynamic **Multiple Choice Menu** command line that lets the user choose the window.

Lines 39 and 40 activate the chosen window.

Line 41 centers it.

Line 42 ends the macro.

The "\r\n" and "\s" strings in the macro are special characters inserted into the dynamic menu string. They represent the CR/LF and "Separator Character" strings. Refer to the *Running Macros from Variables* section within the *Variables* chapter to learn more about these special characters.

The main difference between these to examples is the dynamic menu string is saved and run from a variable rather than a file. This means the macro will run must faster.

Advanced Options

There are certain features about Macro Express that you may want to change, such as the ShortKeys punctuation characters, the "Macro Aborted" message, and so forth. You can change them, but not through the (Options | Preferences) dialog. Instead, Insight Software Solutions has a playable macro utility named *TweakMe3.mxe*

Tweak Macro Express 3 v 3.5

Macro Express 3 v 3.5.0.1

There are several Macro Express 3 options that cannot be adjusted from the Options menu in Macro Express 3. This macro allows you to change these.

Choose one or more items to change.

☐ Online Delay   ☐ Hotkey Abort Macro Message
☐ Activation Prefix   ☐ Right Click Abort Macro Message
☐ Scope Prefix   ☐ Display Gradient Colors
☐ Shortkey Punctuation Chars   ☐ Macro Priority
☐ Shortkey Invalid Chars   ☐ Show Pixel Color in Hex in Mouse Locator
☐ Macro Stop Abort Macro Message

[OK]   [Cancel]

that is available free from their web site. It allows you to change settings stored in a special key in the Registry. Note that it is an *unsupported* utility meant to be used at your own risk. Personally I have not had any problems using it.

If the (Options | Preferences | Miscellaneous | All Users Use the Same Settings) checkbox is *checked*, and if the currently logged in user has read and write privileges to the HKEY_LOCAL_MACHINE area of the Registry, these advanced options are stored in:

> *HKEY_LOCAL_MACHINE\Software\Insight Software Solutions\Macro Express\AdvOptions*

Otherwise they are stored in:

> *HKEY_CURRENT_USER\Software\Insight Software Solutions\Macro Express\AdvOptions*

Here is a short description of each advanced option. Download the macro and read through it to learn more, and to also see some advanced macro programming techniques.

Online Delay

The *If Online* command enables you to test if you are connected to the Internet. As a default, it will wait 5 seconds for a response, then time-out. This option allows you to change the wait time.

Activation Prefix

Determines whether to display the words "Window:" or "ShortKey:" in the Activation column of the *Macro Explorer* window. It affects only the two activation types. The default (setting the value to "1") is to display the words with the ShortKey name or Window title. You can change this to "0" and display the ShortKey name or Window title by itself.

Nickname	Activation
𝖬 TweakMe3	ShortKey: qwerty

Nickname	Activation
𝖬 TweakMe3	qwerty

Scope Prefix

This is similar to the Activation Prefix. It determines whether to display the words "Program Specific:" or "Window Specific" in the Scope column of the *Macro Explorer* window. This affects only the two scopes. The default (setting the value to "1") is to display the words with the Program name or Window title. You can change this to "0" and display the Program name or Window title by itself.

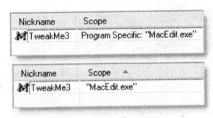

ShortKey Punctuation Chars

Specifies which characters are used to activate a ShortKey macro when **Use Suffix Keys** and **Use Punctuation Chars** are checked in the (Options | Preferences | ShortKeys) dialog. This affects the keys listed in the **Suffix** column of the chart in the *ShortKeys* section of this chapter. By default Macro Express uses ! " ') , - . : ; ?] and ` If you specify the list of punctuation characters to use then you must specify every character you want to use, not just additional characters.

ShortKey Invalid Chars

Specifies which characters are invalid as part of the ShortKey activation sequence when **Use Prefix Keys** is checked in the (Options | Preferences | ShortKeys) dialog. This affects the keys listed in the **Prefix** and **Name** columns of the chart in the *ShortKeys* section of this chapter. By default Macro Express uses ~ (| { } [and : If you specify the list of invalid characters, you must specify every invalid character, not just additional characters.

Macro Stop Abort Message

Hotkey Abort Message

Right Click Abort Message

 These options specifies whether the "Macro Aborted" message is displayed when a *Macro Stop* command executes, or when the **Abort Macro HotKey** is pressed, or when you **right-click** on the Running Man icon in the System Tray. All three choices are handled separately, but the default setting for each is "1", which is to display the message.

The *Macro Stop* command will not display the "Macro Aborted" message from any top-level macro no matter how this advanced option is set. It will only display the message from a lower-level macro, which is any macro run from another macro using the *Macro Run* command.

Display Gradients

Determines whether to display gradient colors the header bars in the Macro Explorer, Scripting Editor, and Direct Editor windows. The default setting is "1", which is to display the gradient.

Macro Priority

This integer value specifies how much time that Macro Express is allowed to use your computer's CPU/processor. The allowable range is 0 through 2,147,483,647. The default value is 1,000. Zero turns this feature off, which gives full priority to Macro Express. You will need to enter a "-1" in the dialog to turn it off, which is then converted and stored as a zero. A "1" gives the lowest priority to Macro Express. The higher the number the more priority is given to running your macros and conversely for the lower the number. Experiment with caution!

Show Pixel Color in Hex in Mouse Locator

This displays both the decimal *and* hexadecimal value of a pixel color on the screen within the *Mouse Locator* tool.

Add a REG_DWORD named **MSLocate Hex Color** to whichever key the advanced options are stored. Give it a value of "**1**" to turn this feature on and a value of "**0**" to turn it off.

Name	Type	Data
(Default)	REG_SZ	(value not set)
Activation Prefix	REG_DWORD	0x00000000 (0)
Gradient	REG_DWORD	0x00000001 (1)
Hotkey Abort Message	REG_DWORD	0x00000000 (0)
Macro Priority	REG_DWORD	0x000003e8 (1000)
Menu Style	REG_SZ	XP
MSLocate Hex Color	REG_DWORD	0x00000001 (1)
Right Click Abort Message	REG_DWORD	0x00000000 (0)
Scope Prefix	REG_DWORD	0x00000000 (0)
Use Stop Message	REG_DWORD	0x00000001 (1)

Mouse Locator

Screen Position
993, 735

Active Window
218, 196

Pixel Color
16777215 / 0xFFFFFF

Banker's Rounding

There is another advanced feature that is not displayed in the *TweakMe3* dialog which affects decimal rounding. Macro Express defaults to a method called *asymmetric arithmetic* rounding; however, it can be changed to *banker's rounding*. Add a REG_DWORD named **Bankers Rounding** to whichever key the advanced options are stored. Give it a value of "**1**" to turn this feature on and a value of "**0**" to turn it off (*asymmetric arithmetic* rounding on). For more on these two types of rounding, please refer to the *Round* section within the *Variables* chapter.

Summary

- There are two types of macro files, library (*.mex*) and playable (*.mxe*).
- An external text editor can be used to create macros.
- Only a single instance of Macro Express will run.
- Only one macro at a time can run.
- Macro Express accepts command line arguments that run macros.
- You can pass variables to a macro from the command line.
- Multiple users can run the same macro at the same time over a network with proper licensing.
- Macro Express recognizes 6 activation types and 4 different scopes.
- More than one activation type can be setup for any given macro.
- Only a single scope is allowed per macro, but it can be a complex one with many different programs included and/or excluded.
- Macro Express recognizes 725 HotKey activation combinations.
- The mouse buttons can be used as HotKeys.
- ShortKeys can be recognized by either their prefix or suffix.
- There are two different types of menus that macros can be run from, Floating and Popup.
- Floating Menus remain on the screen after making a choice.
- Popup Menus disappear after making a choice.
- You can attach your own icons to macros and menus.
- Popup Menus can be scoped just like macros.
- Advanced options can be setup and changed using the *TweakMe3.mxe* macro.

Program Logic and Flow

Like any other good programming language, Macro Express provides the means to control the logic and flow of your macro application. These commands are stored in separate categories named *Logic*, *Repeat*, and *Dialogs*. Each serves a different purpose, but all control what a macro is to do next.

The *Logic* category consists of different *If / Else / End If* commands, *And / Or / Xor* Boolean logic, and *Switch / Case / End Case / End Switch* commands. The *If* commands are each centered around certain Macro Express features such as Variables, Files, Folders, Controls, and so forth. There is no "general" *If* command.

The *Repeat* commands are also centered on different Macro Express features such as Variables, Processes, Counters, and so forth. There is no "general" *Repeat* command.

The *Dialogs* category enables the end user to pick one or more items from a menu using the *Multiple Choice Menu* command. The *Text Box Display* command is used to display messages, and the *Pause* command is used mostly for program development and debugging but is not limited to just those tasks.

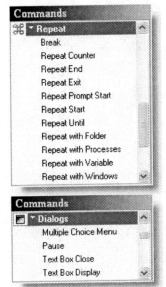

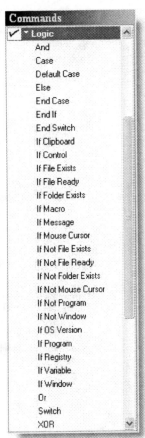

If

Else

End If

The best place to start is with the *If / Else / End If* commands. For those commands that have already been explained elsewhere in this book (which is most of them), you will pointed to the appropriate chapter. The general logic of this programming construct is:

```
If this is true
  Do this
Else
  Do this
End If
```

The **End If** command is required so Macro Express knows where the construct ends. For every **If** command there must be an **End If** command. There are no exceptions to this rule.

You may nest the **If / Else / End If** commands as many times as you wish. The macro below has three nested constructs.

```
If this is true
 Do this "one"
Else
 If this is true
  Do this "two"
 Else
  If this is true
   Do this "three"
  End If
 End If
End If
```

The **Else** command is not required, but is provided to help simplify the flow of the macro. Use it if needed. The results of the following two examples are identical even though the flow of the logic is different because of the use of the **Else** command.

```
// Using the Else command
If Variable %T1% = "Aa"
 Variable Set String %T2% "one"
Else
 If Variable %T1% = "Bb"
  Variable Set String %T2% "two"
 Else
  If Variable %T1% = "Cc"
   Variable Set String %T2% "three"
  End If
 End If
End If
```

```
// Without the Else command
If Variable %T1% = "Aa"
 Variable Set String %T2% "one"
End If
If Variable %T1% = "Bb"
 Variable Set String %T2% "two"
End If
If Variable %T1% = "Cc"
 Variable Set String %T2% "three"
End If
```

AND

OR

XOR

These commands work only with the **If / Else / End If** commands. They are Boolean logic which means that they can return either a *true* or a *false* flag depending on how they are strung together. In all the following examples the variables are set as follows:

```
Variable Set String %T1% "Aa"     // Set T1 to "Aa"
Variable Set String %T2% "Bb"     // Set T2 to "Bb"
Variable Set String %T3% "Cc"     // Set T3 to "Cc"
```

For the **AND** command to return *true*, all statements must be true. There can be as many **AND** commands between the **If** and **End If** commands as needed.

```
If Variable %T1% = "Aa"          // If T1 equals "Aa"
   AND                           // - And -
If Variable %T2% = "Bb"          // If T2 equals "Bb"
   AND                           // - And -
If Variable %T3% = "Cc"          // If T3 equals "Cc" then
   Text Type: True!<ENTER>       // Return true
Else                             // Or else
   Text Type: False!<ENTER>      // Return false
End If                           // End of If test
```

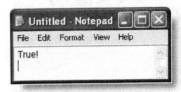

For the **OR** command to return *true*, only one of the statements must be true. There can be as many **OR** commands between the **If** and **End If** commands as needed.

```
If Variable %T1% = "Aa"          // If T1 equals "Aa"
   OR                            // - Or -
If Variable %T2% = "WwXx"        // If T2 equals "WwXx"
   OR                            // - Or -
If Variable %T3% = "YyZz"        // If T3 equals "YyZz" then
   Text Type: True!<ENTER>       // Return true
Else                             // Or else
   Text Type: False!<ENTER>      // Return false
End If                           // End of If test
```

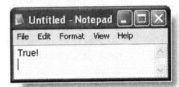

For the **XOR** "exclusive or" command to return *true*, all the statements *except for one* must be true. There should be only one **XOR** command between the **If** and **End If** commands, however, there can be more. They simply cause the *true* or *false* logic flags to be reversed for each one that you add.

```
If Variable %T1% = "Aa"          // If T1 equals "Aa"
   AND                           // - And -
If Variable %T2% = "Bb"          // If T2 equals "Bb"
   XOR                           // - Xor -
If Variable %T3% = "YyZz"        // If T3 equals "YyZz" then
   Text Type: True!<ENTER>       // Return true
Else                             // Or else
   Text Type: False!<ENTER>      // Return false
End If                           // End of If test
```

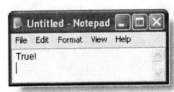

Macro Express evaluates Boolean commands in the order they are written. Consider the next two macro examples. Each Boolean command is evaluated one at a time, with the results being used to compare the next Boolean command, and so forth.

```
// OR evaluated before AND
If Variable %T1% = "Aa"          // If T1 equals "Aa"
   OR                            // - Or -
If Variable %T2% = "WwXx"        // If T2 equals "WwXx"
   AND                           // - And -
If Variable %T3% = "Cc"          // If T3 equals "Cc" then
   Text Type: True!<ENTER>       // Return true
Else                             // Or else
   Text Type: False!<ENTER>      // Return false
End If                           // End of If test
```

In the above macro, the first Boolean compare returns *true* because **%T1%**="Aa" *OR* **%T2%**="WwXx" is *true*. The next one also returns *true* because the *true* that was just returned is compared with the next Boolean command *AND* **%T3%**="Cc", which is also *true*. Therefore, *true AND true* will return *true*.

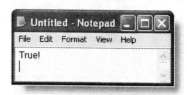

```
// AND evaluated before OR
If Variable %T1% = "Aa"          // If T1 equals "Aa"
  AND                            // - And -
If Variable %T2% = "WwXx"        // If T2 equals "WwXx"
  OR                             // - Or -
If Variable %T3% = "Cc"          // If T3 equals "Cc" then
  Text Type: True!<ENTER>        // Return true
Else                             // Or else
  Text Type: False!<ENTER>       // Return false
End If                           // End of If test
```

In the above macro, the first Boolean compare returns *false* because **%T1%**="Aa" *AND* **%T2%**="WwXx" is *false*. The next one returns *true* because the *false* that was just returned is compared with the next Boolean command *OR* **%T3%**="Cc", which is *true*. Therefore, *false OR true* will return *true*.

If Variable

Use this command to compare variables to literal values or to other variables of the same type. Compare strings to strings, integers to integers, and decimals to decimals.

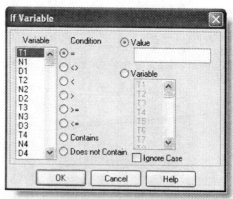

The **Variable** drop-down list (on the left side) contains the target variable to compare. All 297 variables are there to pick from. **T1**, **N1**, and **D1** through **T99**, **N99**, and **D99**.

The **Value** field is for comparing the target variable to a literal value. If you are comparing a string variable then this field will accept either the literal value to compare, or a variable, or a combination of both. Here are three examples.

```
Variable Set String %T1% "AaBbCc"      // Compare literal string in Value field
If Variable %T1% = "AaBbCc"
  Text Type: True!<ENTER>
Else
  Text Type: False!<ENTER>
End If
```

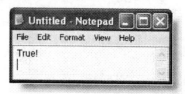

```
Variable Set String %T1% "AaBbCc"
Variable Set String %T2% "AaBbCc"      // Compare just variable in Value field
If Variable %T1% = "%T2%"
  Text Type: True!<ENTER>
Else
  Text Type: False!<ENTER>
End If
```

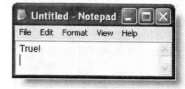

```
// Compare a literal value combined with a variable in the Value field
```

```
Variable Set String %T1% "AaBbCc"
Variable Set String %T2% "Cc"
If Variable %T1% = "AaBb%T2%"
  Text Type: True!<ENTER>
Else
  Text Type: False!<ENTER>
End If
```

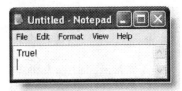

If you are comparing an integer or a decimal variable then the **Value** field will accept only a literal value to compare. For integers, only the characters 0 through 9 and a minus sign are acceptable as input. Any other characters will cause an error to be displayed. For decimals, the dot (or period) is also acceptable.

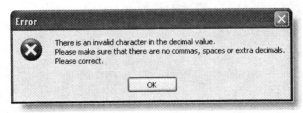

The **Variable** drop-down list (on the right side) is for comparing your target variable to another variable rather than a literal value. This drop-down list changes the listed variables to only those that match the target variable type. Only string, integer, or decimal variables will be listed at any one time.

The **Condition** column of radio buttons contain the comparison choices available to you. There are eight of them. The first six can be used for any variable. The last two (**Contains** and **Does not Contain**) are only available for comparing strings. Comparisons may be equal (=), not equal (<>), less than (<), greater than (>), greater than or equal to (>=), and less than or equal to (<=). And for strings, **Contains** and **Does not Contain**, which simply tests that one string is contained in another … or not. Also, when comparing strings, the **Ignore Case** checkbox can be used for case-insensitive comparisons.

Comparing integers and decimals is straightforward. Strings however are a different matter and there are some things that you should be aware of. What I term as the *target* string variable is always the one chosen from the **Variable** drop-down list found on the left-hand side of the dialog. It is also the one on the left-hand side of the comparison in the command line.

> **If Variable %T1% = "AaBbCc"**

This is important to know when comparing strings in case the strings being compared are of different lengths. In the following examples the variables are set as follows:

Variable Set String %T1% "Aa"	// Set T1 to "Aa"
Variable Set String %T2% "AaBb"	// Set T2 to "AaBb"

When comparing strings of unequal length using the equal (=) operator, the results will always be *false*. The opposite is true of course when using the not equal (<>) operator.

If Variable %T1% = Variable %T2%	// False	**If Variable %T1% <> Variable %T2%**	// True
If Variable %T2% = Variable %T1%	// False	**If Variable %T2% <> Variable %T1%**	// True

When comparing target strings that are shorter than the comparison string using the less than (<) operator, the results will always be *true*. On the other hand, if the target string is longer, then the results will always be *false*. The opposite is true of course when using the greater than (>) operator.

If Variable %T1% < Variable %T2%	// True	**If Variable %T1% > Variable %T2%**	// False
If Variable %T2% < Variable %T1%	// False	**If Variable %T2% > Variable %T1%**	// True

The **Contains** and **Does not Contain** conditions test if a string can, or cannot be, found within another string. Obviously a longer string cannot be found inside a shorter string and will always be *false*, but the opposite may be *true*.

If Variable %T1% contains Variable %T2%	// False	**If Variable %T1% does not contain Variable %T2%**	// True
If Variable %T2% contains Variable %T1%	// True	**If Variable %T2% does not contain Variable %T1%**	// False

If OS Version

This command tests which operating system the macro is running under. There are seven choices and here are the strings that they return:

1. "Win95"
2. "Win98"
3. "WinME"
4. "WinNT"
5. "Win2000"
6. "WinXP"
7. "Win2003"

Not all Microsoft operating systems work the same. Let's say that you want the user to run a certain macro based on which operating system they have. The following sample will tell them which one to run:

```
Activate or Launch: "Notepad" OR "notepad.exe"   // Launch or activate the Windows Notepad application
If OS Version: "Win95"                           // If the operating system is Windows 95
  OR                                             // -OR-
If OS Version: "Win98"                           // If the operating system is Windows 98
  OR                                             // -OR-
If OS Version: "WinME"                           // If the operating system is Windows Me then
    Text Type: Use a Windows 98 macro<ENTER>     // tell user to run the Windows 98 macro
Else                                             // Otherwise
  If OS Version: "WinNT"                          // If the operating system is Windows NT then
     Text Type: Use a Windows NT macro<ENTER>    // tell user to run the Windows NT macro
  Else                                           // Otherwise
    If OS Version: "Win2000"                     // If the operating system is Windows 2000
      OR                                         // -OR-
    If OS Version: "WinXP"                       // If the operating system is Windows XP then
      Text Type: Use a Windows XP macro<ENTER>   // tell user to run the Windows XP macro
    Else                                         // Otherwise
      If OS Version: "Win2003"                   // If the operating system is Windows Server 2003 then
        Text Type: Use a Windows 2003 macro<ENTER> // tell user to run the Windows 2003 macro
```

End If	// End of Win2003 test
End If	// End of Win2000 and WinXP tests
End If	// End of WinNT test
End If	// End Of Win95, Win98, and WinME tests

If Macro Enabled
If Macro Disabled

Both of these commands are found in the Macro Express system-wide *If Commands* dialog. They simply return *true* or *false* based on whether a macro is enabled or disabled. The **Macro Name** field holds the name of your target macro and may contain a literal string, variable, or a combination of both.

You may optionally pick a macro using the **Select** button. When choosing a macro with this button, a *Get Nickname* dialog appears. By default it lists the categories that you have defined. You expand or deflate each category folder in the same way that you would using Windows Explorer to search through folders by clicking on the "+" or "-" symbol.

If you do not want to deal with categories then check the **Display All Macros** checkbox and the dialog immediately changes to an alphabetical list of all macros in the library.

Highlight your target macro and then click the **OK** button. This will record your choice in the **Macro Name** field. You may further edit it from there. Although this field is not case sensitive, it does require an exact match. For example, "{ DateTime - Character DOW }" and "{ DATETIME - CHARACTER DOW }" would both be the same macro because letter-for-letter, they are an exact match. The case does not matter.

```
If Macro "{ DateTime - Character DOW }" Disabled      // If this macro is disabled then
    Macro Enable: { DateTime - Character DOW }         // enable it
End If                                                 // End of disabled test
```

If Message

This command enables you to get an answer from the user. The *If Message* dialog has nice features for tailoring the runtime dialog the user sees.

The **Caption** field stores the window title of the runtime dialog and may contain a literal string, variable, or a combination of both.

The **Message** field stores the question you are presenting to the user and may contain a literal string, variables, or a combination of both. Space for your question is limited to just four lines. You can type as many lines as you want but the user will only see the first four. The rest of the question is simply scrolled off at runtime. The same happens if you use a variable to contain the question, unlike the *Text Box Display* command, which allows for lengthy variables.

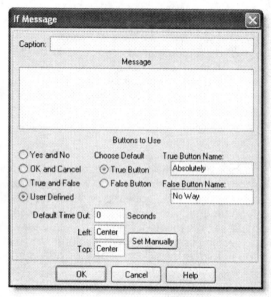

The runtime **Yes | No** buttons can be tailored using other captions. **OK | Cancel**, **True | False**, or a **User Defined** set that you, the developer, create by placing the positive button caption in the **True Button Name** field and the negative button caption in the **False Button Name** field. **Absolutely | No Way** and **Good Idea | Not So Good** make nice user defined captions, but keep the captions short. These two fields will accept literal strings, variables, or a combination of both.

You may also set the "default" response expected at runtime so the user need only press the <Enter> key to answer the question. Choose between the **True Button** and **False Button** radio buttons. Part of the "default" response is a built-in timer feature that will automatically pick the default choice if time elapses. Enter the number of seconds to wait in the **Default Time Out** field. The default value is zero, which means to wait forever. You may enter a value up to 99,999 seconds, which would wait for over a day to get a response. This field will also accept an integer variable.

Macro Express also gives you the ability to place the dialog anywhere you choose on the user's screen at runtime. The **Left** field, **Top** field, and **Set Manually** buttons are used for this placement. The **Set Manually** button will give you access to the system-wide *Dialog Positioner* screen explained in detail within the *Dialog Positioner* section of the *Variables* chapter. The choices made from this dialog are placed into the **Left** and **Top** fields for you. The *If Message* command in this example macro is generated from the *If Message* dialog below.

```
Variable Set String %T1% "What do you think?"      // Set the window title caption
Variable Set String %T2% "Absolutely!"             // Set the positive button
Variable Set String %T3% "Not Really"              // Set the negative button
Variable Set Integer %N1% to 10                    // Timeout after 10 seconds
```

```
If Message: "%T1%"                    // If it is good news then
  Text Type: Good news!<ENTER>        // say it
Else                                  // Or else
  Text Type: Not so good news!<ENTER> // give me the bad news
End If                                // End of user question
```

And this is what the user sees at runtime:

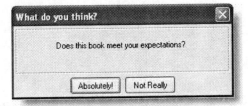

If Clipboard

See the *Clipboard* chapter.

If Control

See the *Window Controls* chapter.

If Mouse Cursor
If Not Mouse Cursor

See the *Mouse* chapter.

If File Exists
If Not File Exists
If File Ready
If Not File Ready
If Folder Exists
If Not Folder Exists

See the *Files and Folders* chapter.

If Registry

See the *Using the Registry* chapter.

If Program
If Not Program
If Window
If Not Window

See the *Windows and Programs* chapter.

Switch
End Switch
Case
Default Case
End Case

The ***Switch / End Switch*** construct is a simple logic structure that allows you to test a variable and branch your macro based on the results. The general logic of this programming construct is:

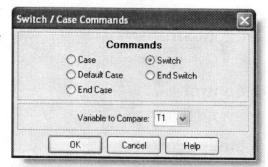

```
Switch (T1)      // Test this variable
  Case:          // If this is a true statement then
    Do this      // run this macro command
  End Case       // End of this test
  Case:          // If this is a true statement -or-
  Case:          // if this is a true statement then
    Do this      // run this macro command
  End Case       // End of this test
  Default Case   // None of the above tests worked so
    Just do this // run this macro command
```

```
End Case          // End of default test
End Switch        // End of test for this variable
```

The **Switch** command marks the beginning of the construct while the **End Switch** command marks the end. For every **Switch** command there must be an **End Switch** command. There are no exceptions to this rule.

Within the construct, the **Case** command marks the beginning of a particular test on a variable while the **End Case** marks the end of the test. There may be more than one **Case** command, or test, for an **End Case** command. This simply works like the **OR** command when dealing with **If / End If** commands. The **Case** statement itself will accept literal values, variables, or a combination of both. If you are going to use a variable to test against the variable contained in the **Switch** command, be sure that it is the same variable type. The Macro Express help system says:

> **Case statements that follow must be consistent with the type of variable you chose for the Switch statement. If the values are not consistent, the result may be unpredictable.**

You may place any number of macro commands within a **Case** command. Thousands of them. Although each macro is limited to 65,000 command lines, you can run some massive macro code within those **Case** commands if it suits your purpose.

You are also allowed an optional default test, named **Default Case**, within a **Switch / End Switch** construct. Like the **Case** command, it uses an **End Case** to mark its end. If all the other **Case** commands, or tests, fail you can count on this one to always be true. This works like the **Else** command when dealing with **If / End If** commands. It must be placed after all the other **Case** commands or else none of them will be tested.

Once either a **Case** or **Default Case** command tests *true* then all other **Case** commands are ignored and processing continues after the last **End Switch** command. By that I mean if you have nested **Switch / End Switch** commands, processing will continue after the main, or primary, **End Switch** command no matter how many times you have nested. This is the reason you do not need to use the **Break** command in a Switch / End Switch construct. The "break" is automatic. You may nest the **Switch / End Switch** commands as many times as you wish. The macro below has a nested construct within the first **Case** command. If the **Case** command tests true then the nested **Switch / End Switch** construct will run.

```
Switch (T1)       // Test this variable
Case:             // If this is a true statement then
  Switch (T2)     // test this variable now
  Case:           // If this is a true statement then
    Do this       // run this macro command
  End Case        // End of this test
  Case:           // if this is a true statement then
    Do this       // run this macro command
  End Case        // End of this test
  End Switch      // End of test for this T2 variable
End Case          // End of this test
Case:             // if this is a true statement then
  Do this         // run this macro command
End Case          // End of this test
End Switch        // End of test for this T1 variable
```

The *Case* command compares for *exact equality* and is case sensitive. There is no *Case* command for "less than", "greater than", or anything else other than "equals".

Variable Set String %T1% "Aa"	// Set the T1 variable
Switch (T1)	// Test this variable
Case: aa	// If this is a true statement then
Text Type: T1 = aa	// run this macro command
End Case	// End of this test
Case: Aa	// If this is a true statement then
Text Type: T1 = Aa	// run this macro command
End Case	// End of this test
End Switch	// End of test for this variable

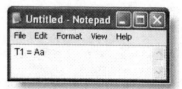

In the above macro, the first *Case* command is *false* because of the exact nature of the "equals" test and is therefore ignored. The macro could have been written as follows because of the "or" nature of stringing multiple *Case* commands with a single *End Case* command.

Variable Set String %T1% "Aa"	// Set the T1 variable
Switch (T1)	// Test this variable
Case: aa	// If this is a true statement -or-
Case: AA	// If this is a true statement -or-
Case: aA	// If this is a true statement -or-
Case: Aa	// If this is a true statement then
Text Type: T1 = Aa	// run this macro command
End Case	// End of this test
End Switch	// End of test for this variable

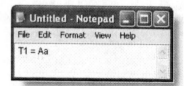

Repeat
Repeat End
Repeat Exit
Break

The *Repeat / Repeat End* construct enables you to repeat a given block of Macro Express commands any given number of times through infinity. The general logic of this programming construct is:

Repeat	// Top of repeat loop construct
Do this 1st command	// Run this macro command
Do this 2nd command	// Run this macro command
Do this 3rd command	// Run this macro command
End Repeat	// Bottom of repeat loop construct

The three command lines while be repeated forever until you stop the macro.

Like the *If* command, there are several different versions of the *Repeat* command. Each marks the beginning of a repeat loop, while the *Repeat End* command marks the end. For every *Repeat* command there must be a *Repeat End* command. There are no exceptions to this rule.

Normally all the commands within any *Repeat / Repeat End* construct will be run at least once. The internal test that Macro Express does to determine if the loop should be exited, is done at the end of the loop when the *Repeat End* command is encountered.

One exception to this rule is if a *Repeat Exit* or *Break* command is encountered. At this point, the loop will be exited without the remainder of the commands being executed. In other words, all the commands before the *Repeat Exit* or *Break* commands are executed at least one time, while those placed beyond the *Repeat Exit* or *Break* commands will not be. The other exception is an illegal value entered into the "counter" field. See the *Repeat Start* command for more information on this exception.

The *Repeat Exit* command tells the repeat loop to exit immediately and continue processing the macro at the first command found beyond the *Repeat End* command. The *Break* command is identical with the *Repeat Exit* command when used inside a *Repeat / Repeat End* construct. However, the *Break* command may also be used within both the *Text File Processing* and *ASCII File Processing* constructs. Refer to the *Files and Folders* chapter.

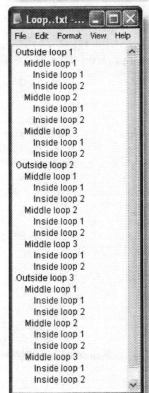

Activate or Launch: "Notepad" OR "notepad.exe"	// Launch the Notepad
Repeat Start (Repeat 10 times)	// Loop 10 times
Text Type: Loop %N1%<ENTER>	// Display the loop number
If Variable %N1% = 5	// If we hit loop 5 then
Repeat Exit	// exit the loop (Break also works)
End If	// End of counter test
Repeat End	// End of the loop

The above macro is set to loop 10 times using the *Repeat Start* command. The loop number is displayed each time through. However, it will loop only 5 times because the *If Variable* command exits the loop when the counter reaches "5".

You may nest the *Repeat / Repeat End* construct as many times as you like. Each nested level is controlled individually. If a nested repeat loop ends, then the one that it was nested within will continue looping until it ends, and then its parent will continue looping until it ends, and so forth. In other words, there is no Macro Express command that instructs a macro to end all the nested *Repeat / Repeat End* constructs at the same time.

01	**Launch: "notepad.exe"**	// Launch the Notepad
02	**Repeat Start (Repeat 3 times)**	// Repeat outside loop 3 times
03	**Text Type: Outside loop %N1%<ENTER>**	// Display loop number
04	**Repeat Start (Repeat 3 times)**	// Repeat middle loop 3 times
05	**Text Type: Middle loop %N2%<ENTER>**	// Display loop number
06	**Repeat Start (Repeat 2 times)**	// Repeat inside loop 2 times
07	**Text Type: Inside loop %N3%<ENTER>**	// Display loop number
08	**Repeat End**	// End of inside repeat loop
09	**Repeat End**	// End of middle repeat loop
10	**Repeat End**	// End of outside repeat loop

The above macro displays how nested loops work. There are 3 loops. Outside, middle, and inside. The outside and middle loops both run 3 times each. The inside loop runs twice. The nature of a loop is to run all the commands within it until it finds a way to exit.

Line 01 launches the Windows Notepad application. Line 02 starts the outside loop. Line 03 records the current outside loop counter to the Notepad. Line 04 begins the middle loop. Line 05 records the current middle loop counter to the Notepad. Line 06 begins the inside loop. Line 07 records the current inside loop counter to the Notepad. By the time line 07 finishes running, the first three lines are recorded in the Notepad window. The rest of the command lines simply end each repeat loop.

So what happens when line 08 runs? The macro loops back to the top of the inside loop (line 06), increments the inside loop counter, and then runs the next command in the loop again (line 07). Now there are four lines recorded in the Notepad window. When line 08 is engaged again the inside loop counter has run twice, and is therefore completed, so the macro moves on to line 09, which is the end of the middle repeat loop. Now the macro loops back to the top of the middle loop (line 04), increments the middle loop counter, and then runs the next command in the loop again (line 05). Now there are five lines recorded in the Notepad window.

The next set of commands is the inside loop again, which runs identical with the first time it ran and adds two more lines to the Notepad window. On and on it goes until all the repeat loops have been satisfied.

Repeat Start

Or, *Start Repeat* as listed in the *Repeat Options* dialog. This **Repeat** command allows you to set a counter for how many times a loop should repeat. The value is stored in the **Repeat Count** field. The default value is 10.

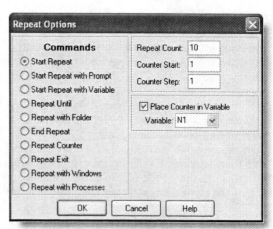

The **Counter Start** field contains the starting number to use for the counter. Say, for example, that you want a loop to repeat 10 times beginning with the number 1. Place a "10" in the **Repeat Count** field and a "1" in the **Counter Start** field ("1" is the default value). When the loop runs, the counter will be incremented each time starting with "1" (1, 2, 3, 4, 5, 6, 7, 8, 9, and 10). You could have also started the counter at 53 by placing "53" into the **Counter Start** field. It still loops only 10 ten times, but the counter will begin at "53" and end at "62" (53, 54, 55, 56, 57, 58, 59, 60, 61, and 62).

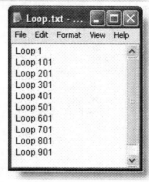

Use the **Counter Step** field if you have a need to increment the counter number by a value greater than the default of "1" each time through the loop. Say, for example, that you want a loop to repeat 10 times beginning with the number 1, but skipping 100 numbers between each loop. Place a "10" in the **Repeat Count** field, a "1" in the **Counter Start** field, and a "100" in the **Counter Step** field. When the macro runs, the counter will begin at "1" and end at "901" (1, 101, 201, 301, 401, 501 601, 701, 801, and 901).

Although negative values are not allowed in the **Repeat Count** field, they are acceptable in both the **Counter Start** and **Counter Step** field. And they would work, as you would imagine, by counting backwards, but counting nonetheless. The reason for the flexibility of counters and counter steps is the *Repeat Start* command enables you to store, and use, the current loop counter. Simply check the **Place Counter in Variable** checkbox and choose the variable that will store the value from the **Variable** drop-down list.

Macro	Comment
Activate or Launch: "Notepad" OR "notepad.exe"	// Launch the Notepad
Repeat Start (Repeat 10 times)	// Loop 10 times
Text Type: Loop %N1%<ENTER>	// Display the loop number
If Variable %N1% = 5	// If we hit loop 5 then
Repeat Exit	// exit the loop (Break also works)
End If	// End of counter test
Repeat End	// End of the loop

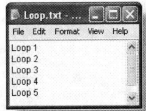

In the above macro, the **N1** variable was picked to hold the current loop counter. We want the loop to run only 5 times (even though the **Repeat Count** field is 10), so we test the loop counter each time to see what the number is. If it is equal to five then we exit the loop. This is possible because the **Place Counter in Variable** feature saves the counter each time through the loop. This feature has been used throughout most of the previous examples to count and display the current loop.

All three fields in the *Repeat Start* command accept literals or integer variables. The minimum value allowed for the **Repeat Count** field is 1. The maximum literal value is 99,999. If you want to loop more times, use an integer variable which may contain values up to 2,147,483,647. An attempt to enter an illegal value in the **Repeat Count** field at design time will result in an error. On the other hand, an illegal integer variable value will be ignored at runtime, which means the *Repeat Start* / *Repeat End* construct, and all the commands between, will not be run. And no error message will be displayed so you must be careful.

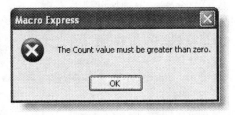

The range of the literal values that may be entered into the **Counter Start** and **Counter Step** fields is -99,999 through 999,999. If you want a greater range, use integer variables which contain values ranging from -2,147,483,648 through 2,147,483,647. There are no "bad" entries possible in these two fields. Macro Express has done a good job with them.

If you place a zero in both the **Counter Start** and **Counter Step** fields the results, although correct, look rather strange. The loop did run 10 times as instructed by the **Repeat Count** field. The **Counter Start** field did start at zero. The **Counter Step** field did step by zero each time.

Again, the **Counter Start** and **Counter Step** fields have nothing to do with the number of loops taken by the *Repeat Start* command. That is controlled strictly by the **Repeat Count** field. However, the **Counter Start** and **Counter Step** fields have *everything* to do with the **Place Counter in Variable** field, which is a feature designed strictly for your use.

Repeat with Variable

Or, **Start Repeat with Variable** as listed in the *Repeat Options* dialog. This **Repeat** command allows you to set a counter for how many times a loop should repeat using an integer variable. The target variable is chosen from the **Repeat Using Variable** drop-down list. The variable is used in the same manner as the value in the **Repeat Count** field of the *Repeat Start* command.

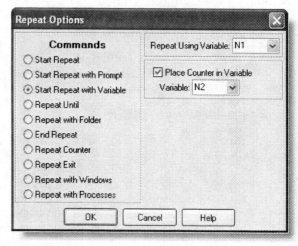

Unlike the **Repeat Start** command, this **Repeat** command always starts with 1 and always increments the counter by 1 each time through the loop.

Integers range from -2,147,483,648 through 2,147,483,647; however, the minimum value needed to cycle through the loop once is 1. Anything less than 1 and the repeat loop, and all the commands within it, will be ignored at runtime. And no error message will be displayed so you must be careful.

As with the **Repeat Start** command, the **Repeat with Variable** command enables you to store, and use, the current loop counter. Simply check the **Place Counter in Variable** checkbox and choose the variable that will store the value from the **Variable** drop-down list.

If you are using the **Place Counter in Variable** feature, the values of both variables will be identical when the loop ends. You can use this information to determine whether a loop runs completely through or has taken an early exit at some point.

Variable Set String %T1% "AEIOU"	// Set a string of vowels
Variable Set Integer %N1% to 10	// Set loop for 10 times
Repeat with Variable using %N1%	// Begin looping
Variable Set String %T2% to Random Letter	// Set a random letter A-Z
If Variable %T1% contains variable %T2%	// If letter is a vowel then
Repeat Exit	// Exit the loop immediately
End If	// End of vowel test
Repeat End	// End of the repeat loop
If Variable %N2% = variable %N1%	// If loop number equals count then
Text Type: No vowels generated!	// no random vowel was generated
End If	// End of counter compare test

Repeat Prompt Start

Or, *Start Repeat with Prompt* as listed in the *Repeat Options* dialog. This **Repeat** command allows the user to set an internal counter *at runtime* for how many times a loop should repeat.

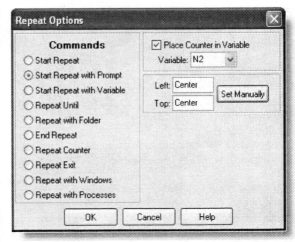

When this command is encountered at runtime, the *Times to Repeat* dialog appears prompting the user to enter a repeat value. The user may enter any value greater than or equal to (>=) zero. Entering zero (or leaving the field blank) means the repeat loop, and all the commands within it, will be ignored. Macro processing continues after the *Repeat End* command line. If the user simply clicks the **Cancel** button, the macro will stop. Macro Express does not test the validity of the value entered by the user. The maximum number of times a loop can repeat is 2,147,483,647 no matter what the user enters. For some perspective, it takes my machine about 100 minutes (1 hr 40 min) to loop 2,000,000,000 (billion) times.

The *Times to Repeat* dialog can be placed anywhere you choose on the user's screen at runtime. The **Left** field, **Top** field, and **Set Manually** buttons are used for this placement. The **Set Manually** button will give you access to the system-wide *Dialog Positioner* screen explained in detail within the *Dialog Positioner* section of the *Variables* chapter. The choices made from this dialog are placed into the **Left** and **Top** fields for you.

As with the *Repeat with Variable* command, the *Repeat Prompt Start* command enables you to store, and use, the current loop counter. Simply check the **Place Counter in Variable** checkbox and choose the variable that will store the value from the **Variable** drop-down list.

This is the same example shown in the *Repeat with Variable* command. The difference is that the user is prompted for the number of loops to run rather than setting it for 10.

```
Variable Set String %T1% "AEIOU"                          // Set a string of vowels
Repeat Prompt Start (Prompt at macro play time)          // Begin looping
  Variable Set String %T2% to Random Letter              // Set a random letter A-Z
  If Variable %T1% contains variable %T2%                // If letter is a vowel then
    Repeat Exit                                          // Exit the loop immediately
  End If                                                 // End of vowel test
Repeat End                                               // End of the repeat loop
If Variable %N2% = variable %N1%                         // If loop number equals count then
  Text Type: No vowels generated!                        // no random vowel was generated
End If                                                   // End of counter compare test
```

Repeat Until

This *Repeat Until* command allows you to create a repeat loop that will continue to run until a particular condition is met. If the condition is not met, then the loop runs forever. The choices are almost identical with the choices presented in the *If Variable* command.

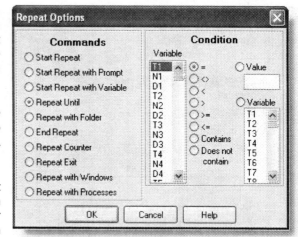

The **Variable** drop-down list (on the left side of the **Condition** pane) contains the target variable to compare. All 297 variables are there to pick from. **T1**, **N1**, and **D1** through **T99**, **N99**, and **D99**.

The **Value** field is for comparing the target variable to a literal value. If you are comparing a string variable then this field will accept either the literal value to compare, or a variable, or a combination of both.

If you are comparing an integer or a decimal variable then the **Value** field will accept only a literal value to compare. For integers, only the characters 0 through 9 and a minus sign are acceptable as input. Any other characters will cause an error to be displayed. For decimals, the dot (or period) is also acceptable.

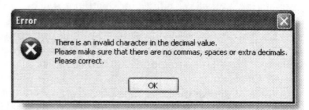

The **Variable** drop-down list (on the right side of the **Condition** pane) is for comparing your target variable to another variable rather than a literal value. This drop-down list changes the variable type available in the list to only those that match the target variable type. Only string, integer, or decimal variables will be listed at any one time.

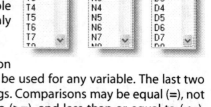

The **Condition** column of radio buttons contains the comparison choices available to you. There are eight of them. The first six can be used for any variable. The last two (**Contains** and **Does not Contain**) are only available for comparing strings. Comparisons may be equal (=), not equal (<>), less than (<), greater than (>), greater than or equal to (>=), and less than or equal to (<=). And for strings, **Contains** and **Does not Contain**, which simply tests that one string is contained in another ... or not. Unlike the *If Variable* command, all string comparisons *are* case sensitive.

Comparing integers and decimals is straightforward. Strings however are a different matter and there are some things that you should be aware of. Please refer to the *If Variable* command earlier in this chapter for expected results when comparing strings.

The ability to loop until a specified condition is met, rather than setting several times to loop, is a nice feature of the Macro Express *Repeat Until* command. With it, you can create an infinite loop. Consider this short macro on the next page, which continues looping until variable **N1** is no longer equal to itself. And since this can never happen, it will loop forever.

```
Repeat Until %N1% <> %N1%          // Repeat until variable N1 does not equal N1
Text Type: Still looping!          // Display "Still looping!"
Repeat End                         // End of infinite loop
```

Getting proper input from the user is another great use of the *Repeat Until* command. Here is a section of code from the free Pop-N-Pass macro library, which is available on the Macro Express web site.

```
Repeat Until %N1% <> %N1%              // Infinite loop begin
  Variable Set String %T1% ""          // Erase the T1 string each time through
  Variable Set String %T1% from Prompt // Ask the user for a macro name
  If Variable %T1% = ""                // If the T1 variable is empty
   OR                                  //  -OR-
  If Variable %T1% = "CANCEL"          // If the user clicked on the Cancel button then
    If Message: "Cancel?"              // ask if user really wants to quit, and if so
     Macro Return                      // quit
    End If                             // End asking user intentions
  Else                                 // Otherwise, the user entered a value and clicked the OK button, so
    Repeat Exit                        // Exit the infinite loop
  End If                               // End of testing user input string
Repeat End                             // End of infinite loop
```

If the user inputs a macro name and clicks on the **OK** button, the loop is exited (third line from the bottom) and no further processing takes place.

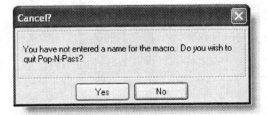

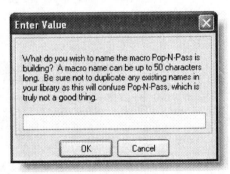

On the other hand, if the value input is blank or if it is "CANCEL" (by clicking the **Cancel** button), then the macro prompts the user for their intentions. If they entered a blank line, or clicked on **Cancel**, by mistake, then this gives them the opportunity to enter the correct information.

Repeat with Processes

This command is similar to the *Repeat with Windows* command. It will loop through all the processes (programs) that are running on your computer, stuffing the name of each into the target variable picked from the **Repeat Using Variable** drop-down list. The program names are returned as uppercase strings.

On your computer, these running processes are found in the Windows *Task Manager* dialog.

The following macro launches the Windows Notepad application and then grabs each program name running on your computer (alphabetically) then stuffs it into the **T1** variable and displays it.

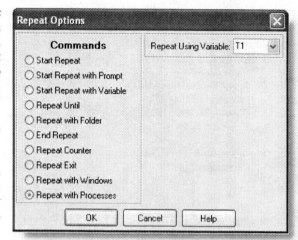

```
Activate or Launch: "Notepad" OR "notepad.exe"    // Launch Notepad
Repeat with Processes: Place process in %T1%       // Stuff T1 with next name
    Text Type: %T1%<ENTER>                          // Display it in Notepad
Repeat End                                         // End of processing loop
```

By the way, these programs are the same ones accessed by the **Select** button in the *If Program* command dialogs. See the *Windows and Programs* chapter for more information on the *If Program* commands.

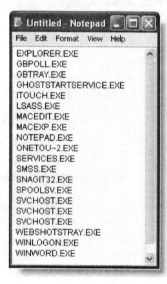

Repeat Counter

This command is no longer supported by Macro Express. By that I mean, it is what it is, and it will never be updated. Here is what the help system says about it:

> **Note: This command is included for backward compatibility only. We recommend that you use the Place Counter in Variable option that is part of the Repeat Start command.**

They are not kidding because I find the command does not work with the newer *Repeat with Windows* and *Repeat with Processes* commands. They remain intact for all the other repeat commands such as the *Repeat Start*, *Repeat with Variable*, *Repeat Until*, and *Repeat with Folder*. It is still a valid command so here goes ...

The *Repeat Counter* command is not a repeat loop like the *Repeat Start* and *Repeat Until* commands. Instead, it is a command placed *inside* a *Repeat* loop like the *Repeat Exit* or *Break* commands, or for that matter any other command.

You must be very careful to know what is going to be on your screen, and where your cursor will be, when this command engages.

Its sole purpose is to increment an internal counter each time though a loop and type it out. The first time through the loop a "1" is typed, the second time through a "2", the third time a "3", and so forth. Whatever the current value is, will be typed out *if possible*. Nothing is typed out unless your cursor is located in a field that accepts text when this command runs. The loop will simply keep repeating.

The **Counter Width** field is used to place leading zeroes in the typed string. The value entered is what the width of the string is to be when it is typed. Only literal values 1, 2, 3, and 4 are accepted as input. Anything else results in a design time error message. Say, for example, you enter a "3" into the **Counter Width** field. The first time through the loop a "001" is typed, the second time through a "002" is typed; the third time a "003", and so forth. So, the largest counter number that can be generated with a leading zero is 999 ("0999").

This does not mean, however, that 999 is the largest counter number that can be generated by looping, only that it is the largest with leading zeros. I have not tested the maximum value that may be generated, but I suspect that it is the largest integer variable that Macro Express allows, which is 2,147,483,647.

The *Repeat Counter* command can be used inside nested *Repeat* commands because each one generates its own internal counter. Here is a simple example of this command using the windows Notepad application to receive the output.

```
Activate or Launch: "Notepad" OR "notepad.exe"   // Launch Notepad
Repeat Start (Repeat 10 times)                   // Loop ten times
  Repeat Counter: Width 3                        // Use leading zeros
  Text Type: <ENTER>                             // Separate the numbers
Repeat End                                       // End of the repeat loop
```

Repeat with Folder

See the *Files and Folders* chapter.

Repeat with Windows

See the *Windows and Programs* chapter.

Multiple Choice Menu

This command enables the user to make a choice, or multiple choices, from a dialog menu. Something like this:

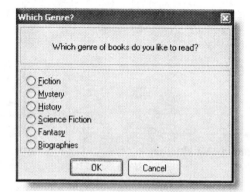

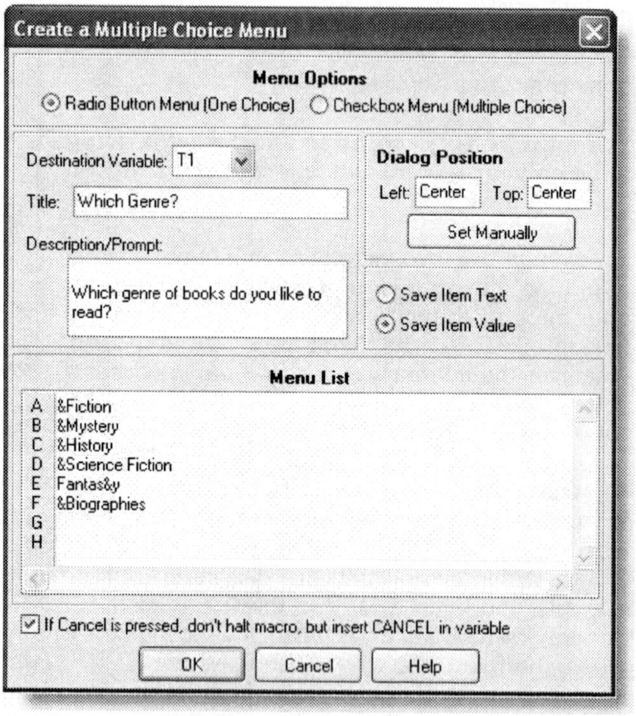

At runtime, the above example asks users to choose which books they like to read. It was generated by the *Create a Multiple Choice Menu* dialog shown to the right.

There are two different types of menus that can be generated. Single-choice and multiple-choice. The above example is a single-choice menu, which means the user can only pick one of the choices presented to them. To create this style of menu, choose the **Radio Button Menu** option at the top of the dialog, which is the default choice. A multiple-choice menu allows the user to pick more than one of the choices presented. To create this style of menu, choose the **Checkbox Menu** option at the top of the dialog. The runtime dialog, as pictured below, changes from using radio buttons to checkboxes.

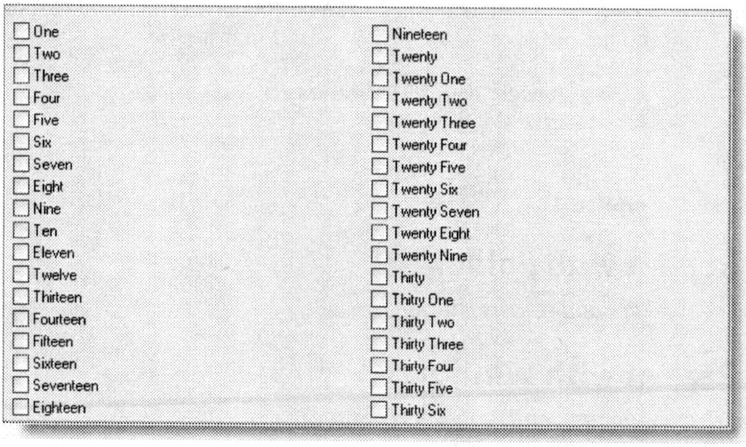

In the **Menu List** field, there are 36 lines, which are numbered **A - Z** and **0 - 9**. Each line stores a choice for the user. This is what it looks like when all 36 lines are filled. Variables can be used in place of literal values when entering choices.

Use the ampersand (**&**) to give the user the ability to choose an option by a single character called an "accelerator key". Place it in front of any character that is to be underlined at runtime.

Whichever underlined character is pressed on the keyboard, that is the option that will be chosen. The example shows the "&Fiction", "&Mystery", and "&History" lines can be chosen by simply pressing the "**F**", "**M**", or "**H**" keys on the keyboard. Be careful not to duplicate the underlined keys in the menu choices because only the first one in the list will be recognized at runtime. If, for example, "Fantas&y" were to be rewritten as "&Fantasy", then it could never be chosen at runtime because the "F" key already belongs to the "&Fiction" line. Also, the ampersand becomes part of the text, like any other character in the string. This becomes important if you choose the **Save Item Text** option, which will be explained in a moment.

No matter which menu style, **Radio Button Menu** (single) or **Checkbox Menu** (multiple) is needed for a particular application, the results from the user's choices are stored in the target variable contained in the **Destination Variable** drop-down list. But what, exactly, is stored in the variable when the choices are made and the **OK** button is clicked? It depends on three things:

1. Which menu style is used, single or multiple.
2. What data is to be saved, **Item Text** or **Item Value.**
3. What to do if the **Cancel** button is clicked instead of **OK.**

The **Save Item Value** options, which is the default choice, stores the letter or number of the user's pick to the target variable. If a user were to choose the "Fantasy" option from our sample, then the target variable would be set to "E". The **Save Item Text** options stores the menu choice itself to the target variable. If a user were to choose the "Fantasy" option from our sample, then the target variable would be set to "Fantas&y". Remember that, if used, the ampersand becomes part of the text.

The same holds true for multiple-choice menus (the **Checkbox Menu** option). For the **Save Item Value** option, if a user were to check both the "Mystery" and "Fantasy" boxes, then the target variable would be set to "BE". Each choice is appended to the target variable string. For the **Save Item Text** option, the target variable would be set to "&MysteryFantas&y".

The **If Cancel is Pressed** checkbox (below the **Menu List** field) instructs Macro Express what to do if the user clicks on the **Cancel** button at runtime. If you leave the box unchecked, and if the user clicks the **Cancel** button, then the macro simply stops running at that point. If, on the other hand, this is option is checked, then the target variable will be set to "CANCEL", and the macro continues running. This feature gives you, the developer, control over what to do next rather than letting the user stop the macro.

```
Repeat Until %N1% <> %N1%            // Infinite loop begin
  Variable Set String %T1% ""        // Erase the T1 string each time through
  Multiple Choice Menu: Which Genre? // Ask the user for a book genre
  If Variable %T1% = "CANCEL"        // If the user clicked on the Cancel button then
    If Message: "Quit"               // ask if user really wants to quit, and if so
      Macro Return                   // quit
    End If                           // End asking user intentions
  Else                               // Otherwise, the user made a choice and clicked the OK button, so
    Replace "&" with "" in %T1%      // Remove the ampersand from the user's pick
    Repeat Exit                      // Exit the infinite loop
  End If                             // End of testing user input string
Repeat End                           // End of infinite loop
```

The above macro is a modified version of the one shown in the *Repeat Until* command. If the user picks a book genre and clicks on the **OK** button, the ampersand is removed from the choice, then the loop is exited (third line from the bottom) and no further processing takes place. On the other hand, if the user clicks the **Cancel** button, then the macro prompts the user for his or her intentions. If they clicked on **Cancel** by mistake, this gives them the opportunity to retry. The following table summarizes what the target variable will be set to at runtime based on the *Multiple Choice Menu* dialog options.

	Save Item Value option	**Save Item Text** option
Radio Button (single)	"A", "B", "C", "D", "E", or "F"	"&Fiction", "&Mystery", "&History", and so forth
Checkbox (multiple)	"ABCDEF"	"&Fiction&Mystery&History ..."
Cancel button pressed	"CANCEL"	"CANCEL"

If you want to set a "default" choice that will automatically be selected when the runtime dialog runs, then simply set the target variable to that value before running the menu. Let's say that you want "Science Fiction" to be the default choice.

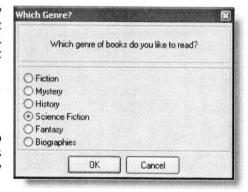

> **Variable Set String %T1% "D"**   // Set default choice to "D"
> **Multiple Choice Menu: Which Genre?**   // Ask user for book genre

The above sample assumes the runtime menu is a **Radio Button Menu** (single pick) and the **Save Item Value** option was chosen. Notice how the "Science Fiction" choice is already picked when the dialog runs.

The **Title** field stores the window title of the runtime dialog and may contain a literal string, variable, or a combination of both.

The **Description/Prompt** field stores the question you are presenting to the user and may contain a literal string, variables, or a combination of both. A literal string is limited to 256 characters, which will create about 6 lines of text. Each line is independently centered within the field. If you need more sentences to explain what you want the user to pick, then use a variable. The runtime dialog expands to fit the variable length. There is sure to be a practical limit of how much information is placed into this field, but I have not tested for it.

Macro Express also gives you the ability to place the dialog anywhere you choose on the user's screen at runtime. The **Left** field, **Top** field, and **Set Manually** buttons are used for this placement. The **Set Manually** button will give you access to the system-wide *Dialog Positioner* screen explained in detail within the *Dialog Positioner* section of the *Variables* chapter. The choices made from this dialog are placed into the **Left** and **Top** fields for you.

There are no options to set the runtime dialog size. The size is calculated internally by Macro Express based on the number of choices on the menu as well as the length of each menu choice. The maximum length of a menu line varies. If it is too long, it will simply be cutoff from the dialog. Normally you will be safe with a line consisting of less than 50 characters.

Text Box Display
Text Box Close

The *Display a Text Box* dialog is used to generate an informational text box that can be launched and displayed at runtime.

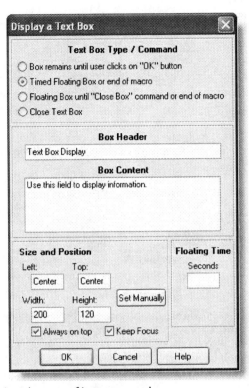

Macro Express provides three ways to close the text box after it is launched and lists them in the **Text Box Type / Command** section at the top. Depending on the option you choose, the text box remains open until:

1. User clicks the **OK** button.
2. The preset timer elapses.
3. A *Close Text Box* command is encountered.

The text box will close automatically whenever the macro stops.

At runtime, if you generate a text box using the first option (**Box remains until user clicks on "OK" button**), the macro will wait until the user clicks **OK** before it continues processing the rest of its commands.

For the second option (**Timed Floating Box or end of macro**), the text box is launched and processing continues while it is being displayed. The text box remains open until the timer lapses or the macro ends. The timer is set using the **Seconds** field in the **Floating Time** section. The allowable range is 1 through 999 seconds (over 16 minutes). This field also accepts integer variables, which can be used if you want the timer to run beyond 999 seconds.

For the third option (**Floating Box until "Close Box" command or end of macro**), the text box is launched, and processing continues while it is displayed. The text box remains open until a matching *Text Box Close* command is encountered or the macro ends.

Multiple text boxes can be displayed at the same time, even those from the third option requiring a *Text Box Close* command to terminate. If you do this, you will need to have a matching *Text Box Close* command for each of them. By "matching" I mean the window caption in the **Box Header** fields must match.

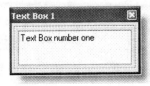

Text Box Display: Text Box 1	// Launch first text box
Text Box Display: Text Box 2	// Launch second text box
Delay 2 Seconds	// Wait for 2 seconds
Text Box Close: Text Box 1	// Close the first text box
Delay 2 Seconds	// Wait another 2 seconds
Text Box Close: Text Box 2	// Close the second text box

The above macro launches and closes two text boxes. The **Box Header** field in each of the *Text Box Close* commands instructs which text box to close. In this case *Text Box 1* is closed first and then *Text Box 2*. The order that they are closed does not matter. However, the **Box Header** field must be an exact match and it *is* case sensitive. The field accepts literal string values, string variables, or a combination of both.

If your macro uses an empty, or blank, **Box Header** field, then the text boxes will be closed in the order they were launched.

Text Box Display:	// Launch first text box
Text Box Display:	// Launch second text box
Text Box Display:	// Launch third text box
Delay 2 Seconds	// Wait for 2 seconds
Text Box Close:	// Close the first text box
Delay 2 Seconds	// Wait another 2 seconds
Text Box Close:	// Close the second text box
Delay 2 Seconds	// Wait for 2 seconds
Text Box Close:	// Close the third text box

Text boxes can also be closed if the user clicks on the [**X**] in the upper-right-hand corner. This is true for any of the three text box options. In other words, you as a developer cannot force a text box to remain on the screen if the user wants it closed.

You do, however, have control over if the text box gains focus when it is launched and/or is forced to always be on top of the window stack. The **Keep Focus** checkbox, if checked (the default), tells Macro Express to set focus to the text box after it launches. If the box is left unchecked, focus will be set back to whichever window had focus when the text box was launched. In other words, focus will be set to the text box for launching and then set back to the other window afterwards.

The **Always on Top** checkbox, if checked, will force the text box to always be on top of all other windows on the stack, even those that may have already been set to remain on top. It has nothing to do with "focus". A window may be on top of all other windows while another one below it retains focus. Even though the default is unchecked, use this option to be sure the user sees the text box when it launches. Without it, the text box may launch behind another window and the user will never see your instructions until it is too late.

If you launch the three text boxes in the last macro example with the **Always on Top** checkbox checked, then the command will appear to have failed because they can be positioned on top of each other. However, other windows on your display will remain behind them. In other words, the three text boxes will remain on top of all other windows in the stack, except for themselves.

Macro Express also gives you the ability to place the dialog anywhere you choose on the user's screen at runtime. The **Left** field, **Top** field, and **Set Manually** buttons are used for this placement. The **Set Manually** button will give you access to the system-wide *Dialog Positioner* screen explained in detail within the *Dialog Positioner* section of the *Variables* chapter. The choices made from this dialog are placed into the **Left** and **Top** fields for you.

The **Width** and **Height** fields are used to set the size of the runtime dialog and will accept any value between 1 and 999,999. If you enter values that are greater than your display size, then the **Box Content** field will be expanded to take up your whole screen, but the titlebar and **OK** button may be inaccessible. These fields will accept integer variables. You may also resize the dialog from the *Dialog Positioner* screen, which is accessed with the **Set Manually** button. Simply resize the dialog with your mouse like any other window, then click the **Save** button. The width and height will be placed into the **Width** and **Height** fields for you.

The **Box Content** field holds the message that you are conveying to the user. It will accept both literal values and variables. The maximum *literal* text length allowed for the **Box Content** field is about 65,500 characters depending on the length of the rest of the command in its native form. Anything over this amount will be truncated. This limit does *NOT* apply if you are using a variable such as %T1% to display a message, although the longer the message, the longer it takes Macro Express to prepare it for display. On my computer 1,000,000 characters takes about 15 seconds before it is displayed in the **Box Content** field.

Vertical elevator bars are used at runtime if the text is more than the dialog size can display in a single screen. There are no text formatting options available.

Here is a section of code from the free Pop-N-Pass macro library, which is available on the Macro Express web site.

```
Variable Set Integer %N21% from Screen Height      // Set the screen height
Variable Modify Integer: %N21% = %N21% / 2         // Set the middle of the screen
Variable Modify Integer: %N1% = %N21% - 270        // Subtract height of text box
Repeat Until %N1% <> %N1%                          // Infinite repeat loop
  Variable Set String %T1% "A"                     // Set the default menu choice
  Text Box Display:  Pop-N-Pass ©                  // Display the text box
  Multiple Choice Menu:  Pop-N-Pass ©              // Display the menu
  Text Box Close:  Pop-N-Pass ©                    // Close the text box now that a choice was made
  Switch (T1)                                      // What did the user choose?
   Case: A                                         // In case the user picked the Window option, then
    Variable Set Integer %N11% to 2                // Set the value for the Window option
    Repeat Exit                                    // Exit the infinite repeat loop
   End Case                                        //End of this test
   Case: B                                         // In case the user picked the Control option, then
    Variable Set Integer %N11% to 3                // Set the value for the Control option
    Repeat Exit                                    // Exit the infinite repeat loop
   End Case                                        //End of this test
   Case: CANCEL                                    // In case the user pressed CANCEL, then
    If Message: "Cancel?"                          // Ask user if they really do want to cancel, if so then
     Macro Return                                  // Quit
    End If                                         // End of user prompt
   End Case                                        // End of this test
  End Switch                                       // End of testing what user has chosen
Repeat End                                         // End of the infinite repeat loop
```

The *Display a Text Box* and the *Create a Multiple Choice Menu* dialogs used to create the **Text Box Display** and **Multiple Choice Menu** commands are shown here:

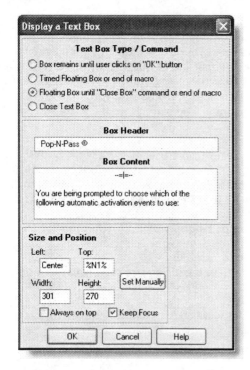

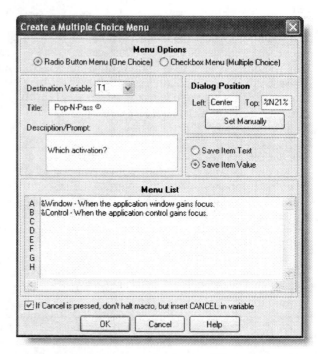

The picture on the right was taken from my Desktop when the above example was run. The demarcation line between the **Text Box** and **Multiple Choice Menu** is the center of my display screen. This is a great way to impart more information to the user than can be placed in just the menu. You need to know where the centerline of your screen is and the height of the text box to subtract, which is what the first three lines of the program do.

An infinite repeat loop is used so the user has a chance to redo their pick in case the **Cancel** button is accidentally chosen.

The first three lines inside the loop set the default menu choice, launches the text box, and then launches the menu. The rest of the code parses what the user has chosen.

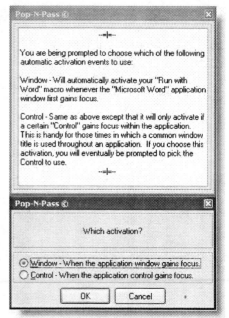

Pause

Macro Express allows a macro to be paused. It will wait forever for a user to click on the **Resume** button (or the macro's HotKey again) to start back up. There are two different **Pause** commands that can be generated from the *Pause Window* dialog.

The first is **Basic Pause**, which has no options to position the runtime dialog and no message field. When the **Basic Pause** command runs, the dialog is positioned in the upper-left-hand corner of the user's display (**0,0**). Period.

The second is the **Complex Pause**, which allows you to set where it will be displayed at runtime. The **Left Coordinate** field, **Top Coordinate** field, and **Set Manually** buttons are used for this placement. The **Set Manually** button will give you access to the system-wide *Dialog Positioner* screen explained in detail within the *Dialog Positioner* section of the *Variables* chapter. The choices made from this dialog are placed into the **Left Coordinate** and **Top Coordinate** fields for you.

The **Keep Focus** checkbox, if checked (the default), tells Macro Express to set focus to the *Macro Paused* dialog after it launches. If the box is left unchecked, focus will be set back to whichever window had it when the dialog was launched. In other words, focus will be set to the runtime dialog for launching and then set back to the other window afterwards.

The **Message** field stores a message to display at runtime and may contain a literal string, variable, or a combination of both. The message is limited to 4 lines of text and each line is independently centered within the field.

Once the runtime dialog is displayed, the macro can be started back up in any of three different ways.

1. Click or press the **Resume** button.
2. Engage the macro's HotKey again (if it has one).
3. Engage the system-wide **Resume Pause** HotKey (**Ctrl-Alt-Shft-Y**).

Clicking or pressing the **Abort** button halts the macro.

Summary

- Macro Express contains logic commands that help structure your macro.
- Compare variables to other variables or literal values
- Determine which operating system the user is running.
- Ask the user questions and, based on the answers, run specific macros.
- Allow the user make choices from a menu.
- Display messages to the user.

Variables

Without variables, Macro Express would not be an easy, or for that matter, practical application to use for any major endeavor. Somewhere along the line, you will begin to use them, if you have not done so already, because they enable you to create *dynamic* and *reusable* macros. Dynamic macros can *adjust* themselves based on choices made by the person running it. Reusable macros are run repeatedly by other macros by the use of the **Macro Run** command.

A variable is simply an object, which holds a value that, for whatever reason, you may want to change within your macro. What values do they hold? Any value. They are called variables for this very reason. How about an example?

Activate or Launch: "Notepad" OR "Notepad.exe"	// Launch the Window Notepad program
Wait For Window Title: "Notepad"	// Wait until it launches and gains focus
Text Type: The quick brown fox jumps over the lazy dog	// Type something into it

This macro launches the Notepad program and types a sentence into it. However, what if the brown fox were to change its color to say, red? You would need to change the last line of your macro.

Text Type: The quick red fox jumps over the lazy dog	// Type something into it

Maybe the dog was not lazy, but was simply sleeping.

Text Type: The quick red fox jumps over the sleeping dog	// Type something into it

This could go on of course, but using variables in your macro will prevent having to change this line of code each time a different fox comes along or the dog wakes up.

Variable Set String %T1% "brown"	// Which fox?
Variable Set String %T2% "lazy"	// A dog's life
Activate or Launch: "Notepad" OR "Notepad.exe"	// Launch the Window Notepad program
Wait For Window Title: "Notepad"	// Wait until it launches and gains focus
Text Type: The quick %T1% fox jumps over the %T2% dog	// Type something into it

Here is the output that results from three different changes to the two variables:

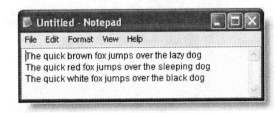

Variable Set String %T1% "brown"	
Variable Set String %T2% "lazy"	
Variable Set String %T1% "red"	
Variable Set String %T2% "sleeping"	
Variable Set String %T1% "white"	
Variable Set String %T2% "black"	

When working with variables, the above example is as basic as one can get because there is a surprising number of tasks they can do, not the least of which is running a macro.

So besides the above example, how do you store or populate variables with information? There are many different ways:

Variable Set String %T1% from Prompt	// Prompt the user for a value
Variable Set String %T1% from Clipboard	// Set a value from the clipboard
Variable Set String %T1% from File: "Data.txt"	// Set a value from a file on your hard drive
Variable Set String %T1% from INI File	// Set a value from an INI file
Variable Set String %T1% from Environment Variable	// Set a value from your environment space

We will examine these commands in detail, plus many more, later in this chapter.

Once variables are populated, they can be used to manipulate other variables and their values. In other words, you can use variables to structure macros logically.

If Variable %N1% = 1	// If the variable N1 is equal to 1 then
Variable Set String %T1% "brown"	// the fox is brown
Else	// or else
Variable Set String %T1% "red"	// the fox is red
End If	// End of structure

As with most scripting languages, variables are surrounded by percent signs, which set them apart from the rest of the command line. In fact, when Macro Express processes a command line, it replaces any variables found (and the surrounding percent signs) with the values stored by the variables. If you have a tough time with the concept of variables, just think of them as shorthand, which will be replaced with something else when the macro runs.

Types of Variables

Macro Express supports string, integer, decimal, window control, and environment variables. The first three types are standard fair that should be familiar to most of you; the last two however, are different. Environment variables are strings that you can name yourself. Window control variables store information about window objects, but will not be covered here because they have their own *Window Controls* chapter where they are discussed in detail.

String Variables

These store text and can contain anything within the range of nothing, to *The Decline and Fall of the Roman Empire*. There are no actual length limits to string variables, but there are both practical limits and limits outside the control of Macro Express such as hard drive space, environment space and Registry limits. All string variables begin with the letter **"T"** and are numbered **1** through **99** (**T1** through **T99**).

Integer Variables

These are whole numbers (numbers containing no decimals) within a 4gb (gigabyte) range. A gigabyte is 4,294,967,296 characters, or bytes. Because they are 32-bit *signed* integers, which means that negative values are allowed, their values can range between -2,147,483,648 ($2^{-32/2}$) and 2,147,483,647 ($2^{(32/2)-1}$). In other words, 2gb on either side of zero. All integer variables begin with the letter **"N"** and are numbered **1** through **99** (**N1** through **N99**).

Decimal Variables

These are decimal numbers ranging from 5×10^{-324} through 1.7×10^{308} with 15 significant digits. This means a negative 5 with 323 trailing zeros on the low-end and a 17 with 307 trailing zeros on the high-end. What does this mean for you? Well most importantly is that you can have numbers containing up to 14 decimal places. For example, Macro Express can calculate the value of *Pi* to be 3.14159265358979, which is 14 decimal places plus the whole number, which are 15 significant digits. If your macros are going to be handling large values then you will need to learn about *exponential notation*, which is outside the scope of this book. Macro Express displays any decimal-only values, like 1E-5 (.00001) and under, in exponential format. However, values such as 1.00000000000001 are still displayed normally. All decimal variables begin with the letter **"D"** and are numbered **1** through **99** (**D1** through **D99**).

Environment Variables

These are special string-type variables, and what wonderful ones they are! You can create and name your own variables over-and-above the native **T1** through **T99** strings. They are stored within the environment space in your computer's memory, which of course has limits. For Windows '95, '98, and Me, the default maximum environment space available is 4,096 bytes (4kb). So this is more than limiting however, on Windows NT, 2000, and XP, the maximum space is 32,768 (32kb) for each user. Some of this space is already used by your operating system to keep information about system paths, your computer, networking environment, and you. This is done whenever you turn your computer on, or switch users. Nevertheless, even with a limited amount of space great things are still possible! How about these examples? **%Secret Identity%** ="Clark Kent", **%Truly Bad Stuff%** ="Kryptonite", **%Truly Good Stuff%** ="Lois Lane". All of which can be used in most places the native **T1** through **T99** variables are used. There is a section devoted to using environment variables towards the end of this chapter.

Scope of Variables

You have just learned that Macro Express provides 297 native variables named **T1**, **N1**, **D1**, and so forth. What you may not realize, is that they are *global* in scope. While running a macro (a "macro session"), any variable created anywhere, any time, in any macro, can be seen, accessed, changed, and used, from any other macro called (run) with the **Macro Run** command. From a programming point-of-view, this can be both good and bad, depending on what you are trying to do. For example, what if you have created a really neat, reusable macro that contains a couple of variables, say **T1** and **N1**, which can be called by any other macro in your library? Then you should expect that, because of the global nature of variables, any variables with the same name in your *main macro* would be overwritten by the ones in the called *really neat macro*. If this sounds confusing, then let me illustrate the point because it is easier to picture than it is to explain it.

```
// Main macro
Variable Set String %T1% "Professional Grade Macros"    // Store a value to T1
Variable Set Integer %N1% to 100                        // Store a value to N1
Macro Run: Really Neat Macro                            // Call the really neat macro that you created
Text Type: T1=%T1%                                      // T1 is now "Insight Software Solutions"
Text Type: N1=%N1%                                      // N1 is now 101


// Really neat macro
Variable Set String %T1% "Insight Software Solutions"   // Store a value to T1
Variable Set Integer %N1% to 101                        // Store a value to N1
Macro Return                                            // Return to caller
```

So, what has happened here? Simple. Your first, or main, macro sets the **T1** and **N1** variables to *Professional Grade Macros* and *100* respectively. Then it calls a submacro, which uses the same variable names, but changes them to *Insight Software Solutions* and *101*. Now, this is not what you want because, after all, the variables in your main macro are being changed. We will create macros in this book that will help you to avoid this situation. Meanwhile, remember that within the native Macro Express variable environment there is only a single **T1**, **N1**, and **D1** variable to be accessed by an unlimited number of macros in your library.

Literal Values vs. Variables

Literal values are fixed bits of information that you use when creating a macro. They can be macro names, window titles, program names, web site names, file and folder names, and almost anything else that you can think of.

> **Activate Window: "Notepad"**   // Literal value
> **Activate Window: "%T1%"**   // Variable value

The first command uses a literal value in the window title field while the second command uses a variable. A variable can be substituted for a literal value in almost every Macro Express command that uses values. This, my friends, is the true power of variables, allowing us to create macros that handle the unknown. Not to mention there are so many things in Macro Express that you simply cannot do with literals, like adding two numbers together. Sure, the numbers that you add may be literal, but the result will always be a variable.

> **Variable Modify Integer: %N1% = 12 + 10**   // Arithmetic operations always result in variables

How about simply finding your mouse pointer? Yes, I know it is on your screen, but where?

> **Variable Set Integer %N1% from Mouse X Position**   // Mouse is X pixels from the left of your screen and
> **Variable Set Integer %N2% from Mouse Y Position**   // Y pixels down from the top

Using only literals would also prevent you from gathering and storing input from the user because, just like arithmetic operations, all input text is stored in variables. It is the nature of the beast.

> **Variable Set String %T1% from Prompt**   // Input variable

How about this? You create a macro to type out *Hello World!* and, since you want to be sure that each letter is typed correctly, you put a delay between each one. Seems simple enough.

After running it once you, you immediately recognize that it takes way to long to type … about 11 seconds. Naturally, you could go back through your macro and change all 11 instances of the **Delay Milliseconds** command to something else, say 250 ms (¼ of a second), and hope that it is not too fast. Alternatively, you could simply replace the literal value with a variable, as in the second macro, which would allow you easily to adjust the speed until you find one that suits your needs.

After making the change and running it again, you find it to be better, but still to slow. However, now you only need to change the value of the variable in the **Variable Set Integer** command to speed things up!

```
// Hello World! with a literal value delay
Text Type: H
Delay 1000 Milliseconds
Text Type: e
Delay 1000 Milliseconds
Text Type: l
Delay 1000 Milliseconds
Text Type: l
Delay 1000 Milliseconds
Text Type: o
Delay 1000 Milliseconds
Text Type: <SPACE>
Delay 1000 Milliseconds
Text Type: W
Delay 1000 Milliseconds
Text Type: o
Delay 1000 Milliseconds
Text Type: r
Delay 1000 Milliseconds
Text Type: l
Delay 1000 Milliseconds
Text Type: d
Delay 1000 Milliseconds
Text Type: !
```

Here is an off-the-subject tip: I have run across too many macros created like what you see here. You do not need to use the *Text Type* command in this manner. To type something out, do this instead:

> **Keystroke Speed: 250 Milliseconds** // 250 ms keystroke delay
> **Text Type: Hello<SPACE>World!**   // Type the text

There is a difference in the size of the macro, eh? I should mention that a ¼-second delay between keystrokes is meant to just illustrate a point. I sincerely doubt that you would ever want to watch something be typed that slowly. Watching grass grow would be more exciting!

Back on the subject, these two examples are basic, and are meant to explain that, one-way or another, you will want to, or have to, use variables when working with Macro Express.

```
// Hello World! with a variable delay
Variable Set Integer %N1% to 250
Text Type: H
Delay %N1% Milliseconds
Text Type: e
Delay %N1% Milliseconds
Text Type: l
Delay %N1% Milliseconds
Text Type: l
Delay %N1% Milliseconds
Text Type: o
Delay %N1% Milliseconds
Text Type: <SPACE>
Delay %N1% Milliseconds
Text Type: W
Delay %N1% Milliseconds
Text Type: o
Delay %N1% Milliseconds
Text Type: r
Delay %N1% Milliseconds
Text Type: l
Delay %N1% Milliseconds
Text Type: d
Delay %N1% Milliseconds
Text Type: !
```

Common Variable Dialogs

The process of adding a variable command line to your macro is handled through dialogs. While in the Scripting Editor, you pick a command from the category list on the left, causing a dialog window to appear, which in turn allows you to define your choice in detail. Which dialog appears, what your choices are, and which, if any, other dialogs appear, all depend on the command line that you are trying to add. However, within all of these different dialogs, you will see some commonality. For example, all dialogs present you with a drop-down list for choosing which of the variables you are targeting. Commands that will prompt the user for information at runtime present you with a positioning dialog used to tell the macro where it is to be placed on the screen at runtime.

Drop-Down List

Naturally, any dialog that concerns variable commands will need to know which variable, or variables, you are targeting. You will nearly always choose the variable through a drop-down list similar to the one you see here, which is for string variables.

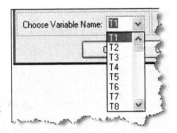

The field names for drop-down lists change depending on which dialog you are using and the action that you are taking. **Choose Variable Name, Variable to Copy from, Variable to Copy to,** and **Variable to Trim**, are only some of the different field names you will encounter.

Some dialogs contain more than one drop-down list, as when you are copying one variable to another, adding two variables together, or concatenating variables. These specify source and target variables.

Most of the time, a drop-down list will display only one variable type: string, integer, or decimal. However, there are certain arithmetic commands that display more than one type within the same drop-down list. Adding an integer and a decimal together is a good example.

Dialog Positioner

As your macro projects progress, there will inevitably come a point that you need to get the user's input during runtime. Their name, a filename, a value … anything. Of course, Macro Express has dialog commands available. What you must do is to tell Macro Express where to place them on the user's screen during runtime, which is done through the dialog positioner … dialog.

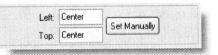

Look at the pictures here on the right. The top picture, or something similar, is part of the dialog that you see when working with the *Prompt for String, Prompt for Integer,* or *Prompt for Decimal* commands. All of which need runtime-positioning information for the picture on the next page. This picture is the input dialog the user interacts with during runtime. The two fields, **Left** and **Top**, will hold the position of the dialog when you are finished. What you see in these two fields depends on what you do to position the dialog. There are three choices:

1. Enter literal, variable, or coordinates, into the two fields.
2. Click on the **Set Manually** button and then use the Dialog Positioner dialog.

3. Click on the **Set Manually** button and then drag the target runtime dialog (this picture) around with your mouse.

Literal Coordinates

Coordinates on your screen are measured in pixels moving left to right (horizontally) in the *X direction* and top to bottom (vertically) in the *Y direction*. The top-left corner of your screen is 0,0 while the bottom-right corner is whatever your screen size is minus 1. Why minus1? Well, coordinates are positions, not sizes, and your screen uses a zero numbering coordinate system, which is why your top-left corner is 0,0 and not 1,1. In my case the bottom-right coordinates of my screen are 1279,1023.

By entering a literal value in the **Left** field, you are telling Macro Express to position the left-hand side of the runtime dialog at that pixel location on the screen. The same logic applies when entering a literal value into the **Top** field. Here though, you are referring the top of the runtime dialog as related to the top of your screen. If, for example, you wanted the runtime dialog to be displayed somewhere in the top-left-hand area of your screen, you would enter, say 25, in both fields. At runtime, Macro Express will place the left-hand side of the dialog 25 pixels from the left-hand side of your screen while placing the top of the dialog 25 pixels from the top of your screen.

Variable Coordinates

Any field in any Macro Express command that accepts a literal value, will accept a variable of the appropriate type. So, both the **Left** and **Top** fields accept variables. Take everything that you just read in the above paragraph and substitute the word "variable" for the phrase "literal value".

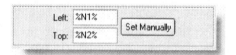

Positional Coordinates

These are words that describe the nine common screen positions, which are more fully explained in the next paragraph. You can manually type coordinates into both the **Left** and **Top** fields. The **Left** field will accept the words **Left**, **Center**, and **Right**. The **Top** field will accept the words **Top**, **Center**, and **Bottom**. In the picture on the previous page, you see the word **Center** is placed in both fields. This is the default and, if left alone, would place the runtime dialog in the center of your screen.

Dialog Positioner

Look again at the *Dialog Positioner* picture on the previous page, which is activated by clicking on the **Set Manually** button in the command dialog. Each button represents one of nine common display positions on your screen. Beginning at noon, and working clockwise, there is **top-center**, **top-right**, **right-center**, **bottom-right**, **bottom-center**, **bottom-left**, **left-center**, **top-left**, and finally just **center**. Simply click on the one that you want and then click the **Save** button. Your choice will be displayed in the **Left** and **Top** fields.

Click-and-Drag

You may also position the runtime dialog by dragging it. Click on the **Set Manually** button in the command dialog then left-click anywhere within the titlebar of the runtime dialog and, while holding down the mouse button, drag the dialog to its position, then release the mouse button. After clicking on the **Save** button, the position will be displayed in the **Left** and **Top** fields.

File-Picker

Another common dialog is the file-picker, which is a real convenience tool. Usually any command that involves a file will present a *File-picker* dialog similar to what is shown here. This example is from the **Set String from File** command. You can either manually type in your target file, or choose it from the picker dialog, which is accessed by clicking on the **ellipses** button (**...**) found next to the **Filename** field. The title of the dialog will change, of course, depending on which command you are working with, as will the file types that you will be allowed to pick.

More likely than not, you are already familiar with how this dialog, or similar ones, work. Just be aware there are plenty of variations to it within Macro Express.

Bypass File Existence Check

This checkbox usually appears when working with a dialog that includes filenames. This is a design time feature for you, the developer. Sometimes when developing macros, the target file will not exist. Maybe it is created at runtime, or maybe it is a file that exists only on the user's computer. If this checkbox is left checked (the default) when you click the **OK** button, the editor will not check for the file in the **Filename** field. However, if you uncheck the box, and if the file does not exist you will be warned.

String Variable Commands

As you have already discovered, every command in Macro Express can use a variable in place of a literal value. This is especially true with string variables. After all, macro names, window titles, programs, web sites, file and folder names, and almost anything else you can think of, are by nature, text strings. Therefore, string variables will have a greater impact on your macro than any other type.

Like most other commands, string variable commands are chosen from a dialog of like, or common, commands. These dialogs pop up the instant that you choose a command from the category list while in the Scripting Editor. Naturally, these dialogs differ from one to another. *Set Text String Variables*, *Modify String Variables*, *Variable Set from File*, and *Read/Write Registry Value* all have different dialogs.

Set Text String Variables

Before you can use them, you need to create them, so let's discover how by first examining the commands within the *Set Text String Variables* dialog on the right. We will then look into other commands in other dialogs that also create string variables.

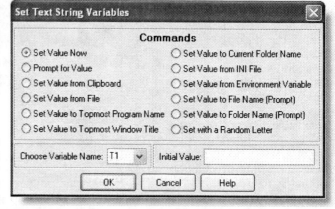

Set Value Now

Use this command to stuff a variable with a value. Start by using the **Choose Variable Name** drop-down list to choose your target variable, and then enter either a literal value or a variable into the **Initial Value** field. You do not need to pick the variable first. As with any of these types of dialogs, you may do anything in any order that works best for you because the command is not written to your macro until after you click the **OK** button.

> **Variable Set String %T1% "The quick brown fox jumps over the lazy dog"**   // Enter a literal value
> **Variable Set String %T1% "%T2%"**   // Enter a variable

Prompt for Value

This command is used when you need to get input from the user at runtime.

The **Prompt Text** field holds instructions for entering information into the field. For example, "Please enter your company name:" There is not an actual limit to the length allowed for your instructions; however, there is a practical limit … the height of your display. You could conceivably enter enough instructions that the dialog is forced off the bottom of your screen.

The **Mask Input** checkbox is used to cover up with asterisks whatever your user is typing, like a password for instance. So, instead of seeing "my secret password", somebody watching would only see "*******************".

The **Prompt Always On Top** checkbox, if used, will force the runtime dialog to always be displayed in front of any other window that may be on your Desktop. This does not mean, however, that it will always have focus, just that it will be on top.

The **Store "CANCEL" if Canceled** checkbox means that your macro will *not* stop if the user clicks the **Cancel** button. Instead, it will place the exact word **CANCEL** in your target variable. This gives you, the developer, a programmatic way to stop the macro by testing the variable's value. You may have some housecleaning to do before stopping a macro, like shutting down some programs, putting the user's Desktop back the way it was, or simply making sure the user wants to cancel the macro. Here is a simple example on how to use this feature:

```
// Enter company name
Repeat Until %N1% <> %N1%                    // Infinite loop
    Variable Set String %T1% ""              // Make sure the input string variable is blank
    Variable Set String %T1% from Prompt     // Prompt the user for a company name
    If Variable %T1% = ""                     // If the input variable is blank
      OR                                      // -or-
    If Variable %T1% = "CANCEL"               // If the user hit the CANCEL button
      If Message: "Cancel?"                   // then ask the user if they want to quit and
        Macro Stop                            // if they do, then quit
      End If                                  // End of message prompt structure
    Else                                      // or else if the user has entered anything else that is valid, then
      Repeat Exit                             // exit out of the loop
    End If                                    // End of CANCEL test structure
Repeat End                                    // End of infinite loop
```

By default, the runtime dialog will be placed in the center of the screen. You can change this by using the **Left** and **Top** fields, or the **Set Manually** button. Please see the *Dialog Positioner* section for more details.

Set Value from Clipboard

This command places whatever text your Windows clipboard currently contains into your target variable.

Macro Express has a special setting in the *Preferences* dialog that forces a delay after any clipboard command, because Windows itself needs extra time to handle the clipboard. The default is 250ms, but you can change this to suit your own needs.

Macro Express handles superlong text strings cleanly and most efficiently! See *Save to Clipboard* within the *Modify String Variables* section for the converse command. For clipboard commands that work with graphics instead of text, see the *Clipboard Graphic Copy* and *Clipboard Save Graphic* commands.

Variable Set String %T1% from Clipboard   // Stuff the T1 variable with whatever is in the Windows clipboard

Set Value from File

Copies the contents of a text file to your target variable. Although there is no actual length limit to the text file, you are sure to run in to a practical limit by taking on something too big. So, what is too big?

That is a personal choice. On my computer, which is not the newest thing out there, I can stuff a variable with a 100mb file, and search for a character string (that I know is at the end), in less than a single second.

Use the **Filename** field to enter which file you are targeting to read into the variable in the **Choose Variable Name** field. You can also use the file-picker **ellipses** button, which sits next to the field. For more information on this dialog, please see the *File-Picker* dialog section.

The **Strip Trailing CR/LF** checkbox is used to remove all *carriage return+line feed* character sequences from the text file as it is read into your target variable. Just in case you do not know what these are, they separate paragraphs in a file within the Windows operating system. In other words, they are the characters that are placed in your text file whenever you hit the *Enter* key on your keyboard.

You can use the **Bypass File Existence Check** checkbox to ignore the filename. Please review the *Common Variable Dialogs* section about this checkbox. See *Save to Text File* within the *Modify String Variables* section for the converse command.

Variable Set String %T1% from File: "Example.txt"   // Stuff the T1 variable with whatever is in the Example.txt file

Set Value to Topmost Program Name

This will stuff your target variable with the filename and extension of whichever program has focus at the point-in-time the command is encountered. It only stuffs the filename and extension and not the program path, in other words *Notepad.exe* and not *C:\Windows\Notepad.exe*. The filename is always written to the variable in an *uppercase* format. Please note the program name returned by this command is the one that has focus, which *may not* be the program that you see on the top of the stack as you look at your screen.

Variable Set String %T1% from Program Name   // Stuff the T1 variable with the program name that has focus

Set Value to Topmost Window Title

This will stuff your target variable with the window title of whichever program has focus at the point-in-time the command is encountered. Please note the window title returned by this command is for the program that has focus, which *may not* be the window that you see on the top of the stack as you look at your screen.

Variable Set String %T1% from Window Title   // Stuff the T1 variable with the window title that has focus

Set Value to Current Folder Name

Use this command to get the current folder (directory) name that your operating system reports you are located in, and place it in your target variable. More than likely, when you first start Macro Express your location will be the Macro Express home folder, something like *C:\Program Files\Macro Express*. The value written to the variable is a Windows full path name without the trailing backslash character.

For those of us old enough to fondly remember *DOS* and yes, *CP/M*, this is nostalgic. Back then, it was important to know where you were located on your hard drive, what folder, or directory you were located in. With Windows, though, it is not that important. However, there are sure to be programs out there that need you to be in a particular folder to work properly. Using this command will tell you if you are there, or not.

```
Variable Set String %T1% from Current Folder Name    // Store the current folder name to the T1 variable
If Variable %T1% <> "c:\My Client's Folder"          // If I am not in my client's folder then
   Change Directory/Folder: "c:\My Client's Folder"  // switch to it now
End If                                                // End of If test
```

Set Value from INI File

Well, the first question here is "what is an INI file"? It is not a file at all, but rather a filename extension used in Windows. It is an acronym, more or less, for *initialization*. INI files are used to initialize, or set parameters for programs. Of course, the Windows Registry has mostly taken this

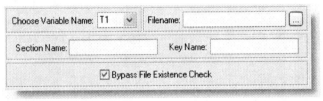

task over since the release of Windows '95, so these are hardly used anymore. Nevertheless "hardly used" does not mean "never used".

An INI file contains *values* stored in *keys*, which are separated into *sections*. If this sounds familiar, and it should, then you are thinking "Registry", and you would be correct.

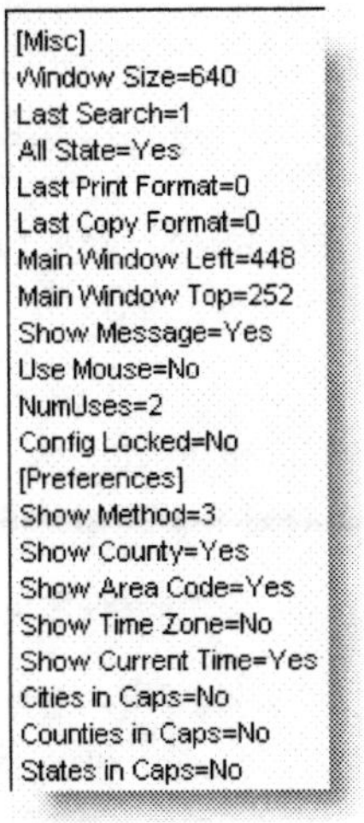

Here is a partial view of these sections, keys, and values from my *Zip Express* INI file. The 1st and 13th line **[Misc]** and **[Preferences]** are both section names, the rest of the lines are the keys and values within each section. Blank lines, although allowed, are not shown here, however, everybody has personal preferences and some developers will separate sections with a blank line to make the file easier to read. Let's say that I wanted to set variable **T1** to whatever value is stored by the *Window Size* key, I would set the fields in the dialog like the picture below.

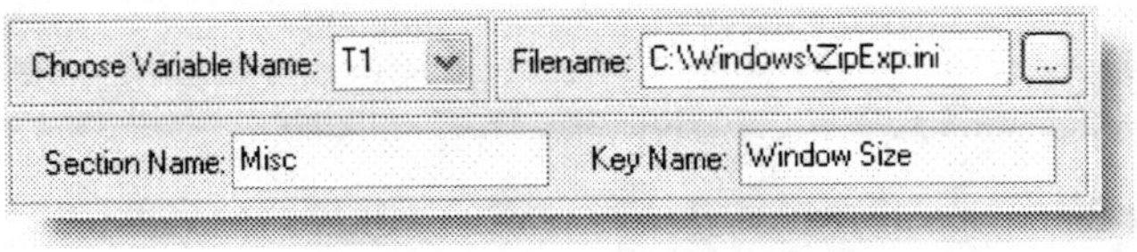

```
[Misc]
Window Size=640
Last Search=1
All State=Yes
Last Print Format=0
Last Copy Format=0
Main Window Left=448
Main Window Top=252
Show Message=Yes
Use Mouse=No
NumUses=2
Config Locked=No
[Preferences]
Show Method=3
Show County=Yes
Show Area Code=Yes
Show Time Zone=No
Show Current Time=Yes
Cities in Caps=No
Counties in Caps=No
States in Caps=No
```

Choose Variable Name: T1   Filename: C:\Windows\ZipExp.ini

Section Name: Misc   Key Name: Window Size

Notice the braces "[]" which surround the *section name* in the INI file are not used in the **Section Name** field in the dialog. In addition, all fields are case-insensitive, in other words, case does not matter. If the section or key name cannot be found within the INI file then a blank string is returned. See ***Save to INI File*** within the *Modify*

String Variables section for the converse command.

> **Variable Set String %T1% from INI File**   // Store something from an INI file to the T1 variable

Set Value from Environment Variable

Again, the first question here should be "what are environment variables"? They are variables stored in the environment space in your computer's memory and contain information about your working environment … information such as paths, names, and printers. There is a partial list of mine on the right.

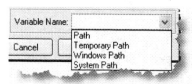

Environment variables are initially set by your computer whenever you login. They are global in scope to other programs, and can be freely accessed by those that have the ability, such as Macro Express. Even though space is limited for environment variables by your operating system, some neat things can be done using them. For now, however, we are simply going to learn how to set string variables with the values that they contain.

The **Variable Name** field is where you enter the environment variable that you are interested in working with. This field also contains a mini drop-down list of some predefined environment variables.

If, for example, I wanted to know what the *ComSpec* environment variable was on my computer, I would simply enter **ComSpec** into the **Variable Name** field. The field is case-insensitive.

ALLUSERSPROFILE=C:\Documents and Settings
APPDATA=C:\Documents and Settings\Joe\Appl
CLIENTNAME=Console
CommonProgramFiles=C:\Program Files\Commor
COMPUTERNAME=XPSERVER
ComSpec=C:\WINDOWS\system32\cmd.exe
HOMEDRIVE=C:
HOMEPATH=\Documents and Settings\Joe
LOGONSERVER=\\XPSERVER
NUMBER_OF_PROCESSORS=1
OS=Windows_NT
Path=C:\WINDOWS\system32;C:\WINDOWS
PATHEXT=.COM;.EXE;.BAT;.CMD;.VBS;.VBE;.JS
PROCESSOR_ARCHITECTURE=x86
PROCESSOR_IDENTIFIER=x86 Family 15 Model 2
PROCESSOR_LEVEL=15
PROCESSOR_REVISION=0207
ProgramFiles=C:\Program Files
PROMPT=PG
SESSIONNAME=Console
SystemDrive=C:
SystemRoot=C:\WINDOWS
TEMP=C:\DOCUME~1\JOE\LOCALS~1\Temp
TMP=C:\DOCUME~1\JOE\LOCALS~1\Temp
USERDOMAIN=XPSERVER
USERNAME=Joe
USERPROFILE=C:\Documents and Settings\Joe
WinDir=C:\WINDOWS

See **Save to Environment Variable** within the *Modify String Variables* section for the converse command.

> **Variable Set String %T1% from Environment Variable**   // Set a string variable from an environment variable

Set Value to File Name (Prompt)

This command places the file-picker in the user's hand at runtime to allow them to choose a file and have its name placed in

the target variable. The value returned is a full-path name. Your only decision is what to name the file-picker when it pops up. Place the window title that you want in the **Title Bar** field.

> **Variable Set String %T1% from File Name**   // Set a string variable from a full-path file name

Set Value to Folder Name (Prompt)

This command places a folder-picker in your user's hands at runtime to allow them to choose a folder and have its name placed in the target variable. The value returned is a full-path name. Unlike the ***Set Value to Folder Name (Prompt)*** command, the **Title Bar** field does not set the runtime window title, but rather it is meant simply for instructions that are placed below the titlebar. Your instructions can take up to two lines before the balance disappears from the instruction area.

  Variable Set String %T1% from Folder Name // Set a string variable from a full-path folder name

Set with a Random Letter

This command places a random letter **A** through **Z** (uppercase only) into the target variable. Nothing else to say about it!

  Variable Set String %T1% to Random Letter // Set a variable to a random letter between A and Z

Modify String Variables

Now let's examine some ways to modify variables. The dialog shown here (Option 1 Tab) and on the next page (Option 2 Tab), hold commands that do more than just "modify", they also save and copy string variables. In addition, this dialog holds converse commands for some of those found in the *Set Text String Variables* section that we just examined.

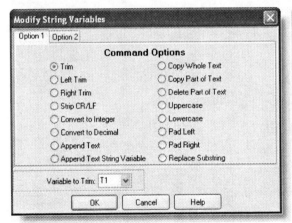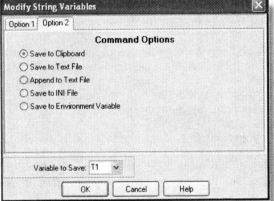

Trim

Strips spaces from both the left and right sides of a string, but not from the middle.

  Variable Set String %T1% " ABC " // Create a text string
  Variable Modify String: Trim %T1% // T1 changed to "ABC"

Left Trim

Strips spaces from just the left side of a string, leaving the right side and middle untouched.

  Variable Set String %T1% " ABC " // Create a text string
  Variable Modify String: Left Trim %T1% // T1 changed to "ABC "

Right Trim

Strips spaces from just the right side of a string, leaving the left side and middle untouched.

> **Variable Set String %T1% " ABC "** // Create a text string
> **Variable Modify String: Right Trim %T1%** // T1 changed to " ABC"

Strip CR/LF

This command is used to remove all *carriage return+line feed* character sequences from a string variable. Just in case you do not know what these are, they separate paragraphs in a file within the Windows operating system. In other words, they are the characters that are placed in your text file whenever you hit the *Enter* key on your keyboard.

> **Variable Set String %T1% "Line1,••Line2,••Line3••"** // Create a string with CR/LF characters
> **Variable Modify String: Strip CR/LF from %T1%** // T1 changed to "Line1,Line2,Line3"

Convert to Integer

Converts a string variable to an integer variable. Use the **Converted Integer** drop-down list to choose the target integer variable to be converted from the **Variable to Convert** drop-down list. Any string can be converted to an integer up to the first character that is not a digit, negative symbol, thousands separator.

Macro Express uses your computer's regional settings (Control Panel | Regional Settings) to determine which characters are used to describe numbers. In other words, which character is used for the negative sign symbol, the thousands separator, and the decimal point symbol.

Any attempt to convert a string that is beyond the allowable integer range (-2,147,483,648 through 2,147,483,647) will be wrong, and there is no runtime error message. The string is truncated to a length that can be converted properly, and then the conversion takes place. For example "3,123,456,789" would be converted to 312,345,678 (the "9" is truncated). The only exception to this is if you convert strings that are only 1 or 2 numbers beyond the allowable limits. These will not be truncated, but instead their values will be wrapped around. By that I mean converting 2,147,483,648, which is 1 greater than the maximum value, will wrap around to -2,147,483,648. The chart shows some different strings and how they are converted.

String	Integer
"-123"	-123
"123abc"	123
"000123abc"	123
"123.456"	123
"-123.456"	-123
"123,456,789"	123456789
"ABC"	zero
"--123"	zero
"1,2,3,4,5,6"	123456
"2,147,483,648"	-2,147,483,648
"2,147,483,649"	-2,147,483,647

> **Variable Set String %T1% "123"** // Create a string
> **Variable Modify String: Convert %T1% to integer %N1%** // Convert

Convert to Decimal

Converts a string variable to a decimal variable. Use the **Converted Decimal** drop-down list to choose the target decimal variable to be converted from the **Variable to Convert** drop-down list.

Any string can be converted to a decimal up to the first character that is not a digit, negative symbol, thousands separator, or decimal point. The chart shows some different strings and how they are converted.

Macro Express uses your computer's regional settings (Control Panel | Regional Settings) to determine which characters are used to describe numbers. In other words, which character is used for the negative sign symbol, the thousands separator, and the decimal point symbol.

String	Decimal
"123.456"	123.456
"-123.456"	-123.456
"123abc.456"	123
".456"	0.456
"000123"	123
"9,123,456.789"	9123456.789
"ABC"	zero
"--123"	zero
"1,2,3,4,5,6"	123456

```
Variable Set String %T1% "123.456"              // Create a string
Variable Modify String: Convert %T1% to decimal %D1%   // Convert
```

Append Text

This command is used to attach a literal text string to the end of a string variable. However, it can also attach a variable to the end of a variable. Use the **Text to Append** field to enter the literal text (or a variable) that you want to append. Also, you are not limited to just entering a string variable to append. An integer or decimal variable is fine also.

```
// Example of appending a literal string
Variable Set String %T1% "The quick"              // Create a string variable
Variable Modify String: Append "brown fox" to %T1%   // Append text to it

// Example of appending an integer variable
Variable Set String %T1% "The value is: "         // Create a string variable
Variable Set Integer %N1% to 10                   // Create an integer variable
Variable Modify String: Append "%N1%" to %T1%     // Append the integer variable to the string variable
```

Append Text String Variable

Use this command to attach one string variable to another. The target variable, or the one to be appended to, is the drop-down list on the left, while the variable that you are going to append from is the drop-down list on the right.

```
Variable Set String %T1% "The quick"          // Create a string variable
Variable Set String %T2% "brown fox"          // Create another string variable
Variable Modify String: Append %T2% to %T1%   // Append the second one to the first
```

Copy Whole Text

Duplicates a string variable. The target variable, or the one to be copied to, is the drop-down list on the left, while the

variable that you are going to copy from is the drop-down list on the right.

> **Variable Set String %T2% "Brown fox"**　　　　// Create a string variable
> **Variable Modify String: Copy %T2% to %T1%**　　// Copy it

Copy Part of Text

Copies part of a string variable. The target variable, or the one to be copied to, is the drop-down list on the left, while the variable that you are going to copy from is the drop-down list on the right. You can copy part of the string, or even the complete string, by controlling values in the **Starting Position** fields and the **Characters**

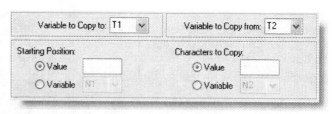

to Copy fields. Both sets of fields accept either literal values (**Value** fields) or variables (**Variable** fields), or a combination of both. They are well protected against bad data entry. An empty text string, a starting position less than 1, and the number characters to copy being greater than the string length are all adjusted to return results that make sense, rather than errors.

Start	Chars	String
0	1,000	exact copy
1,000	0	""
1,000	1,000	""
1	3	"The"
5	11	"quick brown"

The chart shows some different values for the **Starting Position** field and the **Characters to Copy** field, for the string shown in the macro example, and what the copied string would be, based on those values.

> **Variable Set String %T2% "The quick brown fox jumps over the lazy dog"**　　// Create a string variable
> **Variable Modify String: Copy Part of %T2% to %T1%**　　// Copy part of it to

Delete Part of Text

Deletes part of a string variable. You can delete part of the string, or even the complete string, by controlling values in the **Starting Position** fields and the **Characters to Delete** fields. Both sets of fields accept either literal values (**Value** fields) or variables (**Variable** fields), or a combination of both, and are well protected against bad field entries.

An empty text string, a starting position less than 1, and the number characters to delete being greater than the string length, are all adjusted to return results that make sense, rather than errors. The chart shows some different values for the **Starting Position** field and the **Characters to Delete** field, for the string shown in the example Macro Express code, and what, based on those values, the deleted portion would contain.

Start	Chars	String
0	1,000	does nothing
1	1,000	deletes all 43 characters
1,000	0	does nothing (only 43 characters)
1,000	1,000	does nothing (only 43 characters)
1	3	deletes "The"
5	11	deletes "quick brown"

> **Variable Set String %T2% "The quick brown fox jumps over the lazy dog"**   // Create a string variable
> **Variable Modify String: Delete Part of %T2%**   // Delete part of it

Uppercase

Changes the target string variable to all uppercase characters. Nothing more to it than that!

> **Variable Set String %T1% "brown fox"**   // Create a string variable
> **Variable Modify String: Uppercase %T1%**   // Change it to all uppercase characters "BROWN FOX"

Lowercase

Changes the target string variable to all lowercase characters.

> **Variable Set String %T1% "BROWN FOX"**   // Create a string variable
> **Variable Modify String: Lowercase %T1%**   // Change it to all uppercase characters "brown fox"

Pad Left

Adds spaces to just the left side of a string, leaving the right side untouched. The **Width of Text** field is not the number of spaces to

add, but rather what the target variable length should be *after* adding the spaces. If you enter a value that is less than the original string variable width, then the string will not be changed. The **Width of Text** field will accept either a literal value or a variable.

> **Variable Set String %T1% "ABC"**   // Create a string variable
> **Variable Modify String: Pad Left %T1%**   // Pad it on the left to be six characters long "   ABC"

Pad Right

Adds spaces to just the right side of a string, leaving the left side untouched. The **Width of Text** field is not the number of

spaces to add, but rather what the target variable length should be *after* adding the spaces. If you enter a value that is less than the original string variable width, then the string will not be changed. The **Width of Text** field will accept either a literal value or a variable.

> **Variable Set String %T1% "ABC"**   // Create a string variable
> **Variable Modify String: Pad Right %T1%**   // Pad it on the right to be six characters long "ABC   "

Replace Substring

Now this is a great command that can be used in some neat ways. Briefly, it allows you to substitute all, some, or zero parts of a string with another string. The **Text to Replace** field contains the text within the variable that is to be replaced and may contain a literal value, a variable, multiple variables, or a combination of a literal value and variables. The **Replace With** field is the replacement text, and can use literal values and variables in the same manner as the **Text to Replace** field. As usual, these two text fields will accept any variable, and not just string variables. The **Replace All Instances** checkbox, if left unchecked (the default), will only replace the first matching instance of the text in the **Text to Replace** field; otherwise it will replace every instance. The **Ignore Case** checkbox allows the search for instances to be case-insensitive or sensitive, depending on if you leave the box unchecked (the default), or checked.

Here are some examples. For the first one, let's replace the word *brown* with the word *red* in variable **T1**.

> **Variable Set String %T1% "The quick brown fox"**
> **Replace "brown" with "red" in %T1%**

Same example except for substituting string variables for the literal values *brown* and *red*.

> **Variable Set String %T1% "The quick brown fox"**
> **Variable Set String %T2% "brown"**
> **Variable Set String %T3% "red"**
> **Replace "%T2%" with "%T3%" in %T1%**   // "The quick red fox"

This command can also be used easily to reverse words in a sentence. Let's look at an example that will reverse the type and color of the fox.

> **Variable Set String %T1% "The quick brown fox"**
> **Variable Set String %T2% "quick"**
> **Variable Set String %T3% "brown"**
> **Replace "%T2% %T3%" with "%T3% %T2%" in %T1%**   // "The brown quick fox"

Notice something subtle here? Remember earlier it was mentioned that literals could be mixed with variables in this command? Look closer and you will see a *space* between the two variables. The *space* is a literal string between to variables.

You are familiar with the **Append Text** command. Well, this one can be used to *pre*pend text to a string. Let's prepend the word *The* to the sentence *quick brown fox*, using only a single variable. I have mixed a literal "*The*" with a variable for this example.

> **Variable Set String %T1% "quick brown fox"**
> **Replace "%T1%" with "The %T1%" in %T1%**   // "The quick brown fox"

Use this command to append a whole bunch of strings together at once, instead of using several separate appends.

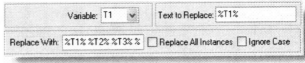

> **Variable Set String %T1% "The"**
> **Variable Set String %T2% "quick"**
> **Variable Set String %T3% "brown"**
> **Variable Set String %T4% "fox"**
> **Replace "%T1%" with "%T1% %T2% %T3% %T4%" in %T1%**

As a final point, there are so many more ways to use this command, but unfortunately, print space is at a premium, so I leave it to you to experiment with.

Save to Clipboard

This command places whatever text is contained by your target variable into your Windows clipboard. Macro Express handles superlong text cleanly and most efficiently! See *Save to Clipboard* within the *Set Text String Variables* section for the converse command, and for information about the automatic delay feature for clipboard commands.

> **Variable Modify String: Save %T1% to Clipboard**   // Stuff the Windows clipboard with whatever is in the T1 variable

Save to Text File

Saves the contents of your target string variable to a text file. There is no actual limit to the string variable; however, you are sure to run in to a practical limit if you take on something too big. What is too big is a

personal choice. On my computer, which is not the newest thing out there, I can have a 100mb long variable and search for a character string within it (that I know is at the end), in less than a single second.

Use the **Filename** field to enter which file you are saving the variable in the **Variable to Save** field to. You can also use the file-picker **ellipses** button, which sits next to the field. For more information on this dialog, please see the *File-Picker* dialog section. If you were to enter a full-path file name, such as *c:\temp\example.txt* then that is where the file will be written. If you enter a file name without a path, it will be created in the current folder or directory. Either way, if the file does not exist, it will be created. If it exists, then it will be overwritten without asking. See the *Append to Text File* to avoid overwriting a file.

The **Add Trailing CR/LF** checkbox is used to add a *carriage return+line feed* character sequence to the end of the target variable. This is a nice feature if you have a whole bunch of lines you want to write but need them separated. See *Set Value from File* within the *Set Text String Variables* section for the converse command.

> **Variable Modify String: Save %T1% to Text File**   // Save the T1 variable to a text file

Append to Text File

Appends the contents of your target string variable to the end of a text file. This is identical with the *Save to Text File* command except that it places the string at the end of the file rather than overwriting the file. If the

file does not exist, it will be created. If it exists then it will be appended to.

Variable Modify String: Append %T1% to Text File   // Append the T1 variable to the end of a text file

Save to INI File

Saves the contents of your target string variable to a *section* and *key name* within an INI file. This is the converse of the *Set Value from INI File* command. Please refer to it for details.

Variable Modify String: Save %T1% to INI File   // Save the T1 variable to an INI file

Save to Environment Variable

Saves the contents of your target string variable to an *environment variable*. This is the converse of the *Set Value from Environment*

Variable command. Please refer to it for details. One difference between the two commands is that this does not have a drop-down list to choose an environment variable name. It must be entered manually into the **Env Var Name** field.

Variable Modify String: Save %T1% to Environment Variable   // Save the T1 variable to an environment variable

Integer Variable Commands

Now let's talk about integers. Just like strings, all integer commands are chosen from dialogs. These dialogs pop up the instant that you choose a command from the category list while in the Scripting Editor. Naturally, these dialogs differ from one to another. *Set Integer Variables*, *Modify Integer Variables*, *Variable Set from File*, and *Read/Write Registry Value* all have different dialogs.

Integers do not affect your macros in the same manner as strings. For example, you cannot use integers to substitute window titles or file names, and neither can they be used as environment variables or variables within INI files. Their greatest impact is that they can be used as screen resolutions, window sizes and positions, color values, timing delays, mouse positions and movements, and much, much more.

The more recent versions of Macro Express has made both design time and runtime changes to the way it handles integers that may be beyond the allowable range of -2,147,483,648 through 2,147,483,647. This can happen because a user may input a bad value, by adding two integers together, and so forth.

Take the *Set Value Now* command as an example. An attempt to enter a value at design time beyond the allowable limits will result in an error after clicking **OK**. It must be changed to continue. This is also true of the *Set a Random Value* command.

There are runtime situations that Macro Express handles with errors, too. Adding two integers together that result in a value beyond the limits will generate a runtime error and the macro will stop.

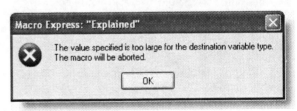

        Variable Set Integer %N1% to 1500000000
        Variable Set Integer %N2% to 1500000000
        Variable Modify Integer: %N3% = %N1% + %N2%

And there are situations that Macro Express cannot handle, and does not produce an error dialog. For example, *Set Value from Clipboard* command which convert strings to integers the same as the *Convert to Integer* string command. Any attempt to enter a string that is beyond the allowable integer range will be wrong, and no runtime error is displayed. The string value is truncated to a length that can be converted properly, and then the conversion takes place. For example "3,123,456,789" would be converted to 312,345,678 (the "9" is truncated). The only exception to this is if you convert values that are only 1 or 2 numbers beyond the allowable integer limits. These will not be truncated, but instead their values will be wrapped around. By that I mean converting 2,147,483,648, which is 1 greater than the maximum value, will wrap around to be -2,147,483,648.

So be aware! Protect your macro from these extreme values.

Set Integer Variables

We will first cover the commands that create integer variables. The two pictures here are from the *Integer Set Variable* choice within the command category list. There are two tabs named Option 1 and Option 2 because not all the available commands will fit onto a single dialog. I imagine that as more commands are added, then so will more tabs be added. In the descriptions below, I will combine some of the more obvious, matched ones together.

Set Value Now

Use the **Initial Value** field to set a value for the target variable named in the **Choose Variable Name** drop-down list. You may enter any value between -2,147,483,648 and 2,147,483,647.

Variable Set Integer %N1% to 10   *// Save 10 to the N1 variable*

Prompt for Value

This command is used when you need to get an integer value from the user during runtime.

The **Prompt Text** field holds instructions for entering information into the field. For example, "Please enter the number of pages." There is not an actual limit to the length allowed for your instructions;

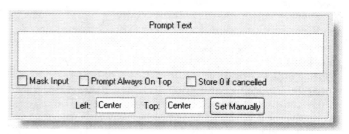

however, there is a practical limit ... the height of your display. You could conceivably enter enough instructions that the dialog is forced off the bottom of your screen.

The **Mask Input** checkbox is used to cover up with asterisks whatever your user is typing, like a secret account number for instance. So, instead of seeing 0123456789, somebody watching would only see **********.

The **Prompt Always On Top** checkbox, if used, will force the runtime dialog to always be displayed in front of any other window that may be on your Desktop. This does not mean it will always have focus, just that it will be on top.

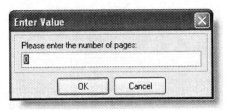

The **Store 0 if Canceled** checkbox means that your macro will *not* stop if the user clicks the **Cancel** button. It will, instead, place a **zero** in your target variable. This gives you, the developer, a way programmatically to stop the macro by testing the variable's value. You may have some housecleaning to do before stopping the macro, like shutting down some programs, putting the user's Desktop back the way it was, or simply making sure the user wants to cancel the macro. Here is a simple example on how to use this feature:

```
// Enter the number of pages
Repeat Until %N2% <> %N2%              // Infinite loop
  Variable Set Integer %N1% to 0       // Make sure the input variable is zero
  Variable Set Integer %N1% from Prompt // Prompt the user for the number of pages
  If Variable %N1% = 0                 // If the user hit the CANCEL button
    If Message: "Cancel?"              // then ask the user if they want to quit and
      Macro Stop                       // if they do, then quit
    End If                             // End of message prompt structure
  Else                                 // or else if the user has entered anything else that is valid, then
    Repeat Exit                        // exit out of the loop
  End If                               // End of CANCEL test structure
Repeat End                             // End of infinite loop
```

It should be pointed out that this example assumes a **zero** would *not* be an acceptable value to enter. Also, only digits and the negative symbol are accepted. Whatever the user enters will be converted to a value. If the value is out of the allowable integer range, an error is displayed. After clicking **OK** the user can try again to enter an acceptable value.

By default, the runtime dialog will be placed in the center of the screen. You can change this by using the **Left** and **Top** fields, or the **Set Manually** button. Please see the *Dialog Positioner* section for more details.

Set Value from Mouse X Position

Set Value from Mouse Y Position

These commands place the coordinate position of the mouse cursor into your target variable (the **Choose Variable Name** field) at the exact time the command runs. The values returned are relative to your screen. See the

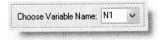

section on *Literal Coordinates* for an explanation of what this means. The **X** direction is left-to-right (horizontally); the **Y** direction is top-to-bottom (vertically). The values returned by these two commands are the same ones returned by the *Get Mouse Position Screen* command.

```
Variable Set Integer %N1% from Mouse X Position   // What is the horizontal position of the mouse
Variable Set Integer %N2% from Mouse Y Position   // What is the vertical position of the mouse
```

Set Value from the Size of a File

This will set a target variable with the size of a file found anywhere on your system. The value returned is in bytes, and is the actual file size, not the space it takes up on your system. Depending

on the structure of your disk (FAT, FAT-32, NTFS), the space that a file takes up on your drive could be larger than the file itself because of minimum file allocation size. A one-byte file could be 1,024 bytes.

Use the **Filename** field to enter which file you are targeting to read into the variable in the **Choose Variable Name** field. You can also use the file-picker **ellipses** button, which sits next to the field. For more information on this dialog, please see the *File-Picker* dialog section. You can use the **Bypass File Existence Check** checkbox to ignore if the named file does not exist. Please review the *Common Variable Dialogs* section about this checkbox.

> **Variable Set Integer %N1% from the size of file "Example.txt"**   // How big is the file?

Set a Random Value

Use this command to set a random integer value. This is similar to the *Set with a Random Letter* command used with string variables. The

Maximum Random Value field is used to set a maximum allowable integer to be returned. Entering a 1 returns a random value of either 0 or 1. The value returned is always positive and the maximum value that can be returned is 2,147,483,647.

Set Value from Screen Width

Set Value from Screen Height

These commands place your screen resolution pair (stated in pixels) into the target variable. 640×480, 800×600, 1024×768, 1280×1024, and 1600×1200 are all common resolution pairs. The first number is the width of your screen and the second is the height.

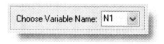

> **Variable Set Integer %N1% from Screen Width**   // What is the width of my screen? 1024
> **Variable Set Integer %N2% from Screen Height**   // What is the height of my screen? 1280

Set Value from Current Window Left

Set Value from Current Window Top

These commands place the coordinate position of the current window, which is the window that has focus, into your target variable (the **Choose Variable Name** field) at the exact time the command runs. The values returned are relative to your screen.

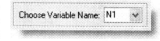

See the section on *Literal Coordinates* for an explanation of what this means. The *left* side of the window is the **X** (horizontally) coordinate, and the *top* of the window is the **Y** (vertical) coordinate.

> **Variable Set Integer %N1% from Left of Window**   // The horizontal position of the focused window
> **Variable Set Integer %N2% from Top of Window**   // The vertical position of the focused window

Set Value from Current Window Width

Set Value from Current Window Height

These commands place either the width or height of the current window, which is the window that has focus, into the target variable displayed in the **Choose Variable Name** field.

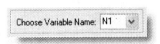

Variable Set Integer %N1% from Window Width   // The width of the focused window
Variable Set Integer %N2% from Window Height   // The height of the focused window

Set Value from Clipboard

Whatever is in the clipboard will be converted to an integer up to the first character that is not a digit, negative symbol, thousands separator.

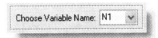

Macro Express uses your computer's regional settings (Control Panel | Regional Settings) to determine which characters are used to describe numbers. In other words, which character is used for the negative sign symbol, the thousands separator, and the decimal point symbol.

If the clipboard contains all nonnumber characters, or is empty, then the value of the integer will be zero. Please refer to the beginning of this section (*Integer Variable Commands*) for possible errors.

Variable Set Integer %N1% from Clipboard   // Convert the clipboard contents to an integer variable

Get Length of a Text Variable

This is an invaluable command when you are manipulating string variables. Eventually, you are going to need to 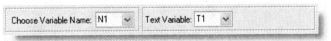 know how long a text string is (how many characters it contains), and this command will retrieve the answer for you.

Variable Set Integer %N1% from Length of Variable %T1%   // Get the length of the T1 text string

Get Position of Text in a Text Variable

Use this command to find the starting position of one string within another. This is another invaluable command when you are manipulating string variables.

The string variable to search is contained in the **Text Variable** drop-down list. What to search for is contained in the **Search Text** field, which will accept either a literal value or any variable. A zero is returned if whatever you are searching for cannot be found within the string. Also, the search is case-sensitive so if you try to find the position of *FOX* in *The quick brown fox*, a zero will be returned.

Variable Set String %T1% "The quick brown fox"   // Create a string to search
Variable Set String %T2% "fox"   // Create something to search for
Variable Set Integer %N1% from Position of Text in Variable %T1%   // Find the position of the string ... 17

Set Value from Current Day

Set Value from Current Month

Set Value from Current Year

These commands return an integer for the day-of-the-month (1 through 31), month number (1 through 12), and year as a 4-digit number (2003, 2004, and so forth) respectively at the time the command runs.

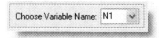

> **Variable Set Integer %N1% from Current Day**   // Today ... 4
> **Variable Set Integer %N2% from Current Month**   // Month ... 7
> **Variable Set Integer %N3% from Current Year**   // Year ... 2003

Set Value from Current Day of Week

Returns an integer for whatever day-of-the-week it is at the exact time the command runs. The first day is Sunday (1) and the last day is Saturday (7).

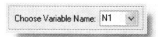

> **Variable Set Integer %N1% from Current Day of Week**   // Day of week ... 6

Set Value from Current Hour

Set Value from Current Minute

Set Value from Current Second

These commands return an integer for the hour (0 through 23) in military time, minute (0 through 59), and second (0 through 59) respectively at the exact time the command runs. If the hour is 23 and the minute and second are each 59, then it is exactly one second before midnight. If the hour, minute and second are all zero then it is midnight. If both the hour and minute are zero and the second is 1 then it is one second after midnight. Here are some different return values and the times they represent.

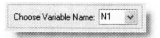

Hr	Min	Sec	Time
23	59	59	11:59:59 pm
0	0	0	midnight
0	0	1	12:00:01 am
11	59	59	11:59:59 am
12	0	0	noon
12	0	1	12:00:01 pm

> **Variable Set Integer %N1% from Current Hour**
> **Variable Set Integer %N2% from Current Minute**
> **Variable Set Integer %N3% from Current Second**

Set Value from Control Left

Set Value from Control Top

Set Value from Control Width

Set Value from Control Height

See the *Window Controls* chapter for a detailed explanation of these commands.

Set Value from Monitor Width

Set Value from Monitor Height

Use these commands to get the screen width and height of a particular monitor in a multi-monitor display system. The **Monitor Number** field contains which monitor that you are referencing and matches the number given by your operating system's *Display Properties* dialog. For single monitor systems, the proper value to enter is zero.

Modify Integer Variables

Now let's examine some ways to modify integer variables. The picture here is from the *Integer Modify Variable* choice within the command category list. In the descriptions below, I will combine some of the more obvious, matching ones together.

Add

Subtract

Multiply

Divide

These four arithmetic commands all work the same. Take two values, perform one of the four operations on them then store the results to a variable.

The numbers to add, subtract, multiply, or divide can be either literal values or variables, or a mixture of both on either side of the big operator sign (shown as a "+" sign in the example picture). Also, if using a variable, you are not limited to just integers. Decimals can also be chosen from either one of the two **Variable** drop-down list, however, any decimal digits will be dropped after the operation is performed.

And because decimal variables can be chosen, you can enter literal values outside the normal integer range. However, no matter which operation you choose, or which variable (integer or decimal) you choose, or the literal values that you may enter, the operation results must always be within the allowable integer range of -2,147,483,648 through 2,147,483,647. If the results are not within these limits, then at runtime an error may, or may not, be displayed even though the answer is wrong. If you enter a literal value beyond one of the limits then no runtime error is displayed. However, if the results of two variables are beyond the limits then a runtime error is displayed. Please refer to the beginning of this section (*Integer Variable Commands*) for possible errors.

The variable displayed in the **Variable to Receive Result** drop-down list will hold the results of the operation.

```
Variable Modify Integer: %N1% = 1000 + 100       // Add two values
Variable Modify Integer: %N1% = 1000 - 100       // Subtract two values
Variable Modify Integer: %N1% = 1000 * 100       // Multiply two values
Variable Modify Integer: %N1% = 1000 / 100       // Divide two values
Variable Modify Integer: %N1% = %N1% + 100       // Add 100 to a variable
Variable Modify Integer: %N1% = %N1% + %D1%      // Add a decimal variable to an integer variable
```

Convert to Text String

This command converts the integer named in the **Variable to Convert** drop-down list to the text string variable named in the **New Text Variable** drop-down list. Literal values cannot be used with this command. If

the integer to convert is zero then the resulting variable string will be "0".

> **Variable Modify Integer: Convert %N1% to text string %T1%**   // Convert a number to a string

Convert to Decimal

This command converts the integer named in the **Variable to Convert** drop-down list to the decimal variable named in the **New Decimal Variable** drop-down list. Literal values cannot be used with this command. Because integers have no decimals, it will appear the newly created decimal value does not either. However, this is just how decimal values are displayed when there is no decimal portion to the number.

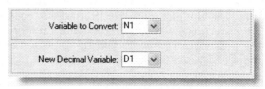

> **Variable Modify Integer: Convert %N1% to decimal %D1%**   // Convert an integer to a decimal

Copy Value

This command simply copies one integer to another. The integer named in the **Variable to Copy** drop-down list is copied to the integer variable named in the **New Variable** drop-down list. Literal values cannot be used with this command.

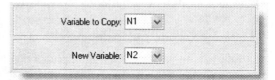

> **Variable Modify Integer: Copy %N1% to %N2%**   // Copy one variable to another

Increment

Decrement

These two commands simply increase or decrease the value of the variable named in the drop-down list by one ("1") without having to do it with the arithmetic operators.

> **Variable Modify Integer: Inc (%N1%)**   // Increase the value by 1
> **Variable Modify Integer: Dec (%N1%)**   // Decrease the value by 1

Decimal Variable Commands

Just like strings and integers, all decimal commands are chosen from dialogs. These dialogs pop up the instant that you choose a command from the category list while in the Scripting Editor. Naturally, these dialogs differ from one to another. *Set Decimal Variables*, *Modify Decimal Variables*, and *Read/Write Registry Value* all have different dialogs.

At design time, if you attempt to enter an illegal value, say in the *Set Value Now* command, an error dialog is displayed.

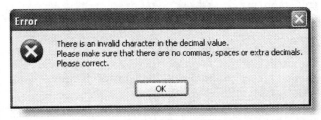

There are also runtime errors generated by decimal commands. Errors are usually caused by the results of calculations being beyond the allowable range of decimal values (5×10^{-324} through 1.7×10^{308}). For example, adding two decimals together that result in this runtime dialog error and then the macro stops. In the macro below, I enter a 17 with 307 zeroes for both the **D1** and **D2** variables (the maximum allowable value), then add them together resulting in the runtime error dialog shown here dialog.

Variable Set Decimal %D1% to
170000000000000000000000000000000000000000000
000000000000000000000000000000000000000000000
000000000000000000000000000000000000000000000
000000000000000000000000000000000000000000000
000000000000000000000000000000000000000000000
000000000000000000000000000000000000000000000
000000000000000000000000000000000000000000000
00000000
Variable Modify Decimal: Copy %D1% to %D2%
Variable Modify Decimal: %D3% = %D1% + %D2%

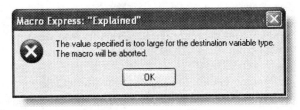

And there are situations that Macro Express cannot handle, and does not produce an error dialog. For example, the *Prompt for Value* and *Set Value from Clipboard* commands which convert strings to decimals the same as the *Convert to Decimal* string command. For example, converting "-123.45.67" will result in 12,345, which is not correct, and there is no error dialog displayed at runtime. So be aware, and protect your macro from strange values.

Set Decimal Variables

We will first cover the commands that create decimal variables. There are fewer than a handful because they are not normally used like string and integer type variables. Mouse positions, window sizes and positions, string lengths, character positions, and timing delays are all specified with whole numbers and not decimals.

Set Value Now

Use the **Initial Value** field to set a value for the target variable named in the **Choose Variable Name** drop-down list. You may enter any value between 5×10^{-324} through 1.7×10^{308}. Please refer to the beginning of this section (*Decimal Variable Commands*) for possible errors.

> **Variable Set Decimal %D1% to 123.456**   // Save 123.456 to the D1 variable

Prompt for Value

This command is used when you need to get a decimal value from the user at runtime.

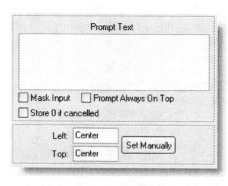

The **Prompt Text** field holds instructions for entering information into the field. For example, "Please enter an amount." There is no actual limit to the length allowed for your instructions; however, there is a practical limit … the height of your display. You could conceivably enter enough instructions the dialog is forced off the bottom of your screen.

The **Mask Input** checkbox is used to cover up with asterisks whatever your user is typing, so instead of seeing 123.456, somebody watching would only see *******.

The **Prompt Always On Top** checkbox, if used, will force the runtime dialog to always be displayed in front of any other window that may be on your Desktop. This does not mean, however, that it will always have focus, just that it will be on top.

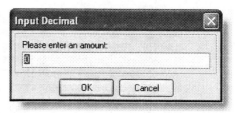

The **Store 0 if Canceled** checkbox means that your macro will *not* stop if the user clicks the **Cancel** button. It will, instead, place a **zero** in your target variable. This gives you, the developer, a way programmatically to stop the macro by testing the variable's value. You may have some housecleaning to do before stopping the macro, like shutting down some programs, putting the user's Desktop back the way it was, or simply making sure the user wants to cancel the macro. Here is an example on how to use this feature:

```
// Enter an amount
Repeat Until %N1% <> %N1%                    // Infinite loop
   Variable Set Decimal %D1% to 0            // Make sure the input variable is zero
   Variable Set Decimal %D1% from Prompt     // Prompt the user for an amount
   If Variable %D1% = 0                       // If the user hit the CANCEL button
      If Message: "Cancel?"                   // then ask the user if they want to quit and
         Macro Stop                           // if they do, then quit
      End If                                  // End of message prompt structure
   Else                                       // or else if the user has entered anything else that is valid, then
      Repeat Exit                             // exit out of the loop
   End If                                     // End of CANCEL test structure
Repeat End                                    // End of infinite loop
```

It should be pointed out that this example assumes a **zero** would *not* be an acceptable value to enter. Also, a user cannot enter just anything into the prompt field at runtime. Only digits, a negative symbol, and a decimal point are allowed. Whatever the user enters will be converted to a value, but please refer to the beginning of this section (*Decimal Variable Commands*) for possible errors.

By default, the runtime dialog will be placed in the center of the screen. You can change this by using the **Left** and **Top** fields, or the **Set Manually** button. Please see the *Dialog Positioner* section for more details.

Set Value from Clipboard

Whatever is in the clipboard will be converted to a decimal up to the first character that is not a digit, negative symbol, thousands separator, or decimal point. If the clipboard contains all nonnumber characters, or is empty, then the value of the decimal will be zero. Please refer to the beginning of this section (*Decimal Variable Commands*) for possible errors.

Variable Set Decimal %D1% from Clipboard   // Convert the clipboard contents to a decimal variable

Modify Decimal Variables

Now let's examine some ways to modify decimal variables. The picture here is from the *Decimal Modify Variable* choice within the command category list. In the descriptions below, I will combine some of the more obvious, matching ones together.

Add

Subtract

Multiply

Divide

These four arithmetic commands all work the same. Take two values and perform one of the four operations on them then store the results to a variable.

The numbers to add, subtract, multiply, or divide can be either literal values or variables, or a mixture of both on either side of the big operator sign (shown as a "+" sign in the example picture). Also, if using a variable, you are not limited to just decimals. Integers can also be chosen from either one of the two **Variable** drop-down lists.

No matter which operation you choose, or which variable (decimal or integer) you choose, or the literal values that you may enter, the operation results must always be within the allowable decimal range of (5×10^{-324} through 1.7×10^{308}). If the results are not within these limits, then at runtime an error may, or may not, be displayed even though the answer is wrong. If you enter an illegal literal value then no runtime error is displayed. However, if the results of two variables are beyond the limits then a runtime error is displayed. Please refer to the beginning of this section (*Decimal Commands*) for possible errors.

The variable displayed in the **Variable to Receive Result** drop-down list will hold the results of the operation.

Variable Modify Decimal: %D1% = 123.456 + 654.321   // Add two values
Variable Modify Decimal: %D1% = 123.456 - 654.321   // Subtract two values

Variable Modify Decimal: %D1% = 123.456 * 654.321   // Multiply two values
Variable Modify Decimal: %D1% = 123.456 / 654.321   // Divide two values
Variable Modify Decimal: %D1% = %D1% + 123.456   // Add 123.456 to a variable
Variable Modify Decimal: %D1% = %D1% + %N1%   // Add an integer variable to a Decimal variable

Round

Decimal variables contain decimal values that can have as many as 14 decimal places. What if you do not want 14 decimal places like when you are working with dollars and cents? Use rounding to get what you want.

Macro Express uses a common type of rounding called *asymmetric arithmetic* rounding, which always rounds a midpoint value to the larger value. What does this mean? Well, we know that a 5 is the midpoint between 1 and 10 and will therefore be rounded up to 10. For example, **1.235**, if rounded to two decimal places, would result in a value of **1.24**. But what if the value was **-1.235** (negative)? If you are thinking **-1.24**, that would be wrong, because when working with negative values, the value closest to *zero* is the larger the number so in this case it would be rounding down. The correct *asymmetric arithmetic* answer would be **-1.23**. Do not be confused. You only need to remember that Macro Express always rounds a midpoint value, positive or negative, to the next *greater* value.

The **Decimal Places to Round to** field contains the number of decimal places to round if the value is positive. If the value is negative, the number of digits on the left-hand side of the decimal point will be rounded. The field accepts either a literal value of -2,147,483,648 through 2,147,483,647 or an integer variable.

The table lists the results of rounding two different decimal numbers. The first eleven rows round the whole number portion of a decimal number. And the bottom twelve rows show the results from rounding the decimal portion of a different number.

Decimal Value	Round	Results
7,890,123,456.1	-1	7,890,123,460
7,890,123,456.1	-2	7,890,123,500
7,890,123,456.1	-3	7,890,123,000
7,890,123,456.1	-4	7,890,120,000
7,890,123,456.1	-5	7,890,100,000
7,890,123,456.1	-6	7,890,000,000
7,890,123,456.1	-7	7,890,000,000
7,890,123,456.1	-8	7,900,000,000
7,890,123,456.1	-9	8,000,000,000
7,890,123,456.1	-10	10,000,000,000
7,890,123,456.1	-11	0
1.7890123456	11	1.7890123456
1.7890123456	10	1.7890123456
1.7890123456	9	1.789012346
1.7890123456	8	1.78901235
1.7890123456	7	1.7890123
1.7890123456	6	1.789012
1.7890123456	5	1.78901
1.7890123456	4	1.789
1.7890123456	3	1.789
1.7890123456	2	1.79
1.7890123456	1	1.8
1.7890123456	0	2

Banker's Rounding

You have another option if you do not like *asymmetric arithmetic* rounding … *banker's* rounding. There is a Windows Registry setting that you can add or to change to force Macro Express to use banker's rounding:

[HKLM] or [HKCU] \Software\Insight Software Solutions\Macro Express\AdvOptions\Bankers Rounding

If this value is set to 1 then banker's rounding is in effect, otherwise, if set to 0 then banker's rounding is off and asymmetric arithmetic rounding is in effect, which is the default. But what is banker's rounding? The following explanation is taken from Microsoft's bulletin 196652 - HOW TO Implement Custom Rounding Procedures.

> When you add rounded values together, always rounding .5 in the same direction results in a bias that grows with the more numbers you add together. One-way to reduce the bias is with banker's rounding. Banker's rounding rounds .5 up sometimes and down sometimes. The convention is to round to the nearest even number, so both 1.5 and 2.5 round to 2, and 3.5 and 4.5 both round to 4. Banker's rounding is symmetric.

Convert to Text String

This command converts the decimal named in the **Variable to Convert** drop-down list to the text string variable named in the **New Text Variable** drop-down list. Literal values cannot be used with this command.

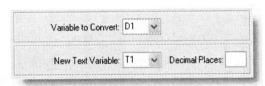

The maximum value that can be typed into the **Decimal Places** field is 99. It will not accept variables. This field can be used either to pad a string with extra zeros or to round a decimal variable before converting it to a string. If the value entered is greater than the number of decimal places in the number itself, then zeros will be added to the length specified, sort of. Sometimes, seemingly at random, there will be other numbers in the "fill" portion of the string, which is the position in the string of zeroes that begins *beyond* the number of decimal places in the original variable. The reason for these random appearances is that some numbers are approximations. In the world of computers, floating-point numbers are broken down and stored by a radix/base, mantissa, and an exponent, making them approximations. Additional information about floating point numbers is beyond the scope of this book.

If the value entered is less than the number of decimal places, then rounding will occur. Rounding follows the same rules as the ***Round*** command.

If the decimal to convert is zero then the resulting variable string will be "0" padded with the zeros to the value in the **Decimal Places** field.

> **Variable Set Decimal %D1% to 1.234**
> **Variable Modify Decimal: Convert %D1% to text string %T1%** // Convert to a string with 2 decimal places ... 1.23
> **Variable Modify Decimal: Convert %D1% to text string %T1%** // Convert to a string with 5 decimal places ... 1.23400

Truncate to Integer

Use this command to convert a decimal to an integer. The name of the command is a warning that this is not a rounding command, but a buzz saw. It removes any decimal places before converting the decimal variable named in the **Variable to Truncate** drop-down list to the integer in the **New Integer Variable** drop-down list. Literal values are not used here. Please refer to the beginning of this section for possible errors.

> **Variable Modify Decimal: Truncate %D1% to integer %N1%**   // Convert a decimal to an integer

Remove Integer

Use this command to strip away the whole number portion of a decimal variable leaving just the decimal part. Be aware that this command can also be used as a command that copies the decimal portion of a variable to a different variable. Now, both of these statements should sound the same, because they are.

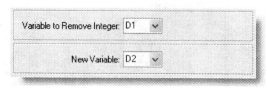

The radio button choice in the main dialog is, in fact, **Remove Integer**; however, look at the example below for what the command line says.

The subtle difference is how you use the **New Variable** drop-down list. If it is set the same as the variable in the **Variable to Remove Integer** drop-down list, then you are simply removing the integer part of a variable. Otherwise, you are using the command to copy the decimal part to another decimal variable, leaving the original variable intact.

        Variable Modify Decimal: Copy fraction part of %D1% to %D1%   // Remove integer portion of a number
        Variable Modify Decimal: Copy fraction part of %D1% to %D2%   // Copy the decimal portion of a number

Copy Value

This command simply copies one decimal to another. The decimal named in the **Variable to Copy** drop-down list is copied to the decimal variable named in the **New Variable** drop-down list. Literal values cannot be used with this command.

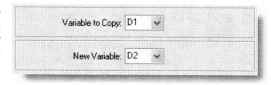

        Variable Modify Decimal: Copy %D1% to %D2%   // Copy one variable to another

Clearing, Saving, and Restoring Variables

Now that you have learned how to create and modify variables, you might want to know how to erase, save, and restore them.

Clear Variables

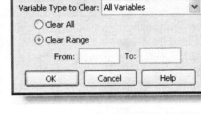

Except for one particular case, which I will discuss later, when a macro first starts, all variables of all types are automatically cleared, erased, emptied, or whatever you prefer to call it ... except for deleted. In Macro Express, there is no "deleted". Variables are not, and cannot be, deleted. They always exist with or without values. "Without" means that integer and decimal variables will be zero and string variables will contain an empty string. This means that you can clear any variable you want by simply setting it to its empty or zero value. For example:

Variable Set String %T1% ""   // Clear text string variable
Variable Set Integer %N1% to 0   // Clear integer variable
Variable Set Decimal %D1% to 0   // Clear decimal variable

Clearing variables in this manner is usually reserved for a small sampling that needs clearing during the operation of your macro. For instance, you may want to be sure a string is empty before prompting the user for input, or an integer used as an error flag is set to zero before calling a submacro.

It would obviously take 297 lines of code to clear all the variables in this manner so Macro Express has provided a way to clear ranges of variables and variable types. The dialog shown here is from the *Clear Variables* choice within the command category list.

Use the **Variable Type to Clear** drop-down list to choose which variables to clear. As shown above, there are five choices. Again, in this chapter we are not concerned with the *Control Variables* type except to say that picking *All Variables* includes them too.

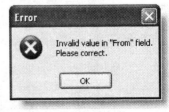

After choosing which variable type to clear, then choose the range to clear. If you want to clear all of them (1 through 99) then simply choose the **Clear All** radio button. This will clear all the variables *only* of the type that you chose.

To clear a specific range of your chosen variable type, click on the **Clear Range** radio button then enter the starting variable number in the **From** field and the ending variable number in the **To** field. Both fields accept either literal values or integer variables. If you enter an illegal value at design time an error message will be displayed.

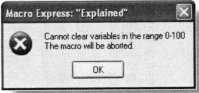

If you use variables, and they are beyond the limits imposed (1 through 99), then an error message will be displayed at runtime, and the macro will stop.

Clear Text Variables: All   //Clear all text variables
Clear Integer Variables: All   // Clear all integer variables
Clear Decimal Variables: All   // Clear all decimal variables
Clear All Variables: All   // Clear all variables
Clear Text Variables: From 10 To 19   // Clear only text variables T10 through T19

Save Variables
Restore Variables

The ability to save and restore variables in Macro Express is a good feature that can be used in different ways. The dialog is accessed from both the *Variable Save* and *Variable Restore* choices within the command category list. Unlike clearing variables, your only choice to save and restore are by variable type (string, integer, and decimal) and not by ranges. In other words, whichever variable type you choose to save or restore, all 99 will be acted on.

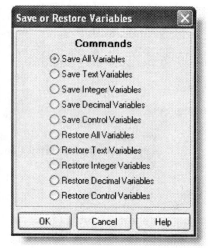

The first, and most obvious, way to use these commands is within a single macro. Instead of creating examples out of all the variable types, which may confuse the issue, I will just use string variables. You can be sure the rest of the variable types work the same. Let's start by setting a string variable with a simple line of text:

> **Variable Set String %T1% "The quick brown fox jumps over the lazy dog"**

Now, for the rest of your macro, **T1** will always be the same, unless you need to use it for something else temporarily, in which case, you would want to save the value before reusing the variable. Do this:

> **Variable Save Text Variables**

You are now free to set the **T1** variable to something different:

> **Variable Set String %T1% "The lazy dog just had fox for dinner"**

Once again, this **T1** variable will not change for the balance of your macro until you change it by either stuffing it with another string or restoring the variables that you saved earlier. Let's do that:

> **Variable Restore Text Variables**   // T1="The quick brown fox jumps over the lazy dog" again

Another reason to use these two commands is when calling a submacro with the **Macro Run** command. First, create a submacro that sets the value of **T1** to the name of my company:

> // Submacro to set a variable with a company name
> **Variable Set String %T1% "Professional Grade Macros"**
> **Macro Return**

Now create the main macro that uses the **T1** variable for a different company name:

```
// Main macro to set a variable with a company name
Variable Set String %T1% "Insight Software Solutions"    // Set T1 with a company name
Variable Save Text Variables                             // Save the variables
Macro Run: Submacro                                      // Run the submacro
Variable Restore Text Variables                          // Restore variables. T1 is back to "Insight Software Solutions"
```

The main macro sets **T1** to a company name then it saves text variables before calling a submacro. The submacro resets **T1** to a different value then returns to the calling main macro. Now the main macro restores the variables that it saved, which puts the **T1** variable back to the way it was.

Another use is between macros, or more accurately, between macro sessions. What is a macro session? It is the continuous running of macros and submacros without interruption or stopping. Once a macro or submacro stops, the session is over.

You can preserve variables between sessions by using these two commands. Briefly, the *Variable Save* command will hold variable values until the next *Variable Save* command is encountered. How does it work? Let's create three macros:

```
// Macro 1
Variable Set String %T1% "The quick brown fox"    // Create a string variable
Variable Save Text Variables                      // Save string variables
Macro Stop                                        // End the macro

// Macro 2
Variable Set String %T1% "AaBbCcDdEeFfGg"         // Create a string variable
Macro Stop                                        // End the macro

// Macro 3
Variable Restore Text Variables                   // Restore string variables
Macro Stop                                        // End the macro
```

Macro 1 creates a string variable then saves all string variables to memory and then stops. After running it, take a look at the variables from inside the debug window and you will see that **T1** is *The quick brown fox*. It should be pointed out the debug dialog is available to you whenever a macro finishes running and will hold the last state of any variable until the next macro is run.

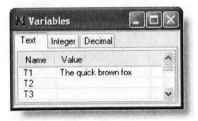

Macro 2 creates another string variable and then stops. After running it, look at the variables from inside the debug window and you will see that **T1** is now *AaBbCcDdEeFfGg*, as you would expect. If you run it again, you will get the same results. Run it as many times as you want, changing the value of the **T1** variable as many times as you want.

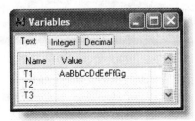

Macro 3 restores variables from memory then stops. Once again, after running the macro, look at the variables from inside the debug window and you will see that **T1** is back to *The quick brown fox*. No matter how many times you changed the **T1** variable in **Macro 2**, no matter how many sessions of **Macro 2** you ran, Macro Express still held the original value of **T1** in memory.

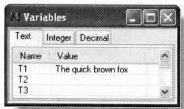

This is what can be expected for all variables when saving and restoring variables between macro sessions … unless you unload Macro Express or reboot your computer between sessions, which will dump anything that Macro Express was saving. Also, this system of saving and restoring variables between sessions does not work across a network because each workstation keeps its own memory and not the memory of another workstation. Running **Macro 1** on a workstation and then **Macro 2** and **Macro 3** on a different workstation does you no good.

Other Variable Dialogs

This section describes using other, miscellaneous dialogs found throughout the Macro Express category command list. They have one thing in common … they all set a variable to a value.

Variable Set from Misc

This is a newer Macro Express command. It is exactly what it says it is … miscellaneous. But what a great bunch of miscellaneous variables they are! For the first time in the history of Macro Express, we have a direct way to discover three things:

1. Where the Macro Express home folder is located.
2. Which Windows Registry key, HKEY_LOCAL_MACHINE or HKEY_CURRENT_MACHINE, contains the current home to all the Macro Express settings.
3. Who is running the macro.

Enter your target variable into the **Variable to Receive Information** field. The miscellaneous value itself is chosen from the **Value to Retrieve** drop-down list.

Set Variable %T1% to "Path to My Documents"	// What is the full path to my "My Documents" folder?
Set Variable %T2% to "Path to Start Menu"	// What is the full path to my "Start Menu" folder?
Set Variable %T3% to "Path to Desktop"	// What is the full path to my "Desktop" folder?
Set Variable %T4% to "Path to Common Documents"	// What is the full path to the common "Documents" folder?
Set Variable %T5% to "Path to Common Start Menu"	// What is the full path to the common "Start Menu" folder?
Set Variable %T6% to "Path to Common Desktop"	// What is the full path to the common "Desktop" folder?
Set Variable %T7% to "Installation Path"	// Where is Macro Express installed?
Set Variable %T8% to "Preferences Registry Key"	// Which Registry key is Macro Express using.
Set Variable %T9% to "Name of Current Macro"	// What is the nickname of the current running macro?
Set Variable %T10% to "Name of Machine"	// Name of the computer
Set Variable %T11% to "Username"	// Name of current user
Set Variable %T12% to "Registered Owner"	// Macro Express registration
Set Variable %T13% to "Registered Company"	// Macro Express registration

ASCII Values and Variables

ASCII (ask-key) is an acronym for **A**merican **S**tandard **C**ode for **I**nformation **I**nterchange, which was first proposed and accepted back in the 60's … yes, the 1960's just after the *Cretaceous Period*. It was originally proposed to create common ground between an unbelievable number of different types of data processing equipment, made by another unbelievable number of different companies.

The standard and extended ASCII character sets, when combined, consist of 256 numbers from 0 through 255. Each is assigned a communication code, punctuation mark, number, letter, or other symbol. The symbols change for values greater than 127, depending on the font set that you are using.

Dec	Hex	Char	Dec	Hex	Char	Dec	Hex	Char	Dec	Hex	Char
0	00	Null	32	20	Space	64	40	@	96	60	`
1	01	Start of heading	33	21	!	65	41	A	97	61	a
2	02	Start of text	34	22	"	66	42	B	98	62	b
3	03	End of text	35	23	#	67	43	C	99	63	c
4	04	End of transmit	36	24	$	68	44	D	100	64	d
5	05	Enquiry	37	25	%	69	45	E	101	65	e
6	06	Acknowledge	38	26	&	70	46	F	102	66	f
7	07	Audible bell	39	27	'	71	47	G	103	67	g
8	08	Backspace	40	28	(	72	48	H	104	68	h
9	09	Horizontal tab	41	29	)	73	49	I	105	69	i
10	0A	Line feed	42	2A	*	74	4A	J	106	6A	j
11	0B	Vertical tab	43	2B	+	75	4B	K	107	6B	k
12	0C	Form feed	44	2C	,	76	4C	L	108	6C	l
13	0D	Carriage return	45	2D	-	77	4D	M	109	6D	m
14	0E	Shift out	46	2E	.	78	4E	N	110	6E	n
15	0F	Shift in	47	2F	/	79	4F	O	111	6F	o
16	10	Data link escape	48	30	0	80	50	P	112	70	p
17	11	Device control 1	49	31	1	81	51	Q	113	71	q
18	12	Device control 2	50	32	2	82	52	R	114	72	r
19	13	Device control 3	51	33	3	83	53	S	115	73	s
20	14	Device control 4	52	34	4	84	54	T	116	74	t
21	15	Neg. acknowledge	53	35	5	85	55	U	117	75	u
22	16	Synchronous idle	54	36	6	86	56	V	118	76	v
23	17	End trans. block	55	37	7	87	57	W	119	77	w
24	18	Cancel	56	38	8	88	58	X	120	78	x
25	19	End of medium	57	39	9	89	59	Y	121	79	y
26	1A	Substitution	58	3A	:	90	5A	Z	122	7A	z
27	1B	Escape	59	3B	;	91	5B	[	123	7B	{
28	1C	File separator	60	3C	<	92	5C	\	124	7C	|
29	1D	Group separator	61	3D	=	93	5D	]	125	7D	}
30	1E	Record separator	62	3E	>	94	5E	^	126	7E	~
31	1F	Unit separator	63	3F	?	95	5F	_	127	7F	□

Dec	Hex	Char	Dec	Hex	Char	Dec	Hex	Char	Dec	Hex	Char
128	80	Ç	160	A0	á	192	C0	└	224	E0	α
129	81	ü	161	A1	í	193	C1	┴	225	E1	ß
130	82	é	162	A2	ó	194	C2	┬	226	E2	Γ
131	83	â	163	A3	ú	195	C3	├	227	E3	π
132	84	ä	164	A4	ñ	196	C4	─	228	E4	Σ
133	85	à	165	A5	Ñ	197	C5	┼	229	E5	σ
134	86	å	166	A6	ª	198	C6	╞	230	E6	µ
135	87	ç	167	A7	º	199	C7	╟	231	E7	τ
136	88	ê	168	A8	¿	200	C8	╚	232	E8	Φ
137	89	ë	169	A9	⌐	201	C9	╔	233	E9	Θ
138	8A	è	170	AA	¬	202	CA	╩	234	EA	Ω
139	8B	ï	171	AB	½	203	CB	╦	235	EB	δ
140	8C	î	172	AC	¼	204	CC	╠	236	EC	∞
141	8D	ì	173	AD	¡	205	CD	═	237	ED	ø
142	8E	Ä	174	AE	«	206	CE	╬	238	EE	ε
143	8F	Å	175	AF	»	207	CF	╧	239	EF	∩
144	90	É	176	B0	░	208	D0	╨	240	F0	≡
145	91	æ	177	B1	▒	209	D1	╤	241	F1	±
146	92	Æ	178	B2	▓	210	D2	╥	242	F2	≥
147	93	ô	179	B3	│	211	D3	╙	243	F3	≤
148	94	ö	180	B4	┤	212	D4	╘	244	F4	⌠
149	95	ò	181	B5	╡	213	D5	╒	245	F5	⌡
150	96	û	182	B6	╢	214	D6	╓	246	F6	÷
151	97	ù	183	B7	╖	215	D7	╫	247	F7	≈
152	98	ÿ	184	B8	╕	216	D8	╪	248	F8	°
153	99	Ö	185	B9	╣	217	D9	┘	249	F9	∙
154	9A	Ü	186	BA	║	218	DA	┌	250	FA	·
155	9B	¢	187	BB	╗	219	DB	█	251	FB	√
156	9C	£	188	BC	╝	220	DC	▄	252	FC	ⁿ
157	9D	¥	189	BD	╜	221	DD	▌	253	FD	²
158	9E	₧	190	BE	╛	222	DE	▐	254	FE	■
159	9F	ƒ	191	BF	┐	223	DF	▀	255	FF	□

Set Variable to ASCII Character

The *Set Variable to ASCII Character* command converts an integer variable, or literal value, to a string variable. Pick the integer variable to convert from the **In Variable** drop-down list, or enter an integer between 0 and 255 into the **Constant** field. A design time error message is displayed if you attempt to enter values beyond these limits. This is a marvelous way to get characters that cannot be entered by the keyboard into string variables like the *carriage return+line feed* character sequence.

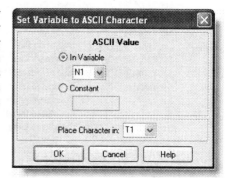

Variable Set %T1% to ASCII Char of 13	// Carriage return
Variable Set %T2% to ASCII Char of 10	// Line feed
Variable Modify String: Append %T2% to %T1%	// Append

Set Variable to ASCII Value

The *Set Variable to ASCII Value* command converts a string variable, or string literal, to an integer variable with the results always between 0 and 255.

Pick the string variable to convert from the **In Variable** drop-down list, or enter a character into the **Character** field. Only a single character will be accepted of course.

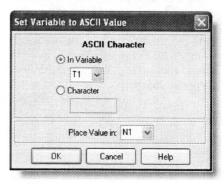

Variable Set %N1% to ASCII Value of "X"   // Convert "X" to 88

Running Macros from Variables

Why would you ever want to run a macro from a variable? To create *dynamic* macros, which adjust themselves to the user's choices at runtime rather than at design time when you have no idea what they are going to choose or use.

Any single command, or even a macro, can be run from a string variable using the *Run Macro in Variable* command. Wow! Good stuff, indeed. This is a good companion to the *Load Macro Text File* command because there is no file I/O to slow things down. Here is a simple example using the *Text Type* command:

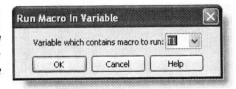

Variable Set String %T1% "<TEXTTYPE:The quick brown fox·>"
Run Macro in Variable %T1%

Wait a minute, what is this? It does not look like the *Text Type* command. Correct! If you have any experience at all with Macro Express, you know that what you see in the Scripting Editor window are not real commands but rather representations of them. To see the real macro commands you need to be viewing them in the Direct Editor window. In the Scripting Editor window, you see:

Text Type: The quick brown fox

In the Direct Editor window, you see the real command:

<TEXTTYPE:The quick brown fox·>

It is the real command, not its representation, that you stuff into string variable to run. So, do you have to pick your way through the Direct Editor to get the real code? No, of course not! While in the Scripting Editor, simply highlight the line, or lines that you want to place in a variable, copy them to the clipboard, then paste the string into the *Set Value Now* command.

Special Characters

Look at the above example. See the "**dot**" like character between the word "**fox**" and the greater-than sign ("**>**") at the end? This is what Macro Express calls the *Separator Character*. It is an ASCII 1, or SOH (Start of Heading), character. A rose by another name ... I will also call it a *Separator Character* to avoid confusion. It is used by Macro Express to separate commands from one another, as well as separating things within a command. The point being, this character cannot be typed directly from your keyboard. It must be pasted in. However,

String	Dec	Hex	Description
\b	8	08h	BS (Backspace)
\n	10	0Ah	LF (Line Feed)
\r	13	0Dh	CR (Carriage Return)
\t	9	09h	HT (Tab)
\s	1	01h	SOH (Separator)
\\	92	5Ch	"\" (Backslash)
\xhh	n/a	n/a	hh = 2 digit hex code

there is an alternative. Use special characters that Macro Express has provided in the table shown here.

Variable Set String %T1% "<TEXTTYPE:The quick brown fox\s>"
Run Macro in Variable %T1%

See how the "**dot**" has been replaced with a "**\s**" after the word "**fox**"? Macro Express will convert this special character string, from within the *Run Macro in Variable* command, to a separator character before it runs.

Let's examine some of the other special characters. What do you suppose the output from this would look like?

> **Variable Set String %T1% "<TEXTTYPE:The quick brown\r\nfox jumps over\r\nthe lazy dog\r\n\s>"**
> **Run Macro in Variable %T1%**

Notice how the *carriage return* and *line feed* special characters (\r\n) were embedded into the **T1** string? Macro Express will convert these in the same exact manner as it does the separator character.

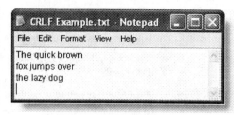

Feel free to experiment with some of the other special characters, but first let's take a closer look at the last two rows in the table.

The "****" is needed so Macro Express does not try to convert a backslash that you want to keep in the string. File paths immediately come to mind. In the example below, the commented line is how the command is normally displayed in the Scripting Editor.

> // Variable Set String %T1% from File: "example.txt"
> **Variable Set String %T1% "<TVAR2:01:04:c:\temp\example.txt>"**
> **Run Macro in Variable %T1%**

When you run this macro, you get an error. Why? Take a closer look at the command line that you are placing into the variable to run. It contains both a "**\t**" and a "**\e**" as part of the normal file path string so Macro Express will interpret the "**\t**" as a tab character rather than what it is. To avoid this situation use the "****" special character string in the command line as shown below.

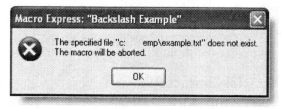

> // Variable Set String %T1% from File: "example.txt"
> **Variable Set String %T1% "<TVAR2:01:04:c:\\temp\\example.txt>"**
> **Run Macro in Variable %T1%**

This could have also been resolved using the special character string sequence "**\xhh**" shown in the last line of the table. But what is it? The "**\x**" portion tells Macro Express the next two characters in the string ("**hh**") are to be interpreted as a 2-digit hex value between **00**h and **FF**h. The "h" in 00h and FFh means hexadecimal or a base 16 number. Hexadecimal numbers are represented by the digits 0, 1, 2, 3, 4, 5, 6, 7, 8, and 9 and the letters A, B, C, D, E, and F. Study the ASCII chart a few pages back for an understanding of how this works. Let's rewrite the example:

> // Variable Set String %T1% from File: "example.txt"
> **Variable Set String %T1% "<TVAR2:01:04:c:\x5Ctemp\x5Cexample.txt>"**
> **Run Macro in Variable %T1%**

The special "**\x5C**" character string will be interpreted by Macro Express as a "\" (backslash) character. Look at the ASCII chart and you will see that **5C**h is indeed a backslash character. You can take this hexadecimal string conversion example to the extreme limit too!

> **Variable Set String %T1%**
> **"\x3C\x54\x45\x58\x54\x54\x59\x50\x45\x3A\x54\x68\x65\x20\x71\x75\x69\x63\x6B\x20\x62\x72\x6F\x77\x6E\x20\x66\x6F\x78\s**
> **\x3E"**
> **Run Macro in Variable %T1%**

What do you suppose the above string means? It means this:

> **Variable Set String %T1% "<TEXTTYPE:The quick brown fox\s>"**
> **Run Macro in Variable %T1%**

Yes, I have taken every character in "**<TEXTTYPE:The quick brown fox\s>**" and converted them to their hexadecimal equivalents (except for the separator character). Like this:

Chr	Hex	Chr	Hex	Chr	Hex	Chr	Hex	Chr	Hex	Chr	Hex
<	3C	T	54	E	45	X	58	T	54	T	54
Y	59	P	50	E	45	:	3A	T	54	h	68
e	65		20	q	71	u	75	i	69	c	63
k	6B		20	b	62	r	72	o	6F	w	77
n	6E		20	f	66	o	6F	x	78	>	3E

Cool, eh? As I said, you can take this feature to extremes. Whole macros can be run in this manner, not just single lines.

Using Environment Variables

As mentioned at the beginning of this chapter, environment variables are a special string type variable. Normally a string variable begins with a "T" and is numbered **1** through **99**, so we have **T1-T99**. Environment variables are not limited to these naming constraints, can have any name you want, and are in no way affected by the *Clear Variables* command. Your operating system has already created some for you. To see what they are, do this:

Click on your *Start* button then choose *Run*. Now type in either "**cmd**" or "**command**" then hit the *<Enter>* key. A DOS window will appear. When it does, simply type, "**set**", and then hit the *<Enter>* key. You will see a list of ready-made environment variables similar to the list found in the *Set Value from Environment Variable* command described earlier in this chapter.

So what if you want to know what the **ComSpec** variable contains on your system? Here is one way:

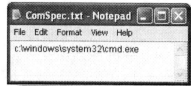

> **Activate Window: "Notepad"**   // Activate the Notepad
> **Text Type: %ComSpec%<ENTER>**   // What is the ComSpec variable?

The important thing to note is that none of the standard string variables were used. All you need to do is wrap a pair of percent signs around any environment name to have Macro Express access and use it.

It is also a simple matter to create an environment variable. Look again at the *Save to Environment Variable* command. You need to use a standard string variable to temporarily hold the value that will be saved to the environment variable. Let's create a secret identity.

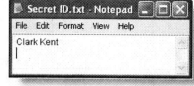

> **Variable Set String %T1% "Clark Kent"**
> **Variable Modify String: Save %T1% to Environment Variable**   // Save
> **%Secret Identity% variable**

So what if somebody wanted to know your not-so-secret **Secret Identity**? Just like before:

> **Activate Window: "Notepad"**   // Activate the Notepad
> **Text Type: %Secret Identity%<ENTER>**   // What is my Secret Identity variable?

How is an environment variable removed or deleted? First, you need to be aware that once Macro Express is unloaded from memory (stopped or shut down), so are your environment variables. This is by design and is mostly to do with your operating system. The way it works is that, whenever you start a Windows program (like Macro Express), it receives a copy of the existing environment variables from the operating system. Any environment variables created by the program are added to the ones received, not to the originals. You can test this for yourself. Create an environment variable from Macro Express, something like the **%Secret Identity%** example, then run the *cmd.exe* or *command.com* program from within Macro Express using the *Program Launch* command.

> **Program Launch: "cmd.exe"**

When the DOS window appears, simply type "**set**" and then hit *<Enter>* and you will see the **Secret Identity** variable in the list. Now look at the environment variable list from the operating system by using the *Start* button (just as you did at the beginning of this section) and you will *not* see any **Secret Identity** in the list. So if Macro Express goes away, then so do the variables it has created.

Other than shutting down Macro Express, you cannot remove a variable that was created, just as you cannot remove any of the **T1** through **T99** variables. You can, however, clear it by simply setting it to an empty value. If, for example, that you wanted to remove the **%Secret Identity%** variable, you would simply create an empty string and then save it to the variable.

Variable Set String %T1% ""	// Create an empty string
Variable Modify String: Save %T1% to Environment Variable	// Save it to the %Secret Identity% variable

There are too many commands to list individually in Macro Express that can use environment variables so here are three general guidelines. An environment variable can be used in any command that:

1. Needs or uses a window title. Use it as the window title.
2. Can accept a literal value in a text field. Use it in the text field.
3. Presents the user with an instruction or prompt. Use it as the instruction or prompt.

Summary

- Macro Express supports string, integer, decimal, window control, and environment variables.
- Use string variables in place of macro names, window titles, program names, file and folder names, and so forth.
- Use integer variables for display and window coordinates, mouse positions, file sizes, string lengths, and so forth.
- Use decimal variables for financial and scientific calculations, or anything else needing a decimal point.
- Variables are global in scope within a Macro Express session.
- Variables enable you to create dynamic and reusable macros.
- Variables can be used to control program flow.
- Variables can be set and cleared but never deleted.
- Variables can be saved and restored between sessions, except for environment variables.
- Whole macros can be run from variables.

Keyboard

W e strongly believe that anything which can be done with a keyboard and mouse can be done with a macro created by Macro Express. The keyboard then, is one of the most important tools you have to create and run macros successfully. Commands to control the keyboard are spread among various categories throughout the Macro Express Editor. The one you will probably use the most is *Text Type*, which Macro Express uses the same way that you do … sending keys to an application one keystroke at a time. In fact, feeding keystrokes into an application is the foundation of macros. And knowing how to use the commands that control these keystrokes is fundamental to using Macro Express effectively.

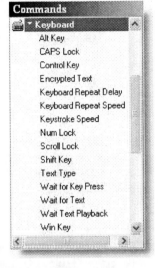

Text Type

Let's start with the one command you will probably use most often to send keystrokes to an application. The intent behind this dialog is to collect the keystrokes and display them in the **Keystrokes** window so you can see them. It looks intimidating, but then so did your keyboard at first. The dialog simply contains all the "special" keys that you have on your keyboard. The section just below the **Keystrokes** display window contains 28 special keys listed alphabetically. Just below that are twelve buttons labeled **F1** through **F12**. Then comes a **Variables** drop-down list, a **Misc Keys** drop-down list, and then a **Symbols** button in the same row. Below that are three choices that we will discuss later.

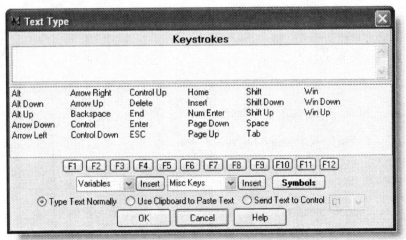

In most word processors today you can instantly move your cursor to the top of the document by holding down the <Ctrl> key and then hitting the <Home> key. This sequence can be produced here with your mouse by first clicking on **Control Down** then **Home** and then **Control Up** from the key list. Each is displayed in the window as you click on it. When you save the dialog (click the **OK** button), the following command line is created.

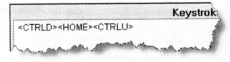

Text Type: <CTRLD><HOME><CTRLU>

This is the purpose of the *Text Type* dialog … to provide you a method to enter keystrokes into your macro using a menu and button style format. If you want <F1>, simply click the **F1** button. For <SPACE> click **Space** in the list. Other keys are listed in the **Misc Keys** drop-down list. Some of these may be unfamiliar to you. They are to me, too. I suspect they were placed here by special

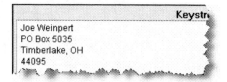

request to Insight Software Solutions. To enter one of these keys, you must pick it from the drop-down list and then click the **Insert** button.

Key	Description
Scroll Lock	Scroll Lock Key
Caps Lock	Caps Lock Key
Num Lock	Num lock Key
Number Pad 0 - 9	Number Pad Keys
Number Pad / * - + .	Number Pad Keys
Print Screen	Print Screen Key
Pause	Pause Key
Application	Menu-looking Key
Left Window	Left-side Windows Key
Right Window	Right-side Windows Key
Left Ctrl	Left-side Control Key
Right Ctrl	Right-side Control Key
F13 - F24	3270 Terminal
Attn	3270 Terminal
CrSel	3270 Terminal
ExSel	3270 Terminal
Erase EOF	3270 Terminal
Play	3270 Terminal
Zoom	3270 Terminal
PA1	3270 Terminal

I have covered inserting special keyboard keys into the **Keystrokes** window, but what about text? Easy! Simply type anything you want into the window. Whatever you enter will be "typed" when the macro runs.

For example, let's say you want a macro to fill in fields on a form. How could you use the *Text Type* command? Try this:

> Keystr…
>
> Joe Weinpert
> PO Box 5035
> Timberlake, OH
> 44095

The following command line is created:

Text Type: Joe Weinpert··PO Box 5035··Timberlake, OH··44095··

The double-dots represent CR/LF. You can see the results in the *Test Window* when the macro is run. Everything is typed, as you would expect, including the CR/LF characters. Entering text in this format works just fine, but there is another format that you should consider:

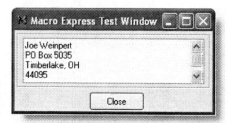

Text Type: Joe Weinpert<ENTER>PO Box 5035<ENTER>Timberlake, OH<ENTER>44095<ENTER>

The output in the *Test Window* is identical, even though <ENTER> replaces the CR/LF characters. I prefer this method because it is, from experience, safer. There are times in the past that I have had trouble when the CR/LF characters were embedded in the text, rather than just represented with <ENTER>.

You do not need to pick special keys such as **Alt**, **Control**, **Space**, **Enter**, and **Tab** from the list. You can, instead, type everything, including the word "<ENTER>", into the **Keystrokes** window as long as you know the correct spelling for each key and do not forget about the "<" and ">" characters. You will be the first to know if something was entered wrong.

The *Text Type* command is meant to combine text, keys, variables, and cursor movements into a single

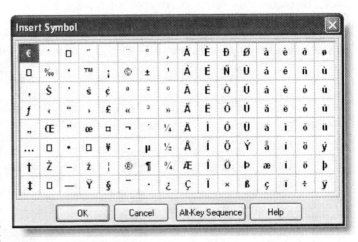

command. Variables can be entered into the **Keystrokes** window by either typing them directly (like "%T1%") or by choosing one from the **Variables** drop-down list, and then clicking on the **Insert** button. Naturally when the macro is run and the text is typed into the application, the contents of the variable will be typed, and not the variable name itself. And any variable can be picked. Strings, integers, and decimals will all be "typed" out as expected.

Not being satisfied with just the ability to enter keys accessible on your keyboard, Macro Express allows us to insert nonkeyboard symbols and characters with the **Symbols** button. The symbols are just the ASCII characters 128 through 255 (there is an ASCII chart in the *Variables* chapter) and are based on which font you are using. More to the point, which font the *target application* is using when the *Text Type* command runs. This is an important point to absorb because symbols work the same as characters. They look different depending on their font family, as do other characters. You would not, for example, expect "AaBbCcDd" to look the same in an Arial font as they do in a Myriad Roman font as is used in this book.

There is another feature to this *Insert Symbol* dialog. The **Alt-Key Sequence** button. This is a throwback to DOS again, but a useful throwback. It allows you to enter any ASCII character from 001 through 255 using the <ALT> key and your numeric keypad. Note that a **null** character (ASCII 000) cannot be entered, although it does exist, meaning that it takes up a character space. If you had a string of 10 **null** characters, your string would be 10 characters long.

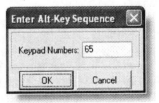

Let's try it. Start Notepad. Now hold the **Alt** key down and press **6** and then **5** on your keypad. Let up on the **Alt** key and you will see an uppercase "A". It is important to know that only the numbers on your keypad will work. The top row of numbers will not, because they send out different keyboard scan codes than those on the keypad. Do the same sequence with **66** and a

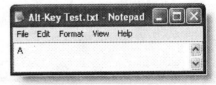

"B" will appear. These, of course, are ASCII numbers that you are entering, so take a look at the chart in the *Variables* chapter to see what the other characters would be fun to enter this way.

This feature will allow you to enter the *unprintable* ASCII characters 1 through 31, which cannot be entered from the

Keystrokes
<ALT:65><ALT:97><ALT:66><ALT:98><ALT:67><ALT:99><ALT:68><ALT:100>

either the **Keys** list, **Misc Keys** drop-down list, or the **Symbols** button.

The **Alt-Key** characters are not displayed in the **Keystrokes** window as characters because they may not be *viewable* or *printable*. Instead, they are displayed as shown above (previous page). What you see on the right is "AaBbCcDd" being output when the macro runs.

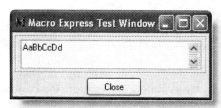

Let's examine the difference between the **Type Text Normally** and the **Use Clipboard to Paste Text** options. The former is the default and the latter is faster … if it can be used. **Type Text Normally** will simply output the string in the **Keystrokes** window one character at a time to your target application. This includes everything and anything from the **Key** list, **Variables** and **Misc Keys** drop-down lists, **Symbols**, and special **Alt-Key** keys.

There is something you need to be aware of when using *Text Type* with the **Type Text Normally** option. If you are typing too much text, too fast, the keyboard buffer could overflow, which is sure to cause havoc with your macro. From the Macro Express help system:

> It is possible when typing back long strings of text the keyboard buffer may overflow. When this happens you will notice some missing or scrambled text among the text that played back. Sometimes you may also hear a strange high-pitched sound. The text is trying to play back too fast. If you are experiencing this problem, you can either select the Use Clipboard to Paste Text option, set a standard Text Type Delay from the Preferences window, or use the Keystroke Speed command to control the text playback speed.

The standard *Text Type* delay is set from this dialog (Options | Preferences | Delays) by the **Use Text Type Delay** field. All *preferences* are global in scope, which means that any setting here will affect the *Text Type* command in every macro that uses it. The default is a zero delay between each character. The timing is specified in microseconds, of which 1,000 equals a single millisecond and 1,000,000 equals just one second. Feel free to experiment with this setting. Start small, with just 1,000 microseconds between each character (keystroke).

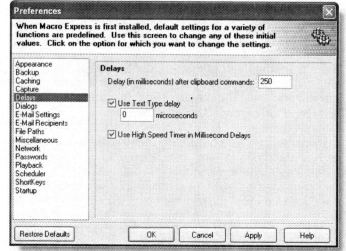

To avoid typing just a single character at a time, delays or no delays, choose the **Use Clipboard to Paste Text** option. It will use your Windows clipboard to paste text directly into the target application all at once, rather than a single character at a time. This option is fast, but cannot be used in certain situations. For example, do not try to fill multiple fields in a form with a single *Text Type* command using this option.

Looking at a previous example, the following command line is created:

> **Text Type: Joe Weinpert··PO Box 5035··Timberlake, OH··44095··**

Joe Weinpert
PO Box 5035
Timberlake, OH
44095

If you were to try this in a form that had fields titled Name, Address, City, and Zip, the macro would possibly fail. I say "possibly" because sometimes it will work, and other times not. The *pasting* will happen too fast for the form to keep pace with the embedded CR/LF characters, or <TAB> characters if they are used in place of CR/LF. Do this instead:

> **Text Type: Joe Weinpert··**
> **Text Type: PO Box 5035··**
> **Text Type: Timberlake, OH··**
> **Text Type: 44095··**

And make sure that you choose the **Use Clipboard to Paste Text** option for each *Text Type*. This will work much faster than the **Type Text Normally** option.

Another situation that *will not work* with this option is where your text string contains something other than text, variables, symbols, <ENTER>, or <TAB>. In other words, you cannot use any keys chosen from the **Misc Keys** drop-down list, **Alt-Key** characters, and all but the two keys from the **Key** list. The Macro Express help system states the following about the **Use Clipboard to Paste Text** option:

> With this option selected, the text will be played back through the Windows clipboard when the macro is run. This option should only be used with text. If you have inserted other keys such as Alt, Ctrl, Shift, etc. into this command when using the Clipboard option, then these keys will paste back as <ALT>, <CONTROL>, <SHIFT>, etc. instead of playing the keystroke.

In other words, the **Use Clipboard to Paste Text** option *will work* with text, variables, symbols, <ENTER> and <TAB>, but nothing else.

The **Send Text to Control** option is covered in detail inside the *Window Controls* chapter. It types text directly into a previously defined Window Control.

Here is a point about using the *Text Type* command effectively. Look back at the example used at the beginning of this chapter.

> **Text Type: <CTRLD><HOME><CTRLU>**

Although this sequence of keystrokes will work by moving the cursor to the beginning of a document, you could have used the simpler <CONTROL><HOME> sequence instead. Macro Express knows the **Control**, **Alt**, and **Shift** keys are always used with one or more other keys. This is also true of the **Win** (Windows) key, with one exception, used by itself, it will engage the *Start* button on your Taskbar. When Macro Express sees something like <CONTROL><HOME>, it automatically holds the <CONTROL> key down while hitting the <HOME> key, then releases it. This is true of any combination that use these keys. <CTRLD><SHIFTD>P<SHIFTU><CTRLU> could be recorded as simply <CONTROL><SHIFT>P.

Using the *Text Type* command to access application menus could use some explaining. Here is the Macro Express Editor menu. It contains **File**, **Macros**, **Category**, **Wizards**, and so forth. To access any of them, use the

Text Type command to type out <ALT> (or sometimes … rarely <ALT><ALT>, depending on the application) to get to the menu bar itself, and then the underlined, *lowercase* letter of your target menu. "f" for the **File** menu, "m" for the **Macros** menu, "c" for **Category**, and "w" for **Wizards**.

Why lowercase? There may be instances where an uppercase character confuses the target application. When you *Text Type* an uppercase "F" the following is sent by Macro Express:

<SHIFTD>f<SHIFTU>

Think about this for a moment. For you to type an uppercase "F", you must hold the **Shift** key down, hit the "f" key, and then let go of the **Shift** key. Macro Express must do this also. So, when you *Text Type* "<ALT>F" this is what is sent:

<ALTD><SHIFTD>f<SHIFTU><ALTU>

The need to add shift keys may confuse an application's menu, so sending a literal lowercase "f" will avoid the need for them. When you *Text Type* "<ALT>f" only the following is sent:

<ALTD>f<ALTU>

Let's go back to the difference between sending a single "<ALT>f" (which you just saw) or double "<ALT><ALT>f" to activate a menu bar and choose, in our example, the File menu. Most of today's applications will work just fine with the former. There may be exceptions. When you find them, try the latter combination. It will send:

<ALTD><ALTU>f

That is correct. Sending two "<ALT><ALT>" keys in a row sends "<ALTD><ALTU>". Again, most applications think this is just fine, and will activate the chosen menu. Try both of these menu-activating keystrokes manually to discover which works best for your application.

It bears repeating that Macro Express needs to do exactly what you do to send keys to an application. Remembering this will make working with Macro Express less harrowing.

Wait Text Playback

Beneath the *Text Type* command is an ideal location to place the description for *Wait Text Playback*, because this is exactly where you want to place it … immediately after the *Text Type* command. The reason to use this command is to stop your macro from continuing until your keyboard buffer reports it is finished typing out the text that was stuffed into it. It does not hurt to place it elsewhere, since it is ignored if the keyboard buffer is already empty. On the other hand, that does not do you much good.

Most of the time this command is not needed because, most of the time you are using simple and short *Text Type* strings. However, the longer these strings become, with or without delays, the better the chance becomes that this command will be useful. I want to repeat that it does not hurt anything to place this command in your macro, especially if you are creating them to run unattended.

There is no dialog for *Wait Text Playback* since it does not contain any settings or parameters. It is chosen directly from the category list.

Wait Text Playback

Keystroke Speed

This command is chosen from the common *Speed* dialog and was mentioned as alternative to setting a global *Text Type* delay from inside the *Preferences* dialog. It lets you control how fast each character is typed into your application from both the *Text Type* and *Encrypted Text* commands.

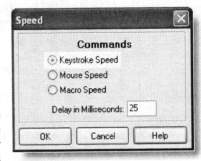

The default is a zero delay between each key sent to the keyboard buffer. It is noteworthy that delays may be needed, *not* because your keyboard is slow (it is not), but rather the software application the keyboard is feeding is slow. Your keyboard buffer must continually wait to send its keys out the front, while keys from *Text Type* are backing up on the other end. Eventually, this will cause the buffer to overflow.

So, you must put the brakes on Macro Express. Slow down feeding the keyboard buffer by placing a small delay between each key sent. Enter a value into the **Delay in Milliseconds** field from zero all the way up to 99,999, which is just a single millisecond under 100 seconds. That is a longtime to wait between keystrokes.

Keystroke Speed: 25 Milliseconds

The delay can be reset to its zero default value by simply adding another *Keystroke Speed* command. It can be changed as often as you like, and will remain in effect until changed with another command, or your macro stops.

Encrypted Text

This is a design time feature. It is used to hide the value of a string variable, or what is to be typed as text into a target application, when viewing, or printing a macro. It does not, however, prevent the viewer from seeing the real text in the debug window if you are using the **Place in a Variable** feature. The **Variable Name**

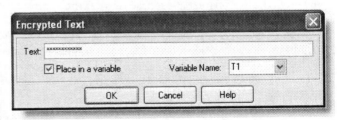

drop-down list is the target variable. The **Text** field contains the encrypted string.

This command is designed to do one of two tasks. If you are *not* using the **Place in a Variable** feature, it will type out the decrypted **Text** field into whichever application is current when the line is run. Otherwise, the **Text** field is decrypted and simply placed into the target **Variable Name**.

Again, this is a design time feature. If you want an encrypted runtime command that can be used to enter passwords and such, see the **Mask Input** feature of the *Prompt for Value* command in the *Set Text String Variables* dialog.

Set Keyboard Repeat Delay
Set Keyboard Repeat Speed

These two commands do *not* affect the **Keystroke Speed** command in any manner. They are instead, a programmatic way to set your computer's keyboard delay and speed settings shown using the Keyboard icon in the *Control Panel*.

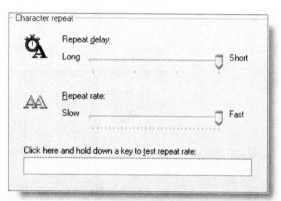

The way the sliding bars in the *Character Repeat* dialog are set, means that I have a quick keyboard. The **Repeat Delay** bar is set to the right tick mark, or what would be the *shortest* delay when holding down a key, before it begins to repeat. Of course the shortest delay means the faster the key will repeat. The **Factor** field in the *Set Keyboard Repeat Delay* command can be set to 3, 2, 1, or 0. These numbers are related to the four tick marks that you see under the **Repeat Delay** bar. A setting of "3" is the longest delay and represents the left tick mark. A setting of "0" is the shortest delay and represents the right tick mark.

The **Repeat Rate** bar is set to the right tick mark, or what would be the *fastest* speed when the key starts repeating. The **Factor** field in the *Set Keyboard Repeat Speed* command can be set from 0 through 31. These numbers are related to the thirty-two tick marks that you see under the **Repeat Rate** bar. A setting of "0" is the slowest repeat speed and represents the left tick mark. A setting of "31" is the fastest repeat speed and represents the right tick mark.

Wait for Key Press
Wait for Text

These two commands are similar in that they stop your macro at runtime to wait for the user to enter something from the keyboard. *Wait for Key Press* waits for a single key and *Wait for Text* waits for a string to be entered. There is no prompt. The macro simply waits whenever, and wherever the command line is encountered and, this is important, passes the keystrokes through to the application.

Your macro can wait for the proper keystrokes forever by choosing the **Wait Indefinitely** option. On the other hand, you may prefer to wait for just a short period of time. If so, use the two **Wait a Maximum** fields (**Minutes** and **Seconds**). Each accepts a value up to 999,999, which means you can have your macro wait for just a little bit over 706 days.

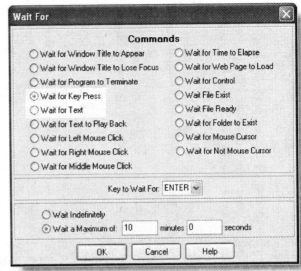

The *Wait for Key Press* command is used to wait for a single key press that can be chosen from the **Key to Wait For** drop-down list. There are 55

A - Z	Tab
0 - 9	Enter
F1 - F12	Control
Space	Alt
Escape	Shift

different keys show here. All the keys, including Control, Alt, and Shift, will report that they have been pressed on the downstroke for passing the key through to the application. This "pass-through" feature can cause a minor problem when using this command.

Take notice of your **Turn CAPS Lock off when starting a macro** setting (Tools | Preferences | Playback). If this feature is used, then any uppercase letter A - Z this command waits for, is passed through as lowercase, unless you use the shift key. I realize this is normal, however, if you are not aware of the setting then you may be thinking that an uppercase letter should be passed through.

The *Wait for Text* command waits for the string named in the **Text to Wait For** field to be typed, rather than just a single character. Again, there is no prompt. The macro simply waits until the correct string is entered. It will not wait for the <Enter> key because it continuously collects keys until it finds the match it is looking for, and then continues. Use the **Case Sensitive** checkbox if all characters must match each upper and lowercase character exactly.

The maximum string length is 32 characters. You will be prevented from going beyond this when entering a literal string. If you place a string variable in the **Text to Wait For** field, and that variable is longer than allowed, an error will be displayed at runtime.

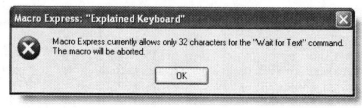

Alt Key

Control Key

Shift Key

Win Key

These commands allow you to control the down or up state of these "control" keys. For every "down", there must be a matching "up", in other words, they work in pairs. This is so important that Macro Express displays each command line between the down and up state indented, like in a *Repeat Loop* or *If / End If* structure.

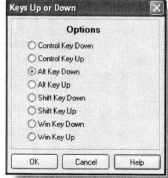

Activate Window: "Microsoft Word"	// Activate Word
Shift Key Down	// Hold the Shift Key down
Repeat Start (Repeat 20 times)	// Loop 20 times
Text Type: <ARROW DOWN>	// Select next line
Repeat End	// Done repeating
Shift Key Up	// Let go the Shift Key

This macro activates Word and then selects the next 20 lines and stops. Notice how the command lines are displayed between **Shift Key Down** and **Shift Key Up**. They are indented to show that all commands between the two lines are carried out *with* the Shift Key down.

You could rewrite the macro to use only the **Text Type** command, however, you would need to place 20 <ARROW DOWN> keys in a row rather than just place a single one in a loop. But the real advantage to using these keys is the format allows you to embed any command needed to get the job done between the "down" and "up" keys. For example, what if you had some mouse movements to embed with one of these keys held down? You could not do that with **Text Type**. So, use these keys when you need to have a series of commands carried out while one of them is being held down.

Caps Lock

Num Lock

Scroll Lock

All these keys have one thing in common; they can be toggled on or off with your keyboard. These commands, however, do not toggle but instead simply turns "on" or "off" a particular key. There is no command to test and return the "on" or "off" state of any of these keys, which would be needed for

"toggling". In other words, nothing happens if you try to "toggle" the
state of a key. If **CAPS Lock** is on, it will remain on if you use the *CAPS Lock
On* command.

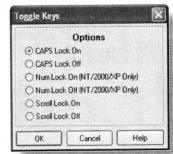

Restore Keyboard Hooks

What is this term "hooks" all about? Well, it means that Macro Express
gets to peek at the keyboard or mouse activity before any other
program, even the one that is active. How else, could Macro Express
process your keyboard and mouse activity? There are certain rules that
are best followed when doing things like this, but sometimes a
program, which is loaded after Macro Express, may not understand these rules. This makes it necessary
for Macro Express to reestablish its dominance over your keyboard and mouse activity.

There is a command to do this at runtime for both keyboard and mouse hooks at the same time. It is
simply called *Reset Hooks* and can be found within the *Macro Express* category in the Macro Express Editor.
To restore both keyboard and mouse hooks at once at design time, click on **Restore Keyboard and Mouse
Hooks** from *Tools* menu in your *System Tray* icon. You could also restore just keyboard hooks from the
Macro Express *Tools* menu by clicking on the **Restore Keyboard Hooks** choice.

Auto Restore Keyboard Hooks

This is not a command, it is an option
found in the *Miscellaneous* dialog in
the *Preferences* screen. Use it to avoid
having to restore hooks manually.

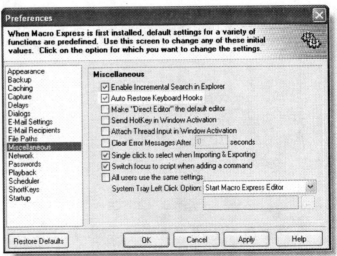

This feature will automatically *try* to
reestablish the Macro Express
dominance of your keyboard, giving it
first look at the keystrokes passed
through the Windows system-wide
keyboard hooks when other programs
are loaded that use these keyboard
hooks. "Try" is used because it is
impossible to guarantee this will work
100% of the time. Three things have to
happen for Macro Express to lose
keyboard dominance:

1. A program is run after Macro Express is loaded -AND-
2. It also uses keyboard hooks -AND-
3. It inserts itself into the system-wide keyboard hooks in an improper fashion.

When an application is launched, and it has a window of some sort, or if an application with a window is
closed, Macro Express will wait 5 seconds before resetting the keyboard hooks if you are using this
feature. Unfortunately, if a new program resets the hooks, but does not display a window, then the
hooks will have to be reset manually. Macro Express cannot detect when a new application is launched
if the application does not display a window. Also, other programs that periodically reset the hooks can

have a similar impact, as they do not alert other running programs, such as Macro Express, when the hooks have been reset. Therefore, the hooks will have to manually be reset as well.

Remap Keyboard

This is not a command, it is an option found in the *Tools* menu. Most of the description you read here is taken directly from the Macro Express help system. There was little that I could do to improve on it other than to add some pictures and bits of information here and there.

The **Remap Keyboard** option will allow you to remap many of the keys on your keyboard, 47 keys to be exact. For instance you could remap the **$** key so every time you press the **$** key, the **£** symbol will be displayed in the application you are running.

Selecting the (Tools | Remap Keyboard) choice from the Macro Explorer menu will activate the *Remap Keyboard* dialog. There are four columns of keys which may be remapped:

1. Uppercase - All letters of the alphabet capitalized.
2. Lowercase - All letters of the alphabet in lowercase.
3. Punctuation - Punctuations, symbol keys, and the space bar found on the keyboard.
4. Numeric - The numbers from 0-9.

Select the key that you want to remap by pointing the mouse at that key and double-clicking on it. The *Select Character* dialog appears.

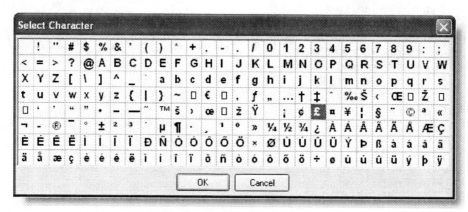

Find the character that will replace your key and double-click on it, or highlight the character with a single mouse click, then click OK. This returns you to the *Remap Keyboard* dialog and the character you selected has been inserted.

For example, double-click on the dollar sign **$** (the right-hand one of the two). The *Select Character* dialog appears. Select the pound **£** symbol. Double-click on it.

You will return to the *Remap Keyboard* dialog. The **£** has replaced the **$** in your list of keys. Now each time you type the **$** key on your keyboard, the **£** symbol will appear.

This option is limited to the alphabet keys, number keys, punctuation keys, and symbols. Keys such as the F1 - F12 keys, Alt, Ctrl, Insert, Home, Page Up, and so forth, cannot be remapped using this feature.

The 47 keys (95 characters) that can be remapped (*Remap Keyboard* dialog):
- Lowercase "a" through "z"
- Uppercase "A" through "Z"
- Punctuation keys plus the space bar
- Numeric keys "0" through "9"

The 224 characters that can be assigned (*Select Character* dialog):
- Normal ASCII characters including "A" through "Z", "a" through "z", "0" through "9" and many punctuation keys such as . , * # ! and dozens more.
- Western European Language characters including â è ö î ú Ö Ë Æ ß ñ and dozens more
- Western European Language punctuation such as ¡ ¿
- Math Symbols such as ÷ × ‰ ± ¼ ½ ¾
- Currency Symbols such as ¢ £ ¥ $
- Typographical Symbols such as ¶ §
- Legal Symbols such as ® © ™
- And various others found in the ANSI set including some of the following ª „ º ¹ ² ³

What if you want to put *un*map your keyboard and put the keys back the way the way they were? You could change the keys back one at a time by remapping them, or you may reset them all at once by taking the following steps:

1. Stop Macro Express.
2. Delete the file **swpkey.mes**, which may be found in the Macro Express home folder.
3. Restart Macro Express.

You could also write a two-line macro:

```
Delete File or Files: "swpkey.mes"    // Delete the keyboard mapping file
Restart Macro Express                 // Reinitialize Macro Express
```

Another option would be to rename the **swpkey.mes** file instead of deleting it. In fact, you could keep several copies of the file and switch them using a macro to load whichever mapping you need.

Summary

- Any task done with a keyboard and mouse can be done with Macro Express.
- The main command to send keystrokes to your application is *Text Type*.
- To avoid overflowing your keyboard buffer, use the *Keystroke Speed* command.
- You can design a macro to stop until a user presses a certain key or types a certain string.
- Actions such as highlighting text or dragging with a mouse can be done with Macro Express by placing the proper commands between the "down" and "up" events of certain control keys.
- Macro Express allows you to remap your keyboard and then reset it to normal.

Mouse

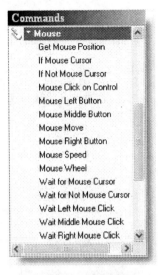

As mentioned in the *Keyboard* chapter, I strongly believe that anything which can be done with a keyboard and mouse can be done with a macro created by Macro Express. The mouse then, like the keyboard, is one of the most important tools you have to create and run macros successfully. Commands to control the mouse are spread among various categories throughout the Macro Express Editor. And knowing how to use them is fundamental to using Macro Express effectively.

Mouse Left
Mouse Right
Mouse Middle

These basic commands, which are called from the *Mouse Command* dialog, are easy to use because they contain no options.

Button Click
Button Double Click

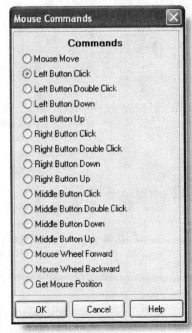

There is a command for each *Left*, *Right*, and *Middle* mouse button that sends a single or double-click. Your mouse will perform the action at the mouse's current position in whichever application is active at the time the command is run. See the *Mouse Move* command to learn how to position your mouse with Macro Express.

> **Mouse Left Button Click**
> **Mouse Left Button Double Click**

If you have no middle mouse button, and you try any of the *Middle* mouse button commands, nothing happens. The command is ignored.

Button Down
Button Up

These commands allow you to hold either the *Left*, *Right*, or *Middle* mouse button *Down*, perform a series of other commands, and then let the mouse button *Up*. The *Down* and *Up* commands work in pairs. This is so important that Macro Express displays each command line between the down and up state indented, like in a *Repeat Loop* or *If / End If* structure. Any commands placed between *Mouse Button Down* and *Mouse Button Up* are performed with the mouse button held down. Click-and-drag is a good example of the operation that can be performed with these commands.

Activate Window: "Microsoft Word"	// Activate Word
Delay 100 Milliseconds	// Let it settle in
Mouse Move To Text Cursor Position	// Position the mouse
Mouse Left Button Down	// Click and hold and
Mouse Move Position 400, 0	// drag
Mouse Left Button Up	//Let go the button

This macro activates *Microsoft Word* and then moves the mouse to wherever the cursor is found. It then holds the left mouse button down, drags the mouse to the right 400 pixels, and then releases the mouse button.

Because there is only one mouse, these two commands cannot be nested. Macro Express will ignore any nesting at runtime. The following macro runs identical with the example above because the inner pair of the *Mouse Left Button Down* and *Mouse Left Button Up* commands are ignored.

Activate Window: "Microsoft Word"	// Activate Word
Delay 100 Milliseconds	// Let it settle in
Mouse Move To Text Cursor Position	// Position the mouse
Mouse Left Button Down	// Click and hold
Mouse Left Button Down	// Click again and hold and
Mouse Move Position 400, 0	// drag
Mouse Left Button Up	//Let go the button
Mouse Left Button Up	//Let go the button again

Mouse Wheel Forward
Mouse Wheel Backward

These two commands move the mouse wheel forward or backward the number of clicks in the **Wheel Clicks** field. Note: This command does not work under Windows 95, 98, or Me.

The **Wheel Clicks** field will accept any value up to 99,999. Although I found anything beyond 150 results in inconsistent behavior. Also, the *Mouse Speed* command has no affect on how fast the wheel turns. The wheel turns as fast as your system allows. You may want to experiment to find a reliable maximum value.

The value entered will give the same results as if you were to move the wheel yourself. On my system, each click of the wheel will move my document up or down by 3 lines. You may have your system set for a different number.

Get Mouse Position

Sets two integer variables with the **X Pos** and **Y Pos** coordinates of your mouse at the time the command is performed. Choose variables from the two drop-down lists. The coordinates saved can be **Relative to Screen** or **Relative to Window**, depending on which option you choose. The "Window", of course, is the active application.

An X or Y coordinate will be negative if **Relative to Screen** is chosen and your mouse is found on a different display in a multiple display system. It can also be negative if you have chosen **Relative to Window** and your mouse is to the left, or above, the active application window. X and Y coordinates are explained more fully in the *Dialog Positioner* section of the *Variables* chapter.

If **Relative to Screen** is chosen then the coordinates returned will be identical with those retuned by the *Set Value from Mouse X Position* and *Set Value from Mouse Y Position* commands described in the *Variables* chapter.

Mouse Move

This dialog is packed with many different ways to move your mouse using Macro Express. Move it based on where the text cursor is found, relative to the display screen, application window, current position, or Window Control.

The **X Pos** and **Y Pos** fields contain the target coordinates of the mouse destination (where the mouse is being moved to) when using **Relative to Screen**, **Relative to Window**, or **Relative to Control** options. When used with **Relative to Last Position**, they represent how far to move the mouse from its current position. The **To Text Cursor Position** option does not use these coordinate fields. Each of them, when used, can be set with a literal value or string variable. A literal value can range from -99,999 through 999,999. When using integer variables, their range is from -2,147,483,648 through 2,147,483,647. These options give you plenty of room to move your mouse, however, the mouse will never be positioned beyond what your computer hardware will allow. If you have a single 1024×768 display, and you set the **X Pos** and **Y Pos** fields for 2000 and 2000, your mouse will be positioned at the bottom-right corner.

The **To Text Cursor Position** option moves the mouse to wherever your text cursor is found, if the text cursor is viewable in the window. There are times when the text cursor may have been scrolled outside the viewable area. If so, then the mouse is repositioned to the top-left corner of the active window, and not to the text cursor, after this command is run. The testing that I have done with this option shows that it is usable with Windows Notepad and Wordpad, Microsoft Excel, and Outlook, and many others. However, it does not work using Microsoft Word. And here is why, from the Macro Express help system:

> **Note: This function will not work on programs that create and use their own text cursor. Programs that do so do not use the built-in Windows Text Cursor functions. Ironically, MS Word appears to fall into this category.**

The **Relative to Screen** option moves the mouse to the coordinates named in the **X Pos** and **Y Pos** fields relative to your display screen. If, for example, these fields are zero and zero, your mouse will be positioned to the top-left corner of your display after the command is run.

The **Relative to Window** option moves the mouse to the coordinates named in the **X Pos** and **Y Pos** fields relative to your active application window. If, for example, these fields are zero and zero, your mouse will be positioned to the top-left corner of the application window after the command is run.

Both the **Relative to Screen** and **Relative to Window** options can make use of the **Ctrl+Space** feature as explained in the paragraph at the bottom of the *Mouse Movement* dialog. This is a great feature because you do not need to know what the coordinates are to populate the **X Pos** and **Y Pos** fields. Do the following steps:

1. Pick which option to use **Relative to Screen** or **Relative to Window**.
2. If **Relative to Window**, activate the application window by clicking on it.
3. Position the mouse to where you want Macro Express to move it.
4. Press the <Control+Space> HotKey combination on your keyboard.

The **X Pos** and **Y Pos** fields will be automatically filled with the correct coordinates. You do not need to know any coordinates and you do not have to fire-up the *Mouse Locator*. Sweet!

The **Relative to Control** option moves the mouse to the coordinates named in the **X Pos** and **Y Pos** fields relative to the Window Control named in the drop-down list. A Window Control may be a command button, entry field, checkbox, and so forth. See the *Window Controls* chapter to learn more. This option, and all of its rules, work identical with the **Relative to Window** option. If, for example your Window Control is a command button, and these fields are zero and zero, your mouse will be positioned to the top-left corner of the command button after the command is run.

The **Relative to Last Position** option moves the mouse the number of pixels named in the **X Pos** and **Y Pos** fields. A positive **X Pos** value moves the cursor to the right, and a negative value to the left. A positive **Y Pos** value moves the cursor down, and a negative value up.

Mouse Locator

The *Mouse Locator* dialog can be launched by clicking on the **Launch Mouse Locator** button, from the Macro Express *Tools* menu, or from the System Tray icon. It displays three pieces of live, dynamic information for you as you drag the mouse across your display.

The **Screen Position** section shows the current mouse coordinates relative to your screen. These values can be used to populate the **X Pos** and **Y Pos** fields when using the **Relative to Screen** option.

The **Active Window** section shows the current mouse coordinates relative to whichever application window has focus. These values can be used to populate the **X Pos** and **Y Pos** fields when using the **Relative to Window** option. But, be sure that your target window *is* the focused window. It is easy to forget which window is focused when you have a screen full of them.

The **Pixel Color** section displays the color of the pixel found at the current mouse coordinates as an integer value. But, what is the color? What does this number represent? Without getting into much detail, you may be aware that colors are displayed in a red-green-blue (RGB) format. Pixels consist of a value from each. Each red and green and blue value is represented by a single byte in the range of 00h through FFh. The "h" earmarks hexadecimal notation.

Color	RGB	Hex	Integer
Black	00h,00h,00h	000000	0
White	FFh,FFh,FFh	FFFFFF	16,777,215
Red	00h,00h,FFh	0000FF	255
Green	00h,80h,00h	008000	32,768
Blue	FFh,00h,00h	FF0000	16,711,680
Yellow	00h,FFh,FFh	00FFFF	65,535
Grey	80h,80h,80h	808080	8,421,504
Orange	00h,66h,FFh	0066FF	26,367

The **Pixel Color** number in the *Mouse Locator* dialog represents the hexadecimal value of all three RGB values concatenated, and then converted to an integer.

Let's examine *white*, which is represented as FFh,FFh,FFh. Concatenating the three values together results in a hexadecimal string "FFFFFF". Converting this to an integer equals 16,777,215, which is the **Pixel Color** number displayed.

Please read the *Advanced Options* section within the *Running and Activating Macros* chapter for a way to display both the integer *and* hexadecimal value of the **Pixel Color**.

Move Mouse to Tray Icon

This is a newer command, which enables you to move the mouse over an icon in your System Tray.

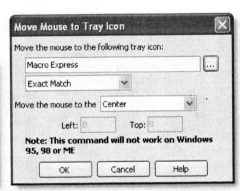

Click on the **ellipses** (...) button to pop up the *Select a Tray Icon* dialog, which will present an alphabetical list of the icons currently in

your System Tray. Select one using your mouse and then double-click. Or select one using the **Up** and **Down** arrows on your keyboard and then hit the **Enter** key. Your choice will be placed into the field.

Or, if you know the name of the icon then you can type it directly into the field. The field will only accept literal strings (no variables), but is not case sensitive. "MACRO EXPRESS", "mAcRo eXpReSs", and "Macro Express" will all find the same icon even when using the **Exact Match** option.

An error will be displayed during development if the field is left blank.

The drop-down list below the name field tells Macro Express to use an **Exact Match** or **Partial Match** when searching for the target icon at runtime. **Exact Match** is the default choice. Using **Partial Match** in the example, "MACRO", "eXpReSs", and "acro Expr" will all find the "Macro Express" icon. Case sensitivity has nothing to do with **Exact Match** or **Partial Match** within Macro Express.

The "**Move the Mouse to The**" drop-down list has two options, which are **Center** and **Specific Coordinates**. The **Center** option is the default choice and will place the mouse cursor in the middle of the icon at runtime. The **Specific Coordinates** options enables you to offset placement of the mouse cursor from the upper-left corner of the icon by values you enter into the **Left** and **Top** fields. Both fields accept literal values and integer variables. The range allowed for literal values is -999,999 through 9,999,999. When using integer variables, their range is from -2,147,483,648 through 2,147,483,647. In other words, more than you will ever need whether using literal values or integer variables.

But why would you want to offset the mouse cursor from the icon? One reason is to pick something from a menu after right-clicking on its icon. Let's use *Capture Express* as an example.

Say that I want to launch its *Configuration* dialog. With the ***Move Mouse to Tray Icon*** command, I can move the mouse cursor over the icon in my System Tray and then right-click on it using the ***Mouse Right Button Click*** command. Using the ***Move Mouse to Tray Icon*** command again, I can move the mouse cursor over the "Configure" choice on the menu by offsetting the coordinates and then click using the ***Mouse Left Button Click*** command.

Move Mouse to Tray Icon: "Capture Express"	// Center on System Tray icon
Mouse Right Button Click	// Click the right mouse button
Variable Set Integer %N1% to -70	// Offset 70 pixels to the left
Variable Set Integer %N2% to -140	// Offset 140 pixels towards the top
Move Mouse to Tray Icon: "Capture Express"	// Use Specific Coordinates N1 and N2
Mouse Left Button Click	// Click the left mouse button

Macro Express warns us the ***Move Mouse to Tray Icon*** command does not work when using Windows 95, 98, or ME. But there is another situation when using Windows XP that can make it look like the command is not working. This is Windows XP ability to hide icons in the System Tray by collapsing it. For example, you may receive an error at runtime stating the Volume icon cannot be found … even though it is in the System Tray.

To avoid this situation, change the behavior of the Volume icon. Right-click on the Taskbar and then choose "Properties". Uncheck the **Hide Inactive Icons** box within the **Notification Area** section to unhide all icons in the System Tray.

Or you can pick icons to unhide by clicking on the **Customize** button, which will pop up the *Customize*

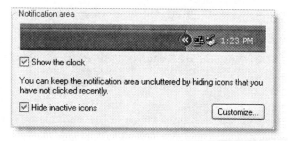

Notifications dialog. The behavior can be set for the Volume icon by clicking in the Behavior column.

There are three choices, which are **Always show**, **Always hide**, and **Hide when inactive**. Change it to **Always show**. This allows the icon to remain visible when the System Tray collapses allowing the *Move Mouse to Tray Icon* command to recognize it.

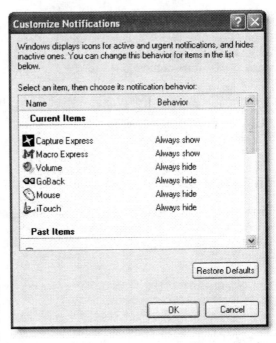

Macro Express allows us to create a Popup Menu and place an icon to access it in the System Tray (refer to the *Popup and Floating Menus* section within the *Running and Activating Macros* chapter). When using the *Move Mouse to Tray Icon* command for a Popup Menu icon, you must specify a **Partial Match**. An **Exact Match** will not work because the name associated with the Popup Menu icon changes when a macro is running.

Mouse Speed

This regulates a delay time *before* each mouse command is carried out. Unlike the *Keystroke Speed* command that places a delay between each character fed into the buffer, this one delays only between commands. Say that you use the *Mouse Move* command to slide the mouse to the right 100 pixels. If *Mouse Speed* is set to 250 milliseconds, then that is how long the macro will pause before sliding the mouse. It does *not* delay between the pixels as the mouse is moved.

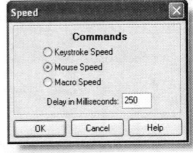

Mouse Speed: 250 Milliseconds	// Set mouse delay
Mouse Move Position 100, 0	// Move 100 pixels to the right
Mouse Move Position 0, 100	// Move 100 pixels down
Mouse Move Position -100, 0	// Move 100 pixels to the left
Mouse Move Position 0, -100	// Move 100 pixels up

This moves the mouse in a square pattern. The macro will pause for 250 milliseconds between each of the *Mouse Move* commands. When it does move the mouse, it will move as fast as your system allows.

Please be aware the delay remains in place until reset with another *Mouse Speed* command, even between macro sessions. This behavior is opposite of the *Keystroke Speed* command, which is automatically resets to zero between sessions. The *Mouse Speed* command will also be set back to zero when Macro Express itself is restarted.

If Mouse Cursor
If Not Mouse Cursor

These two commands, chosen from the system-wide *If Commands* dialog, allow you to branch your macro based on the state of the mouse cursor.

Your mouse cursor can be in any state depending on what you are doing at the moment. It could be "Beam" if you are in a text field, an "Arrow" if in a menu, an "Hourglass" while waiting for an event, and so forth.

There are 21 different mouse cursors that Macro Express can account for, and are listed in the table on the next page. Choose your target mouse cursor from the **Mouse Cursor** drop-down list. Unlike the *Wait for Mouse Cursor* and *Wait for Not Mouse Cursor* commands, the highlighted cursor is not displayed as the list is scrolled.

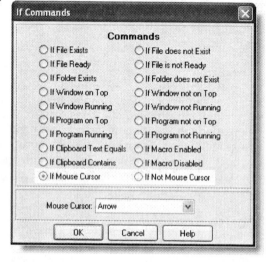

Let's create a macro that uses a change in the mouse cursor to change the size of a window. The example first launches the Windows Notepad, then sets its size to 300×250, centering it on the display and giving you a second to look at it.

A small, 5-millisecond delay is set between each mouse command so you can watch the mouse cursor move down the window, then the mouse cursor is positioned in the titlebar.

Then the mouse cursor is moved down the window a single pixel at a time in a loop. A check is performed each time to find out if it has changed to the "Size NS" mouse cursor. If so, we know the mouse can now be used to resize the Notepad by dragging its bottom line up 100 pixels. The loop is exited and the delay between mouse commands is reset to zero and the macro ends.

Arrow	⇖	Up Arrow	↑	SQL Wait	⏳
Cross	+	Hourglass	⌛	No	⊘
Beam	I	Drag	⬚	App Start	⇖⌛
Size NESW	⤢	No Drop	⊘	Help	⇖?
Size NS	↕	H Split	↔	Hand Point	✋
Size NWSE	⤡	V Split	↕	Size All	✛
Size WE	↔	Multi Drag	⬚	Internet Nav	👆

```
Activate Window: "Notepad"                          // Launch the Notepad
Window Resize: Current Win - (Width: 300, Height: 250)   // Size it
Window Reposition: Center - Current Win         .       // Center it
Delay 1 Seconds                                     // Wait a second to view the Notepad
Mouse Speed: 5 Milliseconds                         // Delay 5 ms between Mouse commands
Mouse Move Window 150, 3                             // Move mouse to titlebar
Repeat Until %N1% <> %N1%                            // Repeat forever
  Mouse Move Position 0, 1                           // Move mouse down a single pixel
  If Mouse Cursor is Size NS                         // If the cursor changed to a Size NS, then
```

```
Delay 1 Seconds              // Wait a second to see it
Mouse Left Button Down       // Hold mouse button down and then
  Mouse Move Position 0, -100 // Drag bottom of Notepad up 100 pixels
Mouse Left Button Up         // Let go the mouse button
Repeat Exit                  // Exit the infinite repeat loop
End If                       // End of mouse test
Repeat End                   // End of infinite repeat loop
Mouse Speed: 0 Milliseconds  // Reset mouse delays back to zero
```

Wait for Mouse Cursor
Wait for Not Mouse Cursor

These two commands, chosen from the system-wide *Wait For* dialog, allow you to halt your macro at runtime until the mouse cursor changes to your target mouse cursor.

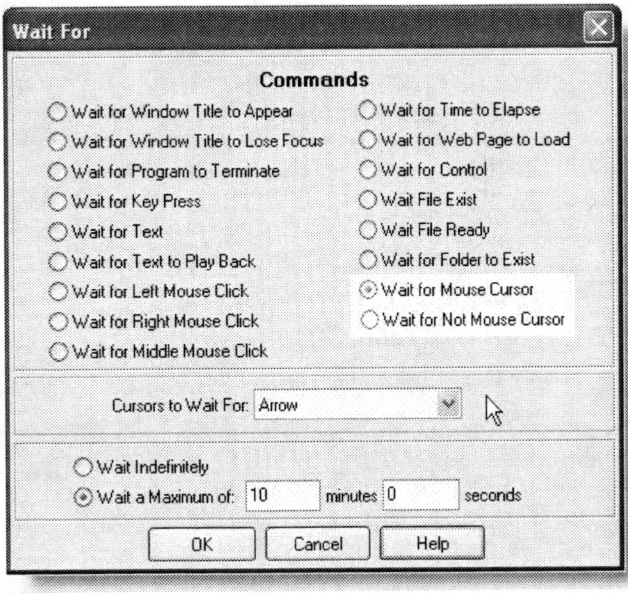

Your macro can wait for the mouse cursor to change forever by choosing the **Wait Indefinitely** option. On the other hand, you may prefer to wait for just a short period of time. If so, use the two **Wait a Maximum** fields (**Minutes** and **Seconds**). Each accepts a value up to 999,999, which means you can have your macro wait for just a little over 706 days.

The mouse cursor can be in any state depending on what you are doing at the moment. It could be "Beam" if you are in a text field, an "Arrow" if in a menu, an "Hourglass" while waiting for an event, and so forth.

There are 21 different mouse cursors that Macro Express can account for, and are listed in the table within the *If Mouse Cursor* command. Choose your target mouse cursor from the **Cursor to Wait For** drop-down list. A picture of the highlighted cursor is displayed to the right of the drop-down box as you scroll through the list.

These commands must be used with caution. Taken from the Macro Express help system:

> **Note: The mouse cursor must remain in the requested state for at least one half second in order for Macro Express to recognize the cursor type.**

The "requested state" is the mouse cursor chosen from the **Cursor to Wait For** drop-down list. Your mouse cursor may change rapidly as your computer allows other tasks to come to the forefront for a few CPU cycles while it is performing an extended task. Without this delay, Macro Express may think the task is completed when the mouse cursor changes the first time.

Let's create a macro that records link positions on a web page. Start the macro and then steadily move your mouse across the web page. The macro waits until the mouse cursor changes to something other than an "Arrow". When it does, it checks to see if the new cursor is "Size WE", which means that you have moved over one of the two side edges with the intent to quit. If, on the other hand, it is an "Internet Navigate" cursor, then we have come across a link. Save the coordinates to the next file line and wait until the mouse cursor is moved off the link and loop again.

```
Repeat Until %N1% <> %N1%                          // Loop forever
  Wait for Not Mouse Cursor: Arrow                 // Wait for something other than an Arrow
  If Mouse Cursor is Size WE                       // If positioned on either window edge, then
    Repeat Exit                                    // Exit the loop
  Else                                             // Or else
    If Mouse Cursor is Internet Navigate           // If we are on a link, then
      Variable Set String %T1% "~"                 // Set T1 to anything
      Get Mouse Position Window: %N1%, %N2%        // Store the link coordinates
      Replace "%T1%" with "%N1%,%N2%" in %T1%      // Create a string from the coordinates
      Variable Modify String: Append %T1% to Text File  // Save link coordinates
      Wait for Not Mouse Cursor: Internet Navigate // Wait until mouse moved off link
    End If                                         // End of link test
  End If                                           // End of window edge test
Repeat End                                         // End of infinite loop
```

Wait Left Mouse Click
Wait Right Mouse Click
Wait Middle Mouse Click

These three commands, chosen from the system-wide *Wait For* dialog, allow you to halt your macro at runtime until one of the mouse buttons is clicked, or double-clicked. As with the other **Wait For** commands, your macro can wait forever by choosing the **Wait Indefinitely** option. On the other hand, you may prefer to wait for just a short period of time. If so, use the two **Wait a Maximum** fields (**Minutes** and **Seconds**). Each accepts a value up to 999,999, which means you can have your macro wait for just a little over 706 days. That is all there is to these three commands.

Restore Mouse Hooks

What is this term "hooks" all about? Well, it means that Macro Express gets to peek at the keyboard or mouse activity before any other program, even the one that is active. How else, could Macro Express process your keyboard and mouse activity? There are certain rules that are best followed when doing things like this, but sometimes a program, which is loaded after Macro Express, may not understand these rules. This makes it necessary for Macro Express to reestablish its dominance over your keyboard and mouse activity.

There is a command to do this at runtime for both keyboard and mouse hooks at the same time. It is simply called *Reset Hooks* and can be found within the *Macro Express* category in the Macro Express Editor.

Reset Hooks

To restore both keyboard and mouse hooks at once at design time, click on **Restore Keyboard and Mouse Hooks** from *Tools* menu in your System Tray icon. You could also restore just mouse hooks from the Macro Express *Tools* menu by clicking on the **Restore Mouse Hooks** choice.

Summary

- Control click, double-click, down, and up events for each individual button on your mouse and individual ticks of the wheel.
- Mouse positioning works with multiple display systems and can be relative to the display, an application, window control, or the current mouse position.
- A mouse can be positioned wherever the text cursor is found.
- A mouse can be positioned over an icon in the System Tray.
- There are 21 mouse cursors that you can trap to control the flow of your macro program.

Clipboard

The Windows clipboard is a versatile tool that can make your macros sing. Most, if not all, Windows applications recognize its existence. And this universal nature allows you to gather text from one application and place it in another. Macro Express can use it to gather text, process it, and then place it back, or do something entirely different with it.

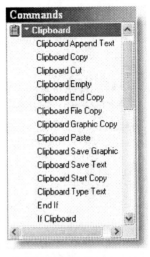

The commands shown here only vaguely match the names of the choices in the main *Clipboard* dialog below. I use the names from the dialog for the command titles, but will match them to the list in the descriptions.

Global Clipboard Delay

This is not a command, but rather a system-wide preference. Windows needs extra time to process the clipboard. So, Macro Express added a global delay that it applies after every *Clipboard* command, and can be found in the *Delays* section of the *Preferences* dialog. (Options | Preferences | Delays).

There is no wait-for-clipboard-to-finish command. With all the other **Wait For** commands that Macro Express has, I am sure if it were possible, we would have it, instead of a global delay. Without this delay, Macro Express would continue processing commands while Windows is still playing with the clipboard, causing your macro possibly to misfire.

All preferences are global in scope, which means that any setting here will affect the **Clipboard** commands in each macro that uses them. The default is a 250 millisecond (1/4-second) delay after each command. I found it to be a perfect setting on my system. But, because no two systems are the same, you will want to experiment to find the best setting for yours.

If you prefer not to use the same delay for every macro, then you can place a **Delay XXX milliseconds** command manually after any **Clipboard** command that does not work correctly. Keep in mind, however, that what may work on one computer, may not be so reliable on another. It is better to "waste" a few milliseconds in a macro than to have a beautiful piece of work inconsistently crash on your client's computer. In other words, it is better to err on the side of caution, and use a global delay.

Nonfile Clipboard Commands

The Macro Express *Clipboard* commands come in two basic flavors, those that do not read from or, write to, a file and those that do. This section covers the nonfile commands highlighted here.

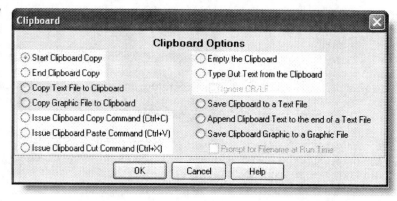

Start Clipboard Copy
End Clipboard Copy

These two commands are listed as *Clipboard Start Copy* and *Clipboard End Copy* in the *Commands* list. They work as a pair. For each *Start* you must have an *End*. This format is so important that Macro Express indents any *Text Type* commands placed between them, plainly showing what is being copied to the clipboard.

Text Type is the *only* command that can be used here. Others that type text, such as *Encrypted Text* and *Date/Time* will not work. Also, you can only type characters, numbers, spaces, punctuations, symbols, and the Enter key (if typed directly into the *Text Type* window). "<TAB>", "<ENTER>", "<SPACE>", and so forth, will not work.

So, this set of commands gives you a way to stuff the clipboard with text entered from your keyboard. Pretty neat!

Clipboard Start Copy	// Start copying to the clipboard
Text Type: Joe Weinpert··	// Name
Text Type: PO Box 5035··	// Address
Text Type: Timberlake, OH··	// City, State
Text Type: 44095··	// Zip code
Clipboard End Copy	// End copying to the clipboard
Clipboard Paste	// Paste clipboard to Test Window

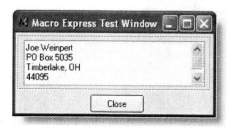

The double-dots represent a CR/LF (Enter key) typed directly into the *Text Type* window. You can see the results in the *Test Window* when the macro is run. The last line pastes the clipboard into the window and everything is as you would expect, including the CR/LF characters.

Type Out Text from the Clipboard

This command is listed as *Clipboard Type Text* in the *Commands* list. It is the polar opposite of the previous command. Instead of gathering text *to* the clipboard, it outputs text *from* the clipboard. How you get the text into the clipboard does not matter. It is similar to pasting text from the clipboard except that it is done one character at a time, and you can skip over any CR/LF (Enter key) characters by checking the **Ignore CR/LF** checkbox.

Because this command places text into the keyboard buffer, it can be used in those applications that do not accept pasting directly from the clipboard. The application will simply think that you can type fast. And because the text is coming from the keyboard buffer, you can adjust the typing speed with the *Keystroke Speed* command detailed in the *Keyboard* chapter.

Here is the same example as before except for the last line, which was changed to this command and the **Ignore CR/LF** checkbox was checked.

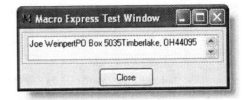

Clipboard Start Copy	// Start copying to the clipboard
Text Type: Joe Weinpert··	// Name
Text Type: PO Box 5035··	// Address
Text Type: Timberlake, OH··	// City, State
Text Type: 44095··	// Zip code
Clipboard End Copy	// End copying to the clipboard
Clipboard Type Text	// Type clipboard to Test Window

Empty the Clipboard

This command is listed as *Clipboard Empty* in the *Commands* list. It simply removes all content from the Windows clipboard. Use it whenever you must be sure the clipboard is empty.

Issue Clipboard Cut Command (Ctrl+X)
Issue Clipboard Copy Command (Ctrl+C)
Issue Clipboard Paste Command (Ctrl+V)

These three commands are listed as *Clipboard Cut*, *Clipboard Copy*, and *Clipboard Paste* in the *Commands* list. They mirror issuing the standard Windows cut, copy, and paste keyboard commands. Using the Windows Notepad as an example, there are three ways to copy selected text to the clipboard.

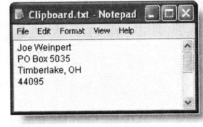

1. Issue a *Ctrl+C* from the keyboard.
2. Choose (Edit | Copy) from the menu.
3. Run the *Clipboard Copy* command.

The *Clipboard Cut*, *Copy*, and *Paste* commands work well for most applications. However, I have found instances where they are not as reliable as choosing the second option (Edit | Copy), although this is rare. I suspect there are some complicated procedures that go on behind the scene when working with the Windows clipboard. The following macro selects all text in the Notepad example, cuts it, and then pastes it.

Activate Window: "Notepad"	// Bring the Notepad window forward
Wait For Window Title: "Notepad"	// Let it settle in
Text Type: <ALT>ea	// Select all text
Wait Text Playback	// Wait until selecting is done
Clipboard Cut	// Cut the text from the Notepad window
Clipboard Paste	// Paste it back in

File Clipboard Commands

These commands read from, or write to, files using the clipboard. They are similar to the *Set Value from File*, *Save to Text File*, and *Append to Text File* commands found within the *String Variable Commands* section in the *Variables* chapter. They of course, use string variables to store the text coming from or going to a file. The *Clipboard* commands use the clipboard for the same tasks.

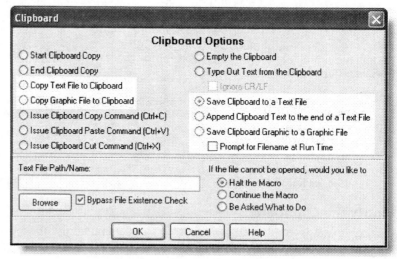

Commands are provided to read from and write to both text and graphic (picture) files. There is no limit on the number of text file types that Macro Express can read; however, there is when it comes to graphic files. There are four graphic file formats that can be copied into the clipboard but only two that can be saved *from* the clipboard:

1. BMP - Windows Bitmap can be copied and saved by the clipboard.
2. JPG - Joint Photographic Experts Group (".jpeg") can be copied and saved by the clipboard.
3. WMF - Windows Metafile Format can only be copied to the clipboard (and pasted), but not saved.
4. EMF - Windows Enhanced Metafile Format can only be copied to the clipboard (and pasted), but not saved.

Any other graphic file type will result in an error ... and what happens next depends on which of the following three options you choose:

File Opening Error Options (Graphic Files Only)

Macro Express has provided three options if the *graphic* file in the **Graphic File Path/Name** field or the file chosen at runtime (using **Prompt for Filename at Run Time**) cannot be opened.

Halt the Macro

The macro will display an error message and then stop. Which error message is displayed depends on what Macro Express has encountered, and whether you are using the *Copy Graphic File to Clipboard* or *Save Clipboard Graphic to a Graphic File* (using **Prompt for Filename at Run Time**) command.

Continue the Macro

This choice allows Macro Express to continue running as if nothing happened. No error message is displayed.

Be Asked What to Do

The macro will display an error message and prompts for what to do next. You have three choices:

Abort - Matches the **Halt the Macro** option.
Retry - Runs the same command line again, which is why there is no reason to ever choose it.
Ignore - Matches the **Continue the Macro** option.

Common Options

There are a handful of options and choices common to these five *Clipboard* commands. The **Text File Path/Name** (or **Graphic File Path/Name**) field contains the name of the file that you are copying from or writing to. It may contain either a literal string or a variable. An error message is displayed at design time if this field is left blank. The **Browse** button will bring forward the *File-Picker* dialog explained within the *Common Variable Dialogs* section in the *Variables* chapter. The resulting file will be placed in the field. The **Bypass File Existence Check** checkbox is also explained in the same section.

The other common option is related to the three commands in the right-hand column of the main *Clipboard* dialog, the ones that write to a file. The **Prompt for Filename at Run Time** checkbox tells Macro Express to let the user choose the target file at runtime. A *Choose Text File* or *Choose Graphic File* dialog will pop up. The **Browse** button will bring forward the Macro Express *File-Picker* dialog explained within the *Common Variable Dialogs* section in the *Variables* chapter. If the user chooses **Cancel** the macro will just stop. If the user chooses **OK** and the **FileName** field is blank, another error message appears warning the user that they must enter a filename.

Copy Text File to Clipboard

This command is listed as *Clipboard File Copy* in the *Commands* list. It copies the contents of the file named in the **Text File Path/Name** field to the clipboard. Although there is no actual length limit to the text file, you are sure to run in to a practical limit if you take on something too big. So, what is too big? That is a personal choice. On my computer, which is not the newest thing out there, I can copy a 50mb file into the clipboard, and paste it another application in about 5 seconds. If the file cannot be found when the macro is run, then a runtime error message will be displayed and your macro will stop.

Clipboard File Copy: "ClipTest.txt"

Save Clipboard to a Text File

This command is listed as *Clipboard Save Text* in the *Commands* list. It saves the contents of the clipboard to the file named in the **Text File Path/Name** field. If the file does not exist it will be created. As with the other commands, there is no actual limit to the contents in the clipboard; however, you are sure to run in to a practical limit if you take on something too big.

Append Clipboard Text to the End of a Text File

This command is listed as *Clipboard Append Text* in the *Commands* list. Instead of copying the clipboard to a file, and in the process overwriting it, it adds the contents to the end of the target file.

If the file cannot be found when the macro is run, then a runtime error message will be displayed and your macro will stop. As with the other commands, there is no actual limit to the contents in the clipboard.

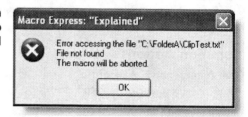

        Clipboard Append Text: "ClipTest.txt"

Copy Graphic File to Clipboard

This command is listed as *Clipboard Graphic Copy* in the *Commands* list. It copies the file named in the **Graphic File Path/Name** field to your clipboard. The file must be one of the four allowable graphic formats mentioned earlier (BMP, JPG, WMF, or EMF).

The table shows error messages displayed when something goes wrong. The first column is related to the file named in the **Graphic File Path/Name** field. You could enter an unknown, or nonsupported, graphic type file. The file entered may not exist, so it cannot be found. Or maybe you just left the field blank. The next two columns are related to your **File Opening Error Option** choice. The **Continue with Macro** option is not represented in the chart because, by definition, there would not be an error message displayed.

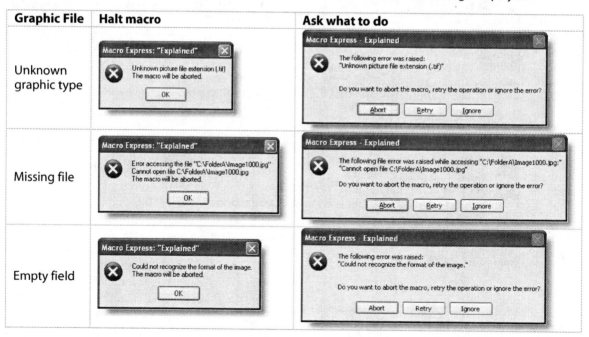

Graphic File	Halt macro	Ask what to do
Unknown graphic type		
Missing file		
Empty field		

    Clipboard Graphic Copy: "Image0000.tif"   // Unknown extension results in error
    Clipboard Graphic Copy: "Image9999.jpg"   // File does not exist results in error
    Clipboard Graphic Copy: ""   // Empty filename results in error

Save Clipboard Graphic to a Graphic File

This command is listed as *Clipboard Save Graphic* in the *Commands* list. It saves the contents of the clipboard to the file named in the **Graphic File Path/Name** field. If the file does not exist it will be created. This command only works with BMP and JPG file types. The saved file will be different from the original because the color-depth setting may be changed by whichever routine Macro Express uses internally. Although this results in a different size, the file remains intact. However, I have encountered problems with Microsoft's Photo Editor when loading BMP files that were saved with this command.

Macro Express will convert graphic file formats. You can load a BMP file into the clipboard and then save it as a JPG file. If you try to save an empty clipboard or one with an illegal file format (like WMF or EMF) then a runtime error is displayed and the macro stops. This is also true if an attempt is made to overwrite a read-only graphic file.

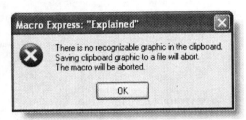

The **Halt**, **Continue**, and **Ask** options are available only if you have checked the **Prompt for Filename at Run Time** checkbox.

If Clipboard Text Equals
If Clipboard Contains

These two commands are listed simply as *If Clipboard* in the *Commands* list. Both are chosen from the system-wide *If Commands* dialog. They are similar to the *If Variable* commands used for strings except the comparisons are limited to only *Equals* and *Contains*. But, they can easily be stretched into *Does Not Equal* and *Does Not Contain* by using the *Else* logic command.

The target text is placed in the **Text to Compare** field, which accepts both literal and variable values. You may also choose an exact character-for-character case match by checking the **Must Match Uppercase and Lowercase** checkbox.

The *If Clipboard Text Equals* command is based on an exact text length and character-for-character match. In other words, if the clipboard text is not the same length as the target text then the match will return "false" no matter what. For example, if the clipboard contains "AaBbCcDdEe" and the target text is "AaBbCcDd" the *If Clipboard Text Equals* match will return "false".

It would, however, return "true" if the *If Clipboard Contains* command were used because the command is based solely on a character-for-character match until it runs out of characters. The target text in the **Text to Compare** field must be less than or equal in length to the text in the clipboard for the command to return "true". Obviously, a shorter string cannot contain a longer string.

```
Clipboard Start Copy                        // Begin placing text into the clipboard
  Text Type: AaBbCcDdEe                     // Type text string into it
Clipboard End Copy                          // End text to clipboard
If Clipboard Text Equals "AaBbCcDd"         // Test if clipboard equals this string
  Text Type: This is true                   // Strings are equal
Else                                        // Or else
  Text Type: This is not true               // Strings are not equal
End If                                       // End test
If Clipboard Contains "AaBbCcDd"            // Test if clipboard contains this string
  Text Type: This is true                   // String is contained
Else                                        // Or else
  Text Type: This is not true               // String is not contained
End If                                       // End test
```

Summary

- Macro Express can use the clipboard to gather text, process it, and then place it back, or do something entirely different with it.
- There is a global delay that can be automatically performed after every *Clipboard* command.
- There are two types of *Clipboard* commands. Those that read from, or write to, a file and those that do not.
- Only the *Text Type* command can be placed between the *Start Clipboard Copy* and *End Clipboard Copy* commands.
- Four graphic file formats are supported, BMP, JPG, WMF, and EMF when using the *Clipboard Graphic Copy* command.
- Two graphic file formats are supported, BMP and JPG when using the *Clipboard Save Graphic* command.

Using the Registry

Registry Overview

What a wonderful tool the Windows Registry can be for you when creating macros. It is the backbone of all the software on your computer and Macro Express includes commands that enable access to the information it contains. Not only can you read information from the Registry into variables, you can also write variables to the Registry.

There was a time when it was advisable not to make too many changes to your Registry. Bad things happened when you did. The stability of the Registry has drastically increased over the years and so, I hope, has your resolve to take precautions when making changes. Here is what the Macro Express help system says about using the Registry commands:

> **"A word of caution is in order here. Only those who have experience working with the Windows Registry should be using these commands. Otherwise you may create some serious problems with your operating system."**

Good advice indeed. But this does not apply to commands that simply read from your Registry. They are harmless. Use caution with those that write or change your Registry.

The commands to be cautious with are *Delete Registry Key*, *Delete Registry Value*, *Write Registry Decimal*, *Write Registry Integer*, and *Write Registry String*. Macro Express does not give warning before overwriting an existing Registry value at runtime. I would also use the *Create Registry Key* command with caution. You do not want to create them unnecessarily. Also, these commands need full Read/Write access to the Registry if you are using Windows NT, 2000, or XP.

The *If Registry, Read Registry Decimal, Read Registry Integer*, and *Read Registry String* commands are harmless and do not need access permissions because they do not change anything.

What is the Registry?

The Registry contains everything about your hardware, operating system, software, and you. Data and information is split into five different root branches (hives or hive keys), which you cannot delete, rename or move.

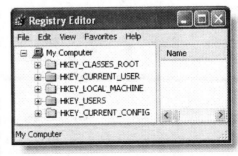

HKEY_CLASSES_ROOT

This contains your registered Window components and installed application information and data on all the Window file types. Windows Explorer uses the information stored here to open the correct application when clicking on a file. It is a link into the **HKEY_LOCAL_MACHINE\Software\Classes** key. When you are looking at this branch, you are looking inside the **HKEY_LOCAL_MACHINE\Software\Classes** key.

HKEY_CURRENT_USER

When you are looking at the this branch, you are looking at a part of the **HKEY_USERS** branch. The part related to the current logged-in user. It is the User Profile. It holds everything about this person. Some of the information includes hardware settings, installed software data, personal settings, Explorer preferences, screen settings, and Desktop layout. It takes many different keys to separate all of this information. For our purposes the most interesting one is the **HKEY_CURRENT_USER\Software** key. Sorted into subkeys by company, it contains a key for almost every application installed on your computer, including Windows itself. This key, and its companion **HKEY_LOCAL_MACHINE\Software** key, are the keepers of all software application settings. Including Macro Express!

HKEY_LOCAL_MACHINE

Contains everything about your computer in different subkeys, including installed hardware and software. None of the information here is specific to a particular user, but rather is the same for all users. **HKEY_LOCAL_MACHINE\Software** is the key of most interest to us within this branch. It, and the **HKEY_CURRENT_USER\Software** key, contains all the information for all the software loaded on your computer, including Windows. So what is the reason behind having more than one key? Nothing, if you are the only user on your computer. On the other hand, if others use your computer they probably have their own software settings for menus, toolbars, colors, and layouts, so these are placed in the **HKEY_CURRENT_USER\Software** key to not interfere with your settings.

There are no rules controlling which software settings to place in which branch. Macro Express uses the **HKEY_LOCAL_MACHINE** branch if its *All Users Use Same Setting* preference is true and if the logged on user has write privileges to **HKEY_LOCAL_MACHINE**. Otherwise it uses the **HKEY_CURRENT_USER** branch.

HKEY_USERS

Contains the Windows profile of the currently logged-in user SID (Security identifier), which is a long unique number like S-1-5-21-1082998407-2300737388-3385321434-1005 or something similar. Any user that logs onto the computer has their profile stored here. This branch has no direct meaning to Macro Express so it is a good idea to ignore it.

HKEY_CURRENT_CONFIG

This branch contains current hardware, software, and device driver configuration information in use by your computer. It is a link into different sections of the other root branches.

What is a Hive?

As it turns out, there are only two real root branches or hives, **HKEY_USERS** and **HKEY_LOCAL_MACHINE**. The others are just links into different parts of them. It would follow then that these two hives are stored someplace on your hard drive.

The **HKEY_USERS** branch is stored in files named *NTUSER.DAT*. There is one for each user found in the user's home folder. On my Windows XP computer for example:

HKEY_USERS\S-1-5-21-1082998407-2300737388-3385321434-1005, which is my login Security ID, is stored in c:\Documents and Settings\Joe Weinpert*ntuser.dat*.

HKEY_LOCAL_MACHINE is stored in separate files within the c:\Windows\System32\Config folder. Each subkey is a file. The *\Software* subkey is stored in a file named *software* (no extension) and *\System* in a file named *system*. The *\Hardware* subkey is not stored because it is created each time you start your computer.

What are Values?

There are perhaps nine types of data contained in the Registry of any importance. Each is stored in a Value designed to hold that particular data type. Branches, or keys, organize these Values in some intelligent way. The following table lists these types. The last two columns show whether Macro Express has support for the Value type in the first column.

Registry Value Type	Common Name	Description of Value Type	Macro Express?	Variable Type
REG_SZ	String	Standard null-terminated text string.	Yes	String
REG_MULTI_SZ	String Array	Concatenated null-terminated text strings ended by two null characters.	No	
REG_EXPAND_SZ	Expandable String	Null-terminated text string that contains unexpanded references to environment variables like %PATH%.	Yes Read-Only	String
REG_DWORD	Dword	A 32-bit number.	Yes	Integer
REG_DWORD_LITTLE_ENDIAN	Dword	A 32-bit number with the least significant value stored first, which is standard Windows architecture.	No	
REG_DWORD_BIG_ENDIAN		A 32-bit number with the most significant value stored first.	No	
REG_BINARY	Binary	Any data stored byte-by-byte.	Yes	Decimal
REG_QWORD	Qword	A 64-bit number.	No	
REG_QWORD_LITTLE_ENDIAN	Qword	A 64-bit number with the least significant value stored first, which is standard Windows architecture.	No	

Here is some nonessential, but interesting, information about the *BIG_ENDIAN* and *LITTLE_ENDIAN* terms. They are from the classic book Gulliver's Travels. The major debate between the Lilliputians was whether soft-boiled eggs should be opened from the big end or the little end. …maybe it was not so interesting.

Even though a discussion of all Value types would be instructional, Macro Express supports 3-1/2 of them, so I will limit the descriptions to those. By the way, three of these Value types were the only ones that could be created with the Windows *RegEdit.exe* program until Windows XP was released (REG_EXPAND_SZ was not one).

REG_SZ

Macro Express supports this Value type through text string variables. A Macro Express text string can be anything. Words, sentences, paragraphs, chapters, or complete books. I do not know the actual string length limit in the Registry, however, I am sure there is a practical limited. All string variables begin with the letter "**T**" and are numbered **1** through **99** (**T1** through **T99**). See the *Variables* chapter for more information. Text string variables are written in a raw format. No conversion is done to them when they are written to, or read from, the Registry, except for the null-termination character at the end.

REG_EXPAND_SZ (Read-Only)

Macro Express supports this Value type through text string variables, but just in a read-only format, and it does not expand the string. "%PATH%" remains as "%PATH%.

** WARNING **
If you write to a value of this type using the ***Write Registry String*** command, the value type *will be changed* in the Registry to REG_SZ.

REG_DWORD

Macro Express supports this Value type through integer variables. A Macro Express integer is a 32-bit signed whole number ranging between -2gb and +2gb (-2,147,483,648 and 2,147,483,647). All integer variables begin with the letter "**N**" and are numbered **1** through **99** (**N1** through **N99**). See the *Variables* chapter for more information. Integer variables are written in a raw format. ***REG_DWORD*** Values do not accept negative numbers, but Macro Express does.

Macro Express uses the highest bit to determine if a value is positive or negative. It is easy to interpret the values while looking in the Registry. If the value you see is 2,147,483,647 or less (7F FF FF FFh), then the value is positive and there is nothing to interpret. If it is greater, then the value being stored is negative. Simply subtract 4,294,967,296 from this value to determine the value in Macro Express.

REG_BINARY

Macro Express supports this Value type through decimal variables. A Macro Express decimal is a 64-bit real number ranging from 5×10^{-324} through 1.7×10^{308}. All decimal variables begin with the letter "**D**" and are numbered **1** through **99** (**D1** through **D99**). See the *Variables* chapter for more information. Decimal variables are written as binary, floating-point numbers. Exponent, mantissa, sign. It is beyond the scope of this book to review binary arithmetic.

Commands

There are ten commands to manipulate the Registry. Manipulating the Registry means to:

- Create Keys
- Delete Keys and Values
- Write to Values
- Read from Values
- Test the existence of Keys and Values

Commands dealing with the first three bullets need full Read/Write permission for those parts of the Registry you are targeting if you are using Windows NT, 2000, or XP. The *HKEY_LOCAL_MACHINE* hive key comes to mind, but there are others. Read/Write permission granted to the *HKEY_CURRENT_USER* hive key is a given. Commands included in the last two bullets do not need special permissions because they do not write to the Registry or change it in any manner.

Registry Picker

This is a tool common to all Registry commands. Everything you do with Registry commands involves telling Macro Express which Key or Value to target. Registry path strings can be lengthy and time-consuming to type into the **Path** field. For example:

HKEY_LOCAL_MACHINE\Software\Professional Grade Macros\Install\PGM Functions\Registration\Name

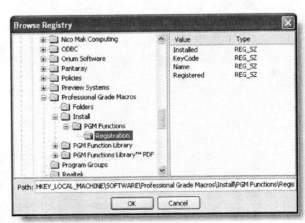

Instead of typing in this rather long string, click on the **Browse** button, which brings up the *Registry Picker* dialog. For those of you who have experience using any file or folder-picker dialog, this will look familiar. Pick your way down through the Registry Keys in the left-hand frame to find your target Key or Value. Each time your choice is added to the **Path** field. It may be the Key or Value does not yet exist, so pick your way down as far as possible and then type the rest in manually.

After clicking the **OK** button, the Registry path string will be built from your choice and placed into the **Path** field for you. If you are picking a Key, Macro Express will add a backslash character "\" to the end of the string. However, it is not needed should you decide instead to type the Registry path string.

Create Registry Key
Delete Registry Key

Both of these commands share the same dialog. You are either going to Create a Registry Key or Delete one using this dialog.

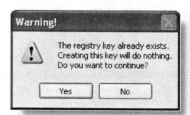

Create Registry Key - This choice will create the Registry Key displayed in the **Path** field. In the example, I want to create a key named **Sub3**. Macro Express will automatically create the rest of the tree needed. _Test, **Sub1**, and **Sub2**. If the **Sub3** Key exists at design time a warning prompt pops up to say the existing Registry Key will *not* be overwritten at runtime.

     Create Registry Key: "Sub3" // Create the Registry Key

Delete Registry Key - This choice is similar to deleting a folder on your hard drive. It will delete the Registry Key displayed in the **Path** field and any subkeys and values associated with it. Be careful with this command. There is no warning at design time or runtime. There is no "undo" feature that we have all come to depend on. **I cannot stress enough the importance of backing up your Registry before testing macros that use this command**. You lose the Registry and you lose your computer. Period. The only way to recover is to reinstall Windows.

    Delete Registry Key: "_Test" // Delete from _Test down
    Delete Registry Key: "Sub1" // Delete from Sub1 down
    Delete Registry Key: "Sub2" // Delete from Sub2 down
    Delete Registry Key: "Sub3" // Delete from Sub3 down

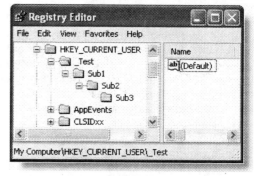

The first command deletes the whole tree from the _**Test** key through the **Sub3** Key and everything between including any Values within any of the Keys. The second command deletes everything from the **Sub1** key through the **Sub3** Key and everything between.

Write Registry String
Write Registry Integer
Write Registry Decimal

These commands write a string, integer, or decimal variable to the target Value found in the **Path** field. The variable to write is chosen from the **Command** drop-down list. As your choice of variable type changes, so do the

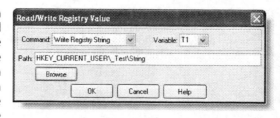

variables types displayed in the **Variable** drop-down list. In the example shown here, the **T1** variable is being written to the *String* value inside the *_Test* Key.

If a Value exists it will be overwritten at runtime without warning. If any Keys or subkeys in the target Registry path do not exist, Macro Express will create them, including the Value, which is why there is *no* *Create Registry Value* command. It is not needed. These commands create the Keys (if needed), create the Value, *and* write the variable all at once. Good stuff!

// Create a string, integer, and decimal
Variable Set String %T1% "AaBbCc"
Variable Set Integer %N1% to 123
Variable Set Decimal %D1% to 123.456

// Write each of them to Registry Values
Write Registry String: "String"
Write Registry Integer: "Integer"
Write Registry Decimal: "Decimal"

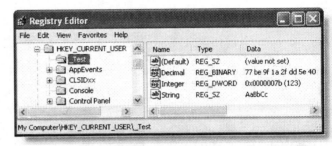

One of each variable type is created in the example. "AaBbCc" for the **T1** string variable, 123 for the **N1** integer variable, and 123.456 for the **D1** decimal variable. They are then written to Values within the *_Test* Key. The Values are named *String*, *Integer*, and *Decimal* respectively, but they could have been named anything. Look at the **Data** column in the right-hand pane of the *Registry Editor* dialog and you can see how the Values are stored. The string is just what it is. The integer is shown in hexadecimal format and decimal format (wrapped in parenthesis). The decimal is shown in binary format.

Read Registry String
Read Registry Integer
Read Registry Decimal

These commands read a string, integer, or decimal variable from the target Value found in the **Path** field. The variable to be read is chosen from the **Command** drop-down list. As your choice of variable type changes, so do the variables types displayed in the **Variable** drop-down list. In the example shown here, the **T1** variable is being read from the *String* value inside the *_Test* Key.

If you try to read from a Registry Value that does not exist, nothing happens. The target variable will not be changed. If you read from one that does exist, but is empty, then your target variable will be empty also. In other words, reading an empty Value is no different from a Value that is not empty; your target variable will be changed in either case.

// Clear existing variables
Variable Set String %T1% ""
Variable Set Integer %N1% to 0
Variable Set Decimal %D1% to 0

```
// Read each Value from the Registry
Read Registry String: "String"          // Variable T1 = "AaBbCc"
Read Registry Integer: "Integer"        // Variable N1 = 123
Read Registry Decimal: "Decimal"        // Variable D1 = 123.456

// Try reading a nonexistent Value
Variable Set String %T2% "Joe Weinpert" // Set a string variable to anything
Read Registry String: "Dummy"           // Variable T2 remains "Joe Weinpert"
```

Delete Registry Value

Use this command to delete any Value from a Key. The command is found as the last choice in the **Command** drop-down list of the *Read/Write Registry Value* dialog. It will delete the Value displayed in the **Path** field. Be careful with this command. There is no warning at design time or runtime. And there is no "undo" feature. Although losing a single Value is not

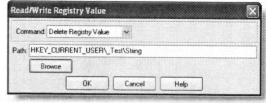

as devastating as losing a whole Registry Key, you should still make a backup of your Registry before testing macros that use this command. "as devastating" does not mean "*not* devastating".

```
Delete Registry Value: "String"
```

The example shows deleting the **String** Value from inside the **_Test** Key. All the other Values remain untouched. If the **String** Value does not exist when the command is performed, then nothing will happen. The macro simply moves on to the next command line.

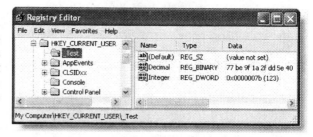

If Registry

This looks inside the Registry to find out if the target string in the **Path** field does, or does not exist. The **If Registry** field has two drop-down lists. The first is a choice between **Key** and **Value**. The second is a choice between **Exists** and **Does not Exist**. In other words, this dialog can create four different commands:

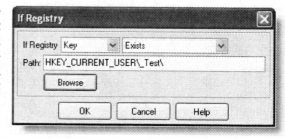

- *If Registry Key Exists*
- *If Registry Key Does not Exist*
- *If Registry Value Exists*
- *If Registry Value Does not Exist*

Use this command to control what actions your macro takes. Let's expand on this.

```
If Registry key, "_Test", exists       // If the "_Test" Key exists then
If Registry value, "String", exists     // If the "String" Value exist then
Read Registry String: "String"          // read it into the T1 variable
```

End If	// End of "String" Value test
If Registry value, "Integer", exists	// If the "Integer" Value exist then
Read Registry Integer: "Integer"	// read it into the N1 variable
End If	// End of "Integer" Value test
If Registry value, "Decimal", exists	// If the "Decimal" Value exist then
Read Registry Decimal: "Decimal"	// read it into the D1 variable
End If	// End of "Decimal" Value test
If Registry value, "Dummy", does not exist	// If the "Dummy" Value does not exist then
Variable Set String %T2% "Joe Weinpert"	// create it and
Write Registry String: "Dummy"	// write it to the Registry
End If	// End of "Dummy" Value test
End If	// End of "_Test" Key test

If the _**Test** Registry Key does not exist then the macro does not perform the remaining commands. It quits. If it does exist then it tests if the **String** Value exists, if true then it reads it into the **T1** variable. Now it tests if the **Integer** Value exists, if it does then it reads it into the **N1** variable. Next it tests if the **Decimal** Value exists; if it finds it then it reads it into the **D1** variable. Finally it tests if the **Dummy** Value does not exist, if missing then it is created from the **T2** variable, otherwise the macro skips to the end.

Saving and Restoring Variables

Now that you know how to use Registry commands, what can be done with them? The Registry is an ideal place to save and restore variables.

- Data common throughout your macros
- Temporary variable storage
- Pass parameters
- Reusable functions

Common Data

Got a name? Address? Login information? All of these bits of data can be saved in the Registry and used when needed without having to re-create them. The advantage for you is your macros need not change when the data they are based on changes. Let's say that you have a handful of macros that are used to login to favorite suppliers on the internet, but you have moved, or your shipping address changed. Now you have to update this handful of macros unless they use information stored in the Registry.

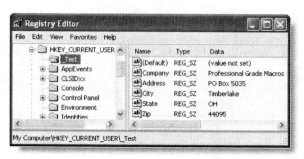

Handful of macros with this code:

```
Text Type: Professional Grade Macros<TAB>   // Type company name
Text Type: PO Box 5035<TAB>                 // Type address
Text Type: Timberlake<TAB>                  // Type city
Text Type: OH<TAB>                          // Type state
Text Type: 44095<TAB>                       // Type zip code
```

Could be changed to this:

```
Read Registry String: "Company"            // Read company name
Text Type: %T1%<TAB>                        // Type company name
Read Registry String: "Address"            // Read address
Text Type: %T1%<TAB>                        // Type address
Read Registry String: "City"               // Read city
Text Type: %T1%<TAB>                        // Type city
Read Registry String: "State"              // Read state
Text Type: %T1%<TAB>                        // Type state
Read Registry String: "Zip"                // Read zip code
Text Type: %T1%<TAB>                        // Type zip code
```

The second macro has double the number of commands, as will the rest of the handful. However, no changes are needed to any of them if your address changes. This is a simple example that should give you some ideas of your own on how to use the Registry to store macro data.

Temporary Variables

The Registry is especially suited to store Macro Express variables. After all, storing variables is what the Registry was designed to do. Use the Registry to save variables so they can be used for some other purpose and then restore them when ready. Let's create two macros. The main macro simply sets the **T1** string variable to "Joe Weinpert" and then calls the shipping macro so the user can input shipping information.

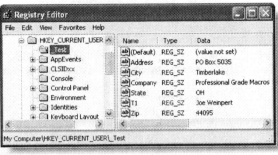

```
// Main macro
Variable Set String %T1% "Joe Weinpert"     // Set T1 to a name
Macro Run: Shipping address                  // Run the shipping input macro


// Shipping address macro
Write Registry String: "T1"                  // Save the current T1 variable
Variable Set String %T1% from Prompt         // Input company name
Write Registry String: "Company"             // Write company name
Variable Set String %T1% from Prompt         // Input address
Write Registry String: "Address"             // Write address
Variable Set String %T1% from Prompt         // Input city
Write Registry String: "City"                // Write city
Variable Set String %T1% from Prompt         // Input state
Write Registry String: "State"               // Write state
Variable Set String %T1% from Prompt         // Input zip code
Write Registry String: "Zip"                 // Write zip code
Read Registry String: "T1"                   // Restore the T1 variable
```

The shipping macro, because it uses the same **T1** variable to prompt for shipping information, saves it to the Registry before overwriting. It is then reused by each command prompt to gather input from the user. The last command in the shipping macro reads the original value from the Registry, which restores it. In other words, the value of **T1** remains the same before and after the shipping macro is called.

Passing Parameters

Use the Registry to pass values back and forth between macros in the form of parameters. This is the first of two steps needed to create true, reusable macros. Macro Express does not have a built-in *modulo* command, which returns the remainder from a division problem. Let's create a function that will do the job instead. A "function" is my term for a "reusable macro".

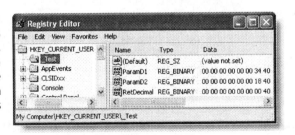

```
// Modulo Function
Read Registry Decimal: "ParamD1"                         // Read the passed dividend (20) into variable D3
Read Registry Decimal: "ParamD2"                         // Read the passed divisor (6) into variable D4
Variable Modify Decimal: %D1% = %D3% / %D4%              // Divide the dividend by the divisor (20/6=3.6667)
Variable Modify Decimal: Truncate %D1% to integer %N1%   // Remove the decimal portion (3.6667=3)
```

Variable Modify Decimal: %D2% = %N1% * %D4%	// Multiply this by the divisor (3*6=18)
Variable Modify Decimal: %D5% = %D3% - %D2%	// Subtract from the dividend to get remainder (20-18=2)
Write Registry Decimal: "RetDecimal"	// Write the remainder to the Registry
Macro Return	// Return to the calling macro

Now whenever we need the remainder from a division problem, we can simply call this function to do the calculation and then read the answer that was written to the Registry.

// Find the remainder of 20/6	
Variable Set Decimal %D1% to 20	// Set D1 to the dividend
Variable Set Decimal %D2% to 6	// Set D2 to the divisor
Write Registry Decimal: "ParamD1"	// Write the dividend to the Registry
Write Registry Decimal: "ParamD2"	// Write the divisor to the Registry
Macro Run: Modulo Function	// Do the calculation
Read Registry Decimal: "RetDecimal"	// Read the answer from the Registry (D3=2)

Reusable Macros

The example *Modulo Function* needs something else to make it a true reusable function. Can you guess what it is? Yes, it needs to save, and then restore, the variables used for its calculations so as not to overwrite the same ones used in any of the other macros. The rewritten function looks like this:

// Modulo Function	
Write Registry Integer: "N1"	// Save the current N1 variable
Write Registry Decimal: "D1"	// Save the current D1 variable
Write Registry Decimal: "D2"	// Save the current D2 variable
Write Registry Decimal: "D3"	// Save the current D3 variable
Write Registry Decimal: "D4"	// Save the current D4 variable
Write Registry Decimal: "D5"	// Save the current D5 variable
Read Registry Decimal: "ParamD1"	// Read the passed dividend (20) into variable D3
Read Registry Decimal: "ParamD2"	// Read the passed divisor (6) into variable D4
Variable Modify Decimal: %D1% = %D3% / %D4%	// Divide the dividend by the divisor (20/6=3.6667)
Variable Modify Decimal: Truncate %D1% to integer %N1%	// Remove the decimal portion (3.6667=3)
Variable Modify Decimal: %D2% = %N1% * %D4%	// Multiply this by the divisor (3*6=18)
Variable Modify Decimal: %D5% = %D3% - %D2%	// Subtract from the dividend to get remainder (20-18=2)
Write Registry Decimal: "RetDecimal"	// Write the remainder to the Registry
Read Registry Integer: "N1"	// Restore the current N1 variable
Read Registry Decimal: "D1"	// Restore the current D1 variable
Read Registry Decimal: "D2"	// Restore the current D2 variable
Read Registry Decimal: "D3"	// Restore the current D3 variable
Read Registry Decimal: "D4"	// Restore the current D4 variable
Read Registry Decimal: "D5"	// Restore the current D5 variable
Macro Return	// Return to the calling macro

It looks like this macro has much work to do to calculate the remainder. Not true. Most of the work is saving and restoring variables. It also looks like it would take a longtime to run. Also not true. This function runs 250 times in a single second on my computer.

Why not simply use the built-in *Variables Save* and *Variables Restore* commands in place of all those *Write Registry* and *Read Registry* commands? Good question. You could. However, the function would no longer be reusable. You would have to be sure the *Variable Save* command used here was not being called in the middle of another *Variable Save* command. Tough to do, especially when making changes and adding macros. Mistakes are easily made, but can be hard to find.

You must use a *Variable Restore* command before using another *Variable Save* command or else you will overwrite the variables in memory. Let me illustrate this.

Variable Set String %T1% "AaBbCc"	// First, set string variable T1 to be "AaBbCc"
Variable Save All Variables	// Now save variables with the built-in command
Variable Set String %T1% "DdEeFf"	// Let us change T1 to be "DdEeFf"
Variables Save All Variables	// Save variables again
Variable Set String %T1% "GgHhIi"	// Finally, change T1 to be "GgHhIi"

At this point, **T1** has been changed three times and is set to "GgHhIi". Now let's restore variables.

Variable Restore All Variables	// T1 is now "DdEeFf" as you would expect, however, let's restore again
Variable Restore All Variables	// T1 is still "DdEeFf"

What happened to "AaBbCc"? It was overwritten in memory by the second *Variables Save* command. Let's create two reusable functions that use the Registry to resolve this issue. They will be called "*Save Variables Function*" and "*Restore Variables Function*". In fact, let's create a system of Registry Values that will enable you to call eight levels of functions or macros without ever having to be concerned that you are overwriting something used somewhere else.

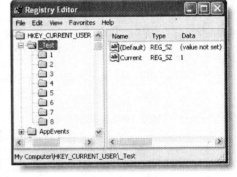

We need two things. A place to store each complete set of 297 variables (99 strings, integers, and decimals) and a pointer to tell us the last set saved. The pointer, which is the **Current** Value, will be numbered 1 through 8 to match the Keys. The plan is to increment the pointer and then save the variables to Values in whichever Key the pointer is set to. When we want to restore a set of variables, the pointer (**Current** Value) tells us which Key to restore them from. This is an LIFO sequence. Last in, first out, which means the last set of saved variables is restored and the pointer is decremented. Let's create the *Save Variables Function* first. I will explain the steps as we go through the macro function.

Set the current cascade pointer (the **Current** Registry key) like this: If we are back at the beginning then the pointer will be blank. Change it to a zero so we can increment it as an integer. If we are at the maximum the pointer will be "8". Loop back around to the beginning level by changing it to a zero.

```
// Save Variables Function
Write Registry String: "T1"          // Save the current T1 variable to a temporary Registry Value
Read Registry String: "Current"      // What is the pointer set to? Read it into T1
If Variable %T1% = ""                // If it is empty then
  Variable Set String %T1% "0"       // set it to 0 so it can be incremented
Else                                 // or else
  If Variable %T1% = "8"             // If it is at the maximum then
    Variable Set String %T1% "0"     // loop back around by setting it to 0
  End If                             // End the T1="" test
End If                               // End the T1="8" test
```

Write Registry Integer: "N1"	// Save the current N1 variable to a temporary Registry Value
Variable Modify String: Convert %T1% to %N1%	// Convert the pointer to an integer
Variable Modify Integer: Inc (%N1%)	// Increment the pointer by one
Variable Modify Integer: Convert %N1% to %T1%	// Now convert it back to a string
Write Registry String: "Current"	// Resave the pointer
Read Registry Integer: "N1"	// Restore the original N1 variable

We want to save all variables but we need variables to do it. For example, we are using **T1** as the *Current* Key pointer, which is not what we want to save. Instead, we want the original that was written to a temporary Value at the start of this function. Macro Express does not have a command to copy Registry Values directly, so we will resolve it by swapping the **T1** and **T2** values back and forth.

Write Registry String: "T2"	// Save the current T2 variable to a temporary Registry Value
Variable Modify String: Copy %T1% to %T2%	// Preserve the pointer. Save it to T2
Read Registry String: "T1"	// Restore the original T1 variable (see first line in function)
Write Registry String: "T1"	// Save it to the Key pointed to by T2 (Path = HKCU_Test\%T2%\T1)
Variable Modify String: Copy %T2% to %T1%	// Recover the contents of T1 back from T2
Read Registry String: "T2"	// Restore the original T2 variable

Now the **T1** variable has been properly saved, write the remaining variables to the Key pointed to by the *Current* Value. Notice how the pointer (variable **T1**) is used in the **Path** field for the remainder of the *Write Registry* commands. I have shortened the command listing to show only the first two and last two commands for each variable type.

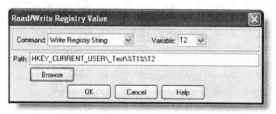

Write Registry String: "T2"	// Save strings T2 - T99
Write Registry String: "T3"	
...	
Write Registry String: "T98"	
Write Registry String: "T99"	
Write Registry Integer: "N1"	// Save integers N1 - N99
Write Registry Integer: "N2"	
...	
Write Registry Integer: "N98"	
Write Registry Integer: "N99"	
Write Registry Decimal: "D1"	// Save decimals D1 - D99
Write Registry Decimal: "D2"	
...	
Write Registry Decimal: "D98"	
Write Registry Decimal: "D99"	

The only thing left to do is restore the original **T1** variable that was saved in the first line of the function.

Read Registry String: "T1"	// Restore the original T1 variable
Macro Return	// Return to the calling macro

Now let's create the *Restore Variables Function* macro. Set the current cascade pointer (the **Current** Registry key) like this: If we are back at the beginning then there is nothing left to restore. This is true even if we have wrapped back around from saving more than eight sets of variables.

```
// Restore Variables Function
Write Registry String: "T1"              // Save the current T1 variable to a temporary Registry Value
Read Registry String: "Current"          // What is the pointer set to? Read it into T1
If Variable %T1% = ""                    // If we are at the start, there is nothing to do (even if we have wrapped)
  Read Registry String: "T1"             // Restore the original T1 variable
  Macro Return                           // Return to the calling macro
End If                                    // End the T1="" test
```

We want to restore all variables but we need variables to do it. For example, we are using **T1** as the **Current** Key pointer, which is not what we want to restore. Instead, we want the value that was saved with *Save Variables Function*. Macro Express does not have a command to copy Registry Values directly, so we will resolve it by swapping the **T1** and **T2** values back and forth.

```
Variable Modify String: Copy %T1% to %T2%    // Preserve the pointer. Save it to T2
Read Registry String: "T1"                   // Restore T1 from Key pointed to by T2 (Path = HKCU\_Test\%T2%\T1)
Write Registry String: "T1"                  // Save it to a temporary Registry Value so it can be restored at the end
Variable Modify String: Copy %T2% to %T1%    // Recover the contents of T1 back from T2 (the pointer)
```

The **T1** variable has been prepared to be restored at the end of the function. Read the remaining variables from the Key pointed to by the **Current** Value. Notice how the pointer (variable **T1**) is used in the **Path** field for the remainder of the **Read Registry** commands. I have shortened the command listing to show only the first two and last two commands for each variable type.

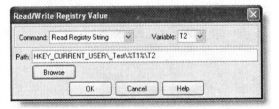

```
Read Registry String: "T2"       // Restore strings T2 - T99
Read Registry String: "T3"
...
Read Registry String: "T98"
Read Registry String: "T99"

Read Registry Integer: "N1"      // Restore integers N1 - N99
Read Registry Integer: "N2"
...
Read Registry Integer: "N98"
Read Registry Integer: "N99"

Read Registry Decimal: "D1"      // Restore decimals D1 - D99
Read Registry Decimal: "D2"
...
Read Registry Decimal: "D98"
Read Registry Decimal: "D99"
```

Decrement the cascade pointer by one. If we are back at the beginning it will be zero, so change it to a blank string before writing it to the Registry.

```
Write Registry Integer: "N1"                       // Save the current N1 variable to a temporary Registry Value
Variable Modify String: Convert %T1% to %N1%       // Convert the pointer to an integer
Variable Modify Integer: Dec (%N1%)                // Decrement the pointer by one
Variable Modify Integer: Convert %N1% to %T1%      // Now convert it back to a string
If Variable %T1% = "0"                             // If it zero then
  Variable Set String %T1% ""                      // set it to a blank string
End If                                             // End the T1="0" test
Write Registry String: "Current"                   // Resave the pointer
Read Registry Integer: "N1"                        // Restore the original N1 variable
```

The only thing left to do is restore the original **T1** variable.

```
Read Registry String: "T1"                         // Restore the original T1 variable
Macro Return                                       // Return to the calling macro
```

You now have functions that will save and restore up to eight sets of variables. The key to using them is to use them in pairs. For every "save" you need a matching "restore". And because this design uses an LIFO sequence, you can call up to eight saves before needing to restore. Like this:

```
Save Variables Function          // Set 1
Save Variables Function          // Set 2
Save Variables Function          // Set 3
Save Variables Function          // Set 4
Save Variables Function          // Set 5
Save Variables Function          // Set 6
Save Variables Function          // Set 7
Save Variables Function          // Set 8
Restore Variables Function       // Set 8
Restore Variables Function       // Set 7
Restore Variables Function       // Set 6
Restore Variables Function       // Set 5
Restore Variables Function       // Set 4
Restore Variables Function       // Set 3
Restore Variables Function       // Set 2
Restore Variables Function       // Set 1
```

Let's rewrite the *Modulo Function* (shown earlier) to use these new save and restore functions.

```
// Modulo Function (save and restore)
Macro Run: Save Variables Function                 // Save variables before overwriting them
Read Registry Decimal: "ParamD1"                   // Read the passed dividend (20) into variable D3
Read Registry Decimal: "ParamD2"                   // Read the passed divisor (6) into variable D4
Variable Modify Decimal: %D1% = %D3% / %D4%        // Divide the dividend by the divisor (20/6=3.6667)
Variable Modify Decimal: Truncate %D1% to integer %N1%   // Remove the decimal portion (3.6667=3)
Variable Modify Decimal: %D2% = %N1% * %D4%        // Multiply this by the divisor (3*6=18)
Variable Modify Decimal: %D5% = %D3% - %D2%        // Subtract from the dividend to get remainder (20-18=2)
Write Registry Decimal: "RetDecimal"               // Write the remainder to the Registry
Macro Run: Restore Variables Function              // Restore variables before returning to caller
Macro Return                                       // Return to the calling macro
```

The rewritten *Modulo Function* saves all variables before doing anything else. It then restores them just before returning to whichever macro called it. In other words, you are wrapping *Modulo Function* within a set of macros that preserves the state of any used variables as it processes its commands. Also, because of the cascaded pointer, you are wrapping the function in a way that does not interfere with any other set of saved variables. Now *Modulo Function* is a true, reusable, *black box*, function that can be used in the same manner as any of the built-in Macro Express commands. It is like extending the Macro Express command library for your own purposes.

It looks like these functions could take a longtime to run. Not true. 12 complete save and restores can be run in a single second on my computer. In other words, saving 297 variables, plus the overhead involved, and then restoring takes only 83 milliseconds.

What if none of your macros or functions use decimal variables? Simply copy these examples to another set of save and restore functions and then delete the lines that save and restore decimals. My company has several different versions of this pair of functions. For example, it is unusual for us to have any reusable, black-box functions that use more than a handful of string and integer variables. So we have created a pair that saves and restores only the first 25 strings and integers. The time to run is much quicker, too. 16ms compared with 83ms.

Summary

- Use Registry commands to write to, and read from, the Windows Registry.
- It is okay to change the Registry, if you are careful.
- Backup your Registry before testing macros that use these commands.
- The Registry is separated into Hives, Keys, and Values.
- Full read/write permissions are needed to access certain regions in the Registry.
- There is no warning given when overwriting Values in the Registry.
- Writing to a nonexistent Value will create the Value.
- Reading from a nonexistent Value will not change the target variable.
- Macro Express supports REG_SZ, REG_EXPAND_SZ (Read-Only), REG_DWORD, and REG_BINARY variable types.
- Using the Registry commands is key to creating reusable macro functions.
- All ten Registry commands are superfast. Processing commands in mere milliseconds.

Windows and Programs

The main purpose for using Macro Express is to control other applications by feeding keystrokes and mouse commands to them. Part of this control involves loading, running, and terminating these applications. Also manipulating their window sizes, positioning them on your Desktop, and changing how they are displayed by maximizing, minimizing, hiding, and unhiding them. And most importantly, setting focus to the one that you want so it receives the keyboard and mouse output from your macro.

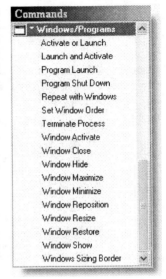

Common Dialogs

There are a handful of different dialogs from which these *Windows/Programs* commands are called. Although each serves a different purpose, there are certain tasks that are common to each, such as the ones shown here.

Current Window
Specific Window

With some commands you can choose whether it is to act on the window that has focus at the time or, optionally, a different window. For example, the following two macros both manipulate the Windows Notepad program:

Activate Window: "Notepad"	// Set focus to the Notepad window
Window Resize: Current Win - (Width: 300, Height: 200)	// Resize it
Window Reposition: Center - Current Win	// Center it on the Desktop
Activate Window: "Microsoft Excel"	// Set focus to Excel
Window Resize: Notepad - (Width: 300, Height: 200)	// Resize Notepad
Window Reposition: Center - Notepad	// Center Notepad on the Desktop

Window Title (May be partial title)

This field holds the name of your target window. The name can be entered as a literal string, string variable, or a combination of both. Whatever you choose, it is *never* case-sensitive. "NOTEPAD" will work as well as "notepad", "NOTEpad", or "NoTePaD".

Most of the time, the name entered into the field is treated by Macro Express as a *partial* name. In other words, when the command is performed, Macro Express searches through the list of running applications until it finds a window title that *contains* whatever is in this field.

Let's say for example that you have three Microsoft Excel spreadsheets opened named *Yearly Expenses*, *Monthly Expenses*, and *Weekly Expenses*, and you wanted to set focus to *Yearly Expenses*. The **Window Title** field would need to contain the word "Yearly" because it is unique to your target window title. If it contained just the word "Expenses" then Macro Express would set focus to the first window it found that contained "Expenses", which may not be the one that you want.

Activate Window: "Yearly Expenses"   // Set focus to the Yearly
Expenses spreadsheet
Activate Window: "Expenses"   // Set Focus to any
window containing the word "Expenses"

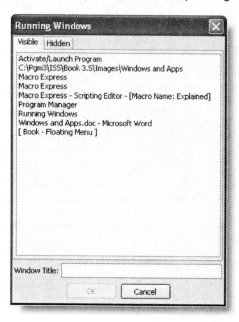

Select Window

If you do not want manually to enter a window name into the **Window Title** field, then you can pick one from the *Running Windows* dialog by clicking on the **Select Window** button. This button may also be called **Browse**, or it may just be an **ellipses** (…) button, depending on which command you are using.

There are two tabs in this dialog. Visible and Hidden. The application windows listed in the Visible Tab are the ones that you can see on your Desktop … the ones that you normally work with. The Hidden Tab contains behind-the-scene windows. These are applications that are running, but are marked as *hidden*.

When you have chosen a window by either picking it from the list, or typing it in manually, click **OK** and the dialog will disappear. The name will be placed into the **Window Title** field for you where it can be further edited to your liking.

Window Activate
Program Launch
Launch and Activate
Activate or Launch

All of these commands are accessed from the *Activate/Launch Program* dialog. It is designed to either run (launch) a program, set focus to (activate) an already running program, or a combination of both actions.

The dialog is separated into three sections. The **Commands** section at the top is where you choose the action to take. These options loosely match what you see in the *Commands* list.

The **Activate Window** section in the middle is available for all but the *Launch Program Only* command because there would be no window to activate.

The bottom portion of the dialog is used for launching programs and contains two tabs named Normal and Advanced. This section is available for all but the *Activate Window Only* command because by definition the program would already be launched and running.

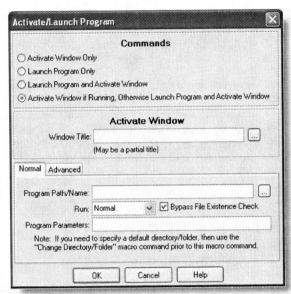

Activate Window Only

Use this command when you want to set focus to an application's window that has already been launched and is running. Setting focus simply means that you bring the window to the top of the stack on your Desktop, the same as if you were to click on it with your mouse. Once focused it is the window that receives all the keyboard and mouse output from your macro. The **Window Title** field contains the target window name. See the *Common Dialogs* section for a description.

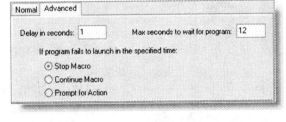

Macro Express will display a runtime error and then stop, if you attempt to activate a nonexistent application window.

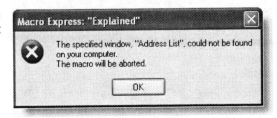

> **Activate Window: "Address List"**   *// Set focus*

Launch Program Only

This command has plenty of choices because it is *the* command used to launch applications from within Macro Express. The Normal and Advanced Tabs accept six different bits of information that applies to launching a program.

1. Name of the program to launch.
2. Where it can be found.
3. How it is to be launched.
4. Command line parameters it will accept.
5. Minimum and maximum launch delay values.
6. What to do if the program fails to launch.

The **Program Path/Name** field holds the name of your target application or file. The name can be entered as a literal string, string variable, or a combination of both. Whatever you choose, it is *never* case-sensitive. The name can be a simple file name, a full path name, or a relative path with a file name. And the name does not have to be a runnable program like those that end with ".exe", ".com", or ".bat". You may enter a file like "C:\Documents\Explained.doc". When Macro Express sees this, it looks for the application that is associated with the ".doc" file extension, which is Microsoft Word on my computer. Once found the application is launched with the named file. A runtime error will be displayed if there is no Windows file association set up for the file extension.

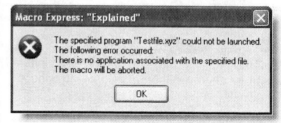

The name in the **Program Path/Name** field must exist if Macro Express is expected to find it. If you enter just a simple file name and extension then it must be found in the *current folder* or somewhere along your computer's *search path*. In fact, the information paragraph within the dialog itself tells you how to change default folders if needed:

> **Note: If you need to specify a default directory/folder, then use the "Change Directory/Folder" macro command prior to this macro command.**

To find your computer's search path use the ***Set Value from Environment Variable*** command. See the *Variables* chapter for a detailed explanation. If the file is anywhere within this path, then Macro Express can launch it. A runtime error will be displayed if Macro Express cannot find the file.

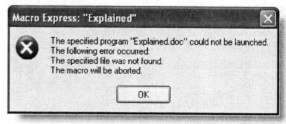

A relative path and file name may also be entered into the **Program Path/Name** field. Relative pathing is done using the *current* (".") and *parent* ("..") folder shortcuts (see the *Common Dialogs* section within the *Files and Folders* chapter). Let's say for example the current folder is "C:\FolderA\Subfolder1" and you want to launch the "C:\FolderA\Weekly Expenses.xls" spreadsheet. You would simply enter "..\Weekly Expenses.xls" into the **Program Path/Name** field.

If you prefer not to manually enter a file name, then use the **ellipses (...)** button on the right-hand side of the **Program Path/Name** field. It displays the standard Macro Express *File-picker* dialog. In this case, however, the choice of file types defaults to runnable programs ".exe", ".com", ".bat", and so forth. Once chosen the dialog will close and the full path and file name will be placed into the **Program Path/Name** field.

The **Bypass File Existence Check** checkbox is a design time option meant to warn you whether your file choice exists. See the *Common Variable Dialogs* section within the *Variables* chapter for a detailed explanation of this option.

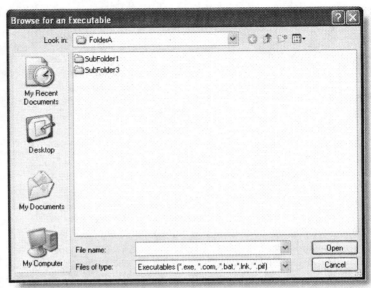

Macro Express has several ways to set the application's window when launched so you do not have to use a separate command to do so. The **Run** drop-down list contains four choices:

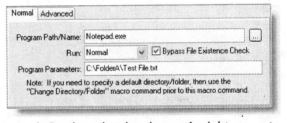

Normal - Launches an application normally. This could be as it was last closed. For example, if it was maximized at the time it was closed, then **normal** might be to launch it maximized. On the other hand, **normal** might mean to launch it as a certain width and height at a particular screen coordinate, no matter how it was positioned when closed. I have not run across any instances where **normal** would launch an application as minimized or hidden if that is how it was last closed.

Minimized - Launches an application directly to the Taskbar. This is the same as launching a program and then clicking the **Minimize** button in the top-right corner of the window.

Maximized - Launches an application as maximized. This is the same as launching a program and then toggling the **Normal/Maximize** button in the top-right corner of the window.

Hidden - Launches an application identical with the **Normal** option but makes the window invisible. The visibility of a window has nothing to do with its accessibility. See the *Hide Window* command later in this chapter.

The **Program Parameters** field is used to pass command line arguments (parameters) to the target application in the **Program Path/Name** field. The Windows Notepad program, for example, allows a command line parameter that instructs it about which file to edit when launched. Simply enter the file name into the **Program Parameters** field.

Each application will handle command line parameter errors differently. Some applications will simply not launch, while others launch anyway, ignoring the error. Still others, like Notepad, will prompt the user with choices to work around the error. Let's say that we have a nonexistent file name in the **Program Parameters** field. Notepad displays this dialog. When this happens, Macro Express *thinks* Notepad has been launched and will continue with the macro. So, you must be certain of the parameters you pass or create your macro to handle errors such as these.

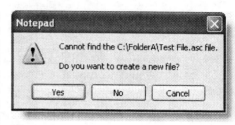

The Advanced Tab for the **Launch Program Only** command contains a delay field named **Delay in Seconds** with three options for what to do if the program fails to launch within the specified period of time. The **Delay in Seconds** value is the number of seconds to wait *after* sending the launch command to check if the program launched. The default value is one second. The maximum value is 99 seconds and the minimum is zero. At the end of this time, Macro Express will test for the program name in memory. If it does not find it, then the **failed to launch** option that you chose will engage.

Stop Macro - This is the default choice, which will display an error message and then stop the macro.

Continue Macro - This will allow the macro to continue as if nothing is wrong. Using this choice means, of course, that you have some other way of trapping for a failed launch and would be the preferred action for unattended operations.

Prompt for Action - Displays a runtime dialog that allows the user to choose which course of action to take. Choosing **No** is the same as the **Stop Macro** option, while choosing **Yes** is identical with **Continue Macro**.

Well, now for the interesting part. I can never get this **Launch Program Only** command to fail except when I purposely enter a bad program name. For example, I use *StyleWriter* as an editor, which always takes at least five seconds to load. Setting the **Delay in Seconds** value to zero or 1 never results in a failed launch. This is true of every program that I have tested. Your results may be different. Macro Express has no control over how Windows launches an application. Macro Express tells Windows what to launch. Windows does the rest … right or wrong.

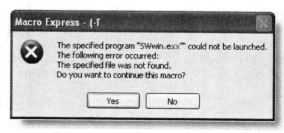

It does not matter though, because if you use this *Launch Program Only* command with zero in the **Delay in Seconds** field and **Continue Macro** chosen, you can reliably and efficiently launch any program on any machine. For example, if it takes a longtime to launch a program on a certain computer, it will probably take longer on a slower one, and not so long on a faster one. Do you create a worse case macro that purposely delays, say, 10 seconds after launching a program to continue? No, of course not.

```
Program Launch: "winword.exe"              // Launch Microsoft Word with Delay=0 and "Continue Macro"
Repeat Start (Repeat 15 times)             // Wait for program to launch 15 times incrementing a counter each time
  If Program Name "winword.exe" is running // If launched, then
    Variable Modify Integer: Dec (%N2%)    // decrement the counter by one, then
    Repeat Exit                            // exit the wait loop
  End If                                    // End launch test
  If Variable %N2% < 15                     // If program launched within 15 wait for loops
    Repeat Exit                            // exit the attempted launch loop
  End If                                    // End counter test
  Delay 1 Seconds                          // Delay 1-second before testing for program name again
Repeat End                                 // End of wait for program to launch loop
```

This macro launches Microsoft Word. It tests 15 times; with a 1-second delay each time, to determine if it has yet launched. There are only 2 ways out of this loop; if Word launches, or if we go beyond 15 seconds to launch it. So, no matter which computer that this macro runs on, fast or slow, Word should always launch without having to have extended and unnecessary delays.

Launch Program and Activate Window

This command combines what you learned about the last two commands into one command line. Launching an application does not necessarily mean that it will automatically gain focus. Macro Express has little, if any, control over the situation. It depends on the mood that Windows is in at the time it gets instructions to launch an application. That is why Macro Express has this two-part command. The first half does the launching, while the second half sets, or attempts to set, the focus to what was just launched.

The Advanced Tab differs from the *Launch Program Only* command in that it contains two delay fields named **Delay in Seconds** and **Max Seconds to Wait for Program**. The **Delay in Seconds** value is the number of seconds to wait after sending the launch command to check if the window named in the **Window Title** field (**Activate Window** section) has been activated and can gain focus. The **Max Seconds to Wait** 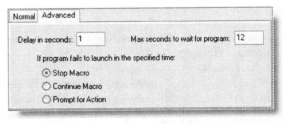 for Program field is the maximum number of seconds to wait for the window to gain focus. The maximum value is 99 seconds and the minimum is zero.

Usually, this command works as advertised, which considering what Windows needs to do to launch and set focus to an application is a great thing! But, you will need to experiment with applications to determine the best values to use, or whether this command will work as you expect with a particular application. I have found that values placed in the **Delay in Seconds** and **Max Seconds to Wait for Program** to be inclusive (5 delay seconds + 5 maximum seconds = 10 seconds) with some applications, while exclusive (5 delay seconds + 5 maximum seconds = 5 seconds) with others. Again, the key to using this command successfully is to experiment with the best values for your application. Each will, more than likely, be different.

Activate Window if Running otherwise Launch Program and Activate Window

This long-winded command does exactly what it claims. It first looks at which applications are running. If it finds a title that matches the **Window Title** field, it runs the *Activate Window Only* command. Otherwise it runs the **Launch Program and Activate Window** command.

Maximize Window

Minimize Window

Restore Window

These three commands are found in the *Window Commands* dialog and are listed as **Window Maximize**, **Window Minimize**, and **Window Restore** respectively in the *Commands* list. They give you the ability to manipulate a window using commands, rather than by using your mouse or keyboard.

You can choose between the **Current Window**, which is the one that has focus at the time the command is run, and a **Specific Window**. The **Window Title** field contains the name of the specific window. You may pick one using the **Select Window** button. The **Window Title** field and **Select Window** button are both explained in the *Common Dialogs* section at the beginning of this chapter.

Maximize Window - This is the same as clicking on the **Maximize** button in the top-right corner of the window. It expands the window to the same size as your Desktop.

Minimize Window - This is the same as clicking on the **Minimize** button in the top-right corner of the window. It removes the window from the Desktop and places on the Taskbar.

Restore Window - This is the same as clicking on the **Restore** button in the top-right corner of the window (if it is maximized) or the program icon/name in the Taskbar (if it is minimized). It resizes and positions the window back to the way it was before maximizing or minimizing.

Window Maximize: Current Window	// Maximize the current window
Window Minimize: Current Window	// Minimize the current window
Window Restore: Current Window	// Normalize the current window

Hide Window

Show Window (unhide)

These two commands are also found in the *Window Commands* dialog and are listed as **Window Hide** and **Window Show** in the *Commands* list. They give you the ability to hide or unhide a window on your

Desktop. Hiding or unhiding a window does not change its position in the stack of windows on your Desktop. Neither does it change which window has focus. It simply makes it visible or invisible.

You can choose between the **Current Window**, which is the one that has focus at the time the command is run, and a **Specific Window**. The **Window Title** field contains the name of the specific window. You may pick one using the **Select Window** button. The **Window Title** field and **Select Window** button are both explained in the *Common Dialogs* section at the beginning of this chapter.

Hide Window - This command makes a window invisible. But, that is all it does. It means the window is still there, is still accessible, is still usable, and works exactly as if were visible. Macro Express can still see it. It can be moved, resized, maximized, minimized, and anything else that can be done to it if it were visible.

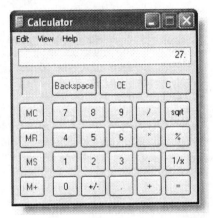

Activate or Launch: "Calculator" OR "calc.exe"	// Launch the calculator
Window Reposition: Center - Current Win	// Center it on the Desktop
Window Hide: Current Window	// Now make it invisible
Text Type: 3*3*3<ENTER>	// Enter a calculation
Window Show: Current Window	// View the results

The above macro activates and/or launches the system calculator, centers it, and then hides it. The *Text Type* command is then used to enter a calculation while the window is still invisible. Finally, the window is made visible.

Show Window - This command makes the window visible if it was previously hidden. It does not, however, set focus to it unless you are using the **Current Window** option.

Close Window
Shut Down Program

These two commands are also found in the *Window Commands* dialog and are listed as *Window Close* and *Program Shut Down* in the *Commands* list. They both shut down a running program and are similar to the **Close Window** and **Close Program** options found in the *Terminate Process* command dialog (explained below). However, they are different in that they cannot guarantee a program will stop. Although, I have yet to encounter a situation where a program did not stop.

You can choose between the **Current Window**, which is the one that has focus at the time the command is run, and a **Specific Window**. The **Window Title** field contains the name of the specific window. You may pick one using the **Select Window** button. The **Window Title** field and **Select Window** button are both explained in the *Common Dialogs* section at the beginning of this chapter.

The *Close Window* command simply sends the WM_CLOSE message to the chosen window, which is the same message that is used when you click on the [X] or choose (File | Close Program). There is no guarantee the program will close, although closing the main window typically does.

The *Shut Down Program* command sends a WM_QUIT message to the chosen window. Typically, when the main thread of an application receives this message, the thread will terminate, thus shutting down the program. This command can only shut down a thread. However, since most programs run their visual elements only on the main thread, this typically shuts the program down.

Window Close: Current Window	*// Stop the program that has focus*
Program Shut Down: Current Window	*// Stop the program that has focus*

Terminate Process

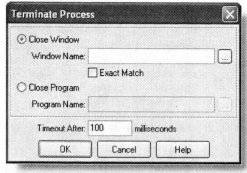

The *Terminate Process* command will make sure the target program is stopped. The **Close Window** and **Close Program** options allow you to select the target process by either its window or program name. Internally it is a complex command using up to three different methods to attempt to close a program. The **Timeout After** value is the amount of time Macro Express waits before attempting the next method. It will accept either a literal value up to 999,999 milliseconds (over 16 minutes), or an integer variable such as **N1, N2**, and so forth. The default value is 100 milliseconds (1/10th of a second).

If you choose the **Close Window** option, the **Window Name** field contains the window title of the target process. There is also an **ellipses** (…) button to pick a window. Both are explained in the *Common Dialogs* section at the beginning of this chapter. By using the **Exact Match** checkbox, you tell Macro Express that the window title has to be an exact match, rather than the usual partial match.

If you choose the **Close Program** option, the **Program Name** field contains the full program name of the target process. There is also an **ellipses** (…) button to pick a program. This option is especially useful for closing a program that does not have a window but may run in the System Tray.

When picking a program, the *Select Program* dialog appears containing a list of currently running applications. Choose one of them and then click the **OK** button. The program name will be placed into the **Program Name** field for you. Although the application names are listed as uppercase, the field itself is *not* case sensitive. "NOTEPAD.EXE" will work as well as "notepad.exe", "NOTEpad.Exe", or "NoTePaD.eXe".

The *Select Program* dialog also gives you a way to choose an application installed on your computer but not currently running. Click on the **Selected from Installed Programs** button and the *List of Installed Programs* dialog appears (shown on the next page) containing a description of each. This is a nice feature! Simply highlight the application name and then click on the **OK** button.

Here are the three methods that this command uses to attempt to stop a program from running.

Method 1. This method sends the Windows WM_CLOSE message to one of the visible windows of the program. It then waits for the **Timeout After** value. If the window did not close, it sends the WM_CLOSE message to the next visible window of that program and waits again for the **Timeout After** value. If the program has not yet closed after repeating this for all visible windows, then it sends a WM_QUIT message to either the window (if it still exists) or the process thread. This method attempts to close visible windows only. It is the same as the *Close Window* and *Shut Down Program* commands discussed previously.

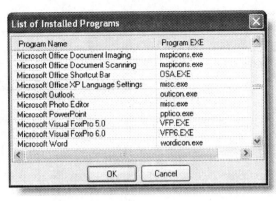

Method 2. If the program was not successfully closed using Method 1, then Macro Express sends the Windows WM_CLOSE message to the program's hidden windows. This method results in waiting only one time for the **Timeout After** value.

Method 3. If the other methods fail to close the program, then Macro Express uses the Windows Terminate Process API command to close the program. This is the same process that is used if you use Ctrl+Alt+Delete to bring up the computer's *Task Manager* dialog, then highlight a program or process, and then click the **End Process** or **End Task** button. If this method is used to close a program, some memory used by that program may not be freed up.

So, one-way or another, this command will terminate any program.

> **Terminate Process: "Microsoft Word"**   // Close Microsoft Word
> **Terminate Process: "WINWORD.EXE"**   // Close Microsoft Word

Window Resize

These commands adjust the size of a window and are called from the *Size or Position a Window* dialog. You may set a window to an exact size or increase or decrease the current size by either a pixel count or percentage. Whichever command you choose the **Width** and **Height** fields are used to set the size and will accept any value between -999 and 9,999. What the values means depends on your choice from the **Resize Commands** section. You may choose to use an integer variable instead of a literal value for either the **Width** or **Height** fields, or both, by clicking on the **Var** radio button, which will activate the integer drop-down list.

The *Specify Exact Size* command will set the window that has focus or the target window in the **Window**

Title field, to the values entered, or the variables chosen, in the **Resize Dimensions** section. The window will never be bigger than your computer's display no matter what you enter for a size. Neither will it ever be smaller than allowed. In other words, you cannot hide a window by setting its size to zero. Use the *Hide Window* command instead.

> **Window Resize: Current Win - (Width: 300, Height: 200)**   *// Set the current window to 300 × 200 pixels*

The *Enlarge/Decrease by Pixels* command will modify the size of the window that has focus, or the target window in the **Window Title** field, by the number of pixels entered, or the variables chosen, in the **Pixels to Resize** section. The window will never be bigger than your computer's display no matter how you adjust the size. And it never be smaller than allowed.

> *// Decrease width by 50 pixels and increase height by 75*
> **Window Resize: Current Win - (-50 Pixels Wider, 75 Pixels Higher)**

The *Enlarge/Decrease by Percentage* command will modify the size of the window that has focus, or the target window in the **Window Title** field, by the percentages entered, or the variables chosen, in the **Percentage to Resize** section.

> *// Decrease width by 15% and increase height by 15%*
> **Window Resize: Current Win - (-15 Percent Wider, 15 Percent Higher)**

Window Reposition

These commands move a window to a certain position on your display and are called from the *Size or Position a Window* dialog. You may move a window to an exact position or by a pixel count or percentage.

The *Specify Exact Location* command will set the window that has focus, or the target window in the **Window Title** field, to the values entered in the **Left** and **Top** fields (within the **Location** section), and will accept any value between -999 through 9,999.

You can optionally use the **Var** drop-down lists to give you more of a range to place the window. This is especially useful for systems that have multiple monitors.

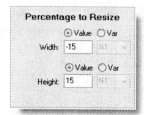

The **Launch Mouse Locator** button launches the *Mouse Locator* dialog, which is explained in detail within the *Mouse* chapter. Use this tool to position your mouse to where you want the window, then press **Ctrl+Space** on your keyboard. The mouse coordinates will be placed into the **Left** and **Top** fields for you. Do not mistake these for being the position of the window. They are not. Let's say for example, that you move your window to some position on the screen by dragging the titlebar with your mouse. Once positioned, you press **Ctrl+Space** on your keyboard. The coordinates that get recorded are *not* the left-hand or top of the window, but rather the position of the mouse.

// Move the current window to 900 pixels from the left and 100 from the top
Window Reposition: Current Win - (Left: 900, Top: 100)

The next nine commands, beginning with *Center on Screen* and ending with *Move to Bottom Right*, position a window exactly as their titles imply. There are no options when using these commands, as they are simply common screen positions of your computer's primary monitor. They cannot be used for the secondary monitors. The Windows Taskbar is considered to be one of the border limits. For example, if the Taskbar is on the bottom of your display and you use the *Move to Bottom Center* command, then the window will *not* be placed at the bottom of your display, but rather the top of the Taskbar. This is also true if your Taskbar is at the top, left, or right of the display.

Window Reposition: Center - Current Win   // Move the current window to the center of the screen
Window Reposition: Bottom Right - Current Win   // Move the current window to the bottom-right corner of the screen

The *Move in Pixels* command will move the window that has focus, or the target window in the **Window Title** field, by the values entered in the **Horizontally** and **Vertically** fields (within the **Pixels to Move** section), and will accept any value between -999 through 9,999. Positive values move the window to the right and down respectively. Negative values move the window to the left and up respectively.

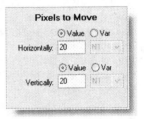

// Move the current window 20 pixels to the right and 20 pixels down
Window Reposition: Current Win - (20 Pixels Horiz, 20 Pixels Vert)

The *Move by Percentage* command will move the window that has focus, or the target window in the **Window Title** field, by the values entered in the **Horizontally** and **Vertically** fields (within the **Percentage to Move** section), and will accept any value between -999 through 9,999. Positive values move the window to the right and down respectively. Negative values move the window to the left and up respectively.

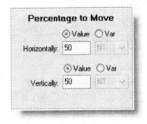

// Move the current window 50 percent to the right and 50 percent down
Window Reposition: Current Win - (50 Percent Horiz, 50 Percent Vert)

A window is moved based on the percentage of the window size placed in the **Horizontally** and **Vertically** fields. The formula is:

New X position = current X position + (window width * Horizontally field)
New Y position = current Y position + (window height * Vertically field)

If your target window is 200 pixels wide and 150 pixels high -AND-
It is positioned at coordinates 100,300 on your screen -AND-
the **Horizontally** field is set to 25 -AND-

the **Vertically** field is set to 30 -THEN-
the window will be moved to 150,345 on your screen

    150 = 100 + (200 * 25%)
    345 = 300 + (150 * 30%)

If your target window is 400 pixels wide and 300 pixels high -AND-
It is positioned at coordinates 200,200 on your screen -AND-
the **Horizontally** field is set to -20 (negative 20) -AND-
the **Vertically** field is set to -10 (negative 10) -THEN-
the window will be moved to120,170 on your screen

    120 = 200 - (400 * 20%)
    170 = 200 - (300 * 10%)

Set Window Order

This command allows you to manipulate the window stack on your Desktop by bringing windows to the top (temporarily or permanently) or sending them to the bottom. However, this command does not set focus to a window. Use the **Window Activate** command to set focus.

You can choose between the **Current Window**, which is the one that has focus at the time the command is run, and a **Specific Window**. The blank field is where the name of the window title is to be placed if you are specifying a window. You may also pick a window using the **Browse** button, which is explained in the *Common Dialogs* section at the beginning of this chapter.

The **Always on Top** command moves the target window to the top of the stack permanently, or at least until you close it or choose a different window. If you open or activate other windows, your target window will remain on top of the stack even though it will not have focus. The following macro launches both the Notepad and Calculator applications. It then sets the Calculator to remain permanently on top of the stack. Finally, it activates the Notepad, which will remain behind the calculator even though it now has focus.

        Activate or Launch: "Notepad" OR "notepad.exe"   // Launch the Notepad application
        Activate or Launch: "Calculator" OR "calc.exe"   // Launch the Calculator application
        Set Window Order: Set Current Window to always be on top // Set Calculator to always be on top
        Activate Window: "Notepad"   // Activate the Notepad (Calculator will still be on top)

The **Remove Topmost Status and Place On Top** command is used in two ways. For those windows that have the "topmost" status set, it removes the setting, otherwise it is used to place a window on top of the stack. If you have a window preset with the "topmost" status, then the status must be removed before another window can be placed on top of the stack. The following macro is identical with the last example except for adding the two commands at the end. The first command removes the "topmost" status of the calculator window. The last command then places the notepad window on top of the stack, giving it focus be default.

Activate or Launch: "Notepad" OR "notepad.exe"   // Launch the Notepad application
Activate or Launch: "Calculator" OR "calc.exe"   // Launch the Calculator application
Set Window Order: Set Current Window to always be on top   // Set Calculator to always be on top
Activate Window: "Notepad"   // Activate the Notepad (Calculator will still be on top)
Set Window Order: Set "Calculator" to on top without topmost status   // Remove the topmost status from the Calculator
Set Window Order: Set "Notepad" to on top without topmost status   // Bring the Notepad to the top of the stack

The *Place On Bottom* command simply shuffles the target window to the bottom of the stack.

Window Sizing Border

This is an interesting system-wide command that affects the width or thickness of the border on any window that can be resized. By system-wide I mean that it affects not only the current windows that are on your Desktop, but also windows that have not yet been launched. The value remains in effect until changed.

The command is called from the Macro Express *System Controls* dialog. It has a field named **Factor** that is the number of pixels added to the window border. Any literal value ranging from 1 though 10 can be placed here, with 1 being the default. Variables are acceptable, too.

The underlying property that this value affects can be found in the *Properties* dialog of your Desktop. Right-click on your Desktop then choose **Properties**. Now click on the **Appearance** Tab and then the **Advanced** button. From the **Item** drop-down list choose **Active Window Border**. The **Size** field is what this Macro Express command changes. Normally it is set to 1. Changing the **Factor** field in Macro Express to 10 will also change it in the **Size** field as shown here.

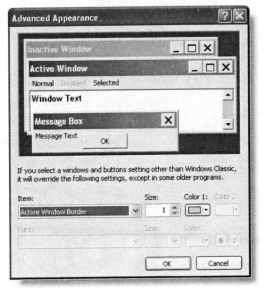

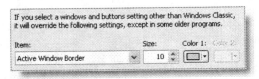

Here, for example, is the Windows Notepad application with the **Factor** field set to the default of 1.

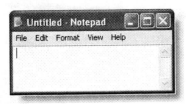

And here it is with the **Factor** field set to the maximum of 10.

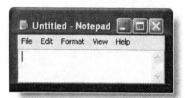

Repeat with Windows

This ***Repeat*** command is chosen from the standard Macro Express *Repeat Options* dialog. Use it to perform operations on any window that is open on your computer.

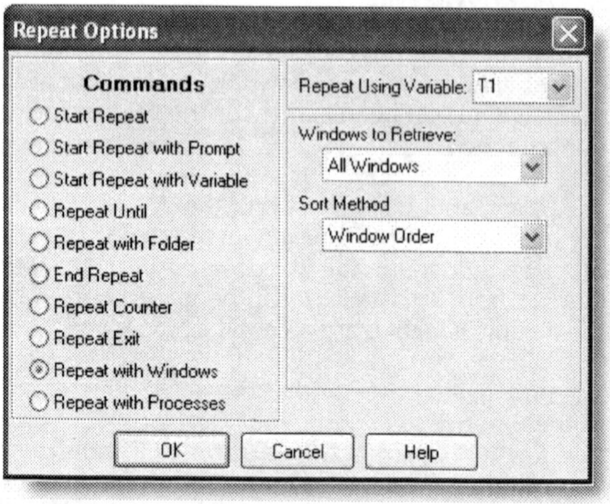

The variable chosen in the **Repeat Using Variable** drop-down list will contain the name of the current window in the repeat loop. The **Windows to Retrieve** drop-down list gives you three choices of which windows are to be accessed by the repeat loop.

1. All Windows
2. Visible Windows
3. Hidden Windows

The default choice is **All Windows**. The visible and hidden windows are what you can see in the *Running Windows* dialog explained at the beginning of this chapter in the *Common Dialogs* section. The **Sort Method** drop-down list allows the repeat loop to go through the windows in the order that they are arranged by your operating system or alphabetically. The default choice is **Window Order**.

This command gives you the ability to loop through the running windows on your computer to place the titles into a variable. What you do with the variable is up to you. It can be used in any command that accepts a window title. You can, for example, use it to close a window, or series of windows that have something common in the name. Maybe you have several Excel spreadsheets open at the same time and want to close all

of them. Using the example from the *Common Dialogs* section at the beginning of this chapter, the following macro closes all the "Expenses" windows.

Repeat with Windows: Place title in %T1%	// Use Visible windows and sort alphabetically
If Variable %T1% contains "Expenses.xls"	// If the title contains and "Expenses.xls" file name then
Window Close: "%T1%"	// close the window
End If	// End of window title test
Repeat End	// End of repeat loop

This example simply lists all the windows open on your computer alphabetically:

```
Activate or Launch: "Notepad" OR "notepad.exe"      // Launch or activate the Windows Notepad application
Window Resize: Notepad - (Width: 400, Height: 800)  // Resize to easily list windows
Window Reposition: Center - Current Win             // Center it on the display
Repeat with Windows: Place title in %T1%            //Repeat with all windows sorted alphabetically
 Text Type: %T1%<ENTER>                             // Type the window title into Notepad
Repeat End                                          // End of repeat loop
```

If Window On Top
If Window Not On Top
If Window Running
If Window Not Running

The *If Window* commands are chosen from the system-wide *If Commands* dialog. The **Window Title** field holds the name of your target window and may contain a literal string, variable, or a combination of both.

You may optionally pick a window using the **Select** button. Unlike the other **Select Window** buttons explained in the *Common Dialogs* section at the beginning of this chapter, this one does not provide for selecting invisible windows, just the visible ones. When choosing a window with this button, a *Select Title* dialog appears. Highlight your target window and then click the **OK** button. This will record your choice in the **Window Title** field. These commands do give you a choice of using an **Exact Match** or **Partial Match** for the window title. Remember, however, that whichever you choose, it is *never* case-sensitive.

The *If Window On Top* command will return *true* if the window named in the **Window Title** field has focus. There is an important distinction between the name of this command and what it tests for, which is "does the target window have *focus*?" Consider this macro:

```
Activate or Launch: "Notepad" OR "notepad.exe"        // Activate or launch the Windows Notepad application
```

```
Activate or Launch: "Calculator" OR "calc.exe"          // Activate or launch the Windows Calculator application
Set Window Order: Set Current Window to always be on top  // Fix the Calculator to always be on top
Activate Window: "Notepad"                               // Set focus to the Notepad
If Window Title "Calculator" is on top                   // If the Calculator is on top then
  Text Type: Calculator is on top<ENTER>                 // say so
Else                                                     // Or else
  Text Type: Notepad is on top<ENTER>                    // Say the Notepad is on top
End If                                                   // End of test
```

After launching both the Windows *Notepad* and *Calculator* applications, the macro sets the calculator to always be on top of all other windows on the stack. However, here is the result of running the macro: The *Notepad* is reported to be *on top* even though it *is not*. It only has *focus*. If you want to test that a window does *not* have focus, then use the opposite *If Window Not On Top* command.

The *If Window Running* command will return *true* if the window named in the **Window Title** field is running on your computer. It does not care if it is on top, has focus, is minimized, maximized, or hidden. It is enough that it is simply running. If you want to test that a window is *not* running, then use the opposite *If Window Not Running* command.

```
Activate or Launch: "Notepad" OR "notepad.exe"   // Launch the Notepad
If Window Title "Calculator" is running          // If Calculator is running
  Text Type: Calculator is running<ENTER>        // say so
Else                                             // Or else
  Text Type: Calculator is not running<ENTER>    // Say that it is not running
End If                                            // End of test
```

If Program On Top
If Program Not On Top
If Program Running
If Program Not Running

The *If Program* commands are chosen from the system-wide *If Commands* dialog. The **Program Name** field holds the name of your target program and may contain a literal string, variable, or a combination of both. These commands are the same as the *If Window* commands except that they use the application's program name.

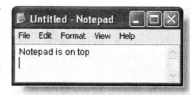

When picking a program with the **Select** button, the *Set Program* dialog appears containing a list of currently running applications. Choose one of them and then click the **OK** button. The program name will be placed into the **Program Name** field for you. Although the application names are listed as uppercase, the field itself is *not* case sensitive. "NOTEPAD.EXE" will work as well as "notepad.exe", "NOTEpad.Exe", or "NoTePaD.eXe".

 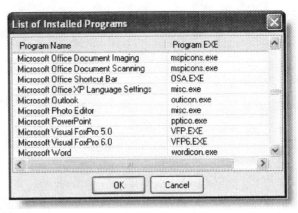

The *Set Program* dialog also gives you a way to choose an application installed on your computer but not currently running. Click on the **Select from Installed Programs** button and the *List of Installed Programs* dialog appears containing a description of each. This is a nice feature! Simply highlight the application name and then click on the **OK** button.

The *If Program On Top* command will return *true* if the program named in the **Program Name** field has focus. There is an important distinction between the name of this command and what it tests for, which is "does the target program have *focus*?" Consider this macro:

Activate or Launch: "Notepad" OR "notepad.exe"	// Activate or launch the Windows Notepad application
Activate or Launch: "Calculator" OR "calc.exe"	// Activate or launch the Windows Calculator application
Set Window Order: Set Current Window to always be on top	// Fix the Calculator to always be on top
Activate Window: "Notepad"	// Set focus to the Notepad
If Program Name "CALC.EXE" is on top	// If the Calculator program is on top then
Text Type: Calculator is on top<ENTER>	// say so
Else	// Or else
Text Type: Notepad is on top<ENTER>	// Say the Notepad program is on top
End If	// End of test

After launching both the Windows *Notepad* and *Calculator* applications, the macro sets the calculator to always be on top of all other windows on the stack. However, here is the result of running the macro: The *Notepad* is reported to be *on top* even though it *is not*. It only has *focus*. If you want to test that a program does *not* have focus, then use the opposite *If Program Not On Top* command.

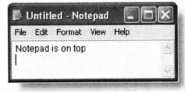

The *If Program Running* command will return *true* if the program named in the **Program Name** field is running on your computer. It does not care if it is on top, has focus, and is minimized, maximized, or hidden. It is enough that it is simply running. If you want to test that a program is *not* running, then use the opposite *If Program Not Running* command.

Activate or Launch: "Notepad" OR "notepad.exe"	// Launch the Notepad
If Program Name "CALC.EXE" is running	// If Calculator is running
Text Type: Calculator is running<ENTER>	// say so
Else	// Or else
Text Type: Calculator is not running<ENTER>	// Say that it is not running
End If	// End of test

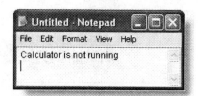

Summary

- Use the Windows/Programs commands to control other programs.
- You can launch programs with command line arguments for those that accept them.
- Windows can be hidden and still be accessible.
- Windows can be resized and repositioned.
- You control the window stack on your Desktop by shuffling windows to the top and bottom.

Files and Folders

Macro Express has a slew of commands for creating, deleting, copying, moving, processing, and manipulating files and folders. The majority are shown here, some of which are duplicated in other command categories. They are so numerous, and cover such a wide range of tasks, that I have broken them down into four subcategories.

1. Disk Operations - Copy, rename, move, delete.
2. File Information - Attributes, names, dates, locations, sizes.
3. Program Logic - Macro flow. If/End If, Wait for.
4. Data Processing- ASCII and text file processing.

Common Dialogs

There are two dialogs common to using these commands. A *File-Picker* and a *Folder-Picker*.

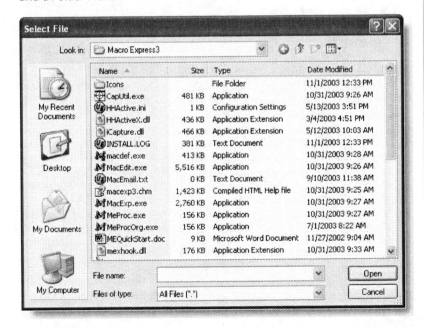

The *File-Picker* dialog is accessed with a **Browse** button from any file command dialog as shown here. Sometimes it is called with an **ellipses (...)** button. The purpose of course, is to save you time, and to make it easy to choose the target file for the current command.

The **Bypass File Existence Check** checkbox works identical with the ones explained in the *Variables* chapter. It is a design time option meant to tell you whether your file choice exists.

The *Folder-Picker* dialog is similar to the *File-Picker* except it is only used to choose folders from your hard drive, ignoring files in the process. Access it with a **Browse** button or an **ellipses (...)** button depending on which command you are using. And, just like the *File-Picker*, is meant to save you much time and effort when accessing folders.

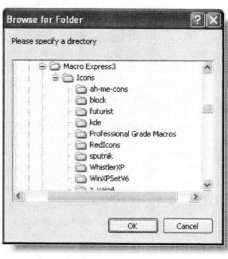

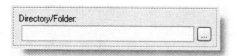

I make the assumption in this chapter that you are already familiar with how both of these common dialogs work from using Window programs, such as Explorer.

The common **Directory/Folder** field will accept either literal values or variables or a combination of both. "c:\TestFolder" or "c:\%T1%" are both acceptable. So are long Window names and short DOS names like "c:\Test Folder\Test Files" and "c:\TestFo~1\TestFi~1".

Standard DOS *current* ("."), and *parent* ("..") folder shortcuts can also be used. For example, to change to the parent folder you would only need to enter ".." in the field. Two parent folders up would be "..\..". If you want to change folders to the next one over, enter "..\Test Files". Network designators ("\\") are also allowed such as "\\Server\Data\Files".

Wildcards ("*" and "?") can be used in some of the file and folder commands. For example, to process all the files in a folder you could enter "c:\TestFolder*.*". If you want just the spreadsheet files use "c:\TestFolder*.xls". Any four character document file would be "c:\TestFolder\????.doc".

Disk Operations

This section covers the eight commands shown here, which are specific to folders and files on your hard drive. They give you direct program control by letting you change, create, rename, and delete folders, and copy, rename, move, and delete files.

For those of you that remember, do these sound like DOS commands? Yes they do ... and this is a good thing! They are simple, easy, and basic commands that make handling your files and folders an easy thing to do with Macro Express.

There is a common warning message for the **Rename Folder**, **Copy File or Files**, **Rename File or Files**, and **Move File or Files** commands that affects the destination name or path field. The warning refers to both absolute *and* relative paths. An absolute path usually begins with "c:\", "\\Server", or just plain "\". A relative path contains shortcuts like ".\SubFolder" or "..\Folder". See the individual command explanations for more details and how each is affected.

If an absolute path is not specified in the New Name/Path field, then the destination will be relative to the current working directory, which can be set using the Change Default Folder command.

There are two common checkboxes for four of the disk operation commands, **Copy File or Files**, **Rename File or Files**, **Move File or Files**, and **Delete File or Files**. When an operation involves many files, check the **Show Progress Dialog Box** checkbox. It will display

a progress bar on the screen while the lengthy operation is occurring. The **Recurse into Subfolders if Using Wildcard Names** checkbox, when checked, will examine each subfolder within the source field name to perform the same operation on files that match the wildcard pattern.

Change Default Folder

This command allows you to change the current, or active, folder on your hard drive to the one that is displayed in the **Directory/Folder** field. The field will accept literal strings, shortcuts, and variables. However, wildcard characters are not acceptable.

Back when DOS was king, it was important to know which directory, or folder was active. In other words, where you were located on the hard drive. It is not so important with Windows unless you are running a program that requires you to be in a certain folder, or you are manipulating files within a folder. Well ... "not so important" may not be the best term to use. It *is* important, although moving from one folder to another is done automatically by Windows as you run different programs from your Desktop.

If a program is started by clicking an icon on your Desktop, you will usually be taken to its home folder before the program starts. This is a view of the *Shortcut* Tab inside the *Properties* dialog of the Macro Express icon on my Desktop.

When Macro Express is started, I am taken to its home folder, which is where it was installed, and then Macro Express is engaged. The folder displayed in the **Start in** field will be my current, or active, folder until I manually change folders, or start a different program. For example, from Macro Express I would run this command to change folders:

Change Directory/Folder: "c:\TestFolder"

This would set my active folder to "c:\TestFolder", if it exists. If it does not exist, then an error message is displayed. Unlike file commands, folder commands do not have an option to check

for existence at design time if you manually fill in the **Directory/Folder** field. So, the error happens at runtime and the macro stops.

Create Folder

Use this command to create a folder or series of folders on your hard drive, or across your network. The **Directory/Folder** field contains the target folder and will accept literal strings, shortcuts, and variables. However, wildcard characters are not acceptable. You can create a whole tree of folders with a single command:

Create Folder: "c:\TempFolder\FolderA\FolderB\FolderC"

The example shows that to create "FolderC", a whole string of folders is created as needed. If the folder you are creating exists, then nothing will happen. Your macro will simply move on to the next line, which also happens if a folder cannot be created. No error message. No warning. This will occur if you attempt to create a folder on a nonexistent drive, or a drive that is no longer mapped to your network, or the field contains wildcard or illegal file name characters.

Rename Folder

This command is used to rename a folder. The **Directory/Folder** field contains the target folder and the **New Name** field contains what it is to be renamed. Either field will accept literal strings, shortcuts, and variables. However, wildcard characters are not acceptable.

The warning message at the bottom of the dialog means that if the **New Name** field contains just a name, then the folder will be renamed and placed in the current folder. Let's assume that you are in a folder named "c:\FolderA" and you want to rename "c:\FolderB" to "c:\FolderC". If you enter just "FolderC" into the **New Name** field, the result will be that "c:\FolderC" is moved to "c:\FolderA\FolderC", which is not what you wanted.

This command is well protected with runtime error messages similar to the one shown here, but there are others (depending on the error). The macro *does NOT* stop when an error occurs, but rather, moves to the next line. An error occurs under the following circumstances:

- The folder in the **Directory/Folder** field cannot be found, or contains wildcard or illegal file name characters.
- The folder in the **New Name** field contains an invalid drive designator, or wildcard or illegal file name characters.
- The folder names are identical in both fields.
- The folder in the **New Name** field exists.
- The folder in the **New Name** field would, after renaming, be at a different *level* in the *same* hierarchy than the folder in the **Directory/Folder** field. Renaming "c:\LevelA" to "c:\LevelA\LevelB" does not work. However, renaming "c:\LevelA" to "c:\LevelB\LevelA" does work because it is a different folder hierarchy. In other words, you moved the folder, and all of its contents, to a new location.

Delete Folder

This command deletes a folder and any files, or other folders that it may contain, *without prompting*. Be careful when testing macros with this command. If you enter a wrong folder name, you could destroy something important on your hard drive. The field will accept literal strings, shortcuts, and variables. However, wildcard characters are not acceptable.

A runtime error occurs and the macro stops *only* if the folder in the **Directory/Folder** field is the current folder. Refer to the *Change Default Folder* command.

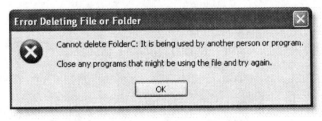

If a folder cannot be found, or the field contains wildcard or illegal file name characters, the macro does not display an error and it *does NOT stop*, but rather, moves to the next line in your macro.

Copy File or Files

This command copies single files, wildcard files, folders, and folder hierarchies. The **File(s) Path/Name** field contains the source and the **New Name** field holds the destination. Files are copied at runtime without warning the user, or prompting to overwrite. Both fields accept literal strings, shortcuts, variables, and wildcards. When copying folders, wildcards are to be inferred (see examples below).

The warning message at the bottom of the dialog means that if the **New Name** field contains just a name, then the file will be copied and placed in the current folder with the new name. Let's assume that you are in a folder named "c:\FolderA" and you want to copy "c:\FolderB\File1.txt" to "c:\FolderB\File2.txt". If you enter just "File2.txt" into the **New Name** field, the result will be that "c:\FolderB\File1.txt" is copied and renamed to "c:\FolderA\File2.txt", which is not what you wanted.

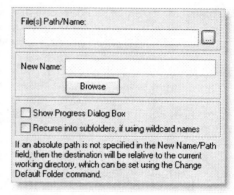

Error messages similar to the one shown here are displayed at runtime. There are others depending on the error. An error occurs under the following circumstances:

- The file or folder in the **File(s) Path/Name** or **New Name** field contains illegal file name characters. An error message is displayed and the macro stops.
- The file or folder in the **File(s) Path/Name** field cannot be found, or does not exist. The macro *does NOT* display an error and it *does NOT* stop, but rather, moves to the next line in your macro.
- The file or folder in the **New Name** field contains an invalid drive designator. An error message is displayed. The macro *does NOT* stop, but rather, moves to the next line in your macro.
- The file or folder names are identical in both fields. An error message is displayed. The macro *does NOT* stop, but rather, moves to the next line in your macro.

Even though the name of this command implies *files*, it is also used to copy *folders*. Let's use the following folder hierarchy, and files, to help illustrate numerous ways to use this command. Assume that you are located in *C:\FolderA* using the ***Change Default Folder*** command.

    C:\FolderA
        SubFolder1
            SubFolder2
            File2.doc
            FileB.txt
        SubFolder3
            File3.doc
            FileC.txt
        File1.doc
        FileA.txt

    FolderA contains SubFolder1, SubFolder3, File1.doc, and FileA.txt
    SubFolder1 contains SubFolder2, File2.doc, and FileB.txt
    SubFolder2 is empty
    SubFolder3 contains File3.doc and FileC.txt

	File(s) Path/Name	New Name	Results	Recurse
1	File1.doc	FileX.doc	C:\FolderA\File1.doc copied to C:\FolderA\FileX.doc	N/A
2	.\File1.doc	.\FileX.doc	Same as above	N/A
3	File1.doc	..\File1.doc	C:\FolderA\File1.doc copied to C:\File1.doc	N/A
4	File1.doc	..\	Same as above	N/A
5	File1.doc	SubFolder1\	C:\FolderA\File1.doc copied to C:\FolderA\SubFolder1\File1.doc	N/A
6	File1.doc	SubFolder1	Same as above	N/A
7	File?.*	File?.sav	C:\FolderA\File1.doc copied to C:\FolderA\File1.sav and C:\FolderA\FileA.txt copied to C:\FolderA\FileA.sav	N/A
8	C:\FolderB\File1.txt	File2.txt	C:\FolderB\File1.txt copied to C:\FolderA\File2.txt	No
9	C:\FolderA	C:\FolderB	Copy all files and folders from C:\FolderA to C:\FolderB	Yes

1. Copy a file to a different name in the same folder.
2. Copy a file to a different name in the same folder using folder shortcuts.
3. Copy a file to its parent folder.
4. Copy a file to its parent folder using folder shortcuts.
5. Copy a file to a subfolder. If the subfolder does not exist then create it.
6. Copy a file to a subfolder if the subfolder exists; otherwise, copy it to a file named "SubFolder1".
7. Copy files beginning with "File" plus any other single character, to files of the same name, but with "sav" as the extension.
8. Copy a file to the current working folder and give it a different name.
9. Copy one folder to another.

Rename File or Files

This command renames single files and files with wildcards. The **File(s) Path/Name** field contains what is to be renamed using the value in the **New Name** field. Both fields accept literal strings, shortcuts, variables, and wildcards. Files are renamed at runtime without warning.

This command was originally meant to be used for files only; however, it can be used on folders, too. In which case it works similar to the *Rename Folder* command.

The warning message at the bottom of the dialog means that if the **New Name** field contains just a name, the file will be placed in the current folder with the new name. Let's assume that you are in a folder named "c:\FolderA". You want "c:\FolderB\File1.txt" renamed to "c:\FolderB\File2.txt". If you enter just "File2.txt" into the **New Name** field, the result will be that "c:\FolderB\File1.txt" is moved and renamed to "c:\FolderA\File2.txt", which is not what you wanted.

Error messages similar to the one shown here are displayed at runtime. There are others depending on the error. An error occurs under the following circumstances:

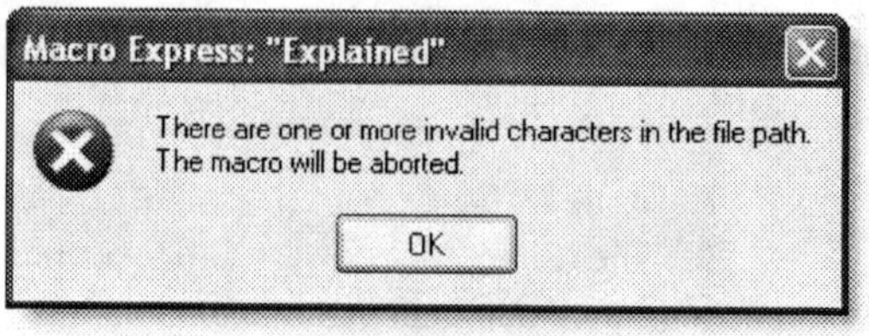

- The file or folder in the **File(s) Path/Name** or **New Name** field contains illegal file name characters. An error message is displayed and the macro stops.
- The file or folder in the **File(s) Path/Name** field cannot be found, or does not exist. The macro *does NOT* display an error and it *does NOT* stop, but rather, moves to the next line in your macro.
- The file or folder in the **New Name** field contains an invalid drive designator. An error message is displayed. The macro *does NOT* stop, but rather, moves to the next line in your macro.
- The file or folder names are identical in both fields. An error message is displayed. The macro *does NOT* stop, but rather, moves to the next line in your macro.

Let's use the same folder hierarchy used in the *Copy File or Files* command to help illustrate this command. Assume that you are located in *C:\FolderA* using the *Change Default Folder* command.

	File(s) Path/Name	New Name	Results	Recurse
1	File1.doc	FileX.doc	C:\FolderA\File1.doc renamed to C:\FolderA\FileX.doc	No
2	.\File1.doc	.\FileX.doc	Same as above	No
3	File?.*	FileX.*	C:\FolderA\File1.doc renamed to C:\FolderA\FileX.doc and C:\FolderA\FileA.txt renamed to C:\FolderA\FileX.txt	No
4	C:\FolderA\File?.*	C:\FolderA\FileX.*	Same as above	No
5	C:\FolderB\File1.txt	File2.txt	C:\FolderB\File1.txt moved as C:\FolderA\File2.txt	No
6	File1.doc	FileX.doc	Rename all File1.doc files to FileX.doc in all subfolders	Yes
7	File?.*	FileX.*	Rename all File?.* files to FileX.* in all subfolders	Yes
8	C:\FolderA	C:\FolderB	Move all files and folders from C:\FolderA to C:\FolderB	N/A

1. Rename a file.
2. Rename a file using folder shortcuts as part of the path.
3. Rename files beginning with "File" plus any other single character, replacing the single character with an "X".
4. Rename files using wildcards and full path names.
5. Move a file to the current working folder and give it a different name.
6. Rename all File1.doc files throughout the FolderA hierarchy.
7. Rename files beginning with "File" plus any other single character throughout the FolderA hierarchy, replacing the single character with an "X".
8. Rename a folder.

Move File or Files

This command moves single files, wildcard files, folders, and folder hierarchies. The **File(s) Path/Name** field contains the source and the **New Path** field holds the destination. Files are moved at runtime without warning the user, or prompting to overwrite. Both fields accept literal strings, shortcuts, variables, and wildcards. When moving folders, wildcards are to be inferred (see examples below).

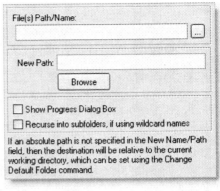

The warning message at the bottom of the dialog means that if the **New Path** field contains just a name, then the file or folder will be placed in the current folder. Let's assume that you are in a folder named "c:\FolderA" and you want to move "c:\FolderB\File2.txt" to "c:\FolderC\File2.txt". If you enter just "FolderC" into the **New Path** field, the result will be that "c:\FolderB\File2.txt" is moved to "c:\FolderA\FolderC", which is not what you wanted.

Error messages similar to the one shown here are displayed at runtime. There are others depending on the error. An error occurs under the following circumstances:

- The file or folder in the **File(s) Path/Name** or **New Path** field contains illegal file name characters. An error message is displayed and the macro stops.
- The file or folder in the **File(s) Path/Name** field cannot be found, or does not exist. The macro *does NOT* display an error and it *does NOT* stop, but rather, moves to the next line in your macro.
- The file or folder in the **New Path** field contains an invalid drive designator. An error message is displayed. The macro *does NOT* stop, but rather, moves to the next line in your macro.
- The file or folder names are identical in both fields. An error message is displayed. The macro *does NOT* stop, but rather, moves to the next line in your macro.

Let's use the same folder hierarchy used in the *Copy File or Files* command to help illustrate this command. Assume that you are located in *C:\FolderA* using the *Change Default Folder* command.

	File(s) Path/Name	New Path	Results	Recurse
1	File1.doc	SubFolder1	C:\FolderA\File1.doc moved to C:\FolderA\SubFolder1	No
2	.\File1.doc	.\SubFolder1	Same as above	No
3	File?.*	SubFolder1	C:\FolderA\File1.doc moved to C:\FolderA\SubFolder1 and C:\FolderA\FileA.txt moved to C:\FolderA\ SubFolder1	No
4	C:\FolderA\File?.*	C:\FolderA\SubFolder1	Same as above	No
5	C:\FolderB\File2.txt	FolderC	C:\FolderB\File2.txt moved to C:\FolderA\FolderC	No

1. Move a file.
2. Move a file using folder shortcuts.
3. Move files beginning with "File" plus any other single character.
4. Move files using wildcards and full path names.
5. Move a file to the current working folder and create the needed subfolder.

Delete File or Files

This command deletes folders and single or wildcard files and moves them to your Recycle Bin. The **File(s) Path/Name** field contains what is to be deleted and will accept literal strings, shortcuts, variables, and wildcards. To delete a folder (and anything it contains) simply enter its name into the field. A file is deleted even if its "Read-Only" flag is set.

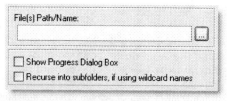

Error messages similar to the one shown here are displayed at runtime. There are others depending on the error. An error occurs under the following circumstances:

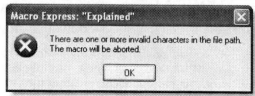

- The file or folder in the **File(s) Path/Name** field contains illegal file name characters. An error message is displayed and the macro stops.

- The file or folder in the **File(s) Path/Name** field contains an invalid drive designator or cannot be found. The macro *does NOT* display an error and it *does NOT* stop, but rather, moves to the next line in your macro.

Let's use the same folder hierarchy used in the *Copy File or Files* command to help illustrate this command. Assume that you are located in *C:\FolderA* using the *Change Default Folder* command.

	File(s) Path/Name	Results	Recurse
1	File1.doc	C:\FolderA\File1.doc deleted	No
2	.\File1.doc	Same as above	No
3	File?.*	C:\FolderA\File1.doc and C:\FolderA\FileA.txt deleted	No
4	C:\FolderA\File?.*	Same as above	No
5	SubFolder1	Delete SubFolder1 and all of its files	N/A

1. Delete a file.
2. Delete a file using folder shortcuts.
3. Delete files beginning with "File" plus any other single character.
4. Delete files using wildcards and full path names.
5. Delete a subfolder and all the files within it.

File Information

This section covers four commands. *Convert Filename*, *File Attributes*, *Get File Version*, and *Variable Set from File*. Also a honorable mention of the *Set Value from the Size of a File* command. These all return some information about a file except for the *File Attributes* command, which *changes* file attributes.

Convert Filename

Windows supports long file and folder names up to 255 characters in length. It generates a DOS (short) file name in **8.3** format, whenever a file or folder is created, to allow DOS or 16-bit Windows programs to access the files. "**8.3**" means eight characters are used for the file name and three for the extension. An **8.3** DOS name will also be generated if a file name is eight characters or fewer, but contains spaces, multiple periods, or anything else that would not be a valid DOS name. Windows generates DOS file names in the following manner:

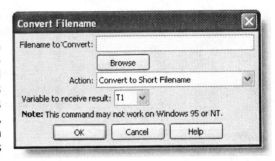

- Any invalid characters (**space " / \ [ ] : ; = ,**) are removed from the file name.
- Because DOS file names can contain only a single period (**.**), all but the last one are removed unless the last one is at the end, then it is removed and the previous one to it is kept. In other words, if a file name ends with a period, then the ending period is ignored. For example "long filename.123.456.789." would be converted to "LONGFI~1.789"
- Windows truncates the file name to six characters and appends a tilde (**~**) and a **digit**. The first attempt is "~1". If this duplicates an existing DOS name in the same folder then "~2" is tried, then "~3", "~4", and so forth. If Windows needs more than a single digit then the file name is truncated to five characters, then four characters, and so forth. For example the DOS file name could be "LONGFI~1.TXT", "LONGF~10.TXT", or "LONG~100.TXT".
- File name extensions are truncated to three characters or fewer. "long filename.123.456.789.script" would be converted to "LONGFI~1.SCR".
- The file name is converted to uppercase.

The **Filename to Convert** field contains the target file or folder name. Since it is your operating system that does the conversion when the file is created (this command just reports it), the file must exist on your hard drive. If not, you will get a handful of weird, meaningless, characters for a conversion or nothing at all. Use the **Action** field drop-down list to choose which conversion to do. *Convert to Short Filename* or *Convert to Long Filename*.

```
Change Directory/Folder: "C:\FolderA"                              // Change folders
Convert Filename "Filename with spaces.txt" to a short filename %T1%   // Windows name to DOS name "FILENA~1.TXT"
Convert Filename "%T1%" to a long filename and store in %T2%       // Convert it back "Filename with spaces.txt"
```

File Attributes

Use this to change file and folder attributes on your hard drive. The **Filename** field contains your target file or folder. The **Attributes** section contains four common file and folder attributes with their **True/False** settings. You can set one, two, three, or all four at the same time with a single command line. Simply check the target attribute or attributes, and then choose either True or False for each.

What are file attributes? Your Windows operating system maintains certain properties associated with every file and folder that exists on your hard drive, including file sizes, dates and times, and attributes.

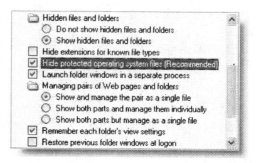

- Archive - Has this been backed up?
- System - Is this a system file?
- Hidden - Is this a hidden file?
- Read-Only - Is it write-protected?
- Directory - Is this a folder or a file?
- Volume Label - Drive volume label.

The first four attributes can be changed using this command. The last two, *Directory* and *Volume Label*, cannot, so I will not be discussing them here.

Archive Attribute

For you history-buffs, this attribute was first used in DOS version 2. It is automatically set whenever a file is created, overwritten, modified, renamed, or moved. Most backup programs can utilize it to control incremental file backup procedures by clearing it when the file is successfully backed up. The file would not be backed up again until reset by the operating system when any one of the five events reoccurs. To set the attribute using this command, click on the **Archive** checkbox and choose the **True** option.

> **Set File Attributes: "ImportantStuff.xls"** // Set Archive attribute to True

System Attribute

This attribute does not affect anything on your system except the capacity to "*see*" certain files from, say, Windows Explorer. Since the early days of DOS, this has perhaps been the most inconsistently used attribute. It usually works with the *Hidden* attribute, by giving one additional security level to a file or folder.

What you see here is the *Advanced Settings* dialog of *Windows Explorer*. (Tools | Folder Options | View). The highlighted choice, if checked, will hide from view all files that are marked with this attribute and any marked with the *Hidden* attribute, too. Having them marked in this manner prevents accidental erasure, because if you cannot see them, then you cannot selected them from within Windows Explorer. To see the effects of this attribute, examine your Windows or Winnt folder with this option checked.

When you uncheck or clear the option, a warning is displayed. Click the **Yes** button then refresh Windows Explorer and you will be able to see

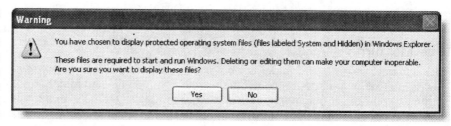

the files marked with this attribute. To set the attribute using this command, click on the **System** checkbox and choose the **True** option.

> **Set File Attributes: "ImportantStuff.xls"** // Set System attribute to True

Hidden Attribute

Like the *System* attribute, this one does not affect anything on your system except the capacity to "*see*" certain files and folders.

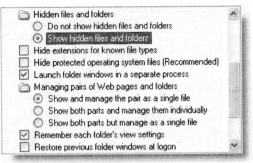

Look again at the *Advanced Settings* dialog. The highlighted choice will hide from view all files that are marked with this attribute. Having them marked in this manner prevents accidental erasure, because if you cannot see them, then you cannot select them from within Windows Explorer. Examine your Windows or Winnt folder with this option chosen. You should not see any of the install folders created from updating your operating system, which are named "*$NtUninstal..*" or something similar. They should appear after clearing the option and refreshing Windows Explorer. To set the attribute using this command, click on the **Hidden** checkbox and choose the **True** option.

> **Set File Attributes: "ImportantStuff.xls"** // Set Hidden attribute to True

Read-Only Attribute

This is a handy attribute. Use it to mark files and folders so they cannot be accidentally overwritten or changed by a program. Maybe you have important data in a *spreadsheet*, *database*, or "*.csv*" file that is used by a macro, but is never to be overwritten. To set the attribute using this command, click on the **Read-Only** checkbox

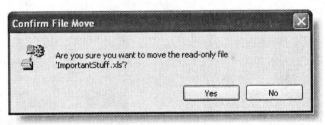

and choose the **True** option. You must remove the Read-Only attribute before changing data in the file.

Windows Explorer will prompt you with this dialog before moving, renaming, or deleting any file or folder that is marked with the Read-Only attribute. The attribute is retained when copying, moving, and renaming files and folders.

> **Set File Attributes: "ImportantStuff.xls"** // Set Read-Only attribute to True

Variable Set from File

This is two commands in one. It retrieves the dates and times of the file or folder contained in the **Filename/Path** field, and will also parse the field into separate file name components. Even though this field accepts both file and folder names, the **Browse** button can only be used to pick a file because it calls the file-picker dialog. Folder names must be entered manually. The field will accept literal strings, shortcuts, and variables. However, wildcard characters are not acceptable.

Get File Date/Time

An error message similar to the one shown here is displayed and the macro stops if the file or folder in the **Filename/Path** field cannot be found for any reason.

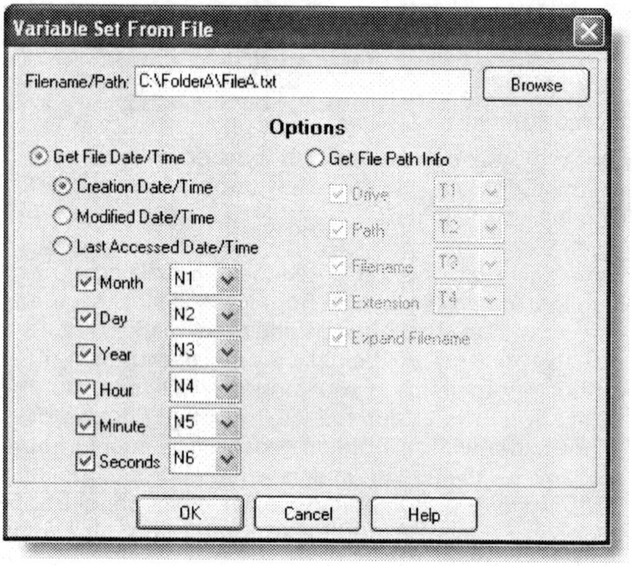

Each file and folder has three different dates and times returned by this command:

1. Creation
2. Modified
3. Last Accessed

Creation Date/Time

This is the date and time stamp given to all three date/time attributes (Creation, Modified, and Last Accessed) when any file is first created. Under normal circumstances it never changes. However, there are free utilities available from the internet that are specifically designed for this. Renaming a file does not change this value, and neither will moving it. Copying it will change it (on the copy) because you are creating another file.

Modified Date/Time

This date and time attribute is updated when a file is edited, lengthened, shortened, changed, or re-saved in any manner. Copying, moving, and renaming it has no effect on this date/time attribute.

Last Accessed Date/Time

This is updated when a file is accessed in any manner such as copying, moving, or renaming it. It may change without you doing anything. Your operating system could change it because you simply clicked on the folder where the file resides.

The **Month, Day, Year, Hour, Minute**, and **Seconds** for each of the three date/time attributes can be returned by this command. The table shows the minimum and maximum values returned for each field. Choose one, some, or all the fields at once. Each value is returned by picking the appropriate checkbox and then using the associated drop-down list to choose the target integer variable to store the value. The Hour field is returned in military time. *Zero* is midnight.

Field	Min	Max
Month	1	12
Day	1	31
Year	4-digits	
Hour	0	23
Minute	0	59
Seconds	0	59

Get File Path Info

File and folder path strings in the **Filename/Path** field can be broken into four components with this command:

- Drive - Drive designator including the colon "**:**"
- Path - Folder portion of path string
- Filename - Name of the file without the extension
- Extension - File name extension including the period "**.**"

Each value is returned by picking the appropriate checkbox and then using the associated drop-down list to choose the target string variable to store the value. The **Expand Filename** checkbox will convert the file or folder in the **Filename/Path** field to a full path string before parsing it. For example, if "File1.txt" is entered and if the current folder is set to "c:\FolderA", internally it will be changed to "C:\FolderA\File1.txt" before parsing. Here are some situations to watch out for:

- The folder or file does not have to physically exist. The path and name will still be parsed.
- Network paths (leading "\\") will be ignored. The **Drive** field variable will be set to an empty string and the leading "\\" remain as part of the path.
- When parsing a folder, the **Filename/Path** field must have a trailing backslash or else it will be parsed as a file name instead of as a folder name.
- Folder shortcuts "**.**" and "**..**" work fine, but only if used with the **Expand Filename** checkbox, otherwise they remain as part of the path.

Here is a simple example of parsing a full path name "C:\FolderA\FileA.txt".

```
Variable Set From File Path// Parse "C:\FolderA\FileA.txt"
// Drive (T1) = "C:"
// Path (T2) = "\FolderA\"
// Filename (T3) = "FileA"
// Extension (T4) = ".txt"
```

Get File Version

This command retrieves a file version number in either a string or an integer format. The **Options** drop-down list controls which format to use.

The **File to Retrieve Version From** field contains your target file name. Although mostly used on *.exe* and *.dll* files, any file type with a version number will work. The field will accept literal strings, shortcuts, and variables. However, wildcard characters are not acceptable.

If the file cannot be found for whatever reason (does not exist, illegal drive designator, and so forth), the macro *does NOT* display an error, and it *does NOT* stop. Instead, it places zero values into your chosen integer variables. If you have chosen to retrieve a string, "0.0.0.0" is returned.

The **Place Result In** drop-down list is used when you are retrieving the file version as a string. Otherwise, each component can be saved to a different integer variable. You can retrieve all the components or just one by putting a check in the correct box and then choosing a variable from the drop-down list.

Get Version of "MacExp.exe" into integer variables

Using Macro Express (*MacExp.exe*) as an example, the following values are retuned:

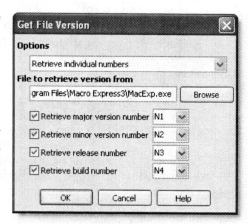

N1 = 3
N2 = 5
N3 = 1
N4 = 1

The major version number is 3, the minor version number is 5, the release number is 1 (which, for Macro Express, is the letter "a"), and the build number is 1. So in this example, Macro Express is "v3.5a build 1", which is represented as 3.5.1.1

Set Value from the Size of a File

This command is more fully explained in the *Variables* chapter. It sets a target integer variable with the size of a file found anywhere on your system. The value returned is in bytes.

Program Logic

Commands such as *If*, *Repeat*, *Break*, and *Wait* control the flow of a program. I use the term "program" to mean a Macro Express script. The *File and Folder* commands include some of these … and more.

Most, if not all, *If* commands are chosen from the system-wide *If Commands* dialog. The top three choices in each column are the ones that we are discussing in this section.

The **Use Search Path** checkbox is a runtime feature. It tells Macro Express to use the Windows search path environment variable (**%PATH%**) to search for a file if it cannot be found in the current folder. The search path is a string of folder names to look through. For example, Notepad.exe is usually found in the "C:\Windows" folder (or something similar), which is in the system search path. So instead of entering "C:\Windows\Notepad.exe" into the **Filename** field, simply enter "Notepad.exe" and Windows will find it for you by looking through the folders in the search path.

If File Exists
If Not File Exists

Use these commands to test for the existence, or nonexistence, of the target file in the **Filename** field. As usual, this field will accept both variables and literal strings. It can be a full path string or just a file name. And folder shortcuts "**.**" and "**..**" are acceptable, but wildcards are not. Here is an example that will create a file if it does not exist.

```
If Not File Exists "TestFile.txt"              // If the file does not exist then
    Variable Modify String: Save %T1% to Text File    // create it
End If                                          //End existence test
```

If Folder Exists
If Not Folder Exists

Use these commands to test for the existence, or nonexistence, of the target folder in the **Folder Name** field. Notice the **Use Search Path** checkbox is not available for folders. As usual, this field will accept both variables and literal strings. It can be a full path string or just a folder name. And folder shortcuts "**.**" and "**..**" are acceptable, but wildcards are not. Here is an example that will create a folder if it does not exist.

```
If Not Folder Exists "C:\FolderA\SubFolder3"    // If the folder does not exist then
    Create Folder: "SubFolder3"                 // create it
End If                                           //End existence test
```

If File Ready
If Not File Ready

These commands test a file to determine if it is, or is not, being used by another application. In other words, is it free to be used by you? Let's say, for example, that you download an update file from the internet regularly. Sometimes it takes one minute, sometimes five minutes, sometimes longer, depending on traffic, and many other factors that you cannot control. Without this command you would need to put a delay in your macro to wait the maximum of time for the file to complete, however impractical the delay may be.

> **FTP Get File: "test"**   // Download file
> **Delay 600 Seconds**   // Delay 10 minutes

This is impractical. If the file takes only a minute to download, then you waste 9 minutes just waiting. If it takes longer than 10 minutes, then more than likely your macro will crash because the file is not yet finished downloading as your macro moves on. Here is a better solution.

> **FTP Get File: "test"**   // Begin downloading file
> **Repeat Until %N1% <> %N1%**   // Infinite loop
>   **If File Ready "test"**   // If the file is finished downloading then
>   **Repeat Exit**   // exit the infinite loop
>   **End If**   // End of test
>   **Delay 10 Seconds**   // Wait 10 seconds before testing file again
> **Repeat End**   // End of infinite loop

The macro continues looping until it reports that it is no longer being written to by the download process. This is much better than wasting time just waiting, or even worse, wasting more time because the file took longer to download than your macro allowed for. However, this solution has a flaw, which is the internet itself. What would happen if the file was delayed longer than 10 seconds during the download process? It would report itself as "finished" when the *If File Ready* command line engages after the delay. But, it is simply waiting for the internet site to continue feeding it. The solution to this problem is the *Wait for File Ready* command explained below.

Wait for File Exist
Wait for Folder to Exist

These commands will stop your macro until the file or folder specified in the **Filename** field exists, or until time runs out, whichever comes first. If the file or folder exists then nothing happens and your macro continues to the next line.

If you are sure the file or folder is going to be created then choose **Wait Indefinitely**, if the file or folder never gets created then your macro will never stop running. On the other hand, you may prefer to only wait for a period of time. Use the **Wait a Maximum** fields (**Minutes** and

Seconds). Each accepts a value up to 999,999, which means you can have the macro wait a tiny bit over 706 days ... although I have not tested this. Whatever value you use, if the time is reached before the file or folder is created then the macro will time-out and display an error dialog like the one shown on the right.

As with many of the **Wait for** commands, Macro Express does not have a graceful way to avoid a time-out. There is nothing to say, for example, "If the file does not get created, then do this, or try that".

Wait for File Ready

This command will wait until a file is not being accessed by another program, or even Macro Express for that matter. The **File must be ready for X Seconds** field is used to set the number of seconds the file must remain untouched for the macro to move on.

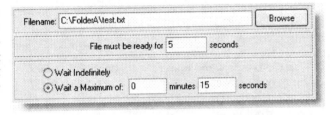

Some programs that create files open and close them often. Think about downloading a file from the internet. Sometimes it downloads smoothly, while other times there may be significant pauses. If, during one these pauses, the **Wait for File Ready** or **If File Ready** commands were to check the status of the file, it would think that it is "ready" when in fact it is not.

Data Processing

This series of commands, *Repeat with Folder*, *Text File Begin Process*, and *ASCII File Begin Process*, will allow you to perform operations on files within folders, process text files a single line at a time, and process data within ASCII files like comma separated value files.

Repeat with Folder

This *Repeat* command is chosen from the standard *Repeat Options* dialog. Use it to perform operations on files or folders that are inside the folder specified in the **Folder** field. If **Return Files** is chosen it will loop through the folder and return each file name it finds to the target variable. On the other hand, if **Return Folders** is chosen, then only folder names will be returned. Files will be ignored.

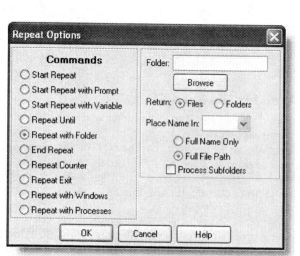

Wildcard characters and folder shortcuts ("." and "..") are not acceptable as input to the **Folder** field. An error dialog will be displayed at runtime if you attempt to use them and your macro will stop. An error dialog is also displayed if the target folder cannot be found.

You may also choose whether to process files or folder names within subfolders by checking the **Process Subfolders** checkbox. Doing so will force Macro Express to retrieve file or folder names from each folder in the **Folder** field hierarchy. In other words, every branch in the tree will be checked.

The file or folder name returned to the variable can be a path name if **Full File Path** is chosen, or simply the file name and extension if **Full Name Only** is chosen. "C:\FolderA\File1.txt" or just "File1.txt".

File or folder names are returned in the order that they are found on your hard drive. They are not returned in alphabetical order (unless your drive is set as NTSF ...maybe). The point is, do not count on the names being returned in the same order that they are displayed with Windows Explorer.

When this command is first engaged, it takes a "snapshot" (more or less) of the target folder. If you are processing names in an active folder, a folder where files are constantly being created as the macro is running, it may miss some of the new file names. Also, if files are being deleted by another program as the macro is running, the new ones may be "placed" into the deleted file slots. Again, causing Macro Express to miss the changes.

Here is a macro that simply counts the number of files in the folder hierarchy that I have been using throughout this chapter.

```
Change Directory/Folder: "C:\FolderA"    // Change folders to the target
Repeat with Folder                       // Loop, return file names and process all subfolders
 Variable Modify Integer: Inc (%N1%)     // Increment the counter
 Text Type: %T1%<ENTER>                  // Type the file name retuned
Repeat End                               // End of loop
```

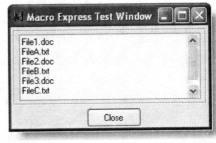

As you can see, six files were counted because we set the **Return** field to return file names to the **T1** target variable. Also, the **Process Subfolders** checkbox was checked, so every file in every subfolder was counted. Now let's try the same with folder names.

```
Change Directory/Folder: "C:\FolderA"    // Change folders to the target
Repeat with Folder                       // Loop, return folder names and process all subfolders
 Variable Modify Integer: Inc (%N1%)     // Increment the counter
 Text Type: %T1%<ENTER>                  // Type the file name retuned
Repeat End                               // End of loop
```

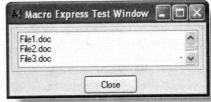

All that was counted were three subfolders because we set the **Return** field to return folder names only. Also, the **Process Subfolders** checkbox remained checked, so every folder in every subfolder was counted. What if we want to count only files that end with ".doc"?

```
Change Directory/Folder: "C:\FolderA"    // Change folders to the target
Repeat with Folder                       // Loop, return file names and process all subfolders
 If Variable %T1% contains ".doc"        // If T1 contains ".doc" then
  Variable Modify Integer: Inc (%N1%)    // Increment the counter
  Text Type: %T1%<ENTER>                 // Type the file name retuned
 End If                                  // End test
Repeat End                               // End of loop
```

As you can see, the concept behind this command is to loop through a folder, grabbing specific files or folders and then process them in some manner. In these examples we simply counted them as the "process". The last example shows how to target specific files within this command loop.

Text File Begin Process
Text File End Process

This command loops through a text file one line at a time loading each line into a variable so you can process, or do something with it. A line is any text that ends with a CR/LF (carriage return+linefeed) character sequence. The CR/LF is not loaded, just the text.

```
Text File Begin Process: "Edit1.txt"    // Load next line
 Text Type: %T1%<ENTER>                 // Process it
Text File End Process                   // Loop again
```

The loop (previous page) starts with the *Text File Begin Process* command and finishes with the *Text File End Process* command. These are like the *Repeat Start* and *Repeat End* commands, which simply control the start and end of a loop.

Each time through the loop the next line from the file is loaded into the target variable, which means you are working, or processing, just a single line of text at a time.

What does "processing" mean? Any operation, or series of operations, performed using any combination of Macro Express commands on the target string variable. The loop simply presents you with the next line in the file, you must decide what to do with it. You must decide which operations to perform on it. There are no limits. There can be thousands of command lines between the *Text File Begin Process* and *Text File End Process* commands. In the example, the "process" I ran on the variable was simply to type it. I could have done a billion things.

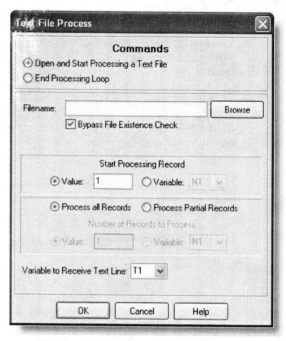

The **Filename** field contains the name of the file to be processed. The **Variable to Receive Text Line** field is the target variable that will be stuffed with the next text line each time through the loop. You do not have to loop through the whole file. Pick and choose where to start and end with the fields in the **Start Processing Records** section. Use the **Value** field to enter the literal line number (0 through 999,999) from the text file to start processing from. Or use the **Variable** drop-down list if the starting line number is contained within a variable.

Now, if you choose **Process all Records**, then each line from the starting line number through the end of the file will be processed. Or you could loop through just a certain number of text lines by choosing **Process Partial Records**, and then entering a literal value in the **Value** field, or using a variable from the **Variable** drop-down list. Both fields are underneath the **Number of Records to Process** line.

There is plenty of flexibility to choose where to begin and end looping through a file. On my computer I can loop through 150,000 text lines in less than one second, so the process itself is fast. But even so, maybe you do not want to loop through the whole file. Maybe you just want to find a certain record (text line) and then exit the loop. Easily done. Say you want to find somebody's phone number in a 1,000-name membership list.

```
Text File Begin Process: "Members.txt"   // Load the next line
  If Variable %T1% = "Joe Weinpert"       // If this member then
    Break                                 // exit the loop
  End If                                  // End of variable test
Text File End Process                     // End of loop
Text Type: %T1%<ENTER>                    // Type phone number
```

The **Break** command allows you to exit out of a Macro Express process or repeat loop. In this example, once the person's name is found, we no longer need to loop through any other text lines, so we exit the loop and then type the name and phone number.

Let's look at how to process your membership list with this command if it is set so each line contains different information about each member, starting with a name, then address, city, and finally the phone number. Again, the phone number is what we are after.

Line	Data
381	Joe Weinpert
382	PO Box 5035
383	Timberlake OH 44095
384	(800) 555-5555
385	Insight Software Solutions
386	PO Box 106
387	Kaysville UT 84037-0106
388	(801) 927-5009

```
Variable Set Integer %N2% to 0           // Not found flag
Variable Set Integer %N1% to 0           // Initialize counter
Text File Begin Process: "Members.txt"   // Load next line
  Variable Modify Integer: Inc (%N1%)    // Increment counter
  If Variable %T1% = "Joe Weinpert"      // If found then
    Variable Modify Integer: Inc (%N2%)  // Set flag to found
    Break                                // exit the loop
  End If                                 // End variable test
Text File End Process                    // End of loop
If Variable %N2% = 1                     // If member found
  Variable Modify Integer: %N1% = %N1% + 3  // Skip 3 more lines
  Text File Begin Process: "Members.txt"    // Process one line
  Text File End Process                   // End of processing
  Text Type: %T1%<ENTER>                  // Type phone number
End If                                    // End test of counter
```

The first two command lines set a "found" flag to zero and then initializes a line counter. The counter is incremented each time through the loop until the member is found. In our example the counter will be 381 when it finds the member, the "found" flag is set to 1, and the loop is exited. The next line following the processing loop tests the "found" flag. If it is zero then the member was not found, and nothing else happens. On the other hand, we add 3 to the line counter, making it 384, because we want to skip 3 lines to get to the phone number.

Now we know which line contains the phone number so we create another processing loop, which we will set to only process a single line. Notice how the **Start Processing Record** is using the **N1** variable to contain the line number. Also, we set the **Number of Records to Process** field to 1 because we only want the phone number. There are no processing commands inside the loop because there is nothing that we are going to do with the **T1** string variable, other than let the loop stuff it with the phone number.

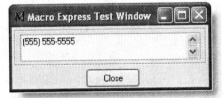

ASCII File Begin Process
ASCII Text File End Process

We have seen that, with the *Text File Begin Process* command, each line of text, up to, but not including the CR/LF, is stuffed into a single variable. The *ASCII File Begin Process* command is similar except that this single line of text can be separated and stored into many different variables. Instead of stuffing, say **T1**, with the whole text line, we could split the text line into different sections, and stuff a different variable with each section. For example, stuff the first section into **T1**, the next section into **T2**, the next into **T3**, then **T4**, and so forth. Of course there needs to be a way to define what these sections are. And of course, there is. Look at the **File Format** field. There are three choices.

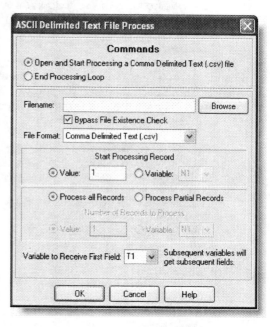

1. Comma Delimited Text (.csv)
2. Tab Delimited Text (.txt)
3. ASCII Delimited Text (.txt)

These are common file formats supported by many different software programs. The examples here use Microsoft Excel.

Besides the **File Format** field, another difference from the *Text File Begin Process* command dialog are the words next to the **Variable to Receive First Field** drop-down list "*Subsequent variables will get subsequent fields.*" It means that whichever string variable you choose to store the next text line from the file, each delimited section will be stored to consecutive string variables. Remember, unlike the *Text File Begin Process* command, each single line of text, each time through the loop, is separated and stored into variables. Here is a sample text file. There are three lines, each with five fields delimited with a comma.

Joe Weinpert, PO Box 5035, Timberlake OH 44095, (800) 555-5555, 123.45
Insight Software Solutions, PO Box 106, Kaysville UT,84037-0106, (801) 927-5009, 543.21
Floyd P Watergil, 123 Street, Cleveland OH 44101, (440) 555-5555, -12.12

A macro to process these text lines may look something like this:

```
ASCII File Begin Process: "Test.csv" (Comma Delimited Text )    // Load next line
  Text Type: %T1%, %T2%, %T3%, %T4%, %T5%<ENTER>                // Display each variable
ASCII File End Process                                          // End of loop
```

Here is what each variable would be each time through the loop:

Loop	T1	T2	T3	T4	T5
1	Joe Weinpert	PO Box 5035	Timberlake OH 44095	(800) 555-5555	123.45
2	Insight Software Solutions	PO Box 106	Kaysville UT 84037-0106	(801) 927-5009	543.21
3	Floyd P Watergil	123 Street	Cleveland OH 44101	(440) 555-5555	-12.12

As you can see, we are using a comma to separate each line into consecutive variables each time through the loop. Obviously there is a limit of 99 string variables (**T1** through **T99**) so there can never be more than 99 sections in a text line. Anything beyond 99 will be ignored, as if they did not even exist.

The text line to begin processing, and how many text lines to process, is handled in the same manner as the *Text File Begin Process* command. Set the fields in both the **Start Processing Records** and **Number of Records to Process** sections.

Comma Delimited Text (.csv)

The file extension ".csv" means **C**omma **S**eparated **V**alue. In this format, every field in each record is separated by a comma. If a field contains a comma, then it must be wrapped in double quotation marks (**"**). The quotation marks are removed automatically by this command when the field is read into the variable. Single quotation marks will not work.

This format is directly supported by Microsoft Excel by simply saving the spreadsheet using the **Save as type** field as shown here. Excel even handles embedded double quotation marks correctly when it is creating the ".csv" file. Look at the last line. Notice how the "P" is wrapped in double quotation marks? This is how the ".csv" file would be created from the example spreadsheet.

Joe Weinpert, PO Box 5035,"Timberlake, OH 44095",(800) 555-5555,123.45
Insight Software Solutions,PO Box 106,"Kaysville, UT 84037-0106",(801) 927-5009,543.21
"Floyd ""P"" Watergil",123 Street,"Cleveland, OH 44101",(440) 555-5555,-12.12

The spreadsheet cells containing commas are quoted fields in the file. And the quoted "P" is quoted again, as is the field created from the cell. Macro Express knows to ignore these quotation marks, except for the "P". When it comes to two double quotation marks in a row, Macro Express removes just the first one and leaves the other. This, in effect, gives you the string exactly as it was in the spreadsheet. Here, for example, is the output from the last line as it was processed by the *ASCII File Begin Process* command. The **T1** string variable is identical with the value in the spreadsheet.

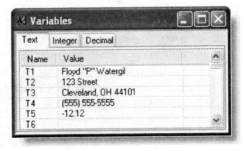

Tab Delimited Text (.txt)

This format is identical with the Comma Delimited Text (.csv) format above, except that <Tabs> are used as field separators instead of commas, and the file has a ".txt" extension. This

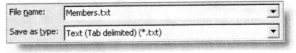

format is also directly supported by Microsoft Excel by simply saving the spreadsheet using the **Save as type** field as shown here. The same quotation mark rules are applied to this format, too.

```
Joe Weinpert      PO Box 5035      "Timberlake, OH 44095"      (800) 555-5555   123.45
Insight Software Solutions   PO Box 106 "Kaysville, UT 84037-0106"  (801) 927-5009   543.21
"Floyd ""P"" Watergil"  123 Street   "Cleveland, OH 44101" (440) 555-5555   -12.12
```

ASCII Delimited Text (.txt)

The ASCII Delimited Text format is the predecessor to the .csv format. In the past, many programs supported the ASCII Delimited format. A properly formatted ASCII Delimited Text file can be read without alteration using the .csv format.

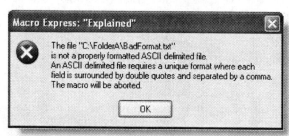

This format, and all of its rules, are identical with the Comma Delimited Text (.csv) format, except that each field must be surrounded by a set of double quotation marks (**"**), and the file has a ".txt" extension. Unlike the other two, this format is not supported by Excel, however, it is the format used and supported by prior versions of Macro Express. Also, this is the only format where a runtime error dialog will appear if something in the file is not formatted correctly.

```
"Joe Weinpert","PO Box 5035","Timberlake, OH 44095","(800) 555-5555","123.45"
"Insight Software Solutions","PO Box 106","Kaysville, UT 84037-0106","(801) 927-5009","543.21"
"Floyd ""P"" Watergil","123 Street","Cleveland, OH 44101","(440) 555-5555","-12.12"
```

Summary

- Standard DOS *current* ("**.**"), and *parent* ("**..**") folder shortcuts can be used in most file and folder commands. Wildcard characters ("**?**"), and ("*****") are supported in many of them.
- For those commands that have both a source field and destination field (copying, renaming, and so forth), if the destination folder cannot be resolved absolutely, then the current working folder is used.
- There is no consistency as to when error messages are displayed at runtime or when a macro will stop after an error. Please refer to the individual commands.
- When using the ***Convert Filename*** command, the file must physically exist.
- When using the ***Get File Path Info*** command, the file does not have to physically exist.
- The ***Get File Version*** command is one of the newer Macro Express commands.

Window Controls

One of the premier features of Macro Express are the Window Control commands. They give you control over … well, Window Controls. So, what is a Window Control?

Window Controls are normally associated with entry fields like those on forms, command buttons like *OK* and *Cancel*, checkboxes for turning features on and off, and radio buttons, which allow a single choice from many. But Windows, subwindows (aka *child* windows), and yes, even your Desktop are also a class of Window Controls. *Almost* anything that you can tab to, click on, or somehow set focus to, is a potential Window Control.

The commands used for these Window Controls, or objects, are some of the easiest Macro Express commands to learn. Although small in numbers, they are powerful. For instance, you can fill in a form without ever having to move your cursor or mouse. Simply stuff the proper text into each field (Window Control) with the command shown here,

which, by the way, is a portion of the **Text Type** command dialog window. Although technically not a Window Control command, this **Send Text to Control** option gives you a direct link into them.

Even better, the fields do not have to be visible, or even have focus for that matter. Contrast this against having to work your way down through an application to get to the form, tabbing to each field, typing in the text, and then moving on to the next field.

Window Controls can also activate macros similar in manner to the way they are activated using program names and window titles. What makes them different, however, is that you can narrow down a macro activation to something as finite as clicking on, or tabbing to, a Window Control. Here is the bottom portion of the *Activation* Tab in the macro properties dialog window, where you decide how best to activate a macro.

Most Window Control commands can be found under the *Window Controls* category shown on the next page. You will find some of these repeated and spread throughout other categories. There are three more commands not shown here, which also handle Window Controls. You will find **Clear Control Variables**, **Save Control Variables**, and **Restore Control Variables** listed under the *Variables* category.

Capture Control and **Get Control** are two different ways to gather information about a Window Control and to stuff it into a variable. This is the first step in using Window Controls.

Set Integer to Control Height, **Width**, **Left**, and **Top** are used to tell exactly where a Window Control is found on your screen.

Mouse Click on Control and *Set Focus* are used to engage a Window Control with your mouse and keyboard. Well, sort of. The *Mouse Click* command does not move to a Window Control and click; it just tells the Window Control that it has been clicked.

Variable Get Control Class, *Variable Get* and *Set Control Text*, and *Variable Modify Control* all manipulate a Window Control by its data. Data being the information saved in the Window Control variable.

The *If Control / End If* structure and the *Wait for Control* commands are used to create macros based on the status of a Window Control, such as *visible*, *enabled*, or *focused*.

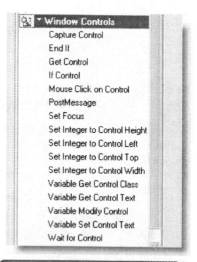

Window Control Variables

Variables are at the heart of Window Controls. This should be no surprise since variables are what give Macro Express its advantage. Let's examine Window Control variables. They all begin with the letter "C" and are numbered **1** through **99** (**C1** through **C99**).

It is important to know, and understand, they are no different from any other variable type in that they simply hold data. The command line *Get Control %C1%* does for Window Control variables what *Set String %T1% "AaBbCc"* does for string variables. The only difference is the steps needed to populate them. For string variables, a dialog pops up and you merrily type in the value. For Window Control variables, a dialog pops up and you drag a set of crosshairs over the Window Control you want. What could be simpler?

In fact the likeness between variable types is so strong that Macro Express has commands to clear, save, restore, and copy Window Control variables much the same as the others.

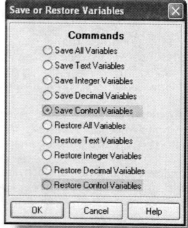

Macro Express has commands that handle applications as they are running such as *Activate Window*, *Wait for Window Title*, and *If Window Title*. And even though these windows are objects, they can be controlled by variables using their titles. For instance, to set focus to one of them, you would use the *Activate Window %T1%* command. If you want one of your Window Controls to gain focus you would use the *Set Focus to %C1%* command. To have your macro wait for a window, use the *Wait For Window Title %T1%* command and for a Window Control, use the *Wait for Control %C1% to Gain Focus* command. See? All the same. Window Controls, and their associated variables, use the same Macro Express ideas and features that you are already familiar with.

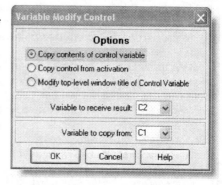

The First Big Step

This section, and the ones that follow, are not follow-the-bouncing-ball, step-by-step, hands-on tutorials. Instead, they are meant to give you as much information as possible about Window Control commands, their variables, and how to use them.

To use a Window Control, you must first tell Macro Express about it with either the *Get Control* or *Capture Control* command. Although they both stuff a variable of your choosing with information from a Window Control, their individual use is different. *Get Control* is used at *design time*, while *Capture Control* is used at *runtime*. Design time is when you are creating, editing, fixing, and otherwise, changing a macro (praying sometimes helps). Runtime is when the macro you just designed, edited, fixed, and prayed over is, well … running … even if it is just sort of running.

Get Control

Let's use your built-in calculator for a simple example of the *Get Control* command, which will be to find the square root of 9. We first have to create three Window Control variables, one each for the **9** and **sqrt** buttons (**C1** and **C2**), and another for the calculator's **display** field (**C3**).

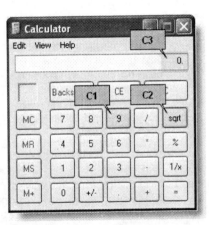

Clicking on the *Get Control* command from the Macro Express Editor displays the *Get Control* dialog. This is what it looks like (below) before capturing a Window Control. At this point, most of the information here is meaningless. But I do want to explain three of the dialog objects now, and the rest after capturing the calculator's **9** button.

Launch Get Control Utility - First notice not the button itself, but rather the informational paragraph above it, which explains exactly what is about to happen. When you click on the button, the *CapUtil.exe* program file (found in the Macro Express home folder) will launch outside Macro Express allowing you to capture, and place into a variable, the information associated with your target Window Control. The **9** button in the *Calculator* for example.

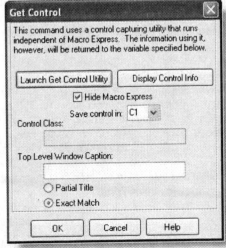

Hide Macro Express - Here is a tip, do it. Make sure this box is checked before launching the capture utility. It removes Macro Express from your screen while you are using the capture utility, and puts it back exactly how it was found when it has finished. Other than capturing something inside the Macro Express Editor (which, other than the main window, you cannot do), there is no good reason to have it displayed.

Save Control In - This is used to tell Macro Express which of 99 Window Control variables to stuff with the information brought back from the Window Control that you are about to capture or have already captured. That is right; the variable can be changed any time before, or after using the capture utility.

Now let's get down to business. Click on the **Launch Get Control Utility** button to launch the *Capture Window Control* dialog. If you have heeded my advice, the Macro Express window will disappear leaving both your target application (in our case the Calculator) and of course, the *Capture Window Control* dialog.

The most important item in this dialog are the *crosshairs* that you see at the bottom. The other, er... most important item is the paragraph at the top. Read it, because it states what it is that you are to do next, redo next, or do as many times as needed next. In other words, you can, while this dialog is running, use the crosshairs to browse over your target application to see which Window Controls you can and, this is important, *cannot* capture. Any capturable Window Control object will display a thick border as you pass the crosshairs over it. Those that cannot be captured display nothing. Here is what the Macro Express help system says:

> **Not every button, menu item or component on a program is a Control. Sometimes the only Control in a given program is the window or dialog that pops up when the program starts. We have also noticed that many of Microsoft's programs have fewer Controls than programs from other manufacturers. How the Controls work depends on the way the program you are trying to control works.**

It says that your high-flying hopes and soaring dreams of being able to create a Window Control variable for all that you see, has just taken a screaming nosedive into the rocks of reality. Sorry, but being able to capture a Window Control depends on how the target application was written and has nothing to do with you, Macro Express, or me.

I have a lot to say later about the **Get Control Using Text** checkbox, but for now leave it checked and use the crosshairs, as directed, to capture the **9** button on the Calculator. What you capture is displayed immediately after releasing the mouse button as you can see here.

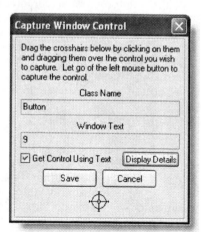

Class Name - Used by Macro Express as part of a unique identifier for each Window Control you capture. This is the internal class name given to a Window Control object by the programmer. Other classes may be called ComboBox, Edit, ListBox, TabControl, and most any other Microsoft Windows class imaginable.

Window Text field - May be used by Macro Express as part of a unique identifier for each Window Control you capture depending on if **Get Control Using Text** is checked or unchecked. If checked, it will contain whatever text is displayed by the Window Control that you are capturing. In our case it will be a **9**, and when you capture the square root button it will contain **sqrt**. There is a 25,000-character limit imposed on any captured text field.

Display Details - Pops up the *Control Details* dialog showing the complete, unique identifier, or *address*, that Macro Express uses to distinguish between Window Controls. It is a simple and effective tree-list structure that gets stored in the Window Control variable itself. At the top will always be the name of the running executable program, then comes the top-level window title. After that, everything is dependent on the program that is running. There are exceptions to this structure, such as your Desktop and Taskbar, because they have no titles.

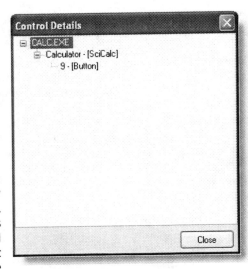

Beginning with the second line, each one starts with whatever is in the **Window Text** field and is followed by (wrapped in brackets) whatever is in the **Class Name** field. When a Window Control command like *Set Focus to %C1%* is used, Macro Express cracks open the **C1** variable and begins running down the tree-list to find the object it needs to act on. First it sees that it must go to the *CALC.EXE* program, and then find a [SciCalc] class named "Calculator", and then a [Button] class named "9", and then sets focus to it.

Want to have some fun? See the "-" symbol at the beginning of each line? Click on one and it will change to a "+" symbol. Go ahead and continue right up the tree, then reverse the process. Now, how much fun can one have?

After you click the **Save** button you are taken back to the *Get Control* dialog where we now have some real information to work with.

Control Class - Identical with the **Class Name** field in the *Capture Window Control* dialog.

Top Level Window Caption - Initially, this contains the main window title of the target application as it was when you captured the Window Control variable. This is tied directly to the *Control Details* dialog shown previously. You can change it, but you will not see the change take place in the *Control Details* dialog until after you click **OK**. The real question is why change it at all? There is no reason to change it in our Calculator example.

But here is a situation where you would want to. Let's say that you are working merrily away on a Word document called "Top Ten Reasons I Love My Job.doc" and you have created a Window Control macro to save it periodically. After a while, you get bored silly staring at a blank document so you start another one called "Top Ten Reasons I Love Macro Express.doc", but the macro does not save it. Why? ... Right! The window title says "Top Ten Reasons I Love Macro Express.doc - Microsoft Word" and the macro you created is looking for "Top Ten Reasons I Love My Job.doc - Microsoft Word". Change this field to

"Microsoft Word", click on **Partial Title**, and then click **OK**. Now your Window Control macro will work for any document at this job, or your next one.

Partial Title or **Exact Match** - This is the same idea used by other Window commands within Macro Express. While looking for the correct Window Control target application, Macro Express can match either a partial or exact window title using the value stored in the **Top Level Window Caption** field.

Display Control Info - Identical with the **Display Details** button in the *Capture Window Control* dialog.

Once you click the **OK** button, Macro Express will add the ***Get Control %C1%*** line to your macro. Repeat the same steps using the crosshairs for the **sqrt** button and the calculator's **display** field. You will have created three Window Control variables, **C1**, **C2**, and **C3**. Now simply add three command lines that will access the Window Controls, which though obvious, will be explained later in this chapter.

Get Control %C1%	// Store 9 button to Window Control variable C1
Get Control %C2%	// Store sqrt button to Window Control variable C2
Get Control %C3%	// Store display window to Window Control variable C3
Mouse Single Left Click on Control %C1%	// Click the 9 button
Mouse Single Left Click on Control %C2%	// Click the sqrt button
Variable Get Control Text: %C3% to %T1%	// Save results to T1

That is it. When the macro is run, the **T1** string will contain your answer, which is 3. How does this compare to a macro that does something similar, but without using Window Controls? Take a look:

Activate Window: "Calculator"	// Set focus to the calculator
Delay 100 Milliseconds	// Allow window to settle in
Mouse Move Window 150, 135	// Position mouse over the 9 button
Mouse Left Button Click	// Click
Delay 100 Milliseconds	// Delay 1/10th of a second
Mouse Move Window 230, 135	// Position mouse over the sqrt button
Mouse Left Button Click	// Click
Delay 100 Milliseconds	// Delay 1/10th of a second
Keystroke Speed: 100 Milliseconds	// Set delay between keystrokes
Text Type: <ALT><ALT>ec	// Copy value in the display window
Keystroke Speed: 0 Milliseconds	// Turn off keystroke delay
Delay 100 Milliseconds	// Delay 1/10th of a second
Variable Set String %T1% from Clipboard	// Save results to T1

In our shorter, Window Controls macro, the calculator does not need focus; in fact, it could be minimized or even hidden. Keystroke delays are not needed because the keyboard is not used. Also, the mouse does not physically have to be moved. And neither do we need the clipboard. I would say that our Window Controls macro is faster and better by far!

Now let's look at the **Get Control Using Text** checkbox object that we alluded to when discussing the *Capture Window Control* dialog. It is key to understanding how Macro Express finds and stores Window Control variables, and can tell one from another.

Just like the houses on your street, each Window Control must have a different address, or more to the point, must somehow be different from any other Window Control. This checkbox tells Macro Express, not what to store (you do that), but rather, which way to store the information just captured.

If the box is checked (Text method) -

The last line in the tree-list inside the *Control Details* dialog will contain the contents the **Window Text** field and the contents of the **Class Name** field (wrapped in brackets). For instance, say you have two Window Control text fields that you want to capture, one named **Name**, and the other named **Address**. We will stuff the **Name** field into **C1** and the **Address** field into **C2**.

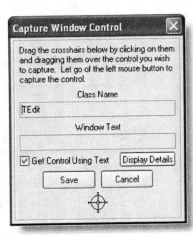

Notice how, after capturing the **Name** field into Window Control variable **C1**, the **Window Text** field is empty? This is because the **Name** field was empty when you captured it. You may also notice that it is empty in the *Control Details* dialog, too.

Now, here is the important part; taking the same steps to capture the **Address** field will result in the same exact information being stored as contained in the **Name** field. No difference. Period. The pictures shown here will be identical for both fields. Macro Express will not be able to decide which is which, even though they are stored in two separate Window Control variables. The following macro will clearly explain this point:

```
// Store Name field to Window Control variable C1
Get Control %C1%
// Store Address field to Window Control variable C2
Get Control %C2%
// Place cursor in the Name field
Mouse Single Left Click on Control %C1%
// Place cursor in the Address field
Mouse Single Left Click on Control %C2%
```

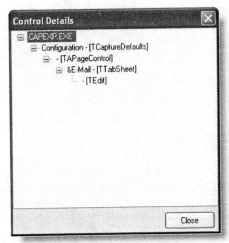

Everything will work as expected until the last line, where the cursor will remain in the **Name** field. Why? Because of what is stored in Window Control variable **C2**. Take another look at the *Control Details* dialog. See the last line that says - [TEdit]? There is nothing before the "-". It is empty, which is exactly what Macro Express searched for; a TEdit **Class** field with nothing in it, and the first one it found was the **Name** field. It is like having two houses on the same street with the same address.

Let's look at another example using the same fields and Window Control variables, only this time the fields are filled with data instead of being blank. Again, we will stuff the **Name** field into **C1** and the **Address** field into **C2**.

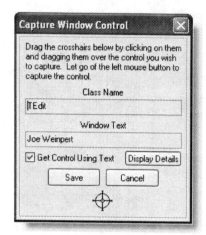

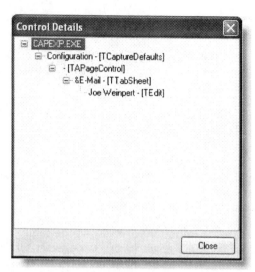

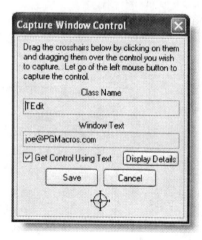

Comparing the tree listings within the *Control Details* dialogs for each variable, we find the lines are identical except for the last one. The Window Control for the **Name** field (**C1**) says "Joe Weinpert - [TEdit]" and the Window Control for the **Address** field (**C2**) says "joe@PGMacros.com - [TEdit]". Now the macro listing on the previous page will run as expected because Macro Express has unique addresses to find.

But, what if the text changes? What if, after capturing a Window Control, you decide to enter a different value into the **Name** or **Address** fields? Can Macro Express still find what it is looking for? Yes ... well sort of, it depends. The Macro Express help system says the following:

> ... if you capture an edit box with the word Test in it, the macro will be looking for the specific edit box with the word Test. If during the playback of the macro the edit box is changed to something else, such as Reset or left blank, then the control (C1) that was captured will not match the actual control ...

In other words, Macro Express will no longer be able to find your Window Control if you change what it contains. Now, technically this is true, but only if you shut down, and then restart, either the application, or Macro Express. As long as they both continue to run, Macro Express will still find the Window Control no matter how you change it. I suspect that internally, after the Window Control is captured, Macro Express caches the information with some internal pointers and that these do not change until the application or Macro Express is restarted. But, do you want to depend on this? I do not.

In my experience, the Index method, which is leaving the box *unchecked* (described next), works better and more reliably when using the *Get Control* command, and I prefer to use it. But, your experience may vary. There may be some rare instances where a Window Control has an inconsistent index; therefore capturing it using text may be the only option. Indeed, I have had forms where several Window Controls captured using the Index method were identical. The only way to distinguish between them was to use the Text method.

If the box is unchecked (Index method) -

It will stuff the Window Control variable with the contents of the **Class Name** field and the *Index* number of the Window Control. Each Window Control in any dialog has an Index number associated with it, which fixes its position in the program hierarchy. Index numbers are ideal for Macro Express to use as an address identifier because each is unique within an application … or they are supposed to be.

I have had cases where the Index number changes. In these cases, it becomes more reliable to use the **Capture Control** command rather than the **Get Control** command. Why? **Capture Control** is a runtime command. It is likely, but not guaranteed, the Index number will be consistent when an application starts (**Get Control** depends on this). But as you use the application, the Index number may change; therefore the **Capture Control** command would be needed to capture these changes as they occur. The next section is dedicated to discussing the **Capture Control** command in detail, but it is good to be aware of it now for these circumstances:

- Some applications assign a single Index number to a specific Window Control and it never changes.
- Other applications assign an Index number to a Window Control and it is always the same when the application first launches, but as you use the program the Index number changes.
- Still other applications assign a seemingly random Index number to a Window Control, and there is no way to predict what that Index number will be at any given time. Sometimes **Get Control** using the Text method will allow the macro to work with these Window Controls. Other times, the macro must use the **Capture Control** command.

So, even though I have had cases involving strange Index number behavior, I still prefer this method to the Text method, whenever possible. But, your experience may be different.

Do not confuse the Index number with *tab order*. Tabbing through a dialog takes you through each Window Control by its tab number (1, 2, and 3). If, while merrily tabbing through a dialog, you have ever wondered, "how the heck did I get here from there?" Now you know. So do not be concerned if the Index number seems out-of-order. It probably is, but is of no importance.

Your Default E-Mail Address

Name

Address

Using the empty fields example again (previous page), we will capture each of them with the **Get Control Using Text** checkbox box *unchecked*, stuffing the **Name** field into **C1** and the **Address** field into **C2** as before.

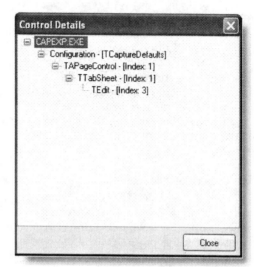

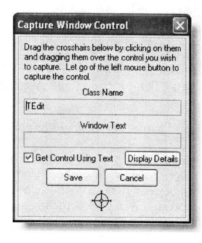

The last line in the *Control Details* dialog are different for the two variables, making them unique, while everything else is the same. The Window Control for the **Name** field (**C1**) says "TEdit - [Index3]" and the Window Control for the **Address** field (**C2**) says "TEdit - [Index4]".

The structure of these lines is different from when capturing by the Text method. It is the application's Index number and not the **Window Text** field that is stored with the contents of the **Class Name** field. The lines are also reversed. The **Class Name** field comes before the Index number. And it is the Index number wrapped in brackets instead of the **Class Name** field. Why? I do not know. What is important is the Index number gives Macro Express a unique identifier.

Capture Control

Use this command to capture Window Controls *at runtime* in any of three different ways. The information is saved to a Window Control variable just like the *Get Control* command. Unlike *Get Control*, there is no *Control Details* dialog to view. There is nothing to see. The macro is running when this command is performed.

Beneath Mouse - Captures whichever Window Control is directly underneath your mouse at the time the command is performed. It does not care what application is active, running, minimized, or anything else for that matter. Whatever is under your mouse is going to be chosen, so be sure it is positioned correctly or you may be surprised at the results.

Control Focused - Whichever button, field, or menu happens to have focus when this command is performed will be captured.

Specific Coordinates - Captures whichever Window Control is directly underneath the named **X** and **Y** **coordinates** at the time the command is performed. This command is directly linked to four other objects in the dialog window, the **X** and **Y coordinate** fields, **Launch Mouse Locator** button, and **Ctrl+Space** instructions. These are not accessible until after picking this choice.

X and **Y coordinates** - The point on the screen at which, whatever is there, will be captured as a Window Control. These are screen coordinates, not window coordinates. Any value between -99,999 and 999,999 is acceptable to allow for multiple display systems.

Launch Mouse Locator - This is the same tool detailed in the *Mouse* chapter.

Ctrl+Space - Although not a button, this instructive paragraph tells you how to make using the **X** and **Y** **coordinate** fields easy. Simply position your mouse over the Window Control to be captured and then press the **Ctrl+Space** key combination. The **X** and **Y** fields will be automatically filled. You do not need to know any coordinates and you do not have to fire-up the Mouse Locator. Sweet!

Capture Using Text - This checkbox is the same as the one in the *Get Control* command. Please refer to it for details. Also, if your goal is to discover what text a Window Control contains or how it is labeled, then you can simply use the *Variable Get Control Text* command explained later in this chapter.

Save to Variable - Used to tell Macro Express which one of 99 Window Control variables to stuff the captured Window Control into.

When you are creating Window Controls at design time using the *Get Control* command you are capturing them manually so you do not need to know any screen or window coordinates. It is different with the *Capture Control* command. You are capturing Window Controls programmatically at runtime, so the macro needs to know where the Window Controls can be found while it is running. Will your application always be in the same position each time it runs? What if it is run on a different computer with a different screen resolution? These are questions that you must consider when creating your macro.

Using the *Capture Control* command, the macro can recapture a Window Control as many times as needed. See the discussion on the **Get Control Using Text** checkbox (Index method) in the **Get Control** section for reasons you might need to do this.

Let's use the built-in calculator again and the **Beneath Mouse** option to build a macro. Notice how you must move the mouse over top of each button that you want to capture.

Activate Window: "Calculator"	// Set focus to the calculator
Mouse Move Window 150, 135	// Position mouse over the 9 button
Capture Control to %C1%	// Store the 9 button to Window Control variable C1
Mouse Move Window 230, 135	// Position mouse over the sqrt button
Capture Control to %C2%	// Store the sqrt button to Window Control variable C2
Mouse Move Window 230, 60	// Position mouse over the display window
Capture Control to %C3%	// Store the display window to Window Control variable C3
Mouse Single Left Click on Control %C1%	// Click the 9 button
Mouse Single Left Click on Control %C2%	// Click the sqrt button
Variable Get Control Text: %C3% to %T1%	// Save results to T1

An example of building a macro with the **Control Focused** option and the Calculator is not possible because the Calculator does not recognize the TAB key. So here is an example using an imaginary application.

Activate Window: "Your Application"	// Activate your application
Text Type: <TAB>	// Set focus to the 1st Control
Capture Control to %C1%	// Store it to Window Control variable C1
Text Type: <TAB>	// Set focus to the 2nd Control
Capture Control to %C2%	// Store it to Window Control variable C2
Mouse Single Left Click on Control %C1%	// Click on the 1st Control
Mouse Single Left Click on Control %C2%	// Click on the 2nd Control

Now let's look at the third and final option. The **Specific Coordinates** option uses screen coordinates unlike the **Beneath the Mouse** example, which used window coordinates.

Activate Window: "Calculator"	// Set focus to the calculator
Window Reposition: Center - Current Win	// Move it to a know position
Capture Control to %C1%	// Store the 9 button at screen location 175,425
Capture Control to %C2%	// Store the sqrt button at screen location 255,425
Capture Control to %C3%	// Store the display window at screen location 255,350
Mouse Single Left Click on Control %C1%	// Click the 9 button
Mouse Single Left Click on Control %C2%	// Click the sqrt button
Variable Get Control Text: %C3% to %T1%	// Save results to T1

Manipulating Window Controls

Now that you have a Window Control, what can you do with it? How can you view its content? How can you change it? Let's look at four Window Control commands; *Variable Get Control Text*, *Variable Set Control Text*, *Variable Get Control Class*, and finally *Variable Modify Control*. Whether you use *Get Control* or *Capture Control* to create a Window Control variable, these commands will work the same.

Variable Get Control Text

The *Variable Get Control Text* command will bring back any current text or caption in any Window Control and place it into any string variable you choose. There is a limit of 25,000 characters. Anything beyond this limit will be truncated.

Place in Text Variable - Choose which one of the 99 string variables to store the value contained in the Window Control variable.

Control to Get Text From - Pick the Window Control variable to act on.

In the **Capture Express** program that I use, there is a dual-use command button that changes from **Abort** to **Done** after a picture is sent to the printer. By using this command I can trap the change to the button's caption (text) to control my macro.

Repeat Until %N1% <> %N1%	// My way of creating an infinite loop
Variable Get Control Text: %C1% to %T1%	// Capture button caption to T1
If Variable %T1% = "&Done"	// If done printing then exit the loop
Repeat Exit	// Exit if Done
End If	// End If test
Delay 250 Milliseconds	// Slight delay before looping again
Repeat End	// End the loop

What is that ampersand in front of the word *Done*? If you were to look at the application you would see the **D** in **Done** is underlined, which tells the user which keyboard equivalent to use in place of the mouse. The ampersand is part of the button's caption. **&Done**, **&Abort**, **&OK**, **&Cancel** are all examples of this technique. This could be a real puzzler if your macro is not working the way you think it should. So remember to watch out for this.

Variable Set Control Text

Use the *Variable Get Control Text* command to change the text in the Window Control variable to something other than what was originally captured. This only works on those Window Controls that have text, such as text boxes and command buttons, and those that were captured using the *Text method* as explained in the **Capture Control** section.

Control Variable to Modify Text - Pick the Window Control variable to act on.

New Text - Use this field to enter the literal text (or any variable) to set the Window Control variable to. This changes only the *Window Control variable*, not the application's object that it was created from with **Get Control** or **Capture Control**. To change the application's text, for those Window Controls that allow it (like an edit box), use the *Send Text to Control* option within the *Text Type* command.

Let's change the last example from the **Capture Express** program used to trap the dual-use command button.

Get Control %C1%	// Control captured while the button displayed "Abort"
Variable Set Control Text %C1% to "&Done"	// Change it internally from "Abort" to "Done"
Activate Window: "Capture Express"	// Activate the window
Text Type: <ALT>p	// Print the image
Wait for Control %C1% to become visible	// Wait for the dual-use button to become visible

The button was captured when it said "Abort". Because it was captured using the Text method, the text in the **C1** Window Control variable is set to "Abort". The next line changes this text to "Done". The last line is the key. It will wait until the **Abort** button changes its caption to **Done**. Which does not occur until after the printing completes.

Variable Get Control Class

Use this command whenever you need to retrieve the contents of the **Class Name** field and place it into a string variable. It works similar to the *Variable Get Control Text* command. Macro Express always saves the **Class Name** field as part of its unique Window Control identifier.

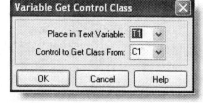

Place in Text Variable - Choose which one of the 99 string variables to store the value contained in the Window Control variable.

Control to Get Text From - Pick the Window Control variable to act on.

Here is a short macro example that captures the contents of the **Control Class** field and places it in a variable to discover its type.

Variable Get Control Class: %C1% to %T1%	// Capture Class Name to T1
Switch (T1)	// Which Class is it?
Case: Tbutton	// Is it a Tbutton class?
Text Type: Class = Tbutton	// Display the class
End Case	// End this Case
Case: Ebutton	// Is it an Ebutton class?
Text Type: Class = EButton	// Display the class
End Case	// End this Case
Default Case	// It is none of the above so wing it!
Text Type: Class = Unknown	// Display the class
End Case	// End this Case
End Switch	// End Class test

Variable Modify Control

This dialog handles three different commands, all of which allow you, in some way to change a Window Control variable.

Copy Contents of Control Variable

As mentioned before, Window Control variables are no different from other variable type. Strings, integers, and decimals can all be copied, and so can Window Control variables.

Variable to Receive Result - Pick the destination Window Control variable.

Variable to Copy From - Pick the Window Control variable to copy.

This is a good command to use when you need a temporary copy of a Window Control to manipulate so the original is not changed.

> **Variable Modify Control %C2%: Copy from %C1%**

Copy Control from Activation

A macro can be automatically activated by a Window Control when the Window Control becomes visible or gains focus. The window snippet shows part of the Activation Tab from a macro that I use for the **Capture Express** program. The Activation Control does not use a Window Control variable like **C1** or **C2**.

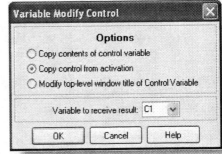

Variable to Receive Result - Pick the destination Window Control variable.

With this command, you can copy the Activation Control to a variable and manipulate it like any other Window Control.
Let's say that you have a macro which automatically activates whenever a certain field in a certain application gains focus and you want to know the coordinates of it. Your macro would like something like this:

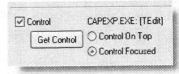

```
// Save activation control to C1
Variable Modify Control %C1%: Copy Activation Control
// Get the X coordinate of the control
Variable Set Integer %N1% from Control %C1% Left
// Get the Y coordinate of the control
Variable Set Integer %N2% from Control %C1% Top
```

Modify Top-Level Window Title of Control

Contrary to popular belief and frustration, this command is not meant to, and cannot, change the title of the window containing the Window Control you targeted. Instead it changes which window the Window Control belongs to. In other words, you can have two different windows with similar Window Controls, and only need to capture them in *one* window for *both* windows. Now that is neat!

Variable to Receive Result - Pick the destination Window Control variable.

Window Title - This field contains the name of the window to attach to the Window Control. The value can be either a literal or a variable. Also, it can be either a partial or exact match depending on which option you choose.

Let's say, for example, that you have two dialog windows, one titled *Cancel* and the other titled *Continue*. Each of them has two Window Control buttons called **Yes** and **No**. Activate the *Cancel* window and capture both buttons.

> **Get Control %C1%**   // Capture Yes button from Cancel window
> **Get Control %C2%**   // Capture No button from Cancel window

Later in your macro the *Continue* window is used. Instead of capturing another set of Window Controls for it, simply change the parent window of the existing **C1** and **C2** Window Controls.

> **Variable Modify Control %C1%: Modify Top-Level Window Title**   // Change C1 to the Continue window
> **Variable Modify Control %C2%: Modify Top-Level Window Title**   // Also change C2

Now when you send a mouse click to the **C1** or **C2** Window Control variable, they will click the *Yes* and *No* buttons in the *Continue* window even though they were originally captured from the *Cancel* window. You can switch them back and forth as often as you like.

> **Mouse Single Left Click on Control %C1%**   // Click the Yes button in Continue window
> **Mouse Single Left Click on Control %C2%**   // Click the No button in Continue window

To avoid chaos and panic, if the *Text method* was used in this example, then both Window Control buttons in both windows must have identical **Yes** and **No** captions. If you use the *Index method*, then they must have identical Index numbers.

Engage!

Okay, you have the Window Control and you have learned how to bend, fold, staple, and mutilate it like nobody's business. Now what? Let's make it do something. Normally, if you wanted a Window object to work, you have to click on it with your mouse or tab to it with your keyboard, or type in its HotKey.

Now there is a fourth choice. We are simply going to tell it what to do with either the *Mouse Click on Control* or the *Set Focus* command.

Mouse Click on Control

The purpose of this command is to have the mouse perform a click somewhere on a Window Control. And it is loaded with features.

Single or Double Click - Clicks or double-clicks whichever button is chosen from the **Button** drop-down list, on whichever Window Control variable is picked from the **Control** drop-down list, at the location displayed in the *Advanced* Tab.

Control - Choose one of 99 target Window Control variables.

Button - This command will work on either the left, middle, or right mouse button. Yes, with this command, you can perform a double-click with the middle or right mouse button. I am sure you will find a reason.

Center of Control - Position the mouse click to be exactly in the middle of the Window Control.

Other X and **Y** - This is a neat option because it allows you to position the mouse click anywhere relative to the target Window Control's screen position. A Window Control can be more than just a button or an edit box. But not all Window Controls can be captured. Here is a prime example:

Take a look at the **Clear History** button picture taken from the (Internet Explorer | Tools | Internet Options | General) Tab. I have been fooled by these types of Window Controls many times.

As you pass the *crosshairs* over this section, the rectangle shown here is as close as you can get to the **Clear History** button. At first glance, it looks like you could use the **X** and **Y** fields to click on the button. Not true! The button is a different Window Control from the History rectangle and cannot be accessed. A Window Control variable cannot be used here because we can only capture the useless rectangle and not the button itself.

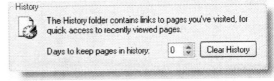

How about an example that *can* be accessed using **X** and **Y** offset coordinates? For this, we will use the *Preferences* dialog from **Zip Express**. Another useful product from Insight Software Solutions.

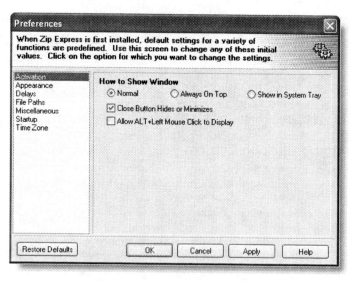

The list in the left-hand pane is a single Window Control with each line being a different option that can be picked, **Activation**, **Appearance**, **Delays**, and so forth.

It would be impossible to pick any of them by just using the default **Center of Control** so we will use an offset coordinate which must be relative to the Window Control.

Activate Window: "Preferences"	// Target window
Variable Set Integer %N1% from Control %C1% Left	// Preference list X coordinate = 5
Variable Set Integer %N2% from Control %C1% Top	// Preference list Y coordinate = 89
Variable Set Integer %N3% from Control %C1% Width	// Preference list width = 121
Variable Set Integer %N4% from Control %C1% Height	// Preference list height = 249
Mouse Single Left Click on Control %C1%	// Activation option offset = 25,9
Mouse Single Left Click on Control %C1%	// Appearance option offset = 25,21
Mouse Single Left Click on Control %C1%	// Delays option offset = 25,33
Mouse Single Left Click on Control %C1%	// File Paths option offset = 25,45

The macro says the upper-left corner of the list Window Control is found at coordinates 5,89 on the display and is 121 pixels wide by 249 high. To do a mouse click on the **Activation** option line, you need to offset the click 25 pixels to the right of the list Window Control coordinate and 9 pixels down. The **Delays** option line is 25 pixels to the right and 33 down. You can pick every option in the list by simply changing the offset of each *Mouse Click* command.

Set Focus

The *Set Focus* command brings whichever Window Control is picked to the top and sets focus as if it was tabbed to or clicked on ... if possible. There are Window Controls that are not meant to ever gain focus. The Calculator's display window for example.

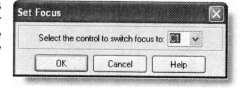

Select the Control to Set Focus To - Pick the destination Window Control variable.

Be careful when setting focus to minimized windows. It will usually work, but there are some situations to be aware of. Set a Window Control variable with the Notepad's text entry area using *Get Control* and the Index method. Minimize the window and then set focus to it. When the *Text Type* command is performed, the window will be normalized, but the text is not typed. I do not know why, however, you would see a text line typed if there were two *Text Type* command lines in a row.

Get Control %C1%	// Capture Notepad
Window Minimize: "Notepad"	// Minimize it
Set Focus to %C1%	// Set Focus while minimized
Text Type: Test Notepad<ENTER>	// Type something

On the other hand, this works fine for the Calculator. You will see "123,456,789" in the display window once the last line is performed.

Get Control %C1%	// Capture the Calculator display
Window Minimize: "Calculator"	// Minimize it
Set Focus to %C1%	// Set Focus while minimized
Text Type: 123456789	// Type something
Window Restore: "Calculator"	// Restore the Calculator

A Window Control cannot be focused if it is located in a different Tab dialog from where you are. Let's say the **Capture Hot Key** field shown here is the Window Control that you want to set focus to. If you use the *Set Focus* command to try get to it from the *Action* Tab, nothing would happen because it is buried inside the *Hot Key* Tab. And there would be no error because Macro Express knows the Window Control exists, it just cannot get to it.

You must first set focus to the *Hot Key* Tab before accessing any Window Controls within it. This is easy to do. You need to capture only one of the four Tabs to a Window Control variable. Any one will do. **H**ot *Key*, **W**hat *Capture*, **A**ction, or **E**-*Mail*. Look at the *Control Details* dialog.

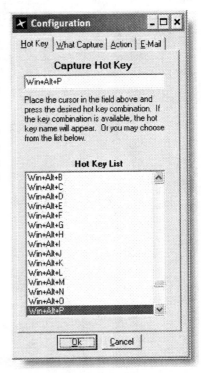

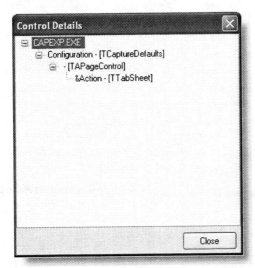

We have captured the *Action* Tab using the Text method. Sending an **A** to it will focus it. However, sending an **E** to it will focus the *E-Mail* Tab, and a **W** the *What Capture* Tab. Why does this work? The Tab dialogs are all on the same access "level" within the dialog much the same as name and address fields are on the same "level" on a form.

To bring forward any of the four Tabs, simply send the correct key to the *Action* Tab Window Control from anywhere in the dialog window.

Back to the problem. You are in the *Action* Tab and you want to set focus to the **Capture Hot Key** field that is in the *Hot Key* Tab. Your macro would send an **H** to the *Hot Key* Tab Window Control using the **Send Text to Control** option inside the **Text Type** command, which will bring it to the top of the stack. Then it will **Set Focus** to the **Capture Hot Key** field Window Control. Nothing could be simpler, eh?

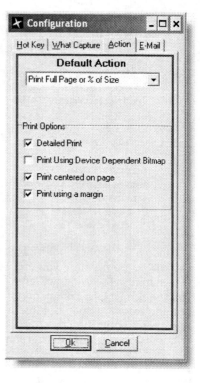

> **Text Type:<ALT><ALT>h**   // Send Text to Control - "H"
> **Set Focus to %C1%**   // Set focus to the Capture Hot Key field

What if? Wait a minute!

There are two Window Control variable commands you can use to gain some control over the flow of your macro. *If Control* and *Wait for Control*. These commands test the following states of a Window Control:

- Focused / Unfocused
- Visible / Invisible
- Enabled / Disabled

Any Window Control can be in any one of these six states, or combination of states, at any particular time. Here are the valid combinations.

- A Visible Window Control can be Enabled or Disabled, Focused or Unfocused
- An Enabled Window Control can be Visible or Invisible, Focused or Unfocused
- A Focused Window Control can be Visible or Invisible, but must be Enabled

The last bullet should be no surprise. Any Window Control can be hidden and yet allowed to gain focus as long as it is enabled. This makes for some wonderful possibilities for using Window Control variables. Take the *Calculator* as an example. You can hide it with the **Window Hide** command, or move it off your display with the **Window Reposition** command, or minimize it with the **Window Minimize** command. Window Control commands will still access it. And math calculations would be done without interfering with your display.

If Control
Wait for Control

Although they serve two different purposes, the underlying theme here is the *state* of the Window Control itself so I am going to cover both commands at the same time. You should already be familiar with how *If* and *Wait* commands work in general.

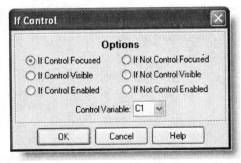

The *If Control* command has its own dialog but, as you can see, the *Wait for Control* command is chosen from the general *Wait For* dialog (next page). The explanations given here are based on what you see in the *Wait For* dialog, but they also apply to the *If Control* dialog.

Gain / Lose Focus - A Window Control gains focus if it is tabbed to, clicked on, or forced with the **Set Focus** command. It loses focus if a different Window Control is tabbed to, clicked on, or forced with the **Set Focus** command. Only one Window Control at a time can have focus. Period. It is the nature of the beast.

Become Visible / Invisible - What is visible to us is not necessarily what is visible to Macro Express. As it turns out, a Window Control is almost always visible no matter where the window containing it is positioned in the Desktop stack. In other words, whether you can see the Window Control or not, Macro Express can, therefore it is visible. This is also true of windows that are hidden or minimized.

It becomes invisible if the window it is part of gets buried behind other windows in the same application. Take a look back at the *Set Focus* section. The **Capture Hot Key** field is only visible as long as the *Hot Key* Tab dialog it belongs to has focus. Once you click on a different Tab, it becomes invisible. On the other hand, if you simply set focus to another window, say *Notepad* or *Calculator*, the Window Control remains visible.

Here is another situation where a Window Control become invisible, but no longer exists … maybe. This occurs with the Calculator's **sqrt** button. It is visible in the *standard view*, but if you switch to the *scientific view*, it no longer exists. It is gone, but will still test as being both invisible and disabled, so is it really gone? I do not know, but it is at least gone enough that Macro Express can no longer get to it.

Become Enabled / Disabled - The application that you are running decides when a Window Control becomes enabled or disabled. You see this occur all the time. Certain fields remain "dimmed" until another field is chosen that enables them. The **X and Y** coordinate fields within the *Mouse Click on Control* command dialog remain disabled until the **Other** radio button is clicked. Say your macro needs to wait until the *Done* button becomes enabled while printing a document. Simply create a Window Control variable from the *Done* button, print the document, and then wait for the Window Control to become enabled. Here is how you would use the *If Control* command to do this:

```
Get Control %C1%                // Capture the Done button
Text Type: <CONTROL>p           // Print the document
Repeat Until %N1% <> %N1%       // Infinite loop until button enabled
  If Control %C1% Enabled       // If the Done button enabled then
    Repeat Exit                 // exit the loop
  End If                        // End If test
  Delay 250 Milliseconds        // Slight delay
Repeat End                      // End infinite loop
```

The *Wait for Control* command is much shorter and does the same thing.

```
Get Control %C1%                        // Capture the Done button
Text Type: <CONTROL>p                   // Print the document
Wait for Control %C1% to become enabled // Wait until the Done button becomes enabled
```

And the rest of the commands

The remaining Window Control commands, and where to find them, are detailed.

Set Integer to Control Left
Set Integer to Control Top
Set Integer to Control Width
Set Integer to Control Height

Listed in the *Window Controls* category, you will find these commands buried in the Option 2 Tab in the *Set Integer Variables* dialog. They retrieve the position and size of any captured Window Control. Here is the important point: the coordinates returned by **Control Left** and **Control Top** are *screen related*, not window related. If you reposition the window containing the target Window Control after setting these integers, then the values are no longer valid, in other words, as the window moves around, the coordinates change, so be careful. Also, some Window Controls such as text boxes may be resizable so the values returned by **Control Width** and **Control Height** may change.

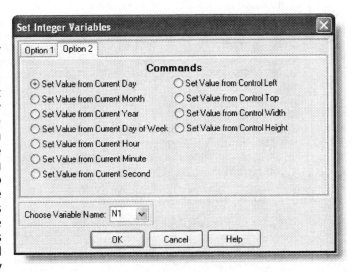

Centering my Calculator on the screen results in these values when capturing it to a Window Control variable:

```
Get Control %C1%                                  // Capture Calculator to Control variable C1
Variable Set Integer %N1% from Control %C1% Left   // X coordinate = 400
Variable Set Integer %N2% from Control %C1% Top    // Y coordinate = 338
Variable Set Integer %N3% from Control %C1% Width  // Width = 480
Variable Set Integer %N4% from Control %C1% Height // Height = 317
```

Send Text to Control

Stuffed within the *Text* category, you will find this one listed as an option within the **Text Type** command. Okay, so

technically it is not a command … a rose by any other name, eh? Use it to stuff any Window Control with a string. That is, any that accept a string. Text fields and edit boxes are good candidates. Unlike the **Variable Set Control Text** command, which changes the Window Control's *variable*, this command changes the Window Control itself.

Here is our old friend from the *Get Control* command section. Window Control variable **C1** is the **Name** field and **C2** the **Address** field. Let's create a macro to fill in the fields using the *Send Text to Control* command.

Get Control %C1%	// Store Name field to Control variable C1
Get Control %C2%	// Store Address field to Control variable C2
Text Type:Joe Weinpert	// Stuff name into the Control variable C1
Text Type:info@pgmacros.com	// Stuff address into the Control variable C2

You could also have used string variables instead of literals.

Get Control %C1%	// Store Name field to Control variable C1
Get Control %C2%	// Store Address field to Control variable C2
Variable Set String %T1% "Joe Weinpert"	// Store Name to string variable T1
Variable Set String %T2% "info@pgmacros.com"	// Store Address to string variable T2
Text Type:%T1%	// Stuff name into the Control variable C1
Text Type:%T2%	// Stuff address into the Control variable C2

Unprintable characters like ENTER, SPACE, and TAB can also be used with this command. There is a 25,000-character limit. The Window Controls that you are targeting can be invisible, disabled, or unfocused, and this command will still work. In other words, without ever having to tab to a field or set focus to it, you can enter information into it … sweet!

Window Control Activation

Window Controls can be used to activate macros in the same way that macros are activated using program names or window titles. Again, this is not a command, but rather an option found on the Activation Tab in the *Properties* window of each macro.

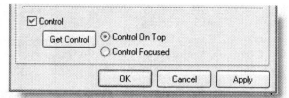

Get Control - Identical with the *Get Control* command explained earlier.

Control On Top - Sort of. It tells Macro Express to activate the macro when the window *containing* the Window Control is activated, or brought to the top. The Window Control itself can be in any state (enabled, disabled).

This is a great solution for situations where you are creating a macro containing identical application window titles, and you need a way to

find the difference. Although both windows on the next page have the same title, they can be distinguished by their Window Controls.

The text box on the right does not contain a **sqrt** button, but the *Calculator* on the left does. Instead of activating a macro based on the window title *Calculator* coming to the top, which would happen in either case, create one that activates when the **sqrt** button comes to the top. And then another one that activates when the text box Window Control comes to the top.

Control Focused - This option will activate a macro when a specific Window Control gains focus and not just when the window containing it comes to the top. It allows you to target macro activation to something as finite as the status of a specific Window Control. And it is great feature … except for some operating system limits. From the Macro Express help system:

> Because of incompatibilities within Windows, the Control Focused feature is only available on Windows 98 and later and Windows NT 4.0 Service Pack 3 and later. This will not work on Windows 95 or Windows NT 4.0 with Service Pack 2 or earlier.

Here is how it works. Create three different macros named **1**, **2**, and **3**. Each one will activate the *Notepad* and type a line into saying "You clicked 1", "You clicked 2", and "You clicked 3" respectively.

```
// Macro 1 activated by button "1"
Activate or Launch: "Notepad" OR "notepad.exe"      // Activate the Notepad
Text Type: You clicked 1<ENTER>                      // Type the line
```

☑ Control — CALC.EXE: 1 [Button]
Get Control — ○ Control On Top / ⊙ Control Focused

```
// Macro 2 activated by button "2"
Activate or Launch: "Notepad" OR "notepad.exe"      // Activate the Notepad
Text Type: You clicked 2<ENTER>                      // Type the line
```

☑ Control — CALC.EXE: 2 [Button]
Get Control — ○ Control On Top / ⊙ Control Focused

```
// Macro 3 activated by button "3"
Activate or Launch: "Notepad" OR "notepad.exe"      // Activate the Notepad
Text Type: You clicked 3<ENTER>                      // Type the line
```

☑ Control — CALC.EXE: 3 [Button]
Get Control — ○ Control On Top / ⊙ Control Focused

Set the activation of each macro to different Window Controls. Macro **1** will be activated by the **"1"** button on the *Calculator*, macro **2** by the **"2"** button, and macro **3** by the **"3"** button.

As you click each of these buttons on the Calculator, the individual macro will be activated, typing its text line into the *Notepad*. Why does this work? Clicking on a button sets focus to it. Each individual macro was told to run whenever its associated button gained focus. So clicking on the **"1"** button causes macro **1** to run, which types a line into the *Notepad*.

Control Activation.txt ...
File Edit Format View Help
You clicked 1
You clicked 2
You clicked 3
|

Clear Control Variables

Listed in the *Variables* category, and accessed from the *Variables Clear* command, *Clear Control Variables* does exactly what the name implies; clears (erases) the contents from Window Control variables. This command works the same for all variable types. You can erase all of them or just a range, say **C10** through **C15**. It has no affect on variables saved with the *Save Control Variables* command. Those are safely packed away in memory until they are restored.

There is a danger to be aware of when using this command. If you choose "All Variables" from the **Variable Type to Clear** drop-down list, it will clear all variable types in your chosen range and not just Window Control variables.

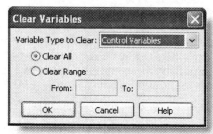

Here is a macro that will clear all Window Control variables, a range of Window Control variables, and every variable type including Window Control variables.

Clear Control Variables: All   // Clear all Control variables
Clear Control Variables: From 10 To 15   // Clear only Control variables C10-C15
Clear All Variables: All   // Clear every existing variable of any type!

Save Control Variables
Restore Control Variables

Listed in the *Variables* category, and accessed from the *Variables Save*, and *Variables Restore* commands respectively, they will save and restore Window Control variables to and from memory. Use them whenever you would like to save the current set of Window Control variables **C1** through **C99**. There is no option to save and restore a range of variables.

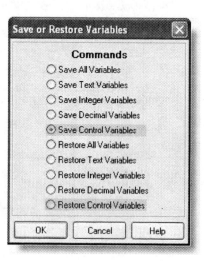

Use the *Save Control Variables* command before calling a submacro that uses the same variable range for its own purposes. And then use the *Restore Control Variables* command to restore them to their previous grandeur when the submacro is finished.

Create two macros. One that captures the **"1"** button on the *Calculator* to Control variable **C1** and the other to capture the **"2"** button using the *same* **C1** variable. Call them **Button1** and **Button2** respectively.

```
// Button1 macro
Activate Window: "Calculator"                  // Activate the calculator
Mouse Move Window 75, 200                       // Move the mouse over the "1" button
Capture Control to %C1%                         // Capture the "1" button to Control variable C1
Mouse Single Left Click on Control %C1%         // Click on it
Macro Return                                    // Return to the calling macro

// Button2 macro
Activate Window: "Calculator"                  // Activate the calculator
Mouse Move Window 115, 200                      // Move the mouse over the "2" button
Capture Control to %C1%                         // Capture the "2" button to Control variable C1
Mouse Single Left Click on Control %C1%         // Click on it
Macro Return                                    // Return to the calling macro
```

Now create another macro called **Main**. This will launch the Calculator, call the **Button1** macro, save variables, call the **Button2** macro, restore variables, and then click on the **"1"** button showing the original variables have been restored.

```
// Main macro
Activate or Launch: "Calculator" OR "calc.exe"   // Start the Calculator
Macro Run: Button1                                // Run Button1 to capture the C1 variable
Variable Save Control Variables                   // Save the Control variables
Macro Run: Button2                                // Run Button2 to overwrite the C1 variable
Variable Restore Control Variables                // Restore the Control variables
Mouse Single Left Click on Control %C1%           // Click on the "1" button again
```

The Calculator will display "121" after running the **Main** macro. The first "1" is entered by calling the **Button1** macro. The Window Control variables are then saved to memory. The "2" is entered by calling the **Button2** macro, which overwrites the **C1** Window Control variable. Next the Window Control variables are restored from memory, which replaces the work done by the **Button2** macro. The next, and last "1", is entered by a call to the *Mouse Click* command, showing the Window Control variables were restored.

Summary

- Anything that you can tab to, click on, or somehow set focus to, is a Window Control candidate.
- There are 99 Window Control variables C1 - C99.
- Window Control variables can be cleared, saved and restored just like any other variable type.
- Window Controls can be captured at design time with the *Get Control* command.
- Window Controls can be captured at runtime with the *Capture Control* command.
- Not all Window Controls can be captured.
- Each Window Control must have a unique "address" for Macro Express to find and act on it.
- Window Controls can be clicked and focused on without using your mouse or keyboard.
- Macros can be automatically activated using Window Controls.

List of Commands

This table is an alphabetical list of categories and matching icons. These are the default categories when Macro Express is installed.

Icon	Category	Icon	Category	Icon	Category
	CD-ROM		Internet Explorer		Registry
	Clipboard		Keyboard		Repeat
	Debug		Logic		System
	Desktop		Macro Control		Text
	Dialogs		Macro Express		Timing
	Explorer		Mouse		Variables
	Files/Folders		Multimedia		Window Controls
	Internet		Network		Windows/Programs

This table is an alphabetical list of commands. The left column is the command. The middle column is a short description of the command's purpose. And the last column displays the category or categories where you will find the command. These are the default categories when Macro Express is installed.

Command	Description	Category
Activate or Launch	Activate a window or launch a program	Windows/Programs
Alt Key	Press key down and let up	Keyboard
And	Boolean AND operator	Logic
ASCII File Begin Process	Start processing lines in an ASCII delimited text file	Files/Folders
ASCII File End Process	Stop processing lines in an ASCII delimited text file	Files/Folders
Audio Balance	Shift audio balance left, center, and right	Multimedia
Audio Bass	Increase or decrease bass	Multimedia
Audio Mute	Mute the audio volume	Multimedia
Audio Mute Toggle	Toggle audio mute on and off	Multimedia
Audio Treble	Increase or decrease treble	Multimedia
Audio Unmute	Unmute the audio volume	Multimedia
Audio Volume	Audio volume increase, decrease, full, and off	Multimedia
Break	Exit out of a Repeat loop or file processing loop	Files/Folders Repeat

Command	Description	Category
		Variables
CAPS Lock	Toggle key on and off	Keyboard
Capture Control	Capture a Window Control programmatically and place it in a Control variable	Window Controls
Case	Switch/Case statement (beginning of Case block)	Logic
CDROM Back	Backtrack a number of seconds	CD-ROM
CDROM Close Tray	Close the tray	CD-ROM
CDROM Eject	Eject	CD-ROM
CDROM Go To Track	Go to a particular track	CD-ROM
CDROM Next Track	Skip to the next track	CD-ROM
CDROM Pause	Pause	CD-ROM
CDROM Play	Play	CD-ROM
CDROM Previous Track	Go back to previous track	CD-ROM
CDROM Step	Fast forward	CD-ROM
CDROM Stop	Stop playing	CD-ROM
Change Directory/Folder	Change the default folder	Files/Folders
Clear Variables	Erase values from specified variables	Variables
Clipboard Append Text	Add text in clipboard to the end of a file	Clipboard
Clipboard Copy	Copy selected text into clipboard	Clipboard
Clipboard Cut	Cut selected text and place it in clipboard	Clipboard
Clipboard Empty	Erase the clipboard	Clipboard
Clipboard End Copy	Stop typing text into clipboard	Clipboard
Clipboard File Copy	Copy text file into clipboard	Clipboard
Clipboard Graphic Copy	Copy graphic file into clipboard	Clipboard
Clipboard Paste	Paste text from clipboard	Clipboard
Clipboard Save Graphic	Save clipboard to a graphic file	Clipboard
Clipboard Save Text	Save clipboard to a text file	Clipboard
Clipboard Start Copy	Begin typing text into clipboard	Clipboard
Clipboard Type Text	Type out text from the clipboard	Clipboard
Control Key	Press key down and let up	Keyboard
Control Panel Open	Open your *Control Panel* dialog	System
Control Panel Run	Run a *Control Panel* applet	System
Convert Filename	Change file names from long to short and from short to long	Files/Folders Variables
Copy File or Files	Copy files	Files/Folders
Create Folder	Create folders	Files/Folders
Create Registry Key	Create a new Registry key	Registry
Date	Set a date to a particular format mask	Text
Date/Time	Set a date or time or both to a particular format mask	Text
Default Case	Switch/Case construct (beginning of Default Case block)	Logic
Default Display Size	Change the resolution of your monitor	System

Command	Description	Category
Default Printer	Change your system's default printer	System
Delay	Halt the macro for a period of time	Timing
Delete File or Files	Delete files	Files/Folders
Delete Folder	Delete folders	Files/Folders
Delete Registry Key	Delete an existing Registry key	Registry
Delete Registry Value	Delete an existing Registry value	Registry
Desktop Cascade	Stack and overlap windows	Desktop
Desktop Minimize All	Place running programs on Taskbar	Desktop
Desktop Restore All	Restore running programs from Taskbar	Desktop
Desktop Tile	Dialog window for the two commands below (this shows only when viewing commands without using categories)	Desktop
Desktop Tile Horizontally	Tile windows left to right across the monitor	Desktop
Desktop Tile Vertically	Tile windows up and down across the monitor	Desktop
Dial Up Networking	Dial a phone book entry	Internet Network
Dial Up Networking:Hang Up	Terminate the dial-up connection (this command is not shown in the Commands Pane)	Internet
Else	If / Else / End If construct	Logic
E-Mail Send	Send E-Mail to recipients	Internet
Empty Macro Recycle Bin	Delete macros in the *Macro Recycle Bin*	Macro Express
Empty Recycle Bin	Empty your computer's recycle bin	System
Encrypted Text	Hide the value of a string variable with asterisks	Text
End Case	End of Case block	Logic
End If	End of If / Else / End If construct	Clipboard Files/Folders Logic Macro Control Network Registry Variables Window Controls
End Switch	End of Switch block	Logic
File Attributes	Set attributes of a file	Files/Folders
FTP Change Directory	Change the working folder on an FTP site	Internet
FTP ChMod	Change attributes of a file on an FTP site	Internet
FTP Delete Directory	Delete a folder on an FTP site	Internet
FTP Delete File	Delete a file on an FTP site	Internet
FTP Get Current Directory	Retrieve the name of the current folder on an FTP site	Internet
FTP Get File	Retrieve a file from an FTP site	Internet
FTP Get Filesize	Retrieve the size of a file on an FTP site	Internet
FTP Keep Alive	Keep the FTP connection open	Internet
FTP List Directory	Retrieve a list of file names in the current folder on an FTP site	Internet

Command	Description	Category
FTP Make Directory	Create a folder on an FTP site	Internet
FTP Rename File	Rename a file on an FTP site	Internet
FTP Send File	Copy a file to an FTP site	Internet
FTP Site Command	Send an unsupported FTP command to an FTP site	Internet
FTP Site Connect	Connect to an FTP site	Internet
FTP Site Disconnect	Disconnect to an FTP site	Internet
Get Control	Capture a Window Control manually and place it into a Control variable	Window Controls
Get File Version	Get the version/release number of a file	Files/Folders Variables
Get IP Address	Retrieve the IP Address of your computer	Internet
Get Mouse Position	Retrieve mouse coordinates	Mouse
Get Pixel Color	Retrieve the color of a pixel on your monitor	System
Hibernate	Place your computer in a hibernate mode	System
If Clipboard	If clipboard text equals	Clipboard Logic
If Control	If a Window Control is focused, visible, or enabled	Logic Window Controls
If Dial Up Successful	If a dial-up connection is successful	Logic Network
If File Exists	If a file exists	Files/Folders Logic
If File Ready	If a file is ready to be accessed	Files/Folders Logic
If Folder Exists	If a folder exists	Files/Folders Logic
If Macro	If macro enabled or disabled	Logic Macro Control
If Message	Create a Yes/No prompt for user to answer at runtime	Logic
If Mouse Cursor	If mouse cursor equals	Logic Mouse
If Not File Exists	If a file does not exist	Files/Folders Logic
If Not File Ready	If a file is not ready to be accessed	Files/Folders Logic
If Not Folder Exists	If a folder does not exist	Files/Folders Logic
If Not Mouse Cursor	If mouse cursor does not equal	Logic Mouse
If Not Program	If a program is not running or not focused	Logic
If Not Window	If a window is not running or not focused	Logic
If Online	If a dial-up connection is active	Logic Network
If OS Version	If operating system is equal to	Logic

Command	Description	Category
If Ping Successful	If address returned a successful "ping"	Logic Network
If Program	If program running or focused	Logic
If Registry	If key or value does or does not exist	Logic Registry
If Variable	True or false based on comparing two variables	Logic Variables
If Window	If window running or focused	Logic
Keyboard Repeat Delay	Sets the keyboard repeat delay	Keyboard Timing
Keyboard Repeat Speed	Sets the keyboard repeat speed	Keyboard Timing
Keystroke Speed	Sets the delay in milliseconds between sending keystrokes	Keyboard
Launch and Activate	Launch a program and activate the window	Windows/Programs
Load Macro Text File	Load an external macro text file to process immediately	Macro Control
Load New Macro File	Load a different macro library file during runtime	Macro Control
Lock Workstation	Lock your computer workstation	System
Log Errors	Record errors to file	Debug
Log Messages	Record messages to file	Debug
Logoff	Logoff as the current user	Network System
Macro Delete	Delete a macro from the macro library file	Macro Control
Macro Disable	Turn off a macro in the macro library file	Macro Control
Macro Enable	Turn on a macro in the macro library file	Macro Control
Macro Playback Speed	Set the playback speed of a macro faster or slower	Macro Control Timing
Macro Return	Return to a previous macro after running	Macro Control
Macro Run	Run a macro in the current macro library file	Macro Control
Macro Stop	Halt a macro	Macro Control
MIDI Balance	Shift MIDI balance left, center, and right	Multimedia
MIDI Mute	Mute the MIDI volume	Multimedia
MIDI Mute Toggle	Toggle MIDI mute on and off	Multimedia
MIDI Unmute	Unmute the MIDI volume	Multimedia
MIDI Volume	MIDI volume increase, decrease, full, and off	Multimedia
Mouse Click on Control	Tell Window Control that it has just been clicked	Mouse Window Controls
Mouse Left Button	Left mouse button click, double-click, down, and up	Mouse
Mouse Middle Button	Middle mouse button click, double-click, down, and up	Mouse
Mouse Move	Move mouse to specified coordinates	Mouse
Mouse Right Button	Right mouse button click, double-click, down, and up	Mouse
Mouse Speed	Sets a delay in milliseconds before each mouse command	Mouse Timing
Mouse Wheel	Spin mouse wheel forward or backward	Mouse

Command	Description	Category
Move File or Files	Move files	Files/Folders
Move Mouse to Tray Icon	Position mouse over an icon in the System Tray	Mouse
Multiple Choice Menu	Create a menu of choices for the user	Dialogs Variables
Network Connect	Connect to a network drive	Network
Network Disconnect	Disconnect from a network drive	Network
Network Toggle	Toggle connection to a network drive on and off	Network
Num Lock	Toggle key on and off	Keyboard
Open Explorer To	Open a special folder in Windows Explorer	Explorer
Open Folder	Open a folder without using Windows Explorer	Explorer
Open Folder in Explorer	Open a folder using Windows Explorer	Explorer
Or	Boolean OR operator	Logic
Password Protection	Set a password for user to enter at runtime	Macro Control
Pause	Temporarily halt macro processing at runtime and display a *Pause* dialog	Debug Dialogs Timing
Ping Site	Send a "ping" to an address	Internet
PostMessage	Send a Windows message to a Window Control	System Window Controls
Power Off	Power down your computer	System
Program Launch	Launch a program	Windows/Programs
Program Shut Down	Shut down or terminate a running program	Windows/Programs
Read Registry Decimal	Retrieve decimal value	Registry
Read Registry Integer	Retrieve integer value	Registry
Read Registry String	Retrieve string value	Registry
Reboot	Restart your computer	System
Reload Macro Express Preferences	Read Macro Express preferences again from your Registry	Macro Express
Remark	Enter a remark line into a macro, which is ignored at runtime	Macro Control
Rename File or Files	Rename files	Files/Folders
Rename Folder	Rename folders	Files/Folders
Repeat Counter	Type out the current Repeat counter	Repeat
Repeat End	End of Repeat loop	Files/Folders Repeat Variables
Repeat Exit	Exit out of Repeat loop	Files/Folders Repeat Variables
Repeat Prompt Start	Get number of Repeat loops from user	Repeat
Repeat Start	Number of times to Repeat a loop	Repeat
Repeat Until	Repeat until value test fails	Repeat
Repeat with Folder	Loop through file and subfolder names in a folder	Files/Folders

Command	Description	Category
		Repeat
Repeat with Processes	Loop through running process (program or task) names	Repeat
Repeat with Variable	Set number of Repeat loops from a variable	Repeat Variables
Repeat with Windows	Loop through running window names	Repeat Windows/Programs
Reset Hooks	Reset Windows keyboard and mouse hooks for Macro Express	Macro Express
Restart Macro Express	Close Macro Express and then start it again	Macro Express
Round Decimal	Rounds a decimal value to a specified number of digits	Variables
Run Dialog Window	Activate your system's *Run* dialog	System
Run Macro in Variable	Run a macro from a variable	Macro Control Variables
Screen Saver	Activate or disable screen saver or set timeout	System
Scroll Lock	Toggle key on and off	Keyboard
Set Focus	Sets focus to a particular Window Control	Window Controls
Set Integer to Control Height	Set an integer to the height of a Window Control	Window Controls Windows/Programs
Set Integer to Control Left	Set an integer to the position of the left side of a Window Control	Window Controls Windows/Programs
Set Integer to Control Top	Set an integer to the position of the top of a Window Control	Window Controls Windows/Programs
Set Integer to Control Width	Set an integer to the width of a Window Control	Window Controls Windows/Programs
Set System Date/Time	Set or reset your system's time and date	System
Set Window Order	Moves active windows to the top and bottom of the stack	Windows/Programs
Shift Key	Press key down and let up	Keyboard
Shutdown	Shut down your computer	System
Sound Beep	Play a "beep" sound	Multimedia
Sound Wave File	Play a WAV file	Multimedia
Suspend Computer	Suspend mode for laptop	System
Switch	Switch/Case statement (beginning of Switch block)	Logic
Terminal Services Session ID	Retrieve the terminal services sessions ID (Windows Terminal Services must be running)	System Variables
Terminate Macro Express	Halts and shuts down Macro Express	Macro Express
Terminate Process	Stops a process (program or task) from running	Windows/Programs
Text Box Close	Close information text window	Dialogs Text
Text Box Display	Create an information text window for the user to read during runtime	Dialogs Text
Text File Begin Process	Start processing lines in a text file	Files/Folders
Text File End Process	Stop processing lines in a text file	Files/Folders
Text Type	Sends keystrokes to the keyboard	Keyboard

Command	Description	Category
		Text
Time	Set a time to a particular format mask	Text
Undock Computer	Undock laptop from docking station	System
Variable Get Control Class	Retrieve the class name of a Window Control and place it in a variable	Variables Window Controls
Variable Get Control Text	Retrieve the text inside a Window Control and place it in a variable	Variables Window Controls
Variable Modify Control	Copy Window Control contents and activation, and change the top-level window	Variables Window Controls
Variable Modify Decimal	Arithmetic and conversion operations on decimals	Variables
Variable Modify Integer	Arithmetic and conversion operations on integers	Variables
Variable Modify String	Operations on strings	Variables
Variable Restore	Restore specified variables after they have been saved	Variables
Variable Save	Save specified variables	Variables
Variable Set Control Text	Set the text of a Window Control	Variables Window Controls
Variable Set Decimal	Set a decimal value	Variables
Variable Set From File	Retrieve file date and time or path information	Files/Folders Variables
Variable Set From Misc	Set a string variable to a miscellaneous value such as current macro, user name, installation path, and so forth	Variables Window Controls
Variable Set Integer	Set an integer value	Variables
Variable Set String	Set a string value	Variables
Variable Set to ASCII Char	Set a string from an ASCII number value	Variables
Variable Set to ASCII Value	Set an integer from an ASCII character	Variables
Video Clip Play	Play an AVI file	Multimedia
Wait For Control	Wait for a Window Control to gain focus or become visible or invisible	Timing Window Controls
Wait For File Exist	Wait for a file to exist	Files/Folders Timing
Wait For File Ready	Wait for a file to be accessible	Files/Folders Timing
Wait For Folder to Exist	Wait for a folder to exist	Files/Folders Timing
Wait For Key Press	Waits until user presses specified key	Keyboard Timing
Wait For Mouse Cursor	Wait for mouse cursor to be a specified cursor	Timing
Wait For Not Mouse Cursor	Wait for mouse cursor to not be a specified cursor	Timing
Wait For Text	Waits until user types expected text	Text Timing
Wait For Web Page	Wait for a web page to load	Internet Explorer Timing
Wait For Window Title	Wait for a particular window to gain focus	Timing

Command	Description	Category
Wait Left Mouse Click	Wait for the left mouse button to click	Mouse Timing
Wait Middle Mouse Click	Wait for the middle mouse button to click	Mouse Timing
Wait Program Terminate	Wait for a program to terminate	Timing
Wait Right Mouse Click	Wait for the right mouse button to click	Mouse Timing
Wait Text Playback	Waits until text typed with the *Text Type* command plays back	Text Timing
Wait Time Delay	Delay macro from continuing for a period of time without expending CPU cycles	Timing
Wait Time Elapse	Delay macro from continuing for an extended period of time without expending CPU cycles	Timing
Wait Window Lose Focus	Wait for the current window to lose focus	Timing
Wallpaper	Set the Desktop wallpaper	System
Web FTP Site	Initiate an FTP transfer	Internet
Web Site	Go to an internet web site	Internet
Win Key	Press key down and let up	Keyboard
Window Activate	Sets focus to a specified window	Windows/Programs
Window Close	Terminate a window	Windows/Programs
Window Hide	Make a window invisible	Windows/Programs
Window Maximize	Maximize a window	Windows/Programs
Window Minimize	Minimize a window to the Taskbar	Windows/Programs
Window Reposition	Move a window	Windows/Programs
Window Resize	Change the size of a window	Windows/Programs
Window Restore	Restore a window from the Taskbar	Windows/Programs
Window Show	Make a window visible again	Windows/Programs
Windows Sizing Border	Sets the border width of all windows on your computer	System Windows/Programs
Write Registry Decimal	Write decimal value	Registry
Write Registry Integer	Write integer value	Registry
Write Registry String	Write string value	Registry
XOR	Boolean XOR operator	Logic

Companion CD

There is a companion CD is included with this book. If it is missing, or if it is defective, please contact us so we can send another one to you. E-Mail me directly at joe@pgmacros.com and I will take care of it.

Macro Express Explained videos

Included on your CD are videos covering different areas of the book. These wonderful tools were all written, produced, and edited by Formaquest Technologies. The videos are ordered by whichever chapters they belong to in the book so they are easy to find. Here is a letter for you, the reader, from Matthew:

LearnMacroExpress.com
A FormaQuest Company

Dear Reader,

I have written these different tutorials to help you understand how to use the various tools in Macro Express. My goal in this training video series was to show similar techniques for implementing these commands in different situations. I want to discuss with you my background knowledge, and how macros have been able to change how I do business.

First, a little bit more about me. I have owned my own company FormaQuest for four years. I started out developing web sites for companies, which I still do, and I run a corporate network of computers for another company based in Salt Lake City.

About two years ago I started working with 360House.com as a digital photographer. I was given the job of finding better methods for processing pictures. By this I mean stitching panoramas, uploading them to a server, running backups, and so forth. I decided that what was needed was a solution which would automate these tasks. And since I am not a C++ or Visual Basic programmer, I figured I would look for an application that could do automation. Shortly after, I found Macro Express and was enthusiastic because of how many different possibilities there were with this product.

I started writing my program, and the first thing that I realized I did wrong was not writing up a plan of action. This should always be the first step because you need to understand what you are developing, and what it needs to do to carry out the goals of the project. This was one of my first projects, and it consisted of around 4,000 lines of code. It was difficult to write, but at the same time I was able to figure out almost all of Macro Express' commands.

Since then I have been able to develop macros for all sorts of things. Whether it being a simply task such as copying a file, or a much more complex project of creating a backup system to run at a certain time of day and that copies the info to a network drive.

The best part of understanding how to make macro scripts is that you can automate almost any job that is based on a computer. Every company that I have visited since knowing about how Macro Express works I have seen possibilities for using automation scripts.

Sincerely,
Matthew Frandsen, CEO
FormaQuest Technologies
LearnMacroExpress.com is a FormaQuest Company

Macro Express examples

The examples that you read in the book are included in a macro library named *Macro Express Explained.mex*. Each chapter is categorized first with a number and then the chapter name. The number keeps the chapters ordered. Within each chapter/category you will find macros named using the same scheme. Each macro name begins with a number and then a section name.

Each macro has a *Macro Stop* command at the beginning to prevent it from running without you examining it first. The macros cannot be expected to run correctly without making minor changes to them. This is because they were developed on my system and not yours. Our monitors and file systems are different. So, feel free to make whatever changes you need.

Pop-N-Pass macro library

Pop-N-Pass is a macro that creates macros that automatically enter User IDs and Passwords into both local and web-based applications.

To install, import the macros into your existing macro file by choosing (File | Import | Macros) from the Main Menu of the Macro Express Editor (*Macro Explorer* window).

To use, bring up the web page or application that requires you to login. When a login dialog is displayed, click on the Pop-N-Pass Builder icon in the System Tray or run the *{ Pop-N-Pass Builder }* macro by pressing **Ctrl+`**. Follow the instructions displayed by the macro.

Pop-N-Pass, while running, is using your keyboard and mouse to build your macro. Do not use the keyboard or mouse until prompted to do so. While it is running, you will see some windows flashing by. This happens because the windows are being hidden immediately after they are loaded to prevent your display from becoming too cluttered and confusing.

Some advanced Macro Express programming techniques were used to create the Pop-N-Pass macro. Feel free to examine the code. It is well documented with plenty of comments. Also, Pop-N-Pass contains extensive help information that describes both how to use it and how it works. Access this information by clicking on the Pop-N-Pass Builder icon in the System Tray.

TweakMe3.mxe utility macro

There are several useful Macro Express features that cannot be adjusted from the (Options | Preferences) dialog. Use the playable macro *TweakMe3.mxe* to change them. Either double-click on *TweakMe3* from Windows Explorer or import it into your macro file by choosing (File | Import | Import a Playable Macro) from the Main Menu of the Macro Express Editor (*Macro Explorer* window).

The *TweakMe3.mxe* macro changes which pane has focus in the Scripting Editor and Direct Editor windows, adjusts what is displayed in Macro Explorer, changes advanced ShortKey options, and suppress the "Macro Aborted" message, and more. Please review the *Advanced Options* section within the *Running and Activating Macros* chapter for a detailed explanation of this utility macro. You may also want to study this macro as a sample of some advanced macro commands and techniques.

Macro Express help file in Word and HTML formats

This is the complete Macro Express help documentation that is found in the Help menu within Macro Express.

The *me3help.exe* file will install the help documentation as a Microsoft Word document. If you prefer, this same installation file

is available in a "zipped" format (*me3help.zip*).
The *macexp3.chm* is the help file in HTML Help format. It can be viewed using the HTML Help program, which is installed by default on Windows XP but may need to be installed for other Windows versions.

Macro Express v 3.5 trial version

Macro Express is the premier Windows macro utility. What this book is all about, eh? We placed this file on your CD as a convenience.

Because Insight Software Solutions updates their software frequently, always check on-line at www.macros.com/download for the latest release.

PGM Functions Library trial version

The PGM Functions Library enhances Macro Express functionality by providing predesigned, callable, reusable functions which may be imported into your macro applications. There are over 100 functions divided into seven categories including variable management, program operations, date and time calculations, math and science functions, string manipulation, file operations and developer tools. Also there are over 50 example macros showing how to use the PGM Functions.

For more information, visit the PGM Functions Library web site www.pgmacros.com or review the *PGM Functions Library.pdf* documentation manual, which is also included on this CD.

ShortKeys trial version

ShortKeys is a utility that allows you to set up replacement text or paragraphs for any given number of user-defined keystrokes. ShortKeys monitors the keyboard activity on a global nature and anytime a user defined keystroke combination is typed in, it will be replaced with the replacement text.

If you find yourself typing the same thing over and over, then this product is for you. Automate tedious and repetitive typing and reduce errors. Type a few characters and ShortKeys will replace them with up to 3000 keystrokes. You will be amazed how much time ShortKeys will save.

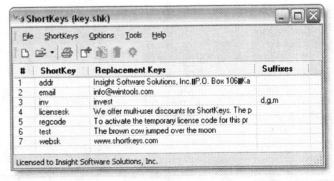

We placed this file on your CD as a convenience. Always check on-line at www.shortkeys.com/download for the latest release.

Capture Express trial version

How many attempts does it take you to capture an image from your screen? If you are using something other than Capture Express, then the answer may very likely be "Several".

Unlike other capture programs which do not permit you to move the "grabber" once you start the capture, Capture Express allows you to toggle between a stretch mode and a move mode by right clicking on the mouse. So if you did not quite get your alignment correct when you started your capture, simply click on the right mouse button and move the grabber to the correct alignment. Other programs will require you to abort the whole capture process and start again in the hope that you get the correct alignment.

Besides capturing basic Screens, Windows and rectangular areas, Capture Express allows you to capture items in a variety of shapes. Optionally place borders around the shapes and choose a masking color for the exterior of the shape. Some of the shapes available include rounded rectangles, circles, ellipses, diamonds, triangles, stars, and other user defined shapes such as an octagon or house figure shape. Print, Save, or E-Mail your captured images. We placed this file on your CD as a convenience. Because Insight Software Solutions updates their software frequently, always check on-line at www.captureexpress.com/download for the latest release.

Zip Express trial version

Zip Express allows easy lookup of U.S. Zip Codes and their associated cities, states, counties, area codes, time zones and current time. Find the current time and time zone for cities around the world.

Paste Zip Code information directly into your Windows applications. Press a HotKey while in your word processor and a Zip Code entry box appears. Type in your Zip Code and the city, state and Zip Code are typed right into your word processor. Press another HotKey to get a Zip Code directly from your database and watch the city, state, and county appear. Automatically!

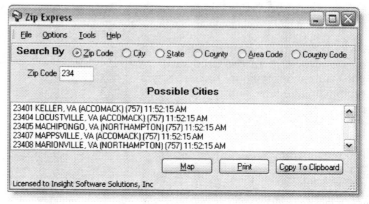

Used by realtors, lawyers, university admissions counselors, call centers and many others. Use with your customer database. Before returning a phone call, enter an Area Code or Country Code into Zip Express to determine where the caller called from and what time it is in their city or country. With the Zip Code information displayed, press the Map button and, with an Internet connection, see a map of that location.

We placed this file on your CD as a convenience. Because Insight Software Solutions updates their software frequently, always check on-line at www.getzips.com/download for the latest release.

Conclusion

Because we here at Professional Grade Macros create so many macros using Macro Express we try to keep pace with all of its changes, updates, and releases. It is difficult! We are beta-testers for Macro Express, and I do not recall a month that has gone by when something has not been added, repaired, or updated in the product. We think this shows a dedication by Insight Software Solutions, Inc. to keep Macro Express moving forward. As good as it is today, the history of Macro Express can only lead us to assume it will continue to expand in scope and abilities throughout the coming years with new features and new commands.

We have learned much about what Macro Express is like today, including what it can, and cannot, do. However, there is more to learn because this book does not cover every possible subject, menu option, or command. To put in writing everything I wanted about Macro Express, this already-late-to-press book would have taken another six months to complete. Here are some subjects that are not covered, or are covered very little:

- Importing and exporting macros from other libraries or playable macro files.
- Backing up Macro Express library files.
- Restoring Macro Express default settings.
- The new built in bug reporter.
- Using the E-Mail settings and recipients feature.
- Multimedia commands (CD-ROM player, audio and MIDI controls, playing WAV and AVI files).
- Internet commands such as Wait for Web page, and the FTP features.
- System commands that reboot, shut down, power off, and suspend your computer.

Because you purchased this book, you are invited to log on to our free web site and download additions and changes. We also plan on publishing papers that cover different aspects of using Macro Express. Please go to http://www.pgmacros.com/members/book. It is free.

We sincerely hope that you have found this book useful. Feel free to e-mail suggestions, criticisms, and ideas on how to make it better! support@pgmacros.com.

Index

/A<nickname>
  section heading, 106
/B
  section heading, 110
/delay;<seconds>
  section heading, 108
/EN
  section heading, 110
  section reference, 110
/EY
  section heading, 110
  section reference, 110
/F<\path\filename>
  section heading, 107
/H
  section heading, 109
  section reference, 109
/IC<filename>
  section heading, 107
/MXE<\path\filename>
  section heading, 106
/N
  section heading, 108
  section reference, 108, 109
/NQS
  section heading, 110
/S
  section heading, 108
/SM<minutes>
  section heading, 109
/T
  section heading, 109
  section reference, 109
/V<variable;value>
  section heading, 106
About this Book
  chapter heading, xvii
Acknowledgments
  chapter heading, xvi
Actions Toolbar
  section heading, 29, 55
  section reference, 55
Activate or Launch, 357
  section heading, 285
Activate Window, 330
Activate Window if Running
  otherwise Launch Program
  and Activate Window
  section heading, 290
Activate Window Only, 285, 290
  section heading, 285
Activate/Launch Program
  dialog, 285

Activating Macros
  section heading, 112
  section reference, 45
Activation Prefix
  section heading, 148
Activation Tab
  section heading, 45
Active
  section heading, 82
Add
  section heading, 211, 215
Add a Category
  section heading, 31
Add Macro
  dialog, 5, 40, 41, 93, 97, 112, 133
Add Macros
  section heading, 40
Add Menu
  dialog, 134, 135
Advanced Installation
  section heading, 16
  section reference, 1
Advanced Options
  section heading, 148
  section reference, 37, 123, 140,
    249, 368
Advanced Settings
  dialog, 314, 315
Alt Key, 357
  section heading, 240
Always on Top, 296
And, 153, 357
AND, 154, 156
  section heading, 154
And the rest of the commands
  section heading, 351
Appearance
  dialog, 25, 30, 34, 35, 88, 140
Appearances
  dialog, 63
Append Clipboard Text to the
  End of a Text File
  section heading, 262
Append Text, 202
  section heading, 199
Append Text String Variable
  section heading, 199
Append to Text File, 203, 260
  section heading, 204
Archive Attribute
  section heading, 314
Area on Screen
  section heading, 128

ASCII Delimited Text (.txt)
  section heading, 328
ASCII File Begin Process, 322,
  326, 327, 357
  section heading, 326
ASCII File End Process, 357
ASCII Text File End Process
  section heading, 326
ASCII Values and Variables
  section heading, 223
  section reference, 77
At Startup
  section heading, 117
Audio Balance, 357
Audio Bass, 357
Audio Mute, 357
Audio Mute Toggle, 357
Audio Treble, 357
Audio Unmute, 357
Audio Volume, 357
Auto Restore Keyboard Hooks
  section heading, 241
Bad Password
  dialog, 85
Banker's Rounding
  section heading, 150, 216
Basic Installation
  section heading, 9
  section reference, 1
Basic Pause, 181
Be Asked What to Do
  section heading, 261
Break, 163, 165, 173, 319, 325,
  357
  section heading, 164
Breakpoints
  dialog, 70
  section heading, 69
Building a Menu
  section heading, 134
Button Click
  section heading, 245
Button Double Click
  section heading, 245
Button Down
  section heading, 245
Button Up
  section heading, 245
Bypass File Existence Check
  section heading, 191
Caching
  dialog, 127
Caps Lock

section heading, 240
CAPS Lock, 358
CAPS Lock On, 241
Capture
dialog, 88, 91
Capture Complete
dialog, 92, 97
Capture Control, 329, 331, 337, 339, 340, 341, 355, 358
section heading, 339
Capture Express trial version
section heading, 369
Capture Icon
section heading, 93
section reference, 95
Capture Macro
dialog, 94, 95, 96, 97, 98, 99
Capture Macros
section reference, 51
Capture Options
section heading, 91
Capture Settings
section heading, 88
section reference, 92, 94
Capture Window
dialog, 93, 95
Capture Window Control
dialog, 332, 333, 334
Capture Wizard
section heading, 95
section reference, 101
Capturing Macros
section heading, 88
section reference, 101
Case, 153, 163, 164, 358
section heading, 162
Categories Pane
section heading, 30
section reference, 35
CDROM Back, 358
CDROM Close Tray, 358
CDROM Eject, 358
CDROM Go To Track, 358
CDROM Next Track, 358
CDROM Pause, 358
CDROM Play, 358
CDROM Previous Track, 358
CDROM Step, 358
CDROM Stop, 358
Center on Screen, 295
Change Default Folder, 307, 308, 310, 311, 312
section heading, 305
Change Directory/Folder, 358
Change Focus Automatically
section heading, 70
Changing Lines
section heading, 69

Character Repeat
dialog, 238
Choose an Activation for the Macro
dialog, 97
Choose Destination Location
dialog, 17
section heading, 12
Choose Graphic File
dialog, 261
Choose Text File
dialog, 261
Clear Control Variables, 329, 353
section heading, 353
Clear Variables, 228, 358
section heading, 219
Clearing, Saving, and Restoring Variables
section heading, 219
Click-and-Drag
section heading, 190
Clipboard, 257, 258, 260, 261, 264
chapter heading, 257
chapter reference, 161
dialog, 257, 261
Clipboard Append Text, 262, 358
Clipboard Copy, 259, 358
Clipboard Cut, 259, 358
Clipboard Empty, 65, 259, 358
Clipboard End Copy, 258, 358
Clipboard File Copy, 261, 358
Clipboard Graphic Copy, 194, 262, 264, 358
Clipboard Paste, 259, 358
Clipboard Save Graphic, 194, 263, 264, 358
Clipboard Save Text, 261, 358
Clipboard Start Copy, 258, 358
Clipboard Type Text, 258, 358
Close Text Box, 177
Close Window, 291, 293
section heading, 291
Columns
section heading, 34
Comma Delimited Text (.csv)
section heading, 327
Command Line
section reference, 111
Command Line Parameters
section heading, 106
Commands
section header, 269
Commands Pane
section heading, 63, 76
section reference, 68
Common Data
section heading, 274

Common Dialogs
section heading, 283, 303
section reference, 285, 286, 290, 291, 292, 296, 298, 299
Common Fields
section heading, 117
Common Options
section heading, 261
Common Variable Dialogs
section heading, 189
section reference, 194, 208, 261, 287
Companion CD
chapter heading, 367
chapter reference, xx
Complex Pause, 181
Components
section header, 105
section reference, 24, 50
Conclusion
chapter heading, 371
chapter reference, xvii, xx
ConfigFilePath
section heading, 19
Configuration
dialog, 250
Confirm Delete
dialog, 31
Contains, 263
Continue the Macro
section heading, 260
Control Details
dialog, 333, 335, 336, 338, 339, 347
Control Key, 358
section heading, 240
Control Panel
dialog, 4, 5, 6, 7, 61, 75, 124, 125, 238, 358
Control Panel Open, 5, 62, 65, 66, 76, 358
Control Panel Run, 358
Convert Filename, 313, 328, 358
section heading, 313
Convert to Decimal, 213
section heading, 199, 212
Convert to Integer, 205
section heading, 198
Convert to Text String
section heading, 211, 217
Copy Command Text
section heading, 74
Copy Contents of Control Variable
section heading, 343
Copy Control from Activation
section heading, 343
Copy File or Files, 305, 310, 311, 312, 358

section heading, 307
Copy Graphic File to Clipboard, 260
section heading, 262
Copy Macro
dialog, 41
Copy Macros
section heading, 40
section reference, 41
Copy Part of Text
section heading, 200
Copy Text File to Clipboard
section heading, 261
Copy Value
section heading, 212, 218
Copy Whole Text
section heading, 200
Create a Macro
section heading, 4
Create a Multiple Choice Menu
dialog, 174, 180
Create Folder, 358
section heading, 306
Create New Macro File
dialog, 4
Create Registry Key, 265, 358
section heading, 270
Create Registry Value, 271
Creating and Editing Macros
chapter heading, 59
chapter reference, xviii, 5, 7, 24, 29, 34, 40, 41, 42, 44, 45, 46, 47, 51
Creation Date/Time
section heading, 316
Credits
section heading, xx
Current Window
section heading, 283
Customize Categories
dialog, 63
Customize Notifications
dialog, 251
Daily
section heading, 119
Data Processing
section heading, 322
Date, 358
Date/Time, 258, 358
Decimal Commands
section reference, 215
Decimal Variable Commands
section heading, 213
section reference, 214, 215
Decimal Variables
section heading, 185
Decrement
section heading, 212
Default Case, 163, 358
section heading, 162

Default Display Size, 358
Default Printer, 359
Delay, 90, 91, 187, 257, 359
Delays
dialog, 234, 257
Delete a Category
section heading, 31
Delete File or Files, 305, 359
section heading, 312
Delete Folder, 359
section heading, 307
Delete Macro(s)
section heading, 56
Delete Macros
section heading, 42
Delete Part of Text
section heading, 200
Delete Registry Key, 265, 359
section heading, 270
Delete Registry Value, 265, 359
section heading, 272
Deleted Macros Pane
section heading, 55
Deleting Lines
section heading, 69
Desktop
section heading, 111
Desktop Cascade, 359
Desktop Minimize All, 359
Desktop Restore All, 359
Desktop Tile, 359
Desktop Tile Horizontally, 359
Desktop Tile Vertically, 359
Destination Location
dialog, 12
Dial Up Networking, 359
Dial Up Networking:Hang Up, 359
Dialog Positioner
dialog, 160, 169, 176, 179, 181, 189
section heading, 189, 190
section reference, 160, 169, 176, 179, 181, 193, 207, 215, 247
Dialogs
dialog, 81, 88
Direct Editor
section heading, 75
section reference, 24, 60
Disabling Lines
section heading, 69
Disk Operations
section heading, 305
Display a Text Box
dialog, 177, 180
Display Gradients
section heading, 149
Display Properties
dialog, 211

Divide
section heading, 211, 215
Do You Wish the Macro to Play Back
dialog, 96
Do You Wish to Capture Keystrokes
dialog, 96
Do You Wish to Capture Mouse Movements and Clicks
dialog, 96
Does Not Contain, 263
Drop-Down List
section heading, 189
Duplicate Name Warning
dialog, 81, 92, 94
Duplicating Lines
section heading, 68
Dynamic Macros
section heading, 141
Editing a Macro
section heading, 42
Editor
section heading, 10
Else, xviii, 153, 154, 163, 263, 359
section heading, 153
E-Mail Send, 359
Empty Macro Recycle Bin, 359
Empty Recycle Bin, 359
section heading, 56
Empty the Clipboard
section heading, 259
Enable and Disable Macros
section heading, 43
Encrypted Text, 237, 258, 359
section heading, 237
End Case, 153, 163, 164, 359
section heading, 162
End Clipboard Copy, 264
section heading, 258
End If, xviii, 7, 72, 153, 154, 155, 163, 240, 245, 330, 359
section heading, 153
End Switch, xviii, 7, 153, 162, 163, 359
section heading, 162
End-User License Agreement
chapter heading, xv
Engage!
section heading, 345
Enter Edit Password
dialog, 83
Environment Variables
section heading, 185
Error Log Viewer
dialog, 48
External Editor
section heading, 87
section reference, 42

File Association Notification
section heading, 14
File Attributes, 313, 359
section heading, 313
File Clipboard Commands
section heading, 260
File Information
section heading, 313
File Opening Error Options (Graphic Files Only)
section heading, 260
File Paths
dialog, 87, 105
File-picker
dialog, 191, 287
File-Picker
dialog, 261, 303
section heading, 191
section reference, 194, 203, 208
Files and Folders
chapter heading, 303
chapter reference, xix, 162, 165, 173, 286
Find
dialog, 38, 39, 56, 67, 73, 77
Finding Text
section heading, 73, 79
section reference, 79
Folder-Picker
dialog, 303, 304
Font
dialog, 73
Fonts used in book
section heading, xxi
FTP Change Directory, 359
FTP ChMod, 359
FTP Delete Directory, 359
FTP Delete File, 359
FTP Get Current Directory, 359
FTP Get File, 359
FTP Get Filesize, 359
FTP Keep Alive, 359
FTP List Directory, 359
FTP Make Directory, 360
FTP Rename File, 360
FTP Send File, 360
FTP Site Command, 360
FTP Site Connect, 360
FTP Site Disconnect, 360
General Tab
section heading, 44
Get Control, 329, 331, 337, 339, 340, 341, 346, 352, 355, 360
dialog, 331, 333
section heading, 331
Get File Date/Time
section heading, 316
Get File Path Info, 328

Get File Version, 313, 328, 360
section heading, 317
Get IP Address, 360
Get Length of a Text Variable
section heading, 209
Get Mouse Position, 360
section heading, 247
Get Mouse Position Screen, 207
Get Nickname
dialog, 159
Get Pixel Color, 360
Get Position of Text in a Text Variable
section heading, 209
Global
section heading, 130
Global Clipboard Delay
section heading, 257
Global Except
section heading, 130
Go To Line
section heading, 72
Go To Line Number
dialog, 67
Halt the Macro
section heading, 260
Help
section heading, 10
Hibernate, 360
Hidden Attribute
section heading, 315
Hide Window, 287, 291, 294
section heading, 290
HKEY_CLASSES_ROOT
section heading, 265
HKEY_CURRENT_CONFIG
section heading, 266
HKEY_CURRENT_USER
section heading, 266
HKEY_LOCAL_MACHINE
section heading, 266
HKEY_USERS
section heading, 266
HotKey
section heading, 113
section reference, 49, 138
Hotkey Abort Message
section heading, 149
Hourly
section heading, 118
Icon
section heading, 81
section reference, 99
Icons
section heading, 11
If, xviii, 7, 153, 154, 155, 163, 164, 240, 245, 319, 349
section heading, 153

If Clipboard, 66, 263, 360
section heading, 161
If Clipboard Contains, 263
section heading, 263
If Clipboard Text Equals, 263
section heading, 263
If Commands
dialog, 159, 252, 263, 299, 300, 319
If Control, 330, 349, 350, 360
dialog, 349
section heading, 161, 349
If Dial Up Successful, 360
If File Exists, 360
section heading, 162, 319
If File Ready, 320, 321, 360
section heading, 162, 320
If Folder Exists, 360
section heading, 162, 319
If Macro, 66, 360
If Macro Disabled
section heading, 159
If Macro Enabled
section heading, 159
If Message, 160, 360
dialog, 160
section heading, 160
If Mouse Cursor, 66, 253, 360
section heading, 161, 252
If Not File Exists, 360
section heading, 162, 319
If Not File Ready, 360
section heading, 162, 320
If Not Folder Exists, 360
section heading, 162, 319
If Not Mouse Cursor, 360
section heading, 161, 252
If Not Program, 360
section heading, 162
If Not Window, 360
section heading, 162
If Online, 148, 360
If OS Version, 360
section heading, 158
If Ping Successful, 361
If Program, xix, 172, 300, 361
section heading, 162
If Program Not On Top, 301
section heading, 300
If Program Not Running, 301
section heading, 300
If Program On Top, 301
section heading, 300
If Program Running, 301
section heading, 300
If Registry, 265, 361
section heading, 162, 272
If Registry Key Does not Exist, 272

If Registry Key Exists, 272
If Registry Value Does not Exist, 272
If Registry Value Exists, 272
If the box is checked (Text method) -
  section heading, 335
If the box is unchecked (Index method) -
  section heading, 337
If Variable, 165, 170, 263, 361
  section heading, 156
If Window, xix, 299, 300, 361
  section heading, 162
If Window Not On Top, 300
  section heading, 299
If Window Not Running, 300
  section heading, 299
If Window On Top, 299
  section heading, 299
If Window Running, 300
  section heading, 299
If Window Title, 330
Increment
  section heading, 212
Insert Symbol
  dialog, 233
Inserting Lines
  section heading, 68
Install
  dialog, 12
Install Older Files
  section heading, 11
Installation
  chapter heading, 9
  chapter reference, xviii, 1
Installation Complete
  dialog, 17
  section heading, 14
Installation Type
  section heading, 10
Installing
  section heading, 13
InstallOlder
  section heading, 17
InstallPath
  section heading, 17
Integer Variable Commands
  section heading, 205
  section reference, 209, 211
Integer Variables
  section heading, 185
Introduction to Macro Express
  chapter heading, 1
  chapter reference, xviii
Issue Clipboard Copy Command (Ctrl+C)
  section heading, 259

Issue Clipboard Cut Command (Ctrl+X)
  section heading, 259
Issue Clipboard Paste Command (Ctrl+V)
  section heading, 259
Keyboard
  chapter heading, 231
  chapter reference, xix, 79, 245, 259
Keyboard Repeat Delay, 361
Keyboard Repeat Speed, 361
Keystroke Speed, xix, 237, 238, 244, 251, 259, 361
  section heading, 237
Last Accessed Date/Time
  section heading, 316
Launch and Activate, 361
  section heading, 285
Launch Program and Activate Window
  section heading, 289
Launch Program Only, 285, 288, 289
  section heading, 286
LaunchNow
  section heading, 17
Left Trim
  section heading, 197
License Agreement
  section heading, 10
LicenseCode
  section heading, 19
LicenseName
  section heading, 18
List of Commands
  chapter heading, 357
  chapter reference, xx, 8
List of Installed Programs
  dialog, 131, 292, 301
Literal Coordinates
  section heading, 190
  section reference, 128, 137, 207, 208
Literal Values vs. Variables
  section heading, 187
Load File
  section heading, 122
Load Macro Text File, 141, 142, 144, 145, 146, 225, 361
  dialog, 141, 142
  section heading, 141
Load New Macro File, 361
Lock Workstation, 361
Log Errors, 361
Log Messages, 361
Log Tab
  section heading, 47
Logoff, 361

Lowercase
  section heading, 201
Macro Commands
  dialog, 81
  section heading, 8
Macro Delete, 361
Macro Disable, 82, 361
Macro Enable, 82, 361
Macro Express Editor
  chapter heading, 23
  chapter reference, xviii, 2, 4, 80, 83, 86
Macro Express examples
  section heading, 367
Macro Express Explained videos
  section heading, 367
Macro Express Explorer and Editors
  section heading, 111
Macro Express help file in Word and HTML formats
  section heading, 368
Macro Express software
  section heading, xvii
Macro Express v 3.5 trial version
  section heading, 369
Macro Nickname
  dialog, 99
Macro Paused
  dialog, 50, 181
Macro Playback Speed, 90, 91, 361
Macro Priority
  section heading, 150
Macro Properties
  section heading, 44
Macro Recycle Bin
  section heading, 52
  section reference, 42
Macro Return, 62, 68, 76, 78, 361
Macro Run, 7, 43, 70, 82, 84, 136, 138, 139, 149, 183, 186, 220, 361
Macro Script Pane
  section heading, 67
Macro Stop, 140, 149, 361, 368
Macro Stop Abort Message
  section heading, 149
Macro Text Pane
  section heading, 77
MacroFileDest
  section heading, 20
Macros Pane
  section heading, 34
Main File Passwords
  section heading, 84
Main Menu
  section heading, 25, 54

Manipulating Window Controls
section heading, 341
Maximize Window, 290
section heading, 290
Menu Builder
dialog, 134, 135
Menu of Macros for Topmost Window
section heading, 49
Menu Toolbar
section heading, 28, 55
section reference, 55
MIDI Balance, 361
MIDI Mute, 361
MIDI Mute Toggle, 361
MIDI Unmute, 361
MIDI Volume, 361
Minimize Window, 290
section heading, 290
Miscellaneous
dialog, 38, 241
Modified Date/Time
section heading, 316
Modify Decimal Variables, 213
section heading, 215
Modify Integer Variables, 205
section heading, 211
Modify String Variables, 192
section heading, 197
section reference, 194, 196
Modify Top-Level Window Title of Control
section heading, 344
Monthly
section heading, 121
Mouse
chapter heading, 245
chapter reference, 128, 161, 294, 339
Mouse Button Down, 245
Mouse Button Up, 245
Mouse Click
section heading, 128
Mouse Click on Control, 330, 345, 350, 361
section heading, 345
Mouse Command
dialog, 245
Mouse Left
section heading, 245
Mouse Left Button, 361
Mouse Left Button Click, 250
Mouse Left Button Down, 246
Mouse Left Button Up, 246
Mouse Locator
dialog, 150, 248, 249, 294
section header, 248
Mouse Middle

section heading, 245
Mouse Middle Button, 361
Mouse Move, 245, 251, 361
section heading, 247
Mouse Move Position, 90
Mouse Move Screen, 89
Mouse Move Window, 89
Mouse Movement
dialog, 248
Mouse Right
section heading, 245
Mouse Right Button, 361
Mouse Right Button Click, 250
Mouse Speed, 246, 251, 361
section heading, 251
Mouse Wheel, 361
Mouse Wheel Backward
section heading, 246
Mouse Wheel Forward
section heading, 246
Move a Category
section heading, 32
Move File or Files, 305, 362
section heading, 311
Move Macro(s) to Category
dialog, 33
Move Mouse to Tray Icon, xix, 250, 251, 362
section heading, 249
Moving Lines
section heading, 68
Multiple Choice Menu, xviii, 144, 147, 153, 180, 362
dialog, 176
section heading, 174
Multiply
section heading, 211, 215
My Computer
dialog, 6
Navigating
section heading, 38
Navigating the Categories Pane
section heading, 32
Navigating the Main Menu
section heading, 26
Network
dialog, 7
Network Connect, 362
Network Disconnect, 362
Network Toggle, 362
Nickname
section heading, 80
section reference, 92, 94
NoEditor
section heading, 16
NoHelp
section heading, 16
NoIcons

section heading, 17
NoIcons File
section heading, 21
Nonfile Clipboard Commands
section heading, 258
NoQuickStart
section heading, 16
NoQuickStart File
section heading, 21
NoQuickStartNow File
section heading, 21
NoStartup File
section heading, 21
Notes on Capturing Macros
section heading, 100
Notes Tab
section heading, 47, 86
section reference, 47, 74
Num Lock, 362
section heading, 240
Once
section heading, 118
Online Delay
section heading, 148
Open Explorer To, 362
Open Folder, 362
Open Folder in Explorer, 362
Open Macro
dialog, 4
Options Pane
section heading, 55
Or, 153, 362
OR, 155, 156, 163
section heading, 154
Other
section heading, 122
Other Variable Dialogs
section heading, 223
Overview
section heading, 265
Pad Left
section heading, 201
Pad Right
section heading, 201
Passing Parameters
section heading, 275
Password Protection, 362
Passwords
dialog, 84
Pause, 50, 153, 180, 362
section heading, 180
Pause Window
dialog, 181
PGM Functions Library trial version
section heading, 369
Ping Site, 362
Place On Bottom, 297
Placing Macros

section reference, 40
Placing Macros in Categories
section heading, 33
Play Back Macro in Specific
Windows
dialog, 98, 99
Playback
dialog, 47, 140, 239
Playing Macros
section heading, 7
Please Select a Wizard
dialog, 95
Please Select New File
dialog, 85
Pop-N-Pass macro library
section heading, 368
Popup and Floating Menus
section heading, 133
section reference, 50, 251
Positional Coordinates
section heading, 190
PostMessage, 362
Power Off, 362
Preferences
dialog, xviii, 18, 19, 30, 35, 38, 42,
44, 47, 81, 88, 91, 92, 94, 95, 99,
108, 110, 119, 123, 124, 142,
148, 193, 237, 241, 257, 346
section heading, 116
PrgLoad.chk File
section heading, 21
Print
dialog, 67, 77, 86
Printing a Macro
section heading, 73, 80
section reference, 80, 86
Program Launch, 228, 362
section heading, 285
Program Logic
section heading, 319
Program Logic and Flow
chapter heading, 153
chapter reference, xviii
Program Shut Down, 291, 362
Program Specific
section heading, 132
Prompt for Decimal, 189
Prompt for Integer, 189
Prompt for String, 189
Prompt for Value, 213, 238
section heading, 192, 206, 214
Properties
dialog, 41, 44, 49, 50, 80, 82, 83,
86, 111, 112, 139, 297, 305, 352
Properties Tab
section heading, 80
section reference, 34, 41, 44, 92,
94, 99
Quick Start Guide

section heading, 11
Quick Wizards
section heading, 101
QuickStartNow
section heading, 18
Read Registry, 276, 279
Read Registry Decimal, 265, 362
section heading, 271
Read Registry Integer, 265, 362
section heading, 271
Read Registry String, 265, 362
section heading, 271
Read/Write Registry Value
dialog, 272
Read-Only Attribute
section heading, 315
Reboot, 362
section heading, 18
Recapture Macro
section heading, 94
REG_BINARY
section heading, 268
REG_DWORD
section heading, 268
REG_EXPAND_SZ (Read-Only)
section heading, 268
REG_SZ
section heading, 268
Registry Editor
dialog, 271
Registry Picker
dialog, 269
section heading, 269
Reload Macro Express
Preferences, 362
Remap Keyboard
dialog, 242, 243
section heading, 242
Remark, 62, 69, 70, 76, 137, 362
Remove Integer
section heading, 218
Remove Topmost Status and
Place On Top, 296
Rename a Category
section heading, 31
Rename File or Files, 305, 362
section heading, 309
Rename Folder, 305, 309, 362
section heading, 306
Rename Macros
section heading, 41
Repeat, xviii, 7, 153, 164, 165,
166, 168, 169, 173, 240, 245,
298, 319, 322
section heading, 164
Repeat Counter, 173, 362
section heading, 172
Repeat End, xviii, 7, 164, 165,
167, 169, 324, 362

section heading, 164
Repeat Exit, 165, 173, 362
section heading, 164
Repeat Options
dialog, 166, 168, 169, 298, 322
Repeat Prompt Start, 169, 362
section heading, 169
Repeat Start, 165, 167, 168, 172,
173, 324, 362
section heading, 166
Repeat Until, 170, 171, 172, 173,
176, 362
section heading, 170
Repeat with Folder, 172, 322, 362
section heading, 173, 322
Repeat with Processes, 172, 363
section heading, 172
Repeat with Variable, 168, 169,
172, 363
section heading, 168
Repeat with Windows, 172, 363
section heading, 173, 298
Replace
dialog, 60, 77, 80
Replace Substring
section heading, 202
Reset Hooks, 241, 255, 363
Restart Macro Express, 15, 363
Restore Control Variables, 329,
354
section heading, 354
Restore Keyboard Hooks
section heading, 241
Restore Macro(s)
section heading, 56
Restore Mouse Hooks
section heading, 255
Restore Variables
section heading, 220
Restore Window, 290
section heading, 290
Resume Pause
section heading, 50
Reusable Macros
section heading, 276
Right Click Abort Message
section heading, 149
Right Trim
section heading, 198
Round, 217
section heading, 216
section reference, 150
Round Decimal, 363
Run
dialog, xvii, xviii, 8, 9, 106, 110,
111, 228, 363
Run Dialog Window, 363
Run Macro, 136
Run Macro Express Editor

section heading, 50
**Run Macro in Variable, 141, 145,
225, 226, 363**
section heading, 145
Run on Windows Startup
dialog, 17
section heading, 13
Running a Macro
section heading, 43, 70, 79
section reference, 43
Running and Activating Macros
chapter heading, 105
*chapter reference, xviii, 2, 5, 6, 7, 8,
24, 34, 37, 40, 41, 43, 45, 46, 49,
50, 79, 80, 83, 87, 89, 92, 93, 99,
249, 251, 368*
Running Macros
section heading, 105
Running Macros from Variables
section heading, 225
section reference, 143, 145, 147
Running Windows
dialog, 127, 284, 298
**Save Clipboard Graphic to a
Graphic File, 260**
section heading, 263
Save Clipboard to a Text File
section heading, 261
Save Control Variables, 329, 354
section heading, 354
Save to Clipboard, 194, 203
section heading, 203
**Save to Environment Variable,
196, 228**
section heading, 204
Save to INI File, 195
section heading, 204
Save to Text File, 194, 204, 260
section heading, 203
Save Variables
section heading, 220
Saving a Macro
section heading, 73, 80
Saving and Restoring Variables
section heading, 274
Schedule
section heading, 115
Scheduler
dialog, 116
Scope
section heading, 129
*section reference, 45, 46, 99, 113,
115, 138, 139*
Scope of Variables
section heading, 186
Scope Prefix
section heading, 149
Scope Tab
section heading, 46, 83

Scoping a Menu
section heading, 139
section reference, 138
Scoping Macros
section heading, 8
Screen Saver, 363
Script Category
dialog, 64
Script Tab
section heading, 46
Scripting Editor
section heading, 61
section reference, 24, 76, 77
Scroll Lock, 363
section heading, 240
Search and Replace Text
section heading, 80
Search Box
section heading, 66, 76
Search for Existing Versions
section heading, 11
Search Results
section heading, 11
Security Tab
section heading, 46, 83
section reference, 45, 46
Select a Tray Icon
dialog, 249
Select an Icon
dialog, 82, 136
Select an Icon File
dialog, 64, 82
Select Character
dialog, 242, 243
Select Components
dialog, 16
section heading, 10
Select Destination Directory
dialog, 12
Select Mouse Activation
dialog, 128
Select Program
dialog, 292
Select Programs
dialog, 130, 132
Select Start Menu Folder
dialog, 17
section heading, 12
Select Title
dialog, 299
Select Window
section heading, 284
Select Window(s)
dialog, 99, 132
Selecting Lines
section heading, 68
**Send Text to Control, 329, 342,
348, 352**
section heading, 351

Separator Character
section heading, 77
Set a Random Value, 205
section heading, 208
Set Control Text, 330
Set Decimal Variables, 213
section heading, 213
**Set Focus, 330, 345, 346, 347,
348, 349, 350, 363**
section heading, 346
Set HotKey Activation
dialog, 49, 113, 115, 138
**Set Integer to Control Height,
329, 363**
section heading, 351
Set Integer to Control Left, 363
section heading, 351
Set Integer to Control Top, 363
section heading, 351
Set Integer to Control Width, 363
section heading, 351
Set Integer Variables, 205
dialog, 351
section heading, 206
Set Keyboard Repeat Delay, 238
section heading, 238
Set Keyboard Repeat Speed, 238
section heading, 238
Set Options
dialog, 37
Set Program
dialog, 300, 301
Set Schedule
dialog, 111, 116
Set String from File, 191
Set System Date/Time, 363
Set Text String Variables, 192
dialog, 192, 238
section heading, 192
section reference, 197, 203
**Set Value from Clipboard, 205,
213**
section heading, 193, 209, 215
Set Value from Control Height
section heading, 210
Set Value from Control Left
section heading, 210
Set Value from Control Top
section heading, 210
Set Value from Control Width
section heading, 210
Set Value from Current Day
section heading, 210
**Set Value from Current Day of
Week**
section heading, 210
Set Value from Current Hour
section heading, 210
Set Value from Current Minute

section heading, 210
Set Value from Current Month
　section heading, 210
Set Value from Current Second
　section heading, 210
Set Value from Current Window Height
　section heading, 209
Set Value from Current Window Left
　section heading, 208
Set Value from Current Window Top
　section heading, 208
Set Value from Current Window Width
　section heading, 209
Set Value from Current Year
　section heading, 210
Set Value from Environment Variable, 204, 228, 286
　section heading, 196
Set Value from File, 203, 260
　section heading, 194
Set Value from INI File, 204
　section heading, 195
Set Value from Monitor Height
　section heading, 210
Set Value from Monitor Width
　section heading, 210
Set Value from Mouse X Position, 247
　section heading, 207
Set Value from Mouse Y Position, 247
　section heading, 207
Set Value from Screen Height
　section heading, 208
Set Value from Screen Width
　section heading, 208
Set Value from the Size of a File, 313
　section heading, 208, 318
Set Value Now, 205, 213, 225
　section heading, 192, 206, 213
Set Value to Current Folder Name
　section heading, 195
Set Value to File Name (Prompt)
　section heading, 196
Set Value to Folder Name (Prompt), 197
　section heading, 196
Set Value to Topmost Program Name
　section heading, 194
Set Value to Topmost Window Title
　section heading, 194

Set Variable to ASCII Character, 224
　section heading, 224
Set Variable to ASCII Value, 224
　section heading, 224
Set Window Order, 363
　section heading, 296
Set with a Random Letter, 208
　section heading, 197
Setting Menu Features
　section heading, 135
Shift Key, 363
　section heading, 240
Shift Key Down, 240
Shift Key Up, 240
ShortKey
　section heading, 123
ShortKey Invalid Chars
　section heading, 149
ShortKey Punctuation Chars
　section heading, 149
ShortKey Settings
　dialog, 126
ShortKeys
　dialog, 123, 149
　section reference, 149
ShortKeys trial version
　section heading, 369
Show Pixel Color in Hex in Mouse Locator
　section header, 150
Show Window, 291
Show Window (unhide)
　section heading, 290
Shut Down Program, 291, 293
　section heading, 291
Shutdown, 363
Size or Position a Window
　dialog, 293, 294
Sort Options
　dialog, 36
Sorting
　section heading, 35
Sound Beep, 363
Sound Wave File, 363
Special Characters
　section heading, 225
　section reference, 77
Special Installation Files
　section heading, 21
Specific Window
　section heading, 283
Specify Exact Location, 294
Specify Exact Size, 293
Speed
　dialog, 237
Start / Stop Capture
　section heading, 51

Start Clipboard Copy, 264
　section heading, 258
Start Installation
　section heading, 13
Start Repeat, 166
Start Repeat with Prompt, 169
Start Repeat with Variable, 168
Starting Macro Express
　section heading, 2
StartMenuFoldr
　section heading, 17
Startup
　dialog, 3, 13, 24, 29
　section header, 17
Startup Preferences
　section heading, 3
Stepping Through a Macro
　section heading, 70
Stopping a Macro
　section reference, 79
Stopping Macros
　section heading, 140
String Variable Commands
　section heading, 192
　section reference, 260
String Variables
　section heading, 185
Strip CR/LF
　section heading, 198
Subtract
　section heading, 211, 215
Summary
　section heading, 22, 57, 103, 151,
　　181, 229, 244, 255, 264, 281,
　　302, 328, 355
Suspend / Resume Macro Express
　section heading, 51
Suspend Computer, 363
Switch, xviii, 7, 153, 162, 163, 363
　section heading, 162
Switching Menu Types
　section heading, 139
Syntax Checking
　section heading, 72
System Attribute
　section heading, 314
System Controls
　dialog, 297
System HotKey
　section heading, 91
System Macros
　section heading, 49
Tab Delimited Text (.txt)
　section heading, 327
Task Manager
　dialog, 172, 293
Technical tools
　section heading, xx
Temporary Variables

section heading, 275
Terminal Services Session ID, 363
Terminate Macro Express, 363
section heading, 51
Terminate Process, 291, 292, 363
section heading, 292
Test Window
section heading, 71, 79
Text Box, 180
Text Box Close, 177, 178, 363
section heading, 177
Text Box Display, xviii, 153, 160, 180, 363
section heading, 177
Text File Begin Process, 322, 324, 326, 327, 363
section heading, 323
Text File End Process, 324, 363
section heading, 323
Text Type, xix, 60, 69, 71, 78, 79, 89, 91, 188, 225, 231, 232, 233, 234, 235, 236, 237, 240, 244, 258, 264, 291, 329, 342, 346, 347, 348, 351, 363, 365
section heading, 78, 231
section reference, 79
The First Big Step
section heading, 331
Time, 364
Time Out
section heading, 122
Times to Repeat
dialog, 169
Trim
section heading, 197
Truncate to Integer
section heading, 217
TweakMe3
dialog, 150
TweakMe3.mxe utility macro
section heading, 368
Type Out Text from the Clipboard
section heading, 258
Types of Variables
section heading, 185
Undock Computer, 364
Uppercase
section heading, 201
Use Log File
section heading, 82
Using Environment Variables
section heading, 228
Using the Registry
chapter heading, 265
chapter reference, xix, 162
Variable Coordinates
section heading, 190

Variable Get Control Class, 330, 341, 364
section heading, 342
Variable Get Control Text, 339, 341, 342, 364
section heading, 341
Variable Modify Control, 330, 341, 364
section heading, 343
Variable Modify Decimal, 364
Variable Modify Integer, 364
Variable Modify String, 364
Variable Restore, 106, 107, 277, 364
Variable Save, 221, 276, 277, 364
Variable Set Control Text, 341, 351, 364
section heading, 341
Variable Set Decimal, 364
Variable Set from File, 192, 205, 313
section heading, 315
Variable Set From File, 364
Variable Set from Misc
section heading, 223
Variable Set From Misc, 364
Variable Set Integer, 187, 364
Variable Set String, 364
Variable Set to ASCII Char, 364
Variable Set to ASCII Value, 364
Variables
chapter heading, 183
chapter reference, xix, 77, 128, 137, 141, 143, 144, 145, 147, 150, 160, 169, 176, 179, 181, 233, 247, 260, 261, 268, 286, 287, 304, 318
dialog, 71, 72
Variables Clear, 353
Variables Restore, 276, 354
Variables Save, 276, 277, 354
Video Clip Play, 364
Viewing Variables
section heading, 71
Views
section heading, 35
Wait, 254, 257, 319, 321, 349
Wait For
dialog, 253, 254, 349
Wait for Control, 330, 349, 350
section heading, 349
Wait For Control, 364
Wait for File Exist
section heading, 320
Wait For File Exist, 364
Wait for File Ready, 320, 321
section heading, 321
Wait For File Ready, 364

Wait for Folder to Exist
section heading, 320
Wait For Folder to Exist, 364
Wait for Key Press, 238, 239
section heading, 238
Wait For Key Press, 364
Wait for Mouse Cursor, 252
section heading, 253
Wait For Mouse Cursor, 364
Wait for Not Mouse Cursor, 252
section heading, 253
Wait For Not Mouse Cursor, 364
Wait for Text, xix, 238, 239
section heading, 238
Wait For Text, 364
Wait for Web Page, 14
Wait For Web Page, 364
Wait for Window, 78
Wait For Window, 70
Wait for Window Title, 330
Wait For Window Title, 364
Wait Left Mouse Click, 365
section heading, 254
Wait Middle Mouse Click, 365
section heading, 254
Wait Program Terminate, 365
Wait Right Mouse Click, 365
section heading, 254
Wait Text Playback, 236, 237, 365
section heading, 236
Wait Time Delay, 365
Wait Time Elapse, 365
Wait Window Lose Focus, 365
Wallpaper, 365
Web FTP Site, 365
Web Site, 365
Weekly
section heading, 120
Welcome
section heading, 9
What are Values?
section heading, 267
What if? Wait a minute!
section heading, 349
What is a Hive?
section heading, 266
What is inside?
section heading, xvii
What is the Registry?
section heading, 265
What was installed?
section heading, 14
What you need to know
section heading, xvii
Win Key, 365
section heading, 240
Window Activate, 67, 296, 365
section heading, 285

Window Close, 67, 70, 291, 365
Window Commands
   dialog, 290, 291
Window Control
   section heading, 129
Window Control Activation
   section heading, 352
   section reference, 129
Window Control Variables
   section heading, 330
Window Controls
   chapter heading, 329
   chapter reference, xx, 129, 161,
      185, 210, 235, 248
Window Hide, 290, 349, 365
Window Maximize, 290, 365
Window Minimize, 290, 349, 365
Window Part
   section heading, 128
Window Reposition, 349, 365
   section heading, 294

Window Resize, 89, 90, 365
   section heading, 293
Window Restore, 290, 365
Window Show, 290, 365
Window Sizing Border, 129
   section heading, 297
Window Title
   section heading, 126
**Window Title (May be partial
   title)**
   section heading, 283
Windows and Programs
   chapter heading, 283
   chapter reference, xix, 129, 162,
      172, 173
Windows Explorer
   section heading, 110
Windows Print
   dialog, 73
Windows Sizing Border, 365

Windows Specific
   section heading, 131
Would You Like the Macro to
   dialog, 98
Write Registry, 276, 278
Write Registry Decimal, 265, 365
   section heading, 270
Write Registry Integer, 265, 365
   section heading, 270
**Write Registry String, 265, 268,
   365**
   section heading, 270
**Write Registry Value, 192, 205,
   213**
Xor, 153
XOR, 155, 365
   section heading, 154
Zip Express trial version
   section heading, 370

ISBN 141203199-0